200 Problems on Languages, Automata, and Computation

Formal languages and automata have long been fundamental to theoretical computer science, but students often struggle to understand these concepts in the abstract. This book provides a rich source of compelling exercises designed to help students grasp the subject intuitively through practice. The text guides the reader through important topics such as finite automata, regular expressions, pushdown automata, grammars, and Turing machines via a series of problems of increasing difficulty. Problems are organised by topic, many with multiple follow-ups, and each section begins with a short recap of the basic notions necessary to make progress. Complete solutions are given for all exercises, making the book well suited for self-study as well as for use as a course supplement. Developed over the course of the editors' two decades of experience teaching the acclaimed Automata, Formal Languages, and Computation course at the University of Warsaw, it is an ideal resource for students who want to understand the subject deeply and for instructors who want to bring new ideas to their teaching.

FILIP MURLAK is Associate Professor at the University of Warsaw, where he lectures on automata, complexity, logic, and databases. His publications include the books *Relational and XML Data Exchange* (2010) and *Foundations of Data Exchange* (2014).

DAMIAN NIWIŃSKI is Professor at the University of Warsaw, where he lectures on automata theory, languages and computations, complexity, algorithmic game theory, and information theory. His publications include the monograph *Rudiments of Mu-calculus* (with A. Arnold, 2001).

WOJCIECH RYTTER is Professor at the University of Warsaw and a member of the Academia Europaea. He is the author of a large number of publications on automata, formal languages, parallel computing, and text algorithms. He is a co-author of several books, including *Efficient Parallel Algorithms* (1987), *Text Algorithms* (1994) and *125 Problems in Text Algorithms* (2021).

200 Problems on Languages, Automata, and Computation

Edited by

FILIP MURLAK
University of Warsaw

DAMIAN NIWIŃSKI
University of Warsaw

WOJCIECH RYTTER
University of Warsaw

CAMBRIDGE
UNIVERSITY PRESS

Shaftesbury Road, Cambridge CB2 8EA, United Kingdom

One Liberty Plaza, 20th Floor, New York, NY 10006, USA

477 Williamstown Road, Port Melbourne, VIC 3207, Australia

314–321, 3rd Floor, Plot 3, Splendor Forum, Jasola District Centre,
New Delhi – 110025, India

103 Penang Road, #05–06/07, Visioncrest Commercial, Singapore 238467

Cambridge University Press is part of Cambridge University Press & Assessment,
a department of the University of Cambridge.

We share the University's mission to contribute to society through the pursuit of
education, learning and research at the highest international levels of excellence.

www.cambridge.org
Information on this title: www.cambridge.org/9781316513460
DOI: 10.1017/9781009072632

First published 2023

A catalogue record for this publication is available from the British Library

ISBN 978-1-316-51346-0 Hardback
ISBN 978-1-009-07378-3 Paperback

Contents

PART II SOLUTIONS

Preface

This book contains problems collected over more than two decades by Damian Niwiński and Wojciech Rytter for the course *Languages, Automata, and Computation* that they alternately taught at the University of Warsaw. Coming from different scientific backgrounds – Wojciech specializing in algorithms and Damian in logic – they shared the idea that the problems should help students develop their skills through the joy of creative thinking. Over the years the collection was gradually expanded and circulated informally in countless versions. Damian and Wojciech always felt that it should be turned into a proper problem book, but this was impossible without written solutions. These were eventually provided by a large group of people, related in various ways to the automata group at the University of Warsaw, under the coordination of Filip Murlak. And thus the long-expected book was born.

A course on formal languages, automata, and computation is present in almost every computer science curriculum around the world, usually in a standardized form based on one of the several classic textbooks. While these textbooks usually complement the expository material with a small set of exercises, sometimes with brief solutions or hints, the present book reverts these proportions: it offers rich problem-solving materials for the course, appropriate both for in-class use and for self-study, accompanied by a minimalistic exposition of the necessary notions.

The book consists of two parts. Part I *Problems* (by D. Niwiński and W. Rytter), contains 200 problems, ranging from easy, marked with ☆, through intermediate (unmarked), to hard and very hard, marked with ★ and ★★, respectively. Some of the harder problems are well-known textbook theorems; we include them because, during the years of teaching the automata course, we have seen that under appropriate guidance students can rediscover a lot of classical material on their own, gaining deeper understanding and a greater sense of accomplishment. Problem statements are interleaved with concise definitions of key notions; for a deeper and broader background we refer to the work listed in the Further Reading section at the end of the book.

Part II, *Solutions* (collectively by 19 authors), contains full solutions to all 200 problems. The focus of the book is on creativity, rather than on practising specific methods, but many solutions build upon previous problems. Some initially simple ideas are further developed in a sequence of problems, the very order of problem statements guiding the students towards powerful methods.

The book has an index. It can help locate the definition of a key notion, like *off-line Turing machine*, and find problems related to a specific topic, like *one-letter alphabet*, or using a specific solution idea, like the *fooling method*.

Notation

$f : A \rightharpoonup B$ — f is a partial function from A to B.

$\#_u(w)$ — the number of (possibly overlapping) occurrences of the word u as a subword of the word w.

$|w|$ — the length of the word w.

$w[i]$ — the ith letter of the word w (counted from 1).

$w[i..j]$ — the infix of the word w from position i to position j, inclusive.

w^R — the reverse of the word w, or w written backwards.

$KL^{-1} = \{u \ : \ \exists v \in L. \, uv \in K\}$ — the right quotient of K by L.

$L^{-1}K = \{v \ : \ \exists u \in L. \, uv \in K\}$ — the left quotient of K by L.

$r \cdot s = \{(x, z) \ : \ \exists y. \, (x, y) \in r \wedge (y, z) \in s\}$ — the left composition of the binary relations r and s.

r^* — the reflective–transitive closure of the binary relation r.

$[w]_2$ — the numerical value of the binary sequence w; e.g., $[011]_2 = 3$.

$\mathrm{bin}(n)$ — the binary representation of $n \in \mathbb{N}$, without leading zeros.

$\$$ — a distinguished letter used as a separator.

PART I

Problems

Damian Niwiński and Wojciech Rytter

1

Words, Numbers, Graphs

Let us fix a finite set Σ; we shall refer to it as the *alphabet*. The elements of Σ are called *letters* or *symbols*. A *word* w over Σ is a finite sequence $a_1 a_2 \ldots a_n$ of letters from Σ. The length of $w = a_1 a_2 \ldots a_n$, denoted by $|w|$, is n. The *empty word*, denoted by ε, is the empty sequence; it has length 0. We write Σ^* for the set of all words over Σ, and Σ^+ for the set of non-empty words over Σ. The *concatenation* of words $u = a_1 a_2 \ldots a_m$ and $v = b_1 b_2 \ldots b_n$, denoted by $u \cdot v$ or simply uv, is the word $a_1 a_2 \ldots a_m b_1 b_2 \ldots b_n$. We write v^n for the word $\underbrace{vv \ldots v}_{n}$.

For a word $w \in \Sigma^*$ and $1 \le i, j \le |w|$, we write $w[i]$ for the ith letter of w and $w[i..j]$ for the infix starting at the ith letter and ending at the jth letter of w; that is, if $w = a_1 a_2 \ldots a_n$, then $w[i..j] = a_i a_{i+1} \ldots a_j$. In particular $w[i..i] = w[i]$ and $w[1..|w|] = w$. For $j < i$ we let $w[i..j] = \varepsilon$.

A *language* (over Σ) is a set of words (over Σ). The *concatenation* of languages L and K is the language $LK = \{uv : u \in L \wedge v \in K\}$. We write L^n for the language $\{w_1 w_2 \ldots w_n : w_1, w_2, \ldots, w_n \in L\}$. The *Kleene star* of a language L is the language $L^* = \bigcup_{n=0}^{\infty} L^n$. Note the case of $n = 0$ in the definition of the Kleene star, which means that the empty word ε belongs to the Kleene star of every language, even the empty one. We write L^+ for $\bigcup_{n=1}^{\infty} L^n$.

Problem 1 ☆
Prove that all languages L and M satisfy

$$(L^* M^*)^* = (L \cup M)^*.$$

Problem 2. PARENTHESIS EXPRESSIONS ☆
Show that the following two ways of defining the set of balanced sequences of parentheses are equivalent:

- The least set L such that the empty sequence ε is in L and if $w, v \in L$ then $(w), wv \in L$.
- The set K of words over the alphabet $\{(,)\}$ in which the number of occurrences of $)$ is the same as the number of occurrences of $($, and in each prefix the number of occurrences of $)$ is not greater than the number of occurrences of $($.

Problem 3. GAME GRAPH

Consider the following game between a barman and a customer. Between the players there is a revolving tray with four glasses forming the vertices of a square. Each glass is either right-side up or upside down, but the barman is blindfolded and wears gloves, so he has no way of telling which of the two cases holds. In each round, the barman chooses one or two glasses and reverses them. Afterwards, the customer rotates the tray by a multiple of 90 degrees. The barman wins if at any moment all glasses are in the same position (he is to be informed about this immediately). Can the barman win this game, starting from an unknown initial position? If so, how many moves are sufficient? Would you play this game for money against the barman? What about an analogous game with three or five glasses?

Problem 4. SEMI-LINEAR SETS

For any fixed $a, b \in \mathbb{N}$, the set of natural numbers $\{a + bn : n \in \mathbb{N}\}$ is called *linear*. A *semi-linear* set is a finite union of linear sets. (The empty set is obtained as the union of the empty family of linear sets.)

(1) Prove that a set A of natural numbers is semi-linear if and only if it is *ultimately periodic*; that is, there exist $c \in \mathbb{N}$ and $d \in \mathbb{N} - \{0\}$ such that for all $x > c$,

$$x \in A \text{ if and only if } x + d \in A.$$

(2) Let $A \subseteq \mathbb{N}$ be arbitrary. Show that the following set is semi-linear:

$$A^* = \{a_1 + a_2 + \cdots + a_k : k \in \mathbb{N}, a_1, \ldots, a_k \in A\}.$$

HINT: *Use congruence* mod m *for a suitably chosen* m.

(3) Prove that the set $A = \{a + b_1 n_1 + \cdots + b_k n_k : n_1, \ldots, n_k \in \mathbb{N}\}$ is semi-linear for all fixed k and $a, b_1, \ldots, b_k \in \mathbb{N}$.

(4) Prove that the family of all semi-linear sets is closed under finite unions, finite intersections, and complement with respect to $\mathbb{N}$.

(5) Prove that (a) any semi-linear set can be represented as the set of lengths of directed paths between two fixed sets of vertices of a finite graph, and (b) any set of numbers obtained in this way is semi-linear.

(6) Give an example of a subset of $\mathbb{N}$ that is not semi-linear.

Problem 5. PRIMITIVE WORDS ★

A word $w \in \Sigma^*$ is *primitive* if it cannot be presented as $w = v^n$ for any $n > 1$.

(1) Prove that for each non-empty word w there is *exactly one* primitive word v such that $w = v^n$ for some $n \geq 1$. We call n the *exponent* of the word w.

(2) For any words w and v, we say that wv is a *cyclic shift* of vw and that wv and vw are *conjugate*. Prove that being conjugate is an equivalence relation and all conjugate words have the same exponent. What is the cardinality of the equivalence class of a word of length m and exponent n?

Problem 6. CODES ★

A language $C \subseteq \Sigma^+$ is a *code* if each word $w \in C^+$ can be *decoded*; that is, w admits exactly one factorization with respect to C: there is exactly one way to present w as $v_1 v_2 \ldots v_n$ with $v_1, v_2, \ldots, v_n \in C$ and $n \in \mathbb{N}$.

(1) Let $\Sigma = \{a, b\}$. Prove that the set $\{aa, baa, ba\}$ is a code and the set $\{a, ab, ba\}$ is not a code.

(2) For a finite set C that is not a code, give an upper bound on the length of the shortest word that admits two different factorizations. Can you find an example meeting your bound?

(3) Show that $\{u, v\}$ is a code if and only if $uv \neq vu$.

See also Problem 75.

Problem 7. THUE–MORSE WORD ★★

(1) Show that the following definitions of the Thue–Morse word are equivalent:
  * the infinite sequence of 0's and 1's obtained by starting with 0 and successively appending the sequence obtained so far with all bits flipped;
  * the infinite word $s_0 s_1 s_2 \ldots$ such that $s_n = 0$ if the number of 1's in the binary representation of n is even, and $s_n = 1$ if it is odd;

- the infinite word $t_0 t_1 t_2 \ldots$, whose letters satisfy the recurrence relation: $t_0 = 0$, $t_{2n} = t_n$, and $t_{2n+1} = 1 - t_n$ for all n.

(2) Show that the Thue–Morse word is *cube-free*; that is, it contains no infix of the form *www* with $w \neq \varepsilon$. In fact, it is *strongly cube-free*; that is, it contains no infix of the form *bwbwb* for $b \in \{0, 1\}$.

   HINT: *First show that it contains neither* 000 *nor* 111 *as an infix, but each infix of length five contains* 00 *or* 11 *as an infix.*

(3) Construct an infinite word over a four-letter alphabet that is *square-free*; that is, it contains no infix of the form *ww* with $w \neq \varepsilon$.

(4) Can it be done with three letters? And two letters?

2

Regular Languages

2.1 Regular Expressions and Finite Automata

A *regular expression* is used to generate a set of words (that is, a language). The most basic regular expression is $\emptyset$, which generates no words. Each individual letter a can be viewed as a regular expression, which generates only one word, namely the one-letter word a. Finally, regular expressions can be combined using the following operators:

$\alpha\beta$ generates $\{wv: \alpha$ generates w and β generates $v\}$,

$\alpha+\beta$ generates $\{w: \alpha$ generates w or β generates $w\}$,

α^* generates $\{w_1 \ldots w_n: n \geq 0$ and α generates all $w_1, \ldots, w_n\}$.

Here is an example of a regular expression that uses all the available operations:

$$\left((a + b)(a + b)\right)^* \left(\emptyset^* + ((a + b)a(a + b))\right).$$

This particular expression generates the set of words over the alphabet $\{a, b\}$ which either have even length, or have an odd length of at least three and penultimate letter a. Note that the subexpression $\emptyset^*$ generates the unique word ε. We write $L(\alpha)$ for the *language generated by* the regular expression α; that is, the set of all words generated by α.

A second formalism for describing sets of words is *finite automata*, which can be deterministic or non-deterministic (deterministic is a special case of non-deterministic). A (non-deterministic) automaton is defined to be a tuple

$$(\Sigma, Q, I, \delta, F),$$

where Σ is the input alphabet, Q is the set of states, $I \subseteq Q$ is the set of initial states, $F \subseteq Q$ is the set of accepting (or final) states, and $\delta \subseteq Q \times \Sigma \times Q$ is the *transition relation*; elements of δ are called transitions, and are written as $q \xrightarrow{a} q'$. An automaton is often drawn as follows:

7

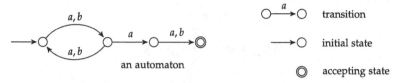

an automaton

transition

initial state

accepting state

The automaton in the picture above has only one initial and one accepting state, but in general there may be more. We extend the notation for transitions to arbitrary words $w \in \Sigma^*$: we write $p \xrightarrow{w} q$ if there is a *run over w* that begins in state p and ends in state q; that is, a path in the automaton which goes from state p to state q, and such that the labels of the edges on the path (that is, the transitions used in the run) are $a_1, \ldots, a_n$ where $w = a_1 a_2 \ldots a_n$. A word w is accepted if there is a run over w from some initial state to some accepting state. For instance, the automaton in the picture above accepts exactly the odd-length words generated by the regular expression from our earlier example. The *language recognized* by $\mathcal{A}$, denoted by $L(\mathcal{A})$, is the set of words accepted by $\mathcal{A}$. Two automata are *equivalent* if they recognize the same languages.

If a non-deterministic automaton has a single initial state q_I (which is often assumed), we use the notation $(\Sigma, Q, q_I, \delta, F)$.

An automaton is called *deterministic* if it has one initial state and its transition relation is a function from $Q \times \Sigma$ to Q, which means that for every $q \in Q$ and $a \in \Sigma$, there is exactly one state p such that $q \xrightarrow{a} p$. Determinism guarantees that for every word there is exactly one run, and thus a word is accepted if and only if this unique run ends in an accepting state. For each non-deterministic automaton one can construct an equivalent deterministic automaton, but the number of states may grow exponentially.

A fundamental result connecting regular expressions and finite automata is that the two formalisms have the same expressive power: a language can be generated by a regular expression if and only if it can be recognized by a finite automaton. Such languages are called *regular languages*.

Problem 8 ☆

Prove that the regular expression

$$\left(00 + 11 + (01 + 10)(00 + 11)^*(01 + 10)\right)^*$$

generates exactly those words over the alphabet $\{0, 1\}^*$ where both 0 and 1 appear an even number of times.

Problem 9 ☆

Construct an automaton that recognizes words over the alphabet $\{0, 1\}$ where the number of 1's on even-numbered positions is even and the number of 1's on odd-numbered positions is odd.

Problem 10. ADDITION

Consider the alphabet $\{0, 1\}^3$, with letters written as columns. Give a regular expression defining the language

$$\left\{ \begin{bmatrix} a_1 \\ b_1 \\ c_1 \end{bmatrix} \begin{bmatrix} a_2 \\ b_2 \\ c_2 \end{bmatrix} \dots \begin{bmatrix} a_n \\ b_n \\ c_n \end{bmatrix} : [a_1 a_2 \dots a_n]_2 + [b_1 b_2 \dots b_n]_2 = [c_1 c_2 \dots c_n]_2 \right\},$$

where $[w]_2$ is the numerical value of the binary sequence w; e.g., $[011]_2 = 3$.

Problem 11. DIVISIBILITY

(1) Construct a deterministic automaton over the alphabet $\{0, 1, \dots, 9\}$ which recognizes decimal representations of numbers divisible by 7. Generalize the above to base-b representations of numbers divisible by k.

(2) Do the same, but with a reverse representation, where the least significant digit comes first. Generalize the above to base-b representations of numbers divisible by k.

Problem 12. ONE-LETTER ALPHABET

(1) Prove that a language $L \subseteq \{a\}^*$ is regular if and only if the set of natural numbers $\{n : a^n \in L\}$ is semi-linear in the sense of Problem 4.

(2) Prove that for an arbitrary set $X \subseteq \{a\}^*$, the language X^* is regular.

Problem 13. BASE-b REPRESENTATION ★

For every $b \in \mathbb{N} - \{0, 1\}$, each word $w \in \{0, 1, \dots, b - 1\}^*$ can be interpreted as a natural number $[w]_b \in \mathbb{N}$ written in base-b representation: $[a_1 \dots a_n]_b = a_1 b^{n-1} + a_2 b^{n-2} + \dots + a_n$ and $[\varepsilon]_b = 0$.

(1) Let $L \subseteq \{0, 1, \dots, b - 1\}^*$ be a regular language. Is

$$\{[w]_b : w \in L\}$$

semi-linear for all b?

(2) Let $M \subseteq \mathbb{N}$ be a semi-linear set. Show that

$$\left\{w \in \{0, 1, \dots, b - 1\}^* : [w]_b \in M\right\}$$

is a regular language for all b.

Problem 14 ★

Prove that for all $a, b, k, r \in \mathbb{N}$, the following language is regular:

$$L = \{\text{bin}(x) \, \$ \, \text{bin}(y) : (a \cdot x + b \cdot y) \equiv r \mod k\}.$$

2.2 Proving Non-Regularity

A finite automaton can only store finite information about the processed prefix of the input word. This limitation can be used to show that a given language is not regular by fooling each deterministic finite automaton. For instance, consider the language $\{a^n b^n : n \in \mathbb{N}\}$. Suppose that it is recognized by a deterministic finite automaton. Because the automaton has finitely many states, there exist $n, m \in \mathbb{N}$ with $n \neq m$ such that the runs over a^n and a^m end in the same state. In consequence, also the runs over $a^n b^n$ and $a^m b^n$ end in the same state. This is a contradiction, because $a^n b^n$ should be accepted and $a^m b^n$ should be rejected. As each deterministic finite automaton can be fooled like this, it follows that $\{a^n b^n : n \in \mathbb{N}\}$ is not a regular language. The above argument can also be interpreted in terms of the Myhill–Nerode equivalence (see Section 2.4).

The pumping lemma provides a property of regular languages which can be used to prove that a given language is not regular, without referring to automata. The lemma says that if a language L is regular, then there exists a constant $N \in \mathbb{N}$ such that, for each word $w \in L$ of length at least N, there is a factorization $w = xyz$ such that

$$|xy| \leq N, \quad |y| \geq 1, \quad \text{and} \quad xy^i z \in L \text{ for all } i \in \mathbb{N}.$$

Let us illustrate how to use the pumping lemma to prove non-regularity. Consider $L = \{a^n b^n : n \in \mathbb{N}\}$. Towards a contradiction, assume that L is regular. Let N be the constant from the pumping lemma. Consider the word $w = a^N b^N$. By the pumping lemma there exists a factorization $w = xyz$ where $|xy| \leq N$, $|y| \geq 1$, and the word $xy^i z$ belongs to L for every $i \in \mathbb{N}$. Because $|xy| \leq N$, the word y consists only of letters a. Because $|y| \geq 1$, for each $i > 1$, the word $xy^i z$ has more letters a than b, which means it cannot belong to L. The obtained contradiction implies that L is not regular.

Sometimes we can deduce that a given language is not regular using non-regularity of some other language and the closure properties of regular languages (see Section 2.3 for an overview). For example, consider the language $L = \{w \in \{a, b\}^* : \#_a(w) = \#_b(w)\}$. Suppose that L is regular. Because regular languages are closed under intersection, by intersecting L with the language K generated by the regular expression $a^* b^*$ we should obtain a regular language as well. However, what we obtain is the non-regular language $\{a^n b^n : n \in \mathbb{N}\}$. The contradiction implies that L is not regular.

Problem 15 ☆
Prove that the following languages are not regular:

(1) $\{a^{2^n} : n \in \mathbb{N}\}$;

(2) $\{a^p : p \text{ is a prime number}\}$;

(3) $\{a^i b^j : \gcd(i,j) = 1\}$;

(4) $\{a^m b^n : m \neq n\}$.

Problem 16 ☆

A *palindrome* is a word that reads the same backwards as forwards. Prove that the set of palindromes over an alphabet with at least two letters is not a regular language.

Problem 17 ☆

A regular expression over an alphabet Σ can be seen as a word over the alphabet $\Sigma \cup \{\emptyset, +, *, (,)\}$. Prove that the set of regular expressions over an alphabet Σ is not a regular language.

Problem 18

Show that if in Problem 10 we consider multiplication instead of addition, then the obtained language is not regular.

Problem 19

Determine whether the following languages are regular:

(1) $\{v \in \{a, b\}^* : \#_a(u) > 2017 \cdot \#_b(u) \text{ for each non-empty prefix } u \text{ of } v\}$;

(2) $\{uv \in \{a, b, c\}^* : \#_a(u) + \#_b(u) = \#_b(v) + \#_c(v)\}$.

Problem 20

Determine whether the following languages are regular:

(1) $\{x \in \{a, b\}^* : \#_{ab}(x) = \#_{ba}(x) + 1\}$;

(2) $\{x \in \{a, b\}^* : \#_{aba}(x) = \#_{bab}(x)\}$.

If so, provide regular expressions for them.

Problem 21 ★

Prove a slightly stronger version of the pumping lemma: If a language L is regular, then there exists a constant N such that for any words v, w, u satisfying $|w| \geq N$ and $vwu \in L$, there exist words x, y, z such that $w = xyz$, $0 < |y| \leq N$, and $vxy^n zu \in L$ for all $n \in \mathbb{N}$. Exhibit a language which satisfies the claim of this stronger lemma, but is not regular.

HINT: *Consider the set of words v over the alphabet $\{b, c\}$ such that the number of letters c in v is prime, or there are two consecutive letters c in v.*

Problem 22. ANTIPALINDROMES ★
A word $w \in \{0, 1\}^*$ is an *antipalindrome* if for some non-empty word $z \in \{0, 1\}^*$ and $s \in \{0, 1\}$,

$$w = z\bar{z}^R \text{ or } w = zs\bar{z}^R,$$

where $\bar{z}$ is obtained from z by flipping the bits. For instance, 0010011 and 0011 are antipalindromes, and the empty word or a single letter are not. Let $L \subseteq \{0, 1\}^*$ be the set of words which do not contain as a subword any antipalindrome of length greater than three whose first letter is 0. Is L a regular language?

Problem 23 ★
Let us assign to each non-empty word $w \in \{0, 1\}^*$ the number $0.w$ in the interval $[0, 1)$ defined as

$$0.w = w[1] \cdot \frac{1}{2} + w[2] \cdot \frac{1}{2^2} + \cdots + w[|w|] \cdot \frac{1}{2^{|w|}}.$$

For a real number $r \in [0, 1]$, let $L_r = \{w : 0.w \le r\}$. Prove that the language L_r is regular if and only if r is rational.

Problem 24 ★
A palindrome is *non-trivial* if its length is at least two. Let Pal_Σ be the set of non-trivial palindromes over the alphabet Σ. Prove that the language $\left(\text{Pal}_\Sigma\right)^*$ is regular if and only if $|\Sigma| = 1$. Is the language $\left\{uu^R : u \in (0 + 1)^*\right\}^*$ regular?

Problem 25 ★
Determine which of the following languages over the alphabet $\{0, 1\}$ are regular:
   (1) words containing a non-trivial palindrome as a prefix;
   (2) words containing a non-trivial palindrome of even length as a prefix;
   (3) words containing a non-trivial palindrome of odd length as a prefix.

Problem 26 ★
Give an example of an infinite language closed under infixes that does not contain an infinite regular language as a subset.

Problem 27 ★★
Is the set of binary representations of prime numbers (without leading 0's) a regular language?

Problem 28 ★★
Let Pump(w) be the least set K such that $w \in K$ and for all words x, y, z, if $xyz \in K$, then $xyyz \in K$. Is Pump(ab) regular? What about Pump(abc)?

2.3 Closure Properties

Each function $f \colon \Sigma \to \Gamma^*$ can be extended to $f \colon \Sigma^* \to \Gamma^*$ by setting

$$h(a_1 a_2 \ldots a_n) = h(a_1)h(a_2)\ldots h(a_n);$$

functions obtained in this way are called *homomorphisms*. A homomorphism $f \colon \Sigma^* \to \Gamma^*$ *preserves length* if $|f(v)| = |v|$ for all $v \in \Sigma^*$.

The class of regular languages is closed under union, intersection, complement, difference, concatenation, Kleene star, homomorphic images, and homomorphic pre-images; that is, if $L, M \subseteq \Sigma^*$ are regular, so are $L \cup M$, $L \cap M$, $\Sigma^* - L$, $L - M$, LM, L^*, $f(L)$, and $g^{-1}(L)$ for all functions $f \colon \Sigma \to \Gamma^*$ and $g \colon \Gamma \to \Sigma^*$.

Problem 29. CONCATENATION ☆
(1) Is there a non-regular language $L \subseteq \{a\}^*$ such that L^2 is regular?
(2) Let $L = \{w \in \{a, b\}^* : \#_a(w) \neq \#_b(w)\}$. Show that L^2 is regular.

Problem 30 ☆
The *reverse* of a word w, denoted by w^R, can be defined recursively: $\varepsilon^R = \varepsilon$ and $(w\sigma)^R = \sigma w^R$ for $w \in \Sigma^*$ and $\sigma \in \Sigma$. Prove that a language $L \subseteq \Sigma^*$ is regular if and only if the language L^R of the reverses of words in L is regular.

Problem 31 ☆
Prove that for every regular language $L \subseteq \Sigma^*$ and every (not necessarily regular) language $X \subseteq \Sigma^*$ the following languages, known as *left* and *right quotients* of L, are regular:

$$X^{-1}L = \{w : \exists v \in X. \, vw \in L\}, \quad LX^{-1} = \{w : \exists u \in X. \, wu \in L\}.$$

Problem 32
Is it true that for each regular language L over Σ there exist two different non-empty words u, v over Σ such that $L\{uv\}^{-1} = L\{vu\}^{-1}$?

Problem 33. CYCLIC SHIFT

For a given automaton $\mathcal{A}$ recognizing a language L, construct an automaton $\mathcal{B}$ that recognizes the language

$$\text{Cycle}(L) = \{vu \ : \ uv \in L\}.$$

Does the fact that $\text{Cycle}(L)$ is regular imply that L is regular as well?

Problem 34

Let L be a regular language over the alphabet $\{0, 1\}$. Prove regularity of the language $L_{\min}$ of words $w \in L$ which are minimal in the lexicographic order among words of length $|w|$ in L.

Problem 35

Let L be a regular language. Prove that the following languages are also regular:

$$\frac{1}{2}L = \{w \ : \ \exists u. \ |u| = |w| \wedge wu \in L\};$$
$$\sqrt{L} = \{w \ : \ ww \in L\}.$$

Problem 36 ★

Let L be a regular language. Prove that the following languages are also regular:

$$\text{Root}(L) = \left\{w \ : \ \exists n \in \mathbb{N}. \ w^n \in L\right\};$$
$$\text{Sqrt}(L) = \left\{w \ : \ \exists u. \ |u| = |w|^2 \wedge wu \in L\right\};$$
$$\text{Log}(L) = \left\{w \ : \ \exists u. \ |u| = 2^{|w|} \wedge wu \in L\right\};$$
$$\text{Fib}(L) = \left\{w \ : \ \exists u. \ |u| = F_{|w|} \wedge wu \in L\right\}.$$

Here F_n is the nth Fibonacci number: $F_1 = F_2 = 1$, $F_{n+2} = F_n + F_{n+1}$.

HINT: Use $n^2 = 1 + 2 + \ldots + (2n - 1)$ and $2^n = 1 + 2^1 + 2^2 + \cdots + 2^{n-1} + 1$.

Problem 37 ★

Prove that for every regular language L, the following language is also regular:
$\left\{w \ : \ w^{|w|} \in L\right\}$.

Problem 38. SUBSTITUTION

Consider regular languages $L \subseteq \Sigma^*$ and $K \subseteq \Gamma^*$, and a function $f \colon \Sigma \to \mathcal{P}(\Gamma^*)$ mapping letters from Σ to languages over Γ. Let $f(w) = f(a_1)f(a_2)\ldots f(a_k)$ for $w = a_1 a_2 \ldots a_k \in \Sigma^*$.

(1) Prove that if $f(a)$ is regular for all $a \in \Sigma$, then so is $f(L) = \bigcup_{w \in L} f(w)$. Show that the assumption is necessary.

(2) Prove that $f^{-1}(K) = \{w \in \Sigma^* : f(w) \subseteq K\}$ is regular.

Problem 39

Let L be a regular language. Prove that the languages

(1) $L_{+--} = \{w : \exists u.\ |u| = 2 \cdot |w| \wedge wu \in L\}$,

(2) $L_{++-} = \{w : \exists u.\ 2 \cdot |u| = |w| \wedge wu \in L\}$,

(3) $L_{-+-} = \{w : \exists u, v.\ |u| = |v| = |w| \wedge uwv \in L\}$

are regular, but the following language may be non-regular:

(4) $L_{+-+} = \{uv : \exists w.\ |u| = |v| = |w| \wedge uwv \in L\}$.

Problem 40

The *Hamming distance* between two words of equal length is the number of positions at which they differ. Prove that for every regular language L over an alphabet Σ and every constant k, the set of words over Σ at a Hamming distance at most k from a word in L is regular.

Problem 41

A *shuffle of words u and v* is any word that can be split into two sub-sequences equal to u and v, respectively. The *shuffle of languages L and M*, denoted by $L \parallel M$, is the set of all possible shuffles of a word from L and a word from M. Prove that if L and M are regular languages then the language $L \parallel M$ is also regular.

Problem 42

Let the *shuffle closure* of a language L be defined as

$$L^\sharp = L \cup (L \parallel L) \cup (L \parallel L \parallel L) \cup \cdots .$$

Give an example of a regular language over a two-element alphabet whose shuffle closure is not regular.

Problem 43

(1) Is it true that for each finite alphabet Σ, the family of regular languages over Σ is the least family containing all finite languages over Σ and closed under union, complement, and concatenation?

(2) What if we additionally assume closure under images through homomorphisms from Σ^* to Σ^* that preserve length?

2.4 Minimal Automata

A deterministic finite automaton that recognizes a language L is *minimal* if no deterministic automaton with fewer states recognizes L. A minimal automaton for a regular language is unique up to isomorphism, so we are justified to speak about *the* minimal automaton for L.

An automaton is minimal for its language if and only if it is

- *reachable*, i.e., every state is reachable from the initial state, and
- *observable*, i.e., from every state a different language is recognized.

Observability can be witnessed by providing for each pair of states a word that *distinguishes* them; that is, it is accepted from exactly one of these states.

Every language $L \subseteq \Sigma^*$ determines the *Myhill–Nerode equivalence* relation on Σ^* which relates words v and v' if and only if for all $w \in \Sigma^*$,

$$vw \in L \Leftrightarrow v'w \in L.$$

A language is regular if and only if its Myhill–Nerode equivalence has finitely many equivalence classes. A transition relation on these equivalence classes can be defined so that from the equivalence class of a word w, upon reading a letter $a \in \Sigma$, one moves to the equivalence class of the word wa. Putting the equivalence class of the empty word as the initial state, and marking equivalence classes of words from L as accepting states, we obtain the minimal automaton for the language L.

Problems related to minimal automata can also be found in Section 2.8.

Problem 44 ☆
Construct the minimal automaton for the language

$$L = \left\{ a^i b^n a^j \ : \ n > 0, i + j \text{ is even} \right\}.$$

Problem 45 ☆
Construct the minimal automaton for the language

$$L = \left\{ w \in \{0, 1, 2, 3, 4\}^+ \ : \ \max_{i,j} \left(w[i] - w[j] \right) \leq 2 \right\}.$$

Problem 46
For $n > 0$ let NPal_n be the set of words over $\{0, 1, \ldots, n-1\}$ that contain no non-trivial palindrome as an infix. How many states does the minimal automaton for NPal_n have?

Problem 47

Let L be a language over the alphabet $\{a, b\}$ that contains the empty word and all words starting with a that do not contain as an infix any palindrome of length strictly greater than three. Draw the minimal automaton for L. How many words are there in L?

Problem 48

Let L be the language of all words over the alphabet $\{0, 1\}$ that do not contain an antipalindrome (see Problem 22) of length strictly greater than two as an infix. Draw the minimal automaton for L.

Problem 49 ★

For $k \in \mathbb{N}$, let $L_k \subseteq \{0, 1\}^*$ be the language of words where each infix of length k contains exactly two 1's and each infix of length at most k contains at most two 1's. Describe the minimal automata for L_k where $k \in \{3, 4\}$.

Problem 50 ☆

Consider a vending machine that accepts coins in two currencies, EUR and PLN with 1 EUR = 4 PLN, and works as follows:

- Every drink costs 1 PLN.
- In the beginning the machine does not contain any coins.
- The machine accepts 1 PLN or 1 EUR; in the latter case the machine gives back 3 PLN if they are available. If the machine cannot give back change, then it signals an error.
- If after the transaction the machine contains an equivalent of at least 8 PLN, then all coins are removed from it, and the machine resumes its operation normally.

A log of the machine is a sequence of inserted coins. A log is *correct* if there was no error signal emitted by the machine while it worked. Construct the minimal automaton over the alphabet $\{$EUR, PLN$\}$ for the language of correct logs.

Problem 51

Football teams A, B, and C compete against each other according to the following rule: the winner of the previous match plays against the team that did not participate in it. Assuming that there are no draws, consider the language over the alphabet $\{A, B, C\}$ of possible sequences of winners. Prove that it is a regular language and describe its minimal automaton.

Problem 52

Mr. X owns stock of three different companies: A, B, and C. Every day, he checks the relative values of his stocks and ranks them from the most to the least valuable (we assume that the values of two stocks can never be the same). Mr. X decided to sell stock of a company if it ever goes down in the ranking for two days in a row. For example, if the stock record in three consecutive days is CBA, ACB, ABC, then Mr. X will sell C. Let Σ be the set of all permutations of $\{A, B, C\}$. Prove that the language L of words over Σ that describes those stock records that do not lead to the sale of any stock owned by Mr. X is regular. Calculate the number of states in the minimal deterministic automaton for L.

Problem 53 ★★

Mr. X decided that every day he will work or not, following the rule that in any seven consecutive days there are at most four working days. A calendar of n consecutive days can be expressed as a word of length n over the alphabet $\{0, 1\}$; where 1 means a working day and 0 means a day off. Prove that the set of all words describing valid calendars forms a regular language over the alphabet $\{0, 1\}$. Construct the minimal automaton for this language.

2.5 Variants of Finite Automata

Automata with ε-transitions are an extension of ordinary finite automata that allows transitions of the form $p \xrightarrow{\varepsilon} q$; using this transition in a run amounts to changing the state from p to q without advancing in the input word.

Problem 54 ☆

Show that for each automaton with ε-transitions there exists an automaton without ε-transitions recognizing the same language.

A *Mealy machine* is a finite automaton with output. Let Σ be a finite input alphabet and let Δ be a finite output alphabet. A Mealy machine can be presented as a deterministic finite automaton $\mathcal{A} = (\Sigma, Q, q_I, \delta)$ with the set of accepting states left unspecified, together with an output function $\gamma: Q \times \Sigma \to \Delta$. When the machine is in a state q and reads an input letter a, it moves to the next state $\delta(q, a)$ while additionally outputting the letter $\gamma(q, a)$. That is, if $q_0, q_1, \ldots, q_n$ is the sequence of states constituting the unique run on an input word $w = a_1 a_2 \ldots a_n \in \Sigma^*$, then the machine outputs the following n-letter word over Δ:

$$\widehat{\gamma}(w) = \gamma(q_0, a_1)\gamma(q_1, a_2) \ldots \gamma(q_{n-1}, a_n).$$

We say that the Mealy machine $\mathcal{A}$ *realizes* the function $\widehat{\gamma}\colon \Sigma^* \to \Delta^*$ defined above. A function $f\colon \Sigma^* \to \Delta^*$ is a *Mealy function* if it is realized by some Mealy machine.

Problem 55 ☆

A function $f\colon \Sigma^* \to \Delta^*$ *reduces* a language $L \subseteq \Sigma^*$ to a language $M \subseteq \Delta^*$ when $w \in L$ if and only if $f(w) \in M$ for all $w \in \Sigma^*$. Construct a Mealy function that reduces the language $\{\varepsilon\} \cup \{w \in \{a,b\}^+ : \#_a(w) \text{ is odd}\}$ to the language $\{\varepsilon\} \cup \{w \in \{a,b\}^+ : \#_a(w) \text{ is even}\}$.

Problem 56

Show the following closure properties:

(1) if $f_1\colon \Sigma_1^* \to \Sigma_2^*$ and $f_2\colon \Sigma_2^* \to \Sigma_3^*$ are Mealy functions, then their composition $f_2 \circ f_1$ is a Mealy function too;
(2) if $f\colon \Sigma^* \to \Delta^*$ is a Mealy function and $L \subseteq \Sigma^*$ is a regular language, then $f(L)$ is a regular language too;
(3) if $f\colon \Sigma^* \to \Delta^*$ is a Mealy function and $L \subseteq \Delta^*$ is a regular language, then $f^{-1}(L)$ is a regular language too.

Moore machines are defined like Mealy machines, except that the output function has the form $\gamma\colon Q \to \Delta$ and the word produced along the run $q_0, q_1, \ldots, q_n$ over a word $w = a_1 a_2 \ldots a_n$ is

$$\widehat{\gamma}(w) = \gamma(q_1)\gamma(q_2)\ldots\gamma(q_n).$$

A *Moore function* is a function that is realized by a Moore machine.

Problem 57 ☆

Show that the class of Moore functions coincides with the class of Mealy functions.

Two-way automata are similar to ordinary finite automata, except that when reading the input word they can go either left or right; that is, their transition relation δ is of the form

$$\delta \subseteq Q \times (\Sigma \cup \{\triangleright, \triangleleft\}) \times \{\leftarrow, \rightarrow\} \times Q.$$

The input word is decorated with markers $\triangleright$ and $\triangleleft$ indicating the left and the right end point of the word, respectively; that is, we run the automata on words of the form $\triangleright w \triangleleft$ for $w \in \Sigma^*$. A *configuration* of the automaton is a pair (q, i), where q is a state and i is a position in the word $\triangleright w \triangleleft$. The automaton can move from configuration (q, i) to configuration (q', i') if either $i' = i + 1$, $(q, a_i, \rightarrow, q') \in \delta$, and $a_i \neq \lhd$ or $i' = i - 1$, $(q, a_i, \leftarrow, q') \in \delta$, and $a_i \neq \rhd$, where a_i is the ith letter of $\rhd w \lhd$. An accepting run on $\rhd w \lhd$ is a sequence $(q_0, i_0), (q_1, i_1), \ldots, (q_k, i_k)$ of configurations like above such that

- q_0 is the initial state of the automaton and $i_0 = 1$,
- for all $j < k$ the automaton can move from (q_j, i_j) to (q_{j+1}, i_{j+1}), and
- q_k is accepting.

Thus, the automaton stops and accepts immediately upon reaching an accepting state, regardless of the current position in the word. The *recognized language* is the set of words w such that there is an accepting run on $\rhd w \lhd$.

Problem 58 ★
For $k \in \mathbb{N} - \{0\}$, let $L_k \subseteq \{a, b, c\}^*$ be the language

$$\big((a + b)^* c\big)^{k-1} (a + b)^* a (a + b)^{k-1} c (a + b + c)^*.$$

(1) Show that each deterministic automaton recognizing L_k has at least 2^k states, and similarly for $(L_k)^R$.
(2) Construct a deterministic two-way automaton recognizing L_k that has $\mathcal{O}(k)$ states and changes the direction of movement only once.

Problem 59 ★★
Show that for each two-way automaton there exists an ordinary finite automaton recognizing the same language.

2.6 Combinatorics of Finite Automata

Problem 60. DETERMINIZATION
Consider the families $\mathcal{A}_n$ and $\mathcal{B}_n$ of non-deterministic finite automata over the alphabet $\{a, b\}$ presented below:

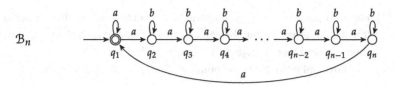

Prove that the minimal deterministic automaton recognizing $L(\mathcal{A}_n)$ has 2^{n-1} states and that the minimal deterministic automaton recognizing $L(\mathcal{B}_n)$ has 2^n states.

Problem 61 ★

For $n \geq 2$, let $\mathcal{A}_n$ be the following deterministic automaton:

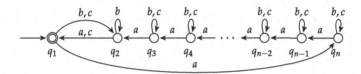

Prove that every deterministic automaton recognizing the reverse of the language recognized by $\mathcal{A}_n$ has at least 2^n states.

HINT: *The group of permutations of a finite set X is generated by any single cycle shifting all elements of X and any transposition of two consecutive elements on the cycle.*

Problem 62. INTERSECTION

Let $\mathcal{A}$ and $\mathcal{B}$ be non-deterministic finite automata, each with at most n states. Show that the intersection of the languages recognized by $\mathcal{A}$ and $\mathcal{B}$ can be recognized by a non-deterministic finite automaton with $\mathcal{O}(n^2)$ states. Is this bound asymptotically tight?

Problem 63 ★

For each positive integer k, let

$$L_k = \left\{ u\$v \: : \: u,v \in \{a,b\}^* \wedge u[1..k] = v[1..k] \right\}.$$

Show that L_k is the intersection of $\mathcal{O}(k)$ languages recognized by a deterministic finite automaton with $\mathcal{O}(k)$ states, the complement of L_k is recognized by a non-deterministic finite automaton with $\mathcal{O}(k^2)$ states, but every non-deterministic finite automaton recognizing L_k has at least 2^k states.

Problem 64 ★

(1) For each positive integer n construct a non-deterministic finite automaton $\mathcal{A}_n$ such that the number of states in $\mathcal{A}_n$ is polynomial in n and the shortest word that $\mathcal{A}_n$ rejects has length $2^{\Omega(n)}$.

(2) As above but ensure that the number of states in $\mathcal{A}_n$ is linear in n.

Problem 65 ★

For every n, find languages $K_1^n, K_2^n, \ldots, K_n^n$ over an alphabet Σ_n such that each language K_i^n can be recognized by a deterministic automaton with at most C states, for some constant C independent of n, and each non-deterministic automaton recognizing $K_n = K_1^n \cap K_2^n \cap \cdots \cap K_n^n$ has $2^{\Omega(n)}$ states.

Problem 66

Show that for all words u, v such that $|u| < |v| = n$ there exists a deterministic finite automaton with $\mathcal{O}(\log n)$ states that accepts u and rejects v.

HINT: *Use the fact that* $\operatorname{lcm}(1, 2, \ldots, \ell) \geq 2^\ell$ *for all* $\ell \geq 7$.[1]

Problem 67 ★

Show that if two states of an n-state deterministic finite automaton are distinguished by some word, then they are distinguished by a word of length at most n.

Problem 68 ★

The *growth* of a language L is the function assigning to each $n \in \mathbb{N}$ the number of words of length n in L. Is there a regular language whose growth is $o(c^n)$ for all $c > 0$, but is not $\mathcal{O}(n^c)$ for any c?

Problem 69 ★★

(1) Prove that for every non-deterministic automaton with n states there exists a regular expression of length $2^{\mathcal{O}(n)}$ that recognizes the same language.

(2) Prove that for a deterministic automaton with n states, the shortest regular expression recognizing its language may have length as high as $2^{\Omega(n)}$.

---

[1] M. Nair. On Chebyshev-type inequalities for primes. *American Mathematical Monthly*, 89(2):126–129, 1982.

2.7 Algorithms on Automata

In this section we compute the running time of algorithms in the random-access machine (RAM) model, where any cell of the memory can be accessed in constant time. In this model the running time can be slightly better than in the Turing machine model, where memory is accessed sequentially by means of a head moving along the tape, one cell at a time (see Section 4.1).

We write $\|\mathcal{A}\|$ for the total size of the representation of the automaton $\mathcal{A}$, when given as input.

Problem 70 ☆
Design an algorithm which, for a given non-deterministic automaton $\mathcal{A}$ and a word w, decides if $w \in L(\mathcal{A})$ in time $\mathcal{O}(\|\mathcal{A}\| \cdot |w|)$.

Problem 71
For a fixed finite automaton $\mathcal{A}$ over the alphabet Σ design a dynamic data structure for a word w that can be constructed in time $\mathcal{O}(|w|)$ and enables the following operations:

- change the letter at position i to $a \in \Sigma$ in time $\mathcal{O}(\log |w|)$;
- decide whether the current word belongs to $L(\mathcal{A})$ in time $\mathcal{O}(1)$.

Problem 72
For a fixed finite automaton $\mathcal{A}$ design a data structure for a word w that can be constructed in time $\mathcal{O}(|w|)$ and enables deciding for given positions $i \leq j$ whether $w[i..j] \in L(\mathcal{A})$ in time $\mathcal{O}(\log |w|)$.

Problem 73 ☆
Let Σ be a fixed alphabet. Design an algorithm that, given two deterministic automata over Σ of sizes N_1 and N_2, respectively, decides in time $\mathcal{O}(N_1 \cdot N_2)$ whether they recognize the same language.[2] The constants hidden in the $\mathcal{O}$-notation may depend on Σ.

Problem 74
Let $\mathcal{A}$ be a fixed deterministic automaton. Design an algorithm that, for a given non-negative integer n, computes the number of words of length n accepted by $\mathcal{A}$ using $\mathcal{O}(\log n)$ arithmetic operations. The constants hidden in the $\mathcal{O}$-notation may depend on $\mathcal{A}$.

---

[2] A better algorithm was proposed by J. E. Hopcroft and R. M. Karp. A linear algorithm for testing equivalence of finite automata. Technical Report 71-114. University of California, 1971.

Problem 75 ★
Design a polynomial-time algorithm for testing whether a given finite set of words $C \subseteq \Sigma^*$ is a code (see Problem 6).

Problem 76 ★★
Design algorithms solving the following two problems (we are interested only in the existence of the algorithms, not their complexity).

(1) Given a finite automaton $\mathcal{A}$ over the alphabet $\{a, b\}$, determine whether $\#_a(w) = \#_b(w)$ for all words w accepted by $\mathcal{A}$.
(2) Given a finite automaton $\mathcal{A}$ over the alphabet $\{a, b\}$, determine whether $\#_a(w) = \#_b(w)$ for infinitely many words w accepted by $\mathcal{A}$.

Problem 77
A word w *synchronizes* a deterministic automaton if there exists a state q such that for all states q' it holds that $q' \xrightarrow{w} q$. Design an algorithm that, given an automaton with n states over a fixed-size alphabet, decides in polynomial time whether there exists a synchronizing word for it. If so, the algorithm should output such a word of length $\mathcal{O}(n^3)$.

Problem 78 ★★
The Černý conjecture, a 50-years-old open problem, states that if a deterministic automaton with n states has a synchronizing word, then it has one of length at most $(n - 1)^2$.

(1) Find a synchronizing word of length $(n - 1)^2$ for the following automaton:

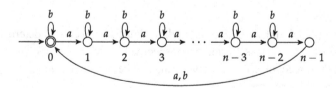

(2) Prove that there is no shorter synchronizing word for this automaton.

Problem 79 ★
Design an algorithm which, for a regular expression β and a word $w \in \Sigma^*$, decides whether β generates w and works in time:

(1) $\mathcal{O}(|\Sigma| \cdot |\beta|^2 \cdot |w|)$;
(2) $\mathcal{O}(|\beta| \cdot |w|)$.

Problem 80

Consider *generalized regular expressions*, which additionally use the binary operators $\cap$ (intersection) and $-$ (set difference). Design an algorithm that, given a generalized regular expression β and a word w, decides in polynomial time whether $w \in L(\beta)$.

2.8 Stringology

Problem 81 ☆

For a given set of words $w_1, w_2, \ldots, w_n$ over an alphabet Σ, construct a deterministic finite automaton with at most $\sum_{i=1}^{n} |w_i|$ states, recognizing the language $\Sigma^*(w_1 + w_2 + \cdots + w_n)$.

Problem 82 ★★

Let $w \in \Sigma^*$ be a word of length $n > 0$ and let $\mathcal{A}$ be the minimal deterministic automaton recognizing the language $\Sigma^* w$.

(1) Show that $\mathcal{A}$ has $n + 1$ states.
(2) Show that in $\mathcal{A}$ all but at most $2n$ transitions go to the initial state.
(3) Show that $\mathcal{A}$ can be computed in time $\mathcal{O}(n)$, provided that the description does not list transitions leading to the initial state.

Problem 83. RECOGNIZING SUBWORDS ★

Let $w \in \Sigma^*$ be a word of length $n > 0$. Let $\mathcal{A}$ be the minimal deterministic automaton recognizing the set of suffixes of w (including the empty word and w itself).

(1) Show that $\mathcal{A}$ has at most $2n + 1$ states.
(2) Show that in $\mathcal{A}$ all except at most $3n$ transitions go to the sink state.
(3) The set of all infixes of w is recognized by a modification of the automaton $\mathcal{A}$ where all states except the sink state are accepting. Give an example of a word w for which this automaton is not minimal.

Problem 84 ☆

Draw minimal automata recognizing the following languages: all infixes of *abbababa* and all suffixes of *abbababa*. For simplicity, omit the sink state. How many states are needed for the analogous automata for the words $ab(ba)^n$, $n \in \mathbb{N}$, including the sink state?

3

Context-Free Languages

3.1 Context-Free Grammars

A *context-free grammar* is a tuple $\mathcal{G} = (\Sigma, \mathcal{N}, S, \mathcal{R})$, where Σ is a finite set of *terminal symbols* (or *terminals*), $\mathcal{N}$ is a finite set of *non-terminal symbols* (or *non-terminals*), $S \in \mathcal{N}$ is a *start symbol*, and $\mathcal{R}$ is a finite set of *rules* that are of the form $X \to \alpha$, where $X \in \mathcal{N}$ is a non-terminal, and α is a sequence of symbols (terminals and non-terminals) from $\Sigma \cup \mathcal{N}$; if the sequence α is empty, we write $X \to \varepsilon$. We often regroup the rules for X, writing them as

$$X \to \alpha_1 \mid \alpha_2 \mid \ldots \mid \alpha_n$$

instead of listing them separately as $X \to \alpha_1$, $X \to \alpha_2$, ..., $X \to \alpha_n$.

Context-free grammars are used to generate (derive) words over the alphabet Σ of terminal symbols. For sequences α and β of terminal and non-terminal symbols, we define a *one-step derivation relation* $\alpha \to \beta$ whenever $\alpha = \alpha_1 X \alpha_3$, $\beta = \alpha_1 \alpha_2 \alpha_3$, and $\mathcal{G}$ has a rule $X \to \alpha_2$. A word $w \in \Sigma^*$ is *generated* by $\mathcal{G}$ if $S \to^* w$, where S is the start symbol of $\mathcal{G}$, and $\to^*$ is the reflexive–transitive closure of $\to$. By $L(\mathcal{G})$ we denote the *language generated by $\mathcal{G}$*; that is, the set of words generated by $\mathcal{G}$. A language is *context-free* if it is generated by some context-free grammar.

A *derivation* for a word w is a sequence

$$S \to \alpha_1 \to \cdots \to \alpha_n = w.$$

The number n is called the length of the derivation. A *derivation from X for w* is defined analogously, except that it begins from the non-terminal X, rather than from the start symbol S.

One can also present derivations as trees. A *derivation tree* for a word w is a tree with nodes labelled by terminal or non-terminal symbols, or the empty word ε. It must satisfy the following conditions:

- the root is labelled by the start symbol S;
- if a node is labelled by a non-terminal X, then
  - either its only child has label ε and $\mathcal{G}$ has a rule $X \to \varepsilon$,
  - or its children, enumerated from left to right, have labels $a_1, \ldots, a_n \in \Sigma \cup \mathcal{N}$ with $n \geq 1$ and $\mathcal{G}$ has a rule $X \to a_1 \ldots a_n$;
- terminal symbols and ε appear only in leaves; by reading these symbols from left to right, we obtain the word w.

A *derivation tree from X* for w is defined analogously, except that the root is labelled with the non-terminal X. We say that a derivation tree *yields* w if it is a derivation tree for w from some non-terminal.

A context-free grammar is called *unambiguous* if it allows at most one derivation tree for every word. We remark that a single derivation tree may be written in a linear form (that is, as a derivation) in multiple ways, depending on the order in which the rules of the grammar are applied. Thus, even if the grammar is unambiguous, words may have multiple (linear) derivations.

Problem 85 ☆
Prove that the set of palindromes over a fixed alphabet, as well as the complement thereof, are context-free languages.

Problem 86 ☆
Given two context-free grammars generating, respectively, languages L and K, construct context-free grammars generating languages $L \cup K$, LK, L^*, and L^R.

Problem 87
Write context-free grammars for the following languages:

(1) $\{a^i b^j c^k : i \neq j \vee j \neq k\}$;
(2) $\{a^i b^j a^k : i + k = j\}$;
(3) $\{a^i b^j c^k d^l : i + j = k + l\}$;
(4) $\{a^i b^j : i < j < 2i\}$;
(5) $\{a^i b^j : 1 \leq i < 2j - 1 \wedge j \geq 1\}$.

Problem 88
Write context-free grammars for the following languages:

(1) the set of words over the alphabet $\{a, b\}$ containing the same number of occurrences of a and b;

(2) the set of words over the alphabet $\{a, b\}$ containing twice as many occurrences of a as occurrences of b;

(3) the set of words over the alphabet $\{a, b\}$ of even length where the number of occurrences of b in even positions is the same as the number of occurrences of b in odd positions.

Problem 89

Write context-free grammars for the following languages:

(1) the set of propositional formulas with one variable p, and constants *true*, *false* (the alphabet is $\{p, true, false, \wedge, \vee, \neg, (,)\}$);

(2) the set of formulas from the previous item that are *tautologies*; that is, they evaluate to *true* under every valuation of p.

Problem 90

Write context-free grammars for the following languages:

(1) the set of fully parenthesized arithmetical expressions over the alphabet $\{0, 1, (,), +, \cdot\}$ that evaluate to 2 under the standard interpretation of the symbols in the alphabet;

(2) the set of arithmetical expressions in the reverse Polish notation (postfix notation), over the alphabet $\{0, 1, +, \cdot\}$, that evaluate to 4.

Problem 91

Give context-free grammars generating those sequences of balanced parentheses (see Problem 2) that:

(1) contain an even number of opening parentheses;

(2) do not contain $(())$ as a subword.

Problem 92 ★

Construct an unambiguous context-free grammar generating the language of balanced sequences of parentheses.

Problem 93 ★

Construct an unambiguous context-free grammar generating the set of words over the alphabet $\{a, b\}$ containing the same number of occurrences of a and b (cf. Problem 88(1)).

Problem 94

Prove that for all $L \subseteq \Sigma^*$ the following conditions are equivalent:

(a) L is regular;

(b) L is generated by a context-free grammar in which every rule is of one of the forms: $X \to \varepsilon, X \to Y, X \to aY$ with $a \in \Sigma$;

(c) L is generated by a *right-linear* context-free grammar; that is, a grammar whose rules are of the form $X \to u$ or $X \to vY$ for $u, v \in \Sigma^*$;

(d) L is generated by a *left-linear* context-free grammar; that is, a grammar whose rules are of the form $X \to u$ or $X \to Yv$ for $u, v \in \Sigma^*$.

Problem 95 ★

Give an example of a context-free grammar with rules of the form $X \to \varepsilon$, $X \to Y, X \to wY, X \to Yw$ with $w \in \Sigma^*$ that generates a non-regular language. Can such grammars generate all context-free languages?

Problem 96 ★

We say that a context-free grammar $\mathcal{G}$ has a *self-loop* if for some non-terminal symbol X we have $X \to^* \alpha X \beta$ where $\alpha, \beta \neq \varepsilon$. Prove that a grammar without self-loops generates a regular language.

Problem 97

Let $\mathcal{G}$ be a context-free grammar with m non-terminals and rules whose right-hand sides have length at most l. Show that if ε is generated by $\mathcal{G}$, then it has a derivation of length at most $1 + l + l^2 + \cdots + l^{m-1}$. Is this bound optimal?

Problem 98 ★

Show that for every context-free grammar $\mathcal{G}$ there is a constant C such that every non-empty word w generated by $\mathcal{G}$ has a derivation of length at most $C \cdot |w|$.

Problem 99

Design an algorithm to decide whether a given context-free grammar generates an infinite language.

Problem 100

Prove that every infinite context-free language can be generated by a context-free grammar such that all of its non-terminals generate infinitely many words.

3.2 Context-Free or Not?

Similarly to the pumping lemma for regular languages (see Section 2.2), there is a pumping lemma which can be used to prove that a given language is not context-free. There are several variants of this lemma. The basic pumping lemma for context-free languages says that, for each context-free language L, there exists a constant N with the following property: every word $w \in L$ of length at least N can be factorized as

$$w = prefix \cdot left \cdot infix \cdot right \cdot suffix,$$

in such a way that

- at least one of the words $left, right$ is non-empty,
- the word $left \cdot infix \cdot right$ has at most N letters, and
- the word $w_k = prefix \cdot left^k \cdot infix \cdot right^k \cdot suffix$ belongs to the language L, for all $k \in \mathbb{N}$.

A stronger variant is the so-called Ogden's lemma, which talks about words with a distinguished set of *marked positions*. It says that, for each context-free language L, there exists a constant N with the following property: every word $w \in L$ with at least N marked positions (in particular, $|w| \geq N$) can be factorized as

$$w = prefix \cdot left \cdot infix \cdot right \cdot suffix,$$

in such a way that

- at least one of the words $left, right$ contains a marked position,
- the word $left \cdot infix \cdot right$ has at most N marked positions, and
- the word $w_k = prefix \cdot left^k \cdot infix \cdot right^k \cdot suffix$ belongs to the language L, for all $k \in \mathbb{N}$.

Notice that marking positions induces a tradeoff: on the one hand, we can guarantee that some position in $left, right$ is marked, but, on the other hand, we know that the length of $left \cdot infix \cdot right$ is bounded by N only with respect to the number of marked positions. The basic pumping lemma is a special case of Ogden's lemma with all positions of w marked. For some languages that cannot be proved not to be context-free using the pumping lemma, Ogden's lemma can be helpful.

In determining whether a given language is context-free it is often useful that the class of context-free languages is closed under homomorphic images, finite unions, and intersections with *regular* languages. Unlike regular languages, context-free languages are not closed under complement.

Problem 101 ☆
Show that the language $\{a^i b^j a^i b^j : i,j \geq 1\}$ is not context-free, but its complement is context-free.

Problem 102
Prove that the following languages are not context-free:

(1) $\{a^i b^j a^k : j = \max\{i,k\}\}$;
(2) $\{a^i b^i c^k : k \neq i\}$;
(3) $\{a^i b^j c^k : i \neq j, i \neq k, j \neq k\}$.

Problem 103
Show that no infinite subset of either of the following languages is context-free, but the complements of these languages are context-free:

(1) $\{a^n b^n c^n : n \geq 1\}$;
(2) $\{(a^n b^n)^n : n \geq 1\}$.

Problem 104
Determine whether the following languages are context-free:

(1) $\{a^i b^j c^k : i,j,k > 0, i \cdot j = k\}$;
(2) $\{a^i b^j c^k d^l : i,j,k,l > 0, i \cdot j = k + l\}$.

Problem 105 ☆
Let L be a context-free language. Is the set of palindromes in L also context-free?

Problem 106
Let $L = \{ww : w \in \Sigma^*\}$. Prove that L is context-free if, and only if, Σ contains at most one letter, and that its complement is always context-free, regardless of the cardinality of Σ.

Problem 107
Prove that for every $k \in \mathbb{N}$, the complement of the language $L_k = \{w^k : w \in \Sigma^*\}$ is context-free.

Problem 108

Prove that the language $L = \{w\$w : w \in \{a, b\}^*\}$ is not context-free, but its complement is.

Problem 109 ☆

Determine whether the following languages are context-free and whether their complements are context-free:

(1) $L_1 = \{w\$v : w, v \in \{a, b\}^*, v$ is an infix of $w\}$;
(2) $L_2 = \{w\$v^R : w, v \in \{a, b\}^*, v$ is an infix of $w\}$.

Problem 110

Is the language

$$L = \{w\$v^R : w, v \in \{a, b\}^*, \ v \text{ is a prefix and a suffix of } w\}$$

context-free? Is its complement context-free?

Problem 111 ★

Prove that $L = \{ww^Rw : w \in \{a, b\}^*\}$ is not context-free. Is its complement context-free?

Problem 112

Determine whether the following languages are context-free:

(1) $\{x\$y : x, y \in \{0, 1\}^+, [x]_2 + 1 = [y]_2\}$;
(2) $\{x\$y^R : x, y \in \{0, 1\}^+, [x]_2 + 1 = [y]_2\}$.

Problem 113

Determine whether the following languages are context-free:

(1) $L_1 = \{\text{bin}(n)\$\text{bin}(2n) : n \geq 1\}$;
(2) $L_2 = \{\text{bin}(n)\$\text{bin}(n^2)^R : n \geq 0\}$.

Problem 114

Determine whether the following languages are context-free:

(1) $\{\text{bin}(n)\$\text{bin}(m) : 1 \leq n \leq m\}$;
(2) $\{\text{bin}(n)\$\text{bin}(m)^R : 1 \leq n \leq m\}$.

Problem 115

Let D_1 and D_2 denote the sets of balanced sequences of parentheses of one type (round) and of two types (round and square), respectively. Determine whether the following languages are context-free:

(1) $\{uv^R : uv \in D_1\}$;

(2) $\{uv^R : uv \in D_2\}$.

Problem 116 ☆

Prove that each language containing only square-free words is context-free if and only if it is finite.

Problem 117

Give an example of a context-free language over a two-letter alphabet, whose complement is infinite and *cube-free*; that is, it contains only cube-free words.

HINT: *Use the Thue–Morse word.*

Problem 118 ★

Consider the ordered alphabet $\{0, 1\}$ with $0 < 1$. A *Lyndon word* is a primitive word which is lexicographically the smallest among all its cyclic shifts. Is the set of all Lyndon words context-free? (See also Problem 5.)

Problem 119 ★

(1) Let V be a finite set of propositional variables. Prove that the set of tautologies over V, interpreted as words over $V \cup \{false, true, \vee, \wedge, \neg, (,)\}$, is context-free (cf. Problem 89(2)).

(2) The set of formulas over a countable set of variables can be represented as the language over the alphabet

$$\{false, true, x, 1, 0, \vee, \wedge, \neg, (,)\}$$

generated by the following grammar:

$$F \to true \,|\, false \,|\, V \,|\, (F \vee F) \,|\, (F \wedge F) \,|\, (\neg F),$$
$$V \to x1 \,|\, V0 \,|\, V1.$$

For example, $((x101 \vee (\neg x1)) \wedge (\neg(false \vee x101)))$ is a formula. Prove that the set of all tautologies is not a context-free language. (It follows easily from the P $\neq$ NP conjecture, but show it without assuming this conjecture.)

A context-free grammar is *linear* if in every rule $A \to w$ the word w contains at most one non-terminal. A context-free language is linear if it is generated by a linear grammar.

Problem 120
Show that for each linear context-free language L there exists a constant N such that each word $w \in L$ of length at least N can be factorized as

$$w = prefix \cdot left \cdot infix \cdot right \cdot suffix,$$

in such a way that $left \cdot right \neq \varepsilon$, $|prefix \cdot left| \leq N$, $|right \cdot suffix| \leq N$, and for all $k \in \mathbb{N}$, the word $w_k = prefix \cdot left^k \cdot infix \cdot right^k \cdot suffix$ belongs to L.

Problem 121 ☆
Show that $L = \{a^i b^i c^j d^j : i, j \in \mathbb{N}\}$ is not a linear context-free language.

Problem 122 ☆
Show that the set of those words w over the alphabet $\{a, b\}$ which have the same number of a's and b's is not a linear context-free language.

3.3 Pushdown Automata

A *pushdown automaton* can be presented as a tuple

$$\mathcal{A} = (\Sigma, \Gamma, Q, q_I, Z_I, \delta, F),$$

where Σ is an *alphabet of input symbols*, Γ is an *alphabet of stack symbols*, Q is a set of states, $q_I \in Q$ is an initial state, $Z_I \in \Gamma$ is an *initial stack symbol*, $\delta \subseteq Q \times (\Sigma \cup \{\varepsilon\}) \times \Gamma \times Q \times \Gamma^*$ is a *transition relation*, and $F \subseteq Q$ is a set of accepting states. All of the above sets are required to be finite. A *transition* $(q, a, Z, q', \gamma) \in \delta$ is usually written as

$$q, a, Z \to q', \gamma.$$

It tells the automaton to first pop the symbol Z from the stack, and then push the sequence γ.

A *configuration* of the pushdown automaton is a triple (q, w, γ), where $q \in Q$ is the current state, $w \in \Sigma^*$ is the word that remains to be read, and $\gamma \in \Gamma^*$ is the stack content (where the first letter is the symbol on the top of the stack, etc.). *Initial* configurations are of the form (q_I, w, Z_I); that is, the state is initial, and the stack contains only the initial symbol. *Final* configurations are of the form (q, ε, γ); that is, the whole input word is already read.

The following *step relation* $\vdash_A$ on configurations reflects a single step of the automaton: we let

$$(q, aw, Z\beta) \vdash_A (q', w, \alpha\beta)$$

whenever A has a transition $q, a, Z \to q', \alpha$ (including the special case of $aw = w$ when $a = \varepsilon$). Notice that A can reach a configuration (q, w, ε) with empty stack, but it can make no further transitions from this configuration. By $\vdash_A^*$ we denote the reflexive–transitive closure of $\vdash_A$.

A sequence of configurations $(q_0, w_0, \gamma_0), (q_1, w_1, \gamma_1), \ldots, (q_m, w_m, \gamma_m)$ is a *run* of A on a word $w \in \Sigma^*$ if (q_0, w_0, γ_0) is the initial configuration with $w_0 = w$, and $(q_i, w_i, \gamma_i) \vdash_A (q_{i+1}, w_{i+1}, \gamma_{i+1})$ for all $i < m$. The run is *accepting* if (q_m, w_m, γ_m) is a final configuration (that is, $w_m = \varepsilon$) and $q_m \in F$. The language recognized by A is defined as the set of those words on which there exists an accepting run:

$$L(A) = \left\{ w \in \Sigma^* : (q_I, w, Z_I) \vdash_A^* (q_F, \varepsilon, \gamma) \text{ for some } q_F \in F, \gamma \in \Gamma^* \right\}.$$

Two automata are *equivalent* if they recognize the same language.

Problem 123 ☆
Construct pushdown automata recognizing previously introduced context-free languages:

(1) palindromes (Problem 85);
(2) balanced sequences of parentheses (Problem 92);
(3) words containing twice as many a's as b's (Problem 88(2));
(4) words that are not of the form ww (Problem 106).

Problem 124
Construct a pushdown automaton recognizing the language

$$\left\{ \mathrm{bin}(n) \, \$ \, \mathrm{bin}(n+1)^R : n \in \mathbb{N} \right\}.$$

Problem 125 ★
Construct a pushdown automaton recognizing the language

$$\left\{ \mathrm{bin}(n) \, \$ \, \mathrm{bin}(3 \cdot n)^R : n \in \mathbb{N} \right\}.$$

Generalize this construction.

Problem 126 ★★
Prove that for every pushdown automaton one can construct an equivalent pushdown automaton with two states only.

Problem 127 ☆
Prove that for each pushdown automaton one can construct an equivalent automaton (with the same states) that in each transition replaces the topmost stack symbol with at most two stack symbols.

Problem 128 ★★
Prove that for each pushdown automaton one can construct an equivalent pushdown automaton that has only *push* transitions and *pop* transitions; that is, only transitions of the form

$$q, a, Z \rightarrow q', YZ \quad \text{and} \quad q, a, Z \rightarrow q', \varepsilon.$$

Can one limit the number of states for such automata as well?

Problem 129 ☆
Given a pushdown automaton recognizing a language L, construct pushdown automata recognizing the following languages:

(1) $\text{Prefix}(L) = \{w : \exists v. \, wv \in L\}$;
(2) $\text{Suffix}(L) = \{w : \exists u. \, uw \in L\}$;
(3) $\text{Infix}(L) = \{w : \exists u, v. \, uwv \in L\}$.

Problem 130

(1) Give an example of a non-regular context-free language L such that the set of infixes of words from L is regular.
(2) Give an example of a non-regular context-free language L such that the set of infixes of words from L is not regular.

Problem 131
Given a pushdown automaton recognizing a language L, construct a pushdown automaton recognizing the language

$$L^R = \left\{w^R : w \in L\right\}.$$

Problem 132 ★★
Given a pushdown automaton recognizing a language L, construct a pushdown automaton recognizing the language

$$\text{Cycle}(L) = \{vw : wv \in L\}.$$

Problem 133 ★

Given a pushdown automaton recognizing a language L, and a finite automaton recognizing a language K, construct pushdown automata recognizing the following languages:

(1) $L \cap K$;
(2) LK^{-1};
(3) $K^{-1}L$.

Can this be done also when K is only assumed to be context-free?

Problem 134

Let $max(w)$, $min(w)$, and $med(w)$ denote, respectively, the maximum, the minimum, and the median of the numbers $\#_a(w)$, $\#_b(w)$, and $\#_c(w)$. Determine which of the following languages are regular, and which are context-free:

(1) $\{u \in \{a, b, c\}^* : max(w) - min(w) \leq 2017 \text{ for each prefix } w \text{ of } u\}$;
(2) $\{u \in \{a, b, c\}^* : max(w) - med(w) \leq 2017 \text{ for each prefix } w \text{ of } u\}$.

Problem 135 ★

Prove that for every pushdown automaton $\mathcal{A}$ there exists a constant C such that for every non-empty word $w \in L(\mathcal{A})$ there exists an accepting run of length at most $C \cdot |w|$.

Problem 136 ★

Prove that for each pushdown automaton $\mathcal{A}$ the set of words that are the possible contents of the stack in runs of $\mathcal{A}$ is regular. Then, deduce that the set of words that are the possible contents of the stack in *accepting* runs of $\mathcal{A}$ is also regular.

A pushdown automaton over the input alphabet Σ is *deterministic* if from every configuration there is at most one possible move; that is, for each state p and each stack symbol Z,

- for each symbol $a \in \Sigma \cup \{\varepsilon\}$ there is at most one transition of the form $p, a, Z \to q, \gamma$, and
- if there is a transition of the form $p, \varepsilon, Z \to q, \gamma$, then there is no transition of the form $p, a, Z \to q', \gamma'$ for $a \neq \varepsilon$.

Problem 137 ★

Prove that the language

$$\left\{a^n b^n \; : \; n \in \mathbb{N}\right\} \cup \left\{a^n b^{2n} \; : \; n \in \mathbb{N}\right\}$$

cannot be recognized by a deterministic pushdown automaton.

Problem 138 ★

Prove that the set of palindromes over the alphabet $\{a, b\}$ cannot be recognized by a deterministic pushdown automaton.

3.4 Properties of Context-Free Languages

Problem 139

Give an example of a context-free language L such that the language $\frac{1}{2}L = \{u \; : \; \exists v. \, |u| = |v| \wedge uv \in L\}$ is not context-free (cf. Problem 35).

Problem 140

The shuffle of two regular languages is regular (see Problem 41).

(1) Prove that the shuffle of a context-free language and a regular language is context-free.

(2) Construct an example of two context-free languages whose shuffle is not context-free.

Problem 141

In Problem 42 we construct a finite language whose shuffle closure is not regular; however, it is context-free. Construct a finite language whose shuffle closure is not context-free.

Problem 142

Prove that if K and L are regular languages then the language $\bigcup_{n \in \mathbb{N}} K^n \cap L^n$ is context-free, but need not be regular.

Problem 143

Give an example of regular languages K, L, M such that the language $\bigcup_{n \in \mathbb{N}} K^n \cap L^n \cap M^n$ is not context-free.

Problem 144

Give an example of a context-free language L such that the language $\sqrt{L} = \{w \; : \; ww \in L\}$ is not context-free (cf. Problem 35).

Problem 145

Give an example of a context-free language L such that the language $\text{Root}(L) = \{w : w^k \in L \text{ for some } k\}$ is not context-free (cf. Problem 36).

Problem 146 ☆

Let L be a regular language. Show that $\{uv^R : uv \in L, u \neq v\}$ is a context-free language.

Problem 147 ☆

Let $L \subseteq \{a, b\}^*$ be a regular language and let h_1 and h_2 be homomorphisms. Show that $\{h_1(u)(h_2(u))^R : u \in L\}$ is a linear context-free language.

Problem 148 ☆

Let h_1 and h_2 be homomorphisms on $\{a_1, b_1, a_2, b_2\}^*$ defined by $h_i(a_i) = a$, $h_i(b_i) = b$, and $h_i(a_j) = h_i(b_j) = \varepsilon$ for $i \neq j$. Show that the language $\{w : h_1(w) = h_2(w)\}$ is not context-free.

Problem 149

Show that for every pair of homomorphisms, h_1 and h_2, both $\{xy^R : h_1(x) = h_2(y)\}$ and $\{xy^R : h_1(x) \neq h_2(y)\}$ are linear context-free.

Problem 150

Show that the class of linear context-free languages is closed under intersections with regular languages.

Problem 151 ☆

For a given language L, let $\min(L)$ be the language of words from L that are minimal in the prefix order; that is, $u \in \min(L)$ if and only if $u \in L$ and no strict prefix of u belongs to L. Prove that if L is recognizable by a deterministic pushdown automaton, then so is $\min(L)$.

Problem 152 ☆

Show that for $L = \{a^i b^j c^k : k \geq i \text{ or } k \geq j\}$ the language $\min(L)$, defined in Problem 151, is not context-free.

Problem 153

In analogy to Problem 151, we define the language $\max(L)$ of words in L that are maximal in the prefix order; that is, $u \in \max(L)$ if $u \in L$ and no word having u as a strict prefix belongs to L. Give an example of a context-free language L such that $\max(L)$ is not context-free.

Problem 154

Prove that for every regular language L over an alphabet Σ the set M of words v over Σ at a Hamming distance at most $|v|/2$ from a word in L is context-free, but it need not be regular (cf. Problem 40).

Problem 155. PARIKH'S THEOREM ★★

Fix an alphabet $\Sigma = \{a_1, \ldots, a_d\}$. The *Parikh image of a word* $w \in \Sigma^*$ is $(\#_{a_1}(w), \ldots, \#_{a_d}(w)) \in \mathbb{N}^d$. The *Parikh image of a language* $L \subseteq \Sigma^*$ is the set of Parikh images of all $w \in L$. Prove that for every context-free language over Σ there is a regular language over Σ with the same Parikh image.

Problem 156 ☆

Prove that each context-free language over a one-letter alphabet is regular.

Problem 157 ☆

Prove that if L is a context-free language, then $\{a^{|w|} : w \in L\}$ is a regular language.

Problem 158 ☆

A language has the *prefix property* if, for every two words from that language, one is a prefix of the other. Show that if a context-free language has the prefix property then it is a regular language.

Problem 159

(1) Is there a language L over a finite alphabet such that neither L nor the complement of L contain an infinite regular language?

(2) What if we additionally require L to be context-free?

4

Theory of Computation

4.1 Turing Machines

A *Turing machine* is essentially a non-deterministic finite automaton enriched with external memory in the form of an infinite sequence of cells, called the *tape*. At every stage of the computation, the machine's *head* is placed over one of the cells. In every step, the machine changes its state, overwrites the contents of the current cell, and possibly moves its head to a neighbouring cell.

Formally, a Turing machine $\mathcal{M}$ over an input alphabet Σ has a finite set of states Q with a distinguished initial state $q_0 \in Q$, a subset $F \subseteq Q$ of *accepting states*, a finite tape alphabet $T \supseteq \Sigma$ with a distinguished *blank* symbol $\text{B} \in T - \Sigma$, and a transition relation

$$\delta \subseteq Q \times T \times Q \times T \times \{\leftarrow, \circlearrowleft, \rightarrow\}.$$

A transition $(q, a, p, b, d) \in \delta$ is applicable in state q if the machine's head sees the tape symbol a in its current cell. The transition allows the machine to overwrite a with b, change the state to p, and either keep the head over the same cell or move it left or right, depending on d.

A *configuration* of the machine specifies the tape contents, the machine's state, and the position of the head: for $w, v \in T^*$ and $q \in Q$, the configuration wqv describes the situation where the tape contains the word wv with all remaining cells empty (that is, containing the blank symbol B), the state is q, and the head is placed over the cell containing the first symbol of the word v.

Given an input word w, the machine starts its computation in its initial state q_0, with its head over the first (left-most) symbol of w. The initial configuration is thus $c_0 = q_0 w$. The computation consists in applying transitions sequentially, starting from the initial configuration c_0. The application of a single transition of $\mathcal{M}$ is captured by the *step relation* $\vdash_{\mathcal{M}}$: we write $c \vdash_{\mathcal{M}} c'$ if configuration c' is the result of applying a transition of machine

41

$\mathcal{M}$ in configuration c. A *run of* $\mathcal{M}$ *over* w is a finite or infinite sequence of consecutive configurations,

$$c_0 \vdash_{\mathcal{M}} c_1 \vdash_{\mathcal{M}} c_2 \vdash_{\mathcal{M}} \cdots .$$

A configuration wqv is accepting if the state q is accepting; a run is accepting if it is finite and its last configuration is accepting. The language $L(\mathcal{M})$ recognized by a machine $\mathcal{M}$ consists of all those words $w \in \Sigma^*$ for which $\mathcal{M}$ has an accepting run starting in the initial configuration $q_0 w$. Two Turing machines are *equivalent* if they recognize the same language.

Unless stated otherwise, we assume that the tape is infinite in both directions; however, one could also consider a model with *right-infinite* tape, where there are no tape cells to the left of the initial position of the head. The two models are computationally equivalent (see Problem 164).

A *multi-tape* Turing machine can have multiple tapes. Transitions of a machine with k tapes are in the following format:

$$\delta \subseteq Q \times T^k \times Q \times T^k \times \{\leftarrow, \circlearrowright, \rightarrow\}^k.$$

Thus such a machine has k heads, moving independently, but a common state is used to determine their moves. A machine with any constant number of tapes can be simulated by a machine with a single tape. Therefore, the one-tape model is computationally equivalent to the k-tape one, for all k.

The Turing machines discussed so far are *non-deterministic*. A machine is *deterministic* if its transition relation δ satisfies the following condition: for every state q and tape symbol a, there is at most one state p, tape symbol b, and direction t such that $(q, a, p, b, t) \in \delta$ (equivalently, there is *exactly* one p, b, and t). Thus, in every state q and for every tape symbol a, a deterministic machine has at most one possible transition to apply.

Problem 160 ☆
Construct Turing machines over the input alphabet $\{0, 1\}$ recognizing the following languages:

(1) $\{ww : w \in \{0, 1\}^*\}$;
(2) the set of palindromes;
(3) the set of binary representations of prime numbers.

Problem 161
A directed graph with n vertices $\{0, \ldots, n-1\}$ can be represented by a word over $\{0, 1\}$ of length n^2, whose kth letter is 1 if and only if there is an edge in the graph from vertex i to vertex j, where $k = n \cdot i + j + 1$.

(1) Construct a *non-deterministic* Turing machine that recognizes the language of all those words over $\{0, 1\}$ that represent a graph with a path from vertex 0 to vertex $n - 1$.
(2) Construct a *deterministic* Turing machine recognizing the same language.

Problem 162 ☆

We say that a deterministic one-tape Turing machine over input alphabet $\{a\}$ computes a function $f : \mathbb{N} \to \mathbb{N}$ in *unary* representation if, for each $n \geq 0$, the computation of the machine starting in the initial configuration $q_0 a^n$ terminates in the configuration $q_f a^{f(n)}$, where q_f is a distinguished final state.

(1) Construct a Turing machine computing the function $n \mapsto 2^n$.
(2) Construct a Turing machine computing the function $n \mapsto \lceil \log_2 n \rceil$.

Problem 163

Given two deterministic Turing machines $\mathcal{M}_1$ and $\mathcal{M}_2$ over the alphabet Σ, construct deterministic machines recognizing the following languages:

(1) $L(\mathcal{M}_1) \cup L(\mathcal{M}_2)$;
(2) $L(\mathcal{M}_1) \cap L(\mathcal{M}_2)$;
(3) $L(\mathcal{M}_1)L(\mathcal{M}_2)$;
(4) $L(\mathcal{M}_1)^*$.

Problem 164

Prove that every Turing machine is equivalent to a machine with a right-infinite tape; that is, a tape that has no cells to the left of the initial position of the head.

Problem 165

Given a *non-deterministic* Turing machine, construct an equivalent *deterministic* one.

Problem 166

Prove that every Turing machine $\mathcal{M}$ over the input alphabet $\{0, 1\}$ is equivalent to a Turing machine $\mathcal{M}'$ with tape alphabet $\{0, 1, \text{B}\}$ which never writes the blank symbol B.

Problem 167 ★

Given a Turing machine, construct an equivalent one-tape Turing machine with four states.

Problem 168 ★★
In a *write-once* Turing machine, whenever a transition overwrites a symbol a with a symbol b, either $a = $ B $\neq b$ or $a = b \neq$ B holds.

(1) Given a one-tape Turing machine, construct an equivalent two-tape write-once machine.
(2) Prove that one-tape write-once Turing machines only recognize regular languages.

Problem 169 ★★
Prove that a deterministic one-tape Turing machine that makes $\mathcal{O}(n)$ steps on each input of length n recognizes a regular language (cf. Problem 185).

Problem 170
The notion of pushdown automaton can be naturally extended to automata with multiple stacks. Show that every Turing machine is equivalent to an automaton with two stacks. Deduce further that every automaton with k stacks is equivalent to an automaton with two stacks.

An *automaton with a queue* is similar to pushdown automata, except that it performs operations on a queue, not on a stack. Transitions are of the forms

$$(q, a, p), \qquad (q, \text{get}(s), p), \qquad (q, \text{put}(s), p),$$

where q and p are states, a is an input symbol, and s is an element of a finite queue alphabet S. The first one reads a from the input; the second one is only enabled when s is the first symbol in the queue and it removes this symbol from the queue; the last one adds s to the queue as the last symbol. We assume that the queue is initially empty.

Problem 171
Prove that every Turing machine is equivalent to an automaton with a queue.

A *k-counter automaton*, for $k \geq 1$, is a non-deterministic finite automaton additionally equipped with k *counters* $c_1, \ldots, c_k$. Each counter stores a non-negative integer; initially, all the counters are set to 0, except for a distinguished counter c_1 whose initial value is understood as the input of the counter automaton. Thus, counter automata recognize sets of non-negative integers, rather than sets of words. Transitions of counter automata do not read input, but manipulate counters: every transition performs an operation on one of the counters c_i. The allowed operations are

$$c_i \overset{?}{=} 0 \quad \text{(zero test)},$$

$$c_i\text{++} \quad \text{(increment)},$$

$$c_i\text{--} \quad \text{(decrement)},$$

but the transition c_i-- can be executed only if the current value of c_i is strictly positive. That is, counter values are not allowed to drop below 0.

Problem 172 ★

Turing machines over a one-letter input alphabet can be viewed as acceptors of sets of natural numbers, written in unary representation. Prove that such Turing machines are equivalent to three-counter automata.

4.2 Computability and Undecidability

A machine *halts* on an input word w if it has no infinite run starting from the initial configuration $q_0 w$. A language $L \subseteq \Sigma^*$ such that $L = L(\mathcal{M})$ for some Turing machine $\mathcal{M}$ that may or may not halt on all input words is called *recursively enumerable* or *semi-decidable*. Problem 173 justifies the common use of both these rather different names: it implies that a language L is accepted by a Turing machine if and only if there exists a (different) Turing machine that outputs all words in L one by one. A machine that halts on all inputs is called *total*. If $L = L(\mathcal{M})$ for a total machine $\mathcal{M}$, then L is called *decidable*. Unsurprisingly, a language that is not decidable is called *undecidable*.

It is standard to identify a language with the computational problem of checking whether a given word belongs to the language. For example, one may say that 'it is decidable whether a given number is prime', meaning that the language of all (representations of) prime numbers is decidable. In such statements one typically neglects to specify a concrete representation schema for numbers (or for automata, grammars, Turing machines, or other input objects) as words, since decidability properties usually do not depend on the chosen method of representation.

Many natural computational problems are known to be undecidable, the halting problem for Turing machines being the archetypical example. Consider a representation of Turing machines as words over some fixed finite alphabet (for instance, as a list of alphabet letters followed by a list of transitions). The *halting problem* is then the problem of checking, given a representation $[\mathcal{M}]$ of a machine $\mathcal{M}$ and a word w over the input alphabet of $\mathcal{M}$, whether $\mathcal{M}$ halts on input w. Other undecidable problems include checking whether a given machine accepts a non-empty language, a regular or context-free language, etc. In fact, the well-known Rice theorem says that every non-trivial question about the language accepted by a given Turing machine is undecidable.

Deterministic Turing machines can be seen as devices for computing functions. One way to do that, for functions on natural numbers, is used in Problem 162. Another, more general, way is to consider functions mapping words to words. If a one-tape deterministic machine $\mathcal{M}$, given input word w, halts in an accepting configuration with a word v written on its tape, then we write $\mathcal{M}(w) = v$. Assuming that the input alphabet of $\mathcal{M}$ is Σ and each v above is a word over Γ, this gives a function f from Σ^* to Γ^* defined as $f(w) = v$; we say that $\mathcal{M}$ *computes* f. In general, the function computed by a machine is partial, because the machine may reject some inputs and may not halt on some inputs. Such a function is called a *partial computable function*. If the machine accepts every input, then the function is total, and is simply called a *computable function*.

Problem 173
Prove that the following conditions on a non-empty language L are equivalent:

(a) L is recursively enumerable;
(b) L is the domain of some partial computable function;
(c) L is the image of some partial computable function;
(d) L is the image of some computable function.

Problem 174 ★
Prove that a set $L \subseteq \mathbb{N}$, treated as a language L over the alphabet $\{0, 1\}$ via the standard binary representation of natural numbers, is decidable if and only if it is finite or it is the image of some strictly increasing computable function $f: \mathbb{N} \to \mathbb{N}$.

Problem 175 ☆
Prove the following Turing–Post theorem: if a language and its complement are both recursively enumerable, then they are both decidable.

Problem 176 ★★
Prove that there exists a recursively enumerable language whose complement is infinite but does not contain any infinite, recursively enumerable language.

HINT: *Construct the language by choosing, for every Turing machine $\mathcal{M}$ that accepts an infinite language, a single word accepted by $\mathcal{M}$. Choose wisely, so that the complement of your language remains infinite.*

Problem 177 ★

Recall the definition of a k-counter automaton from just before Problem 172. Prove that there exists a two-counter automaton $\mathcal{A}$ such that it is undecidable whether $\mathcal{A}$ halts on a given input number n.

Problem 178 ★★

Prove that the following *Post correspondence problem* is undecidable: Given two lists of words $u_1, \ldots, u_n \in \Sigma^*$ and $w_1, \ldots, w_n \in \Sigma^*$, is there a sequence of indices $i_1, \ldots, i_m \in \{1, \ldots, n\}$ such that

$$u_{i_1} \ldots u_{i_m} = w_{i_1} \ldots w_{i_m}?$$

If such a sequence exists then the word $u_{i_1} \ldots u_{i_n}$ (equal to $w_{i_1} \ldots w_{i_n}$) is called a *solution* of the instance of the Post correspondence problem.

HINT: *As an intermediate step, use a modification where i_1 has to be 1.*

Problem 179 ★

Prove that the following *universality problem* is undecidable: Given a context-free grammar $\mathcal{G}$ over an alphabet Σ, is it the case that $L(\mathcal{G}) = \Sigma^*$?

Problem 180

Are the following problems decidable?

(1) Given a context-free grammar $\mathcal{G}$, does $L(\mathcal{G})$ contain a palindrome?
(2) Given two context-free grammars $\mathcal{G}_1$ and $\mathcal{G}_2$, is it the case that

$$L(\mathcal{G}_1) \cap L(\mathcal{G}_2) = \emptyset?$$

(3) Is a given context-free grammar $\mathcal{G}$ unambiguous?

HINT: *Use the Post correspondence problem.*

Problem 181 ☆

Is it decidable whether a given word is accepted by a given one-tape deterministic Turing machine, assuming that we know that the machine never changes the direction of head movements more than once?

Problem 182 ★

Is the following problem decidable: Given words $u, w \in \Sigma^*$ and a number k, is there a word $x \in \Sigma^*$ of length at least k such that $\#_u(x) = \#_w(x)$?

Problem 183

Fix an encoding of Turing machines that represents a machine $\mathcal{M}$ as a word $[\mathcal{M}]$. Consider a function C that maps each pair $([\mathcal{M}], v)$ to the minimal length of a word w such that $\mathcal{M}(w) = v$, or to a special symbol ∞ if there is no such w. Prove that the function C is not computable but it can be approximated in the following sense: there is a Turing machine that, for input $([\mathcal{M}], v)$, produces an infinite sequence of numbers that eventually stabilizes at the value $C([\mathcal{M}], v)$.[1]

4.3 Chomsky Hierarchy

Context-sensitive grammars are defined like context-free grammars, with the exception that their rules are of the form

$$\alpha X \beta \to \alpha \gamma \beta,$$

where $X \in \mathcal{N}$, $\alpha, \beta, \gamma \in (\Sigma \cup \mathcal{N})^*$, and $\gamma \neq \varepsilon$, for a set $\mathcal{N}$ of non-terminal symbols and a set Σ of terminal symbols. Languages generated by context-sensitive grammars are called *context-sensitive languages*.

Under the above definition, context-sensitive languages cannot contain the empty word. One can easily extend the definition slightly to allow the empty word. In this section, however, we prefer to keep this simple definition and restrict our attention to non-empty words.

The *Chomsky hierarchy* consists of four classes of languages:

        Type 0 : Recursively enumerable languages,

        Type 1 : Context-sensitive languages,

        Type 2 : Context-free languages,

        Type 3 : Regular languages.

Ordered by inclusion, they form a strictly increasing chain:

$$\text{Type } 3 \subsetneq \text{Type } 2 \subsetneq \text{Type } 1 \subsetneq \text{Type } 0.$$

---

[1] There is no contradiction here, since an observer of an infinite sequence can never tell whether it has already stabilized.

Problem 184

A *monotonic* grammar has rules of the form $\alpha \rightarrow \beta$, where α and β are sequences of terminal and non-terminal symbols and $|\beta| \geq |\alpha|$. Prove that each monotonic grammar can be transformed into an equivalent context-sensitive grammar (possibly using different non-terminal symbols).

Problem 185

Prove that context-sensitive languages are exactly the languages recognized by non-deterministic *linear bounded automata*; that is, one-tape Turing machines working over input words with marked first and last positions, accessing only the part of the tape occupied by the input word[2] (cf. Problem 169).

Problem 186 ★

Prove that the quotient of a context-sensitive language by a regular language may be an undecidable language.

HINT: *Use the language of runs of a Turing machine that recognizes a recursively enumerable but undecidable language.*

Problem 187 ☆

Prove that recursively enumerable languages are closed under quotients by recursively enumerable languages.

Problem 188 ★★

Which of the four classes of the Chomsky hierarchy are closed under union, intersection, and complement?

4.4 Computational Complexity

We assume the standard model of Turing machines defined in Section 4.1. All machines are multi-tape by default, unless explicitly stated otherwise. We write P, NP, and PSPACE for the classes of languages recognized by, respectively, deterministic Turing machines working in polynomial time, non-deterministic Turing machines working in polynomial time, and deterministic Turing machines working in polynomial space. That is, a language L belongs to P if it is recognized by a deterministic Turing machine that makes $\mathcal{O}(n^c)$ steps on inputs of length n for some constant c, and similarly for NP and PSPACE. A language L is NP-*hard* if each language in NP can be reduced

---

[2] One can equivalently take Turing machines using $\mathcal{O}(n)$ space.

to L by means of a *polynomial-time reduction*; that is, a reduction computable in P. A language is NP-*complete* if it is NP-*hard* and belongs to NP. The notions of PSPACE-*hardness* and PSPACE-*completeness* are defined analogously.

A famous NP-complete problem is the satisfiability of propositional formulas. We write CNF-SAT for the variant of this problem where the formula is in the conjunctive normal form; that is, it is a conjunction of clauses. In 3SAT we additionally assume that each clause has at most three literals.

We will commonly use the concept of an *off-line Turing machine*. In this setting, the input word w is given on a special *input tape*, which contains w delimited by the start marker ▷ on the left and the end marker ◁ on the right. The input tape is read-only, which means that the head, initially placed over the start marker, can only move over the tape reading its contents, but cannot write on it. The machine, however, also has a constant number of work tapes, initially filled with blanks, which can be used for storing intermediate results of computations. The transitions are defined as usual for multi-tape machines; that is, a transition consists of simultaneous moves of all the heads over all the tapes.

The class L contains all languages recognized by an off-line Turing machine working in logarithmic space; that is, the working space used for inputs of size n is bounded by $k \cdot \log n$ for some constant k. Similarly, we can define functions $f \colon \Sigma^* \to \Gamma^*$ computable in logarithmic space, for some fixed alphabets Σ and Γ. We say that such a function f is *computable in* L if there exists an off-line Turing machine that, given input w of size n, uses at most $k \cdot \log n$ working space and outputs the word $f(w)$ in the following sense. Selected transitions of the machine are enriched with annotations 'output γ' for some $\gamma \in \Gamma$. When such a transition is executed, the symbol γ is written to the output. The machine has to accept and the word consisting of all consecutive output letters has to be equal to $f(w)$.

A function $f \colon \mathbb{N} \to \mathbb{N}$ is *space-constructible* if there exists an off-line Turing machine that on input 1^n produces the word $1^{f(n)}$ on the first work tape while visiting only $\mathcal{O}(f(n))$ cells of the work tapes in total. Analogously, f is *time-constructible* if there exists an off-line Turing machine that on input 1^n produces the word $1^{f(n)}$ on the first work tape while performing $\mathcal{O}(f(n))$ steps in total.

Problem 189
Which of the following functions are space-constructible: $2n$, n^2, n^k for a constant k, 2^n, 2^{2^n}, $\lceil \log_2(n+1) \rceil$?

Problem 190
Which of the following functions are time-constructible: $2n$, n^2, n^k for a constant k, 2^n, 2^{2^n}, $\lceil \log_2(n + 1) \rceil$?

Problem 191
Prove that the composition of two functions computable in L is also computable in L.

Problem 192
Prove that the classes P, NP, and PSPACE are closed under Kleene star in the following sense: if a language L belongs to the class, then so does L^*.

Problem 193 ★
Show that L is closed under Kleene star if and only if L = NL.

Problem 194
Prove that the following problem is NP-complete: given a regular expression over an alphabet Σ, decide if it generates word containing all letters from Σ.

Problem 195 ★
In the EXACT COVER problem, one is given a finite universe U and a family $\mathcal{F}$ of subsets of U. The task is to determine whether there is a subfamily of $\mathcal{F}$ consisting of pairwise disjoint sets whose union is equal to U. Prove that this problem is NP-complete.

Problem 196 ★
In the SUBSET SUM problem, one is given a set S of non-negative integers and a target non-negative integer t, all encoded in binary. The task is to verify whether there exists a subset of S such that the sum of elements of the subset is equal to t. Prove that this problem is NP-complete.

Problem 197 ★
Prove that every problem in NP can be reduced to 3SAT by a reduction working in logarithmic space.

Problem 198 ★★
In the TILING problem, we are given a set of square tiles $S \subseteq \{0, 1, \ldots, n\}^4$ and an integer N, represented in unary. Each tile x is represented as a quadruple of integers $x = (x[\leftarrow], x[\uparrow], x[\rightarrow], x[\downarrow])$ from the range between 0 and n, which we will treat as *colours* of the respective sides of the tile. A tiling of an $N \times N$

square is called *proper* if it consists of N^2 tiles from S aligned side-to-side, and the following two conditions are satisfied:

- if two tiles share a side, the colours of their corresponding sides match;
- the sides of the $N \times N$ square are coloured with 0.

Tiles cannot be rotated. The question is whether such a proper tiling exists. Prove that this problem is NP-complete.

Problem 199 ★
Prove that the following problem is PSPACE-complete: given a non-deterministic automaton $\mathcal{A}$ over an alphabet Σ, decide if $\mathcal{A}$ rejects some word from Σ^*.

Problem 200 ★
Prove that the following problem is PSPACE-complete: given a finite set of deterministic automata, decide if there is a word accepted by all automata from the set.

PART II

Solutions

*Mikołaj Bojańczyk, Lorenzo Clemente, Wojciech Czerwiński,
Piotr Hofman, Szczepan Hummel, Bartek Klin,
Leszek Kołodziejczyk, Eryk Kopczyński, Sławomir Lasota,
Filip Mazowiecki, Henryk Michalewski, Filip Murlak,
Joanna Ochremiak, Paweł Parys, Michał Pilipczuk,
Michał Skrzypczak, Szymon Toruńczyk, Igor Walukiewicz,
and Joost Winter*

5

Words, Numbers, Graphs

Solution to Problem 1

Let us begin with the left-to-right inclusion. If a word belongs to $(L^*M^*)^*$, then it can be factorized into several pieces, each one from L^*M^*. The number of pieces might be zero. Let us look at one such piece. Since it belongs to L^*M^*, it can be factorized into several even smaller pieces, the first ones from L, and the remaining ones from M, as in the following picture:

Combining these two observations, every word in $(L^*M^*)^*$ can be factorized into pieces, each one of them from $L \cup M$, as in the following picture:

This proves the left-to-right inclusion.

For the right-to-left inclusion, take some word in $(L \cup M)^*$. This word can be factorized into several pieces, each one from either L or M, as in the following picture:

Each such piece belongs to L^*M^*, because L^*M^* contains both L and M, by unfolding one of the stars one time, and unfolding the other star zero times. Therefore, the entire word belongs to $(L^*M^*)^*$. ∎

Solution to Problem 2. PARENTHESIS EXPRESSIONS

Let us first show that $L \subseteq K$. Since $\varepsilon \in K$, it suffices to show that if $w, v \in K$, then $(w), wv \in K$. We shall use the notation $\#_($(u)$ and $\#_)$(u)$ for the numbers of opening and closing parentheses in u, respectively. Clearly, $\#_($(wv)$ = $\#_($(w)$ + $\#_($(v)$ = $\#_)$(w)$ + $\#_)$(v)$ = $\#_)$(wv)$. For any prefix u of wv, either u is a prefix of w and satisfies the required condition by the initial assumption, or $u = wv_0$ for some prefix v_0 of v and we have $\#_($(u)$ = $\#_($(w)$ + $\#_($(v_0)$ \geq $\#_)$(w)$ + $\#_)$(v_0)$ = $\#_)$(u)$. For (w) the argument is similar.

To show that $K \subseteq L$, we shall prove by induction on the length of the word that each word in K belongs to L. Clearly, $\varepsilon \in L$. For a word u over the alphabet $\{(,)\}$ let $f_u(i)$ denote the difference between the number of the opening and closing parentheses in the prefix of u of length i. Then, $u \in K$ if and only if $f_u(|u|) = 0$ and $f_u(i) \geq 0$ for all $i \in \{1, \ldots, |u| - 1\}$. Note also that $f_u(0) = 0$ for all u. Assume that $u \in K$. There are two cases.

Assume first that $f_u(i) \geq 1$ for all $i \in \{1, 2, \ldots, |u| - 1\}$. Since $u \in K$, $f_u(1) = f_u(|u| - 1) = 1$, which means that $u = (w)$ for some w. Note that $f_w(i) = f_u(i+1) - 1$ for $i \in \{0, 1, \ldots, |w|\}$. It follows that $f_w(|w|) = f_w(|u| - 2) = f_u(|u| - 1) - 1 = 0$ and $f_w(i) = f_u(i+1) - 1 \geq 0$ for $i \in \{0, 1, |u| - 2\}$, so $w \in K$. By the induction hypothesis, $w \in L$. By the definition of L, $u = (w) \in L$.

The remaining case is that $f_u(i) = 0$ for some $i \in \{1, 2, \ldots, |u| - 1\}$. Let $u = wv$ and $|w| = i$. Since $f_w(j) = f_u(j)$ for all $j \in \{0, 1, \ldots, |w|\}$ and $f_v(j) = f_u(j + i)$ for all $j \in \{0, 1, \ldots, |v|\}$, it follows immediately that $w, v \in K$. By the induction hypothesis, $w, v \in L$. By the definition of L, $u = wv \in L$. ∎

Solution to Problem 3. GAME GRAPH

Observe first that, since after each move of the barman the customer rotates the tray, the barman never knows exactly which glasses were reversed, except that if he chose two glasses, he knows whether they formed an edge or a diagonal of the square. Thus, we can equivalently consider a game in which the barman only chooses one of three options, *vertex*, *edge*, or *diagonal*, and the customer chooses which glasses to reverse, always respecting the barman's decision.

We shall model this game as a graph. Its vertices will correspond to all possible situations in the game (configurations of the tray with glasses), edges will have labels v, e, or d, representing the barman's choice, and there will be multiple edges with the same label starting in a given vertex, leading to vertices representing possible situations after the customer has reversed the glasses of his choice. A winning strategy for the barman can be represented as a word w over the alphabet $\{v, e, d\}$ such that each path whose label sequence is w passes through one of the two situations in which all glasses are in the same position.

Since each glass can be in one of two positions, we have 2^4 different situations in the game. This leads to a graph with 16 vertices, which is difficult to analyse. Observe, however, that since the customer chooses the glasses to reverse, and we treat right-side up and upside down symmetrically, there are only four *types* of situations in the game: all glasses have the same position, one glass has a different position from the other three, glasses across diagonals have the same positions, glasses across two parallel edges have the same positions. The graph corresponding to this level of abstraction looks like this:

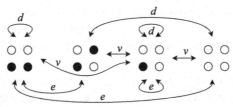

The graph is so small that we can use direct examination to find words that guarantee reaching a situation in which the barman wins (all glasses in the same position). The shortest such word is *dedvded*.

For the cases with three and five glasses, one constructs analogous graphs with two and four vertices, respectively. Both these graphs contain a cycle (of length one and three, respectively) which avoids a situation with all glasses in the same position, and in which each step between successive vertices can be made over any letter (v, e or v, e, d, respectively). Hence, the barman does not have a winning strategy in these cases. ∎

Solution to Problem 4. SEMI-LINEAR SETS

(1)   Each linear set $\{a + bn : n \in \mathbb{N}\}$ is ultimately periodic with $c = a$ and $d = b$ if $b > 0$; if $b = 0$, the set is finite (a singleton, in fact) and each finite set $A \subseteq \mathbb{N}$ is ultimately periodic with $c = \max A$ and $d = 1$. Moreover, if the sets A and A' are ultimately periodic with witnessing constants c, d and c', d', respectively, then each of them is ultimately periodic with witnessing constants $\max(c, c')$ and $d \cdot d'$. Consequently, their union is also ultimately periodic, with the same witnessing constants. It follows that all semi-linear sets are ultimately periodic. For the converse implication, let $A \subseteq \mathbb{N}$ be an ultimately periodic set with witnessing constants c and d. Then

$$A = A \cap [0, c] \cup \bigcup_{i \in A \cap (c, c+d]} \{i + dn : n \in \mathbb{N}\}.$$

(2) If A is empty, then $A^* = \{0\}$ is semi-linear. Let us assume A is non-empty. Let a be any number from A and let us consider the partition $A^* = A_0 \cup A_1 \cup \cdots \cup A_{a-1}$, where A_r contains numbers from A^* with remainder r modulo a. If A_r is non-empty, then $A_r = \{a_r + an : n \in \mathbb{N}\}$, where a_r is the least element of A_r. It follows that A^* is semi-linear, as required.

(3) Let $B = \{b_1, \ldots, b_k\}$. By the second point, B^* is semi-linear; that is, it is a finite union of linear sets. We obtain A by shifting each of these linear sets by a.

(4) The family of semi-linear sets is closed under finite union by definition. Closure under finite intersection follows from closure under union and complement. To prove closure under complement, observe that a set $A \subseteq \mathbb{N}$ is ultimately periodic if and only if $\mathbb{N} - A$ is ultimately periodic (with the same witnessing constants).

(5) For the first part (a), let $A = \{a + bn : n \in \mathbb{N}\}$ be a linear set. Let G_A be the graph having a path of length a from a source vertex u to a target vertex v (if $a = 0$, then $u = v$), plus additionally a cycle of length b starting and ending in the target vertex v. Then, the set of lengths of finite paths from u to v is precisely A. If A is a semi-linear set $A = A_1 \cup \cdots \cup A_k$ with $A_1, \ldots, A_k$ linear, then let $G_1, \ldots, G_k$ be the corresponding graphs constructed with the method above. Let s_i and t_i be the source and target vertices of G_i. We obtain G_A by taking the disjoint union of the G_i's, the source set is $\{s_1, \ldots, s_k\}$, and the target set is $\{t_1, \ldots, t_k\}$.

For the second part (b), fix a directed graph G. Since semi-linear sets are closed under finite unions, it suffices to consider a starting vertex u and a target vertex v. Recall that a path or a cycle is *simple* if it visits each vertex at most once. For each simple path P from u to v and each set $\mathcal{C} = \{C_1, C_2, \ldots, C_k\}$ of simple cycles in G define the set

$$A_{P,\mathcal{C}} = \{|P| + |C_1| \cdot n_1 + \cdots + |C_k| \cdot n_k : n_1, \ldots, n_k \in \mathbb{N} - \{0\}\}.$$

This is a semi-linear set. Let A be the union of $A_{P,\mathcal{C}}$ over all P and $\mathcal{C}$ such that the union of P and all cycles in $\mathcal{C}$ is a connected graph. We claim that A is the set of lengths of all paths from u to v. Indeed, the union of P and all cycles in $\mathcal{C}$ can be interpreted as a path from u to v, as follows. Since the union is connected, there is a cycle in $\mathcal{C}$ that has a common vertex with P: remove this cycle from $\mathcal{C}$ and insert it into P, obtaining a longer path. Continuing in this way, we obtain a path of length $|P| + |C_1| + \cdots + |C_k|$. For a path of length $|P| + |C_1| \cdot n_1 + \cdots + |C_k| \cdot n_k$, go through each cycle the appropriate number of times. Conversely, each path P from u to v can be decomposed into a simple path P_0 from u to v and a multiset of simple cycles $C_1, C_2, \ldots, C_n$, for some n, based on the fact that each non-simple path contains a simple cycle. The union of P_0 and $C_1, C_2, \ldots, C_n$ is connected, as they form the original path P. Hence, the length of P belongs to A.

(6) The sets of squares, powers of 2, and prime numbers are not semi-linear. In fact, one can show that most subsets of $\mathbb{N}$ are not semi-linear using a counting argument. Indeed, we have uncountably many subsets of $\mathbb{N}$, but only countably many semi-linear sets. ∎

Solution to Problem 5. PRIMITIVE WORDS

(1) A word v such that $w = v^n$ for some n is called a *period* of w. Hence, we must prove that each non-empty word has exactly one primitive period. For existence, consider the following recursive procedure. If w has no period other than itself, it is primitive (by definition) and we are done. Otherwise, let $v \neq w$ be a period of w and start again with w replaced by v. Since $|v| < |w|$, this procedure terminates. And since $w = v^n$ and $v = u^m$ implies $w = u^{mn}$, the primitive word output by the procedure is a period of w. For uniqueness, let u and v be periods of w. Consider a graph C_w consisting of a single cycle with vertices $\{1, 2, \ldots, |w|\}$ labelled with the corresponding letters $w_1, w_2, \ldots$ of w. An example for $w = abaabaabaaba$ looks like this:

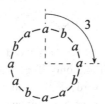

Since u and v are periods of w, rotating the cycle C_w by $|u|$ or $|v|$ vertices (clockwise), or $-|u|$ or $-|v|$ vertices (anticlockwise), does not change the labelling. Hence, we can rotate the cycle by $\alpha \cdot |v| + \beta \cdot |u|$ vertices for any $\alpha, \beta \in \mathbb{Z}$. It follows from the correctness of Euclid's algorithm that the greatest common divisor d of $|u|$ and $|v|$ can be written as $\alpha \cdot |u| + \beta \cdot |v|$ for some $\alpha, \beta \in \mathbb{Z}$. Hence, we can rotate the cycle C_w by d vertices without changing the labelling. Since d divides $|u|$ and $|v|$, $w_1 w_2 \ldots w_d$ is a period of u and v. If u and v are primitive, we must have $u = w_1 w_2 \ldots w_d = v$, which proves that w has at most one primitive period.

In fact, we have proved a stronger claim: the primitive period of w is also the shortest period of w, which in turn is the prefix of w of length d, where d is the minimal positive number such that rotating C_w by d

vertices does not change the labelling. In particular, $d = |w|/n$, where n is the exponent of w.

(2) Note that the graph C_{vw} can be obtained from C_{wv} by rotating by $|w|$ vertices. More generally, two words are conjugate if and only if their graphs are identical up to rotation. It follows immediately that being conjugate is an equivalence relation. Also, if u and w are conjugate, the minimal positive d such that rotation by d vertices does not change the labelling is the same for both graphs. Consequently, the primitive periods of u and w have the same length, which implies that their exponents are equal. Finally, the cardinality of the equivalence class of a word w is equal to the number of different rotations of the graph C_w. By the previous item, if $|w| = m$ and the exponent of w is n, then $d = m/n$ is the minimal positive number such that rotation by d vertices does not change the labelling in C_w. Then, rotations by $0, 1, 2, \ldots, d - 1$ vertices are all different, but for $i \equiv j \pmod{d}$ the rotations are identical. Hence, the cardinality of the equivalence class of w is m/n. ∎

Solution to Problem 6. CODES

(1) The set $\{a, ab, ba\}$ is not a code because the word aba admits two factorizations, $a \cdot ba$ and $ab \cdot a$. To see that the set $\{aa, baa, ba\}$ is a code, let us consider a word $w \in \{a, b\}^*$ with m occurrences of the letter b. We can then write w as

$$a^{n_0} ba^{n_1} ba^{n_2} \ldots ba^{n_m}$$

for some $n_0, n_1, \ldots, n_m \in \mathbb{N}$. This word admits a factorization with respect to $\{aa, baa, ba\}$ if and only if n_0 is even and $n_1, n_2, \ldots, n_m \geq 1$. Let us see that each such word admits exactly one factorization. The word to cover the ith occurrence of b is uniquely determined by the parity of the block of a's immediately to the right: we must use ba for odd n_i, and baa for even n_i. Having done this, we are left with blocks of letters a of even length, and we cover them with aa in a unique way.

(2) Let $C = \{u_1, u_2, \ldots, u_n\}$. We shall see that the upper bound for the minimal length of a word with two different factorizations is

$$N = \left(\sum_{i=1}^{n} |u_i| \right)^2.$$

Assume that w is a word with two different factorizations with respect to C and has the smallest length among all such words. We shall see that $|w| \leq N$. Let us label each position k of w with a quadruple (i, j, i', j') such that position k in w corresponds to position j in u_i in the first factorization and to position j' in $u_{i'}$ in the second factorization. Note that the number of different quadruples of this form is exactly N. Hence, by the pigeonhole principle, if $|w| > N$, there are two positions k, ℓ with $k < \ell$, labelled with the same quadruple (i, j, i', j'). Let v be the word obtained from w by removing the infix starting at position $k + 1$ and ending at position ℓ. We shall see that v also has two different factorizations, which contradicts the minimality of w.

First, note that both factorizations of w can be modified into factorizations of v. Indeed, the two parts of u_i, the one to the left of position k and the one to the right of position $\ell + 1$, form the whole word u_i. Hence, the first factorization can be modified simply by removing the part corresponding to the removed infix. Similarly for the second factorization.

Are these new factorizations different? By the minimality of w, the first factors of the two factorizations of w are different, as otherwise we would be able to shorten w by removing them. Since the first letter of w is never contained in the removed infix, the first factors of the two factorizations are not changed (other than possibly being split and put back together), and they remain different. Hence, the two factorizations of v are different.

(3) If $uv = vu$, then clearly $\{u, v\}$ is not a code. For the converse implication, we prove the following claim, which immediately implies that if $\{u, v\}$ is not a code, then $uv = vu$.

Claim. If $\{u, v\}$ is not a code, then $u = t^m$ and $v = t^n$ for some word t and some $m, n \in \mathbb{N}$.

Assume that the claim is false and let $\{u, v\}$ be a counterexample with the smallest possible value of $|u| + |v|$. Let w have minimal length among words with two different factorizations using $\{u, v\}$. By the minimality of $|w|$, one of these factorizations begins with u and the other with v. If $|u| = |v|$, it follows directly that $u = v$. Assume that $|u| < |v|$, the other case being symmetric. Since both u and v are prefixes of w, it follows that u is a proper prefix of v, say $v = uv'$. By replacing each v with uv' in the two factorizations of w using $\{u, v\}$, we obtain two factorizations of w using $\{u, v'\}$, which are distinct because one begins with uv' and the other with uu. Since $|u| + |v'| < |u| + |v|$, the set $\{u, v'\}$ is not a counterexample to the claim, so $u = t^m$ and $v' = t^n$ for some t and $m, n \in \mathbb{N}$. It follows that $u = t^m$ and $v = t^{m+n}$, which is a contradiction. $\blacksquare$

Solution to Problem 7. THUE–MORSE WORD

(1) Let us look at positions 2^{n-1} to $2^n - 1$ in the Thue–Morse word as given by the first definition. These are exactly those produced in the nth step

of the procedure (step 0 is producing the initial 0 at position 0). Observe that the binary representations of the numbers 2^{n-1} through $2^n - 1$ can be obtained by putting 1 in front of the $(n-1)$-bit representations of the numbers 0 through $2^{n-1} - 1$. This corresponds exactly to copying the word produced in steps 0 through $n - 1$, with all bits flipped. Hence, the first two definitions are equivalent.

It is straightforward to check that the sequence $s_0, s_1, \ldots$ from the second definition satisfies the recurrence relation from the third definition. Since this recurrence relation has only one solution, the two definitions are equivalent.

The remainder of the solution follows a proof by Carl D. Offner.[1]

(2) To verify the first assertion of the hint, that no three consecutive letters in the Thue–Morse word are equal, it suffices to note that the recurrence relation implies $t_{2n+1} \neq t_{2n}$ for all n.

For the second assertion of the hint, suppose towards a contradiction that the Thue–Morse word contains 01010 as an infix. If the infix starts at position $2n$, then $t_{2n} = t_{2n+2} = t_{2n+4} = 0$, and by the recurrence relation, $t_n = t_{n+1} = t_{n+2} = 0$, which contradicts the first assertion. Similarly, if the infix starts at position $2n + 1$, then $t_n = t_{n+1} = t_{n+2} = 1$, again contradicting the first assertion. A symmetric argument rules out a 10101 infix. All the remaining five-bit sequences contain 00 or 11. Therefore, so does the Thue–Morse word.

Let us now see that the Thue–Morse word is strongly cube-free. Towards a contradiction, assume that

$$t_n t_{n+1} \ldots t_{n+k} = t_{n+k} t_{n+k+1} \ldots t_{n+2k} \qquad (\diamond)$$

for some $n \geq 0$ and $k > 0$, and let k be minimal such that $(\diamond)$ holds. If k is even, we can use the recurrence relation and we obtain that $(\diamond)$ holds with n and k replaced by $\lfloor n/2 \rfloor$ and $k/2$, respectively, contradicting the minimality of k. Assume that k is odd. If $k = 1$, it follows that $t_n = t_{n+1} = t_{n+2}$, which contradicts the first assertion. Hence, $k \geq 3$ and, by the second assertion, between n and $n + 2k$ there is a pair of consecutive positions holding the same letter. By $(\diamond)$, there are in fact two such pairs, starting at positions differing by k. As k is odd, one of the pairs starts at an even position. That is, $t_{2m} = t_{2m+1}$ for some m, which contradicts the recurrence relation.

[1] Carl D. Offner. *Repetitions of Words and the Thue–Morse sequence.* See the author's webpage: https://www.cs.umb.edu/~offner/.

(3)   A square-free word can be obtained by taking the infinite word

$$[t_0 t_1] [t_1 t_2] [t_2 t_3] \cdots$$

over the alphabet $\{[00], [01], [10], [11]\}$. Indeed, for all $n \geq 0$ and $k > 0$,

$$[t_n t_{n+1}] \cdots [t_{n+k-1} t_{n+k}] = [t_{n+k} t_{n+k+1}] \cdots [t_{n+2k-1} t_{n+2k}]$$

immediately implies $(\diamond)$.

(4)   It is not too difficult to reduce the alphabet to three letters. We claim that in the word constructed above,

- [00] is always preceded by [10] and followed by [01],
- [11] is always preceded by [01] and followed by [10].

Indeed, by construction, [00] can be followed only by [00] or [01], but [00][00] would mean 000 in the Thue–Morse word, which is impossible. The remaining three cases are entirely analogous.

Consider the word obtained from $[t_0 t_1] [t_1 t_2] [t_2 t_3] \cdots$ by replacing all occurrences of [00] and [11] with [??]. We claim that the new word is also square-free. Suppose it is not and let it contain uu as an infix. The word u cannot consist of a single letter, because $u = [01]$ or $u = [10]$ would imply that uu is an infix of the old word, and $u = [??]$ is excluded by the previous claim. If u has at least two letters, each occurrence of [??] in u has a preceding or a following letter within u. Hence, by the previous claim we can reconstruct the word v corresponding to u in the old word. It follows that the old word contains vv as an infix, which is a contradiction.

Over a two-letter alphabet, no word of length four (or more) is square-free. ∎

6

Regular Languages

Solution to Problem 8

Let us write L for the set of words where both 0 and 1 appear an even number of times. Let us first prove that the regular expression in question generates a language contained in L. To prove this, we observe that the regular expression inside the outermost star generates a language contained in L, and concatenating many words from L gives another word in L.

We now show that all words in L are captured by the regular expression. Take some word in L. Since L contains only words of even length, this word can be factorized into two-letter blocks as follows:

$$b_1 b_2 \ldots b_n \qquad \text{with } b_1, b_2, \ldots, b_n \in \{0, 1\}^2.$$

The number of two-letter blocks from $\{01, 10\}$ must be even, since otherwise the word would have an odd number of 0's (and 1's). Let us group the two-letter blocks from $\{01, 10\}$ into consecutive pairs; each consecutive pair is separated by two-letter blocks from $\{00, 11\}$. Here is an example of such a grouping:

$$00 \; \underbrace{01 \; 00 \; 11 \; 10}_{\text{pair}} \; 00 \; 11 \; \underbrace{10 \; 11 \; 10}_{\text{pair}} \; \underbrace{01 \; 10}_{\text{pair}} \; 00 \; 00$$

Every two-letter block that is not captured by the grouping is in $00 + 11$, and every group is in

$$(01 + 10)(00 + 11)^*(01 + 10).$$

Therefore, we have managed to split the word into pieces, each one from

$$00 + 11 + (01 + 10)(00 + 11)^*(01 + 10),$$

which proves that the entire word is captured by the Kleene star of the above expression. ∎

Solution to Problem 9

We give two solutions, the second being more optimized. After reading a prefix of the input, the first automaton stores:

- the number of 1's on even positions, modulo 2;
- the number of 1's on odd positions, modulo 2;
- the number of positions, modulo 2.

Therefore, the state space of the automaton is $\{0, 1\}^3$. The initial state is $(0, 0, 0)$. The transition function is

$$\delta((a, b, c), d) = \begin{cases} (a + d, b, c + 1) & \text{if } c = 0, \\ (a, b + d, c + 1) & \text{if } c = 1, \end{cases}$$

with all arithmetic being modulo 2. The accepting states are

$$(0, 1, c) \quad \text{for } c \in \{0, 1\}.$$

The previous automaton had eight states. Let us show one that has four states. In the state, we store two bits (a, b), where:

- a is the number of 1's that need to be seen in the future on even-numbered positions, modulo 2;
- b is the number of 1's that need to be seen in the future on odd-numbered positions, modulo 2.

In the above, counting of positions refers to the part of the input that has not been read yet, and therefore the next position to be read is always odd-numbered. The initial state is $(0, 1)$, and the unique accepting state is $(0, 0)$. The transition function is

$$\delta((a, b), c) = (b, a + c)$$

with arithmetic modulo 2. A picture of the automaton is given below.

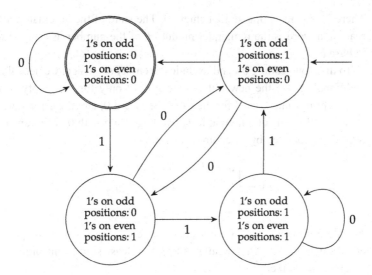

As a side note, observe that the above automaton is not only deterministic, but also reverse deterministic, in the sense that reversing the arrows gives a deterministic automaton. ∎

Solution to Problem 10. ADDITION

The following solution allows leading columns full of 0's:

$$\left(\begin{bmatrix} 0 \\ 0 \\ 0 \end{bmatrix} + \begin{bmatrix} 1 \\ 0 \\ 1 \end{bmatrix} + \begin{bmatrix} 0 \\ 1 \\ 1 \end{bmatrix} + \begin{bmatrix} 0 \\ 0 \\ 1 \end{bmatrix} \cdot \underbrace{\left(\begin{bmatrix} 1 \\ 0 \\ 0 \end{bmatrix} + \begin{bmatrix} 0 \\ 1 \\ 0 \end{bmatrix} + \begin{bmatrix} 1 \\ 1 \\ 1 \end{bmatrix} \right)^* \cdot \begin{bmatrix} 1 \\ 1 \\ 0 \end{bmatrix}}_{\text{carry}} \right)^* .$$

To disallow leading 0's, prepend the above expression with the subexpression under the external star, removing the column full of 0's. ∎

Solution to Problem 11. DIVISIBILITY

(1) We go straight for the general solution: the digits are $\{0, 1, \ldots, b-1\}$ and we want the number to be divisible by k, with k being possibly greater than $b-1$. We allow leading 0's and we include the empty word ε in the language (treated as yet another representation of the number 0).

   The states of the automaton are remainders modulo k; that is, numbers in $\{0, 1, \ldots, k-1\}$. The initial state is 0. The transition function is

$$\delta(q, a) = b \cdot q + a \bmod k.$$

There is one accepting state, namely 0. The state of the automaton after reading a word is the remainder modulo k of the number as represented in base b.

To disallow leading 0's and exclude the empty sequence, we need three additional states: the new initial state $\underline{\varepsilon}$ used only for the empty word, an accepting state $\underline{0}$ used for the one-letter word 0, and the error state $\bot$ used for all words of length at least two beginning with 0. The transition relation is obtained by extending δ as follows:

$$\delta(q, a) = \begin{cases} a \bmod k & \text{for } q = \underline{\varepsilon}, a \neq 0, \\ \underline{0} & \text{for } q = \underline{\varepsilon}, a = 0, \\ \bot & \text{for } q \in \{\underline{0}, \bot\}. \end{cases}$$

(2) As in the previous item, we consider the general case where the parameters are b and k. After reading the $i + 1$ least significant digits that represent a number

$$a_0 b^0 + a_1 b^1 + \cdots + a_i b^i,$$

the automaton keeps in its state the pair

$$(x, y) \in \{0, \ldots, k - 1\}^2,$$

where x is the value of the number modulo k, and y is b^{i+1} modulo k. The initial state is $(0, 1)$ and the accepting states are those that have 0 on the first coordinate. The transition function is defined by

$$\delta((x, y), a) = (x + ya, yk),$$

where all arithmetic is modulo k. If we want to avoid accepting the empty word or avoid accepting 0's on the most significant digit, we need to add information in the state for that. ∎

Solution to Problem 12. ONE-LETTER ALPHABET

(1) Let us first do the right-to-left implication. Recall that a semi-linear set is a finite union of linear sets, where a linear set is a set of the form

$$\{i + j \cdot n : n \in \mathbb{N}\}$$

for some choice of parameters $i, j \in \mathbb{N}$. To describe such a linear set, we use a regular expression of the form

$$a^i (a^j)^*.$$

For a semi-linear set, we take a union of finitely many such expressions. Let us now do the left-to-right implication: for every regular language L

over a one-letter alphabet, the lengths of words in L form a semi-linear set. Here it is convenient to assume that L is represented by a deterministic automaton. A deterministic automaton over a one-letter alphabet looks like this:

In general, the lengths of the prefix and the loop depend on L, and similarly for the distribution of accepting states. The lengths of words accepted by such an automaton clearly form a semi-linear set. More precisely, by closure of semi-linear sets under finite unions, it suffices to consider the case when there is only a single accepting state, say at distance i from the initial state. If the accepting state is in the prefix, then the set of lengths of accepted words is the singleton $\{i\}$, which is a special case of a semi-linear set of the form $\{i + 0 \cdot n : n \in \mathbb{N}\}$. If the unique accepting state is on the loop, then the set of lengths is $\{i + j \cdot n : n \in \mathbb{N}\}$, assuming that j is the length of the loop.

(2) Let $A \subseteq \mathbb{N}$ be the set of lengths of words in X. By Problem 4(2), $A^* \subseteq \mathbb{N}$ is semi-linear, and thus by the previous point $X \subseteq \{a\}^*$ is regular. ∎

Solution to Problem 13. BASE-b REPRESENTATION

(1) The set $\{[w]_b : w \in L\}$ is not necessarily semi-linear for a regular language L. For instance, for $b = 2$ and the language L generated by the regular expression 10^*, we get the set of all powers of 2, which is not semi-linear.

(2) By definition, a semi-linear set is a finite union of sets of the form

$$\{i + j \cdot n : n \in \mathbb{N}\}.$$

Since regular languages are closed under finite unions, it suffices to show that for all numbers $i, j \in \mathbb{N}$, the following language is regular:

$$\{w \in \{0, 1, \ldots, b - 1\} : [w]_b = i + j \cdot n \text{ for some } n \in \mathbb{N}\}.$$

A word belongs to the above language if and only if it satisfies the following conditions, all of which can be checked by finite automata:

- the word represents a number greater than or equal to i, which can be checked by an automaton that reads $\log(i)$ least significant bits;
- the word represents a number that is congruent to i modulo j, for which we use the automaton from Problem 11(1), except that the accepting state is changed to $i \bmod j$.

Therefore the entire language is regular, by closure of regular languages under finite intersection.   ∎

Solution to Problem 14

Recall that, in Problem 11(1), we showed that there is an automaton with states

$$\{\varepsilon, \underline{0}, \bot, 0, 1, \ldots, k - 1\}$$

such that after reading a non-empty binary word, its state is $\underline{0}$ if it is a one-letter word 0, $\bot$ if it is a longer word beginning with 0, and otherwise it is the value of the represented number modulo k. (Note that we disallow leading 0's and do not treat ε as an alternative representation of the number 0.) We can use this automaton to recognize the present language L as follows. In a first phase, we run this automaton on the part before \$, and then do a second phase where the automaton is run on the part after \$, while storing the results of the first phase. At the end, we check that the results of the two phases are such that the modulo equation is satisfied.

Here is a more formal construction. Let Q and δ be the set of states and the transition function of the automaton from Problem 11(1), as applied to base 2 and divisibility by k. The set of states of the automaton for the language in this problem will be

$$Q \cup \{\underline{0}, 0, 1, \ldots, k - 1\} \times Q.$$

The transition function for the new automaton, call it γ, extends the transition function δ; that is, for states from Q and input letters from $\{0, 1\}$, the functions γ and δ agree. When reading \$, the automaton goes from the first phase to the second phase, assuming the first phase results in a state other than $\{\varepsilon, \bot\}$, otherwise the automaton enters the error state:

$$\gamma(q, \$) = \begin{cases} (q, \varepsilon) & \text{if } q \in \{\underline{0}, 0, 1, \ldots, k - 1\}, \\ \bot & \text{otherwise.} \end{cases}$$

Note how the result of the first phase is stored in the first coordinate of the second phase state. Finally, in the second phase, we also use the original divisibility automaton, but we keep the result of the first phase in memory as well:

$$\gamma((q,p),a) = (q,\delta(p,q)).$$

After reading an input word, the automaton is in a state of the form $(p,q) \in \{\underline{0},0,1,\ldots,k-1\}^2$ if and only if the input is $w\$v$ such that w and v are binary representations of numbers congruent, respectively, to p and q modulo k (with $\underline{0}$ treated as 0). Such a pair (p,q) is accepting if and only if

$$a \cdot p + b \cdot q \equiv r \mod k. \qquad \blacksquare$$

Solution to Problem 15

(1) Let us use the fooling method. Assume that the language $\{a^{2^n} : n \in \mathbb{N}\}$ is regular and let $\mathcal{A}$ be a deterministic automaton recognizing it. Because $\mathcal{A}$ has finitely many states, there exist $m,n \in \mathbb{N}$ with $m \neq n$ such that the runs of $\mathcal{A}$ over a^{2^m} and a^{2^n} end in the same state. Then, the runs over $a^{2^m} a^{2^m}$ and $a^{2^n} a^{2^m}$ end in the same state as well. This is a contradiction. Indeed, $a^{2^m} a^{2^m}$ should be accepted because $2^m + 2^m$ is a power of 2, but $a^{2^n} a^{2^m}$ should be rejected because $2^n + 2^m$ is not a power of 2 for $m \neq n$.

(2) Assume that $L = \{a^p : p \text{ is a prime number}\}$ is regular. Let N be the constant from the pumping lemma. Consider a word w of length at least $N + 2$ that belongs to L and let xyz be a factorization of w such that $|xy| \leq N$, $|y| \geq 1$, and the word $xy^i z$ belongs to L for every $i \in \mathbb{N}$. Let $k = |xz|$. Since $|xyz| \geq N + 2$ and $|xy| \leq N$, we have that $k \geq 2$. The word $xy^k z$ has length $k + k \cdot |y| = k \cdot (1 + |y|)$, which gives us a contradiction.

(3) We use the fooling method. Assume that $\{a^i b^j : \gcd(i,j) = 1\}$ is a regular language and let $\mathcal{A}$ be a deterministic automaton recognizing it. For each prime number p, consider the word $w_p = a^p$. Since $\mathcal{A}$ has finitely many states, there exist prime numbers $p \neq r$ such that the runs over w_p and w_r end in the same state q. If we start in q and read p letters b, then we reach an accepting state, because $\mathcal{A}$ accepts the word $a^r b^p$. But this means that also the word $a^p b^p$ gets accepted, and we obtain a contradiction.

(4) Assume that the language $\{a^m b^n : m \neq n\}$ is regular. By taking the intersection of its complement with the regular language $a^* b^*$ we obtain the language $\{a^n b^n : n \in \mathbb{N}\}$, which is not regular. This gives us a contradiction, since the complement of a regular language is regular and the intersection of two regular languages is also regular. $\qquad \blacksquare$

Solution to Problem 16

Let Σ be an alphabet with at least two letters. Let a and b be two different letters from Σ. Assume that the language of palindromes over Σ is regular. Let N be the constant from the pumping lemma. Consider the palindrome $w = a^N bba^N$. By the pumping lemma we can write $w = xyz$ where $|xy| \leq N$, $|y| \geq 1$, and $xy^i z$ is a palindrome for every $i \in \mathbb{N}$. Since $|xy| \leq N$, the word y consists only of letters a and thus for $i = 0$ the word $xy^i z$ is not a palindrome (in fact, any $i \neq 1$ would do). ∎

Solution to Problem 17

Assume that the set of regular expressions over an alphabet Σ is a regular language. Let N be the constant from the pumping lemma. Consider the regular expression

$$r = \underbrace{((\ldots (\emptyset)^* \emptyset)^* \ldots)^*}_{N}.$$

Since $|r| \geq N$, by the pumping lemma we can write $r = xyz$ with $|xy| \leq N$, $|y| \geq 1$, in such a way that, for all $i \geq 0$, the word $xy^i z$ is a regular expression. Take any $i > 1$. The word $xy^i z$ does not have balanced parentheses: it begins with more than N left parentheses and contains only N right parentheses. Therefore $xy^i z$ is not a regular expression. We obtain a contradiction. ∎

Solution to Problem 18

Recall that in Problem 10 we view letters of the alphabet $\{0, 1\}^3$ as columns. Assume that the language

$$\left\{ \begin{bmatrix} a_1 \\ b_1 \\ c_1 \end{bmatrix} \begin{bmatrix} a_2 \\ b_2 \\ c_2 \end{bmatrix} \ldots \begin{bmatrix} a_n \\ b_n \\ c_n \end{bmatrix} : [a_1 a_2 \ldots a_n]_2 \cdot [b_1 b_2 \ldots b_n]_2 = [c_1 c_2 \ldots c_n]_2 \right\}$$

is regular and let N be the constant from the pumping lemma. Consider the following word w of length $2N + 1$, representing multiplication $2^N \cdot 2^N = 2^{2N}$:

$$\overbrace{\begin{bmatrix} 0 \\ 0 \\ 1 \end{bmatrix} \begin{bmatrix} 0 \\ 0 \\ 0 \end{bmatrix} \ldots \begin{bmatrix} 0 \\ 0 \\ 0 \end{bmatrix}}^{N-1} \overbrace{\begin{bmatrix} 1 \\ 1 \\ 0 \end{bmatrix} \begin{bmatrix} 0 \\ 0 \\ 0 \end{bmatrix} \ldots \begin{bmatrix} 0 \\ 0 \\ 0 \end{bmatrix}}^{N}.$$

By the pumping lemma there exists a factorization $w = xyz$ such that $|xy| \leq N$, $|y| \geq 1$, and the word $xy^i z$ belongs to the language for every $i \in \mathbb{N}$. Since $|xy| \leq N$, for every $i \in \mathbb{N}$, the first two rows of the word $xy^i z$ are the binary representations of the number 2^N. On the other hand, for any $i > 1$, the last row of the word xy^iz is the binary representation of a number greater than 2^{2N}, so we obtain a contradiction. ∎

Solution to Problem 19

(1) Let L_1 be the language in question. Assume that L_1 is regular. Since the reverse of a regular language is also a regular language (see Problem 30), the language L_1^R, given as

$$\left\{ v \in \{a, b\}^* : \#_a(u) > 2017 \cdot \#_b(u) \text{ for each non-empty suffix } u \text{ of } v \right\},$$

is a regular language. Let N be the constant from the pumping lemma. Consider the word

$$v = \underbrace{b \dots b}_{N} \underbrace{a \dots \dots a}_{2017N+1}.$$

By the pumping lemma there exists a factorization $v = xyz$ where $|xy| \le N$, $|y| \ge 1$, and the word xy^iz belongs to L_1^R for any $i \in \mathbb{N}$. Take some $i > 1$. The word xy^iz starts with at least $N + 1$ letters b followed by exactly $2017N + 1$ letters a. Hence, taking the suffix u to be the whole word xy^iz shows that xy^iz does not belong to L_1^R. We get a contradiction.

(2) Let L_2 be the language in question. Assume that L_2 is regular and consider the constant N from the pumping lemma. The word

$$w = a^N b^N c^{2N+1}$$

is in L_2, as $w = uv$ with $u = a^N b^N c$ and $v = c^{2N}$. The pumping lemma now gives some $k \in \{1, 2, \dots, N\}$ such that

$$z = a^{N+2k} b^N c^{2N+1}$$

is in L_2 again. However, it is not possible to factorize z into two words u and v that satisfy the condition from the definition of L_2. Indeed, if u contains only a's, then

$$\#_a(u) + \#_b(u) \le N + 2k < 3N + 1 = \#_b(v) + \#_c(v).$$

If u contains both a's and b's, but not c's, then either $\#_a(u) + \#_b(u)$ is odd and $\#_b(v) + \#_c(v)$ is even, or vice versa. If u contains a's, b's, and c's, then

$$\#_a(u) + \#_b(u) = 2N + 2k > 2N + 1 \ge \#_b(v) + \#_c(v).$$

Hence, L_2 is not regular. ∎

Solution to Problem 20

(1) Let L_1 be the language in question. In the definition of L_1 we care about the number of times the letters change from a to b and from b to a. If the word x starts with b, then $\#_{ba}(x) \geq \#_{ab}(x)$ and $x \notin L_1$. Assume that x starts with a. If x ends with a, then $\#_{ab}(x) = \#_{ba}(x)$ and $x \notin L_1$, but if x ends with b, we have $\#_{ab}(x) = \#_{ba}(x) + 1$ and $x \in L_1$. Therefore, $L_1 = a(a+b)^*b$.

(2) Let L_2 be the language in question. Consider a word x of the form

$$(aabaa)^n (bbabb)^m.$$

For such a word we have $\#_{aba}(x) = n$ and $\#_{bab}(x) = m$. Therefore, $x \in L_2$ if and only if $n = m$. By the closure of regular languages under homomorphic pre-images, if L_2 were regular, the set $\{a^n b^n : n \in \mathbb{N}\}$ would also be regular as it is the pre-image of $L_2 \cap (aabaa)^*(bbabb)^*$ under the homomorphism $a \mapsto aabaa$, $b \mapsto bbabb$; a contradiction. ∎

Solution to Problem 21

Consider a regular language L. There exists a deterministic finite automaton $\mathcal{A}$ recognizing L. Let N be the number of states of $\mathcal{A}$. Take any words v, w, u satisfying $|w| \geq N$ and $vwu \in L$. Let us analyse the run of the automaton $\mathcal{A}$ over the word vwu. The automaton starts in its initial state. After reading v it is in some state q. In the segment of the run starting in this position and ending just after the last letter of w, the automaton must see some state at least twice, since the length of w is at least equal to the number of states. Let p be the first state visited twice. Starting in the state q, the automaton reads some prefix of w and reaches state p for the first time. Let us denote this (possibly empty) prefix of w by x. Then $\mathcal{A}$ continues reading w and reaches p for the second time. We let y be the subword of w read by $\mathcal{A}$ in between its first and second visits to p. Clearly, $0 < |y| \leq N$. After reading y, the automaton reads the final (possibly empty) part z of w, continues its run reading u, and finally arrives in an accepting state.

While analysing the run of $\mathcal{A}$ over vwu we defined a factorization $w = xyz$. Now it suffices to prove that for all $n \in \mathbb{N}$ the word $vxy^n zu$ is in L. Take any $n \geq 0$. Let us analyse the run of $\mathcal{A}$ over $vxy^n zu$. From the analysis above it follows that after reading the prefix vx the automaton is in state p. Since $\mathcal{A}$ is deterministic, any run over y that starts in p ends in p. Therefore, after reading y^n the automaton is back in state p. Finally, reading zu leads to an accepting state, which shows that the word $vxy^n zu$ belongs to L.

Now, let L be the language from the hint. We will show that L satisfies the claim of the stronger lemma with $N = 3$ but it is not regular. Take any words v, w, u satisfying $|w| \geq 3$ and $vwu \in L$. There are two possibilities:

- if w contains the letter b, then $vxy^n zu \in L$ for $y = b$, because repeating and deleting the letter b never makes the two conditions above false;
- if $w = c^k$, where $k \geq 3$, then $vxy^n zu \in L$ for $y = c$, because even after deleting one letter c there are still two consecutive letters c.

Therefore, L satisfies the claim of the stronger lemma.

The language L is not regular. One way to see this is to consider its intersection with the regular language $K \subseteq \{b, c\}^*$ of words which do not contain any two consecutive letters c. The language $L \cap K$ is the set of words which contain a prime number of letters c and have at least one letter b between any two letters c. This language is easily seen not to be regular, via an argument similar to the one in Problem 15(2). Therefore, L cannot be regular, since the intersection of two regular languages is a regular language. ∎

Solution to Problem 22. ANTIPALINDROMES

We use the fooling method. Assume that L is regular and let $\mathcal{A}$ be a deterministic automaton that recognizes L. For each $i > 0$ consider the word $w_i = 01^i$. Since the automaton $\mathcal{A}$ has finitely many states, there exist i and j such that $j \geq i + 2$ and the runs of $\mathcal{A}$ over the words w_i and w_j end in the same state q. If we start from the state q and read a word $0^j 1$, then we reach an accepting state, because the word $01^i 0^j 1$ does not contain as a subword any antipalindrome of length greater than three whose first letter is 0. This gives us a contradiction: the automaton $\mathcal{A}$ accepts also the word $01^j 0^j 1$, which is itself an antipalindrome of length greater than three whose first letter is 0. ∎

Solution to Problem 23

Assume that r is rational. Let $0.b_1 b_2 \ldots$ be the infinite binary expansion of r (if there are two, take the one with infinitely many 0's). Since r is rational, the sequence $b_1 b_2 \ldots$ is *ultimately periodic*; that is, there exists i_0 and $k \geq 1$ such that $b_i = b_{i+k}$ for all $i \geq i_0$. Consequently, the set Q of suffixes of the sequence $b_1 b_2 \ldots$ is finite. Consider a deterministic automaton with the set of states $Q \cup \{\bot, \top\}$. The initial state is $b_1 b_2 \ldots$. The states $\top$ and $\bot$ are sink states, and all the states except $\bot$ are accepting. From a state $b_n b_{n+1} \ldots$, over a letter $a \in \{0, 1\}$, the automaton moves to

- the state $b_{n+1} b_{n+2} \ldots$, if $a = b$,
- the state $\top$, if $a < b_n$,
- the state $\bot$, if $a > b_n$.

Notice that after reading a word w the automaton reaches

- the state $\top$, if for every n we have $0.w1^n \leq r$,
- the state $\bot$, if $0.w > r$,
- the state $b_n b_{n+1} \ldots$, if $r - 0.w = 0.\underbrace{00\ldots0}_{|w|} b_n b_{n+1} \ldots$.

Thus, the above automaton recognizes the language L_r.

Now assume that the language L_r is regular for some r and let $0.b_1 b_2 \ldots$ be the infinite binary expansion of r (again, if there are two, take the one with infinitely many 0's). Consider the words $w_i = b_1 b_2 \ldots b_i$ for $i = 1, 2, \ldots$. Notice that $w_i^{-1} L_r = L_{0.b_{i+1} b_{i+2} \ldots}$. Because L_r is regular, it has only finitely many left quotients. (Indeed, if L_r is recognized by an automaton $\mathcal{A}$, then each left quotient of L_r is recognized by $\mathcal{A}$ with the initial state replaced by some state of $\mathcal{A}$. Hence, the number of different left quotients of L_r is bounded by the number of states of $\mathcal{A}$.) Consequently, $w_i^{-1} L_r = w_j^{-1} L_r$ for some $i < j$. That is, $L_{0.b_{i+1} b_{i+2} \ldots} = L_{0.b_{j+1} b_{j+2} \ldots}$ for some $i < j$. We would like to conclude that $0.b_{i+1} b_{i+2} \ldots = 0.b_{j+1} b_{j+2} \ldots$, which would imply that the binary expansion of r is ultimately periodic and r is rational. Assume to the contrary that $0.b_{i+1} b_{i+2} \ldots > 0.b_{j+1} b_{j+2} \ldots$ (the remaining case is analogous). Then, there exists $k \geq 1$ such that $b_{i+k} > b_{j+k}$ and $b_{i+\ell} = b_{j+\ell}$ for all $\ell = 1, 2, \ldots, k-1$. Hence, $b_{i+1} b_{i+2} \ldots b_{i+k} \in L_{0.b_{i+1} b_{i+2} \ldots} - L_{0.b_{j+1} b_{j+2} \ldots}$, which is a contradiction. ∎

Solution to Problem 24

Clearly, if $\Sigma = \{a\}$ then $(\text{Pal}_\Sigma)^*$ contains all words over Σ except the word a and the empty word. Therefore, the language is regular.

Assume that $|\Sigma| \geq 2$ and let a and b be two distinct letters in Σ. Notice that $ab^n ab^m a \in (\text{Pal}_\Sigma)^*$ if and only if $ab^n ab^m a \in \text{Pal}_\Sigma$. This in turn holds if and only if $n = m$. That is, by intersecting $(\text{Pal}_\Sigma)^*$ with the regular language $ab^* ab^* a$ we obtain $\{ab^n ab^n a : n \in \mathbb{N}\}$, which is obviously not regular (a straightforward application of the pumping lemma). By the closure properties of regular languages, $(\text{Pal}_\Sigma)^*$ is not regular either.

Let us turn to the language $\{uu^R : u \in (0+1)^*\}^*$. Note that it is an analogue of $(\text{Pal}_{\{0,1\}})^*$ defined using palindromes of even length. Consider a word of the form $(01)^n (10)^m$. As each word in $\{uu^R : u \in (0+1)^*\}$ has even length, and begins and ends with the same letter, all infixes of $(01)^n (10)^m$ that are in $\{uu^R : u \in (0+1)^*\}$ are of the form $(01)^i (10)^i$ or $1(01)^i (10)^i 1$. Consequently, $(01)^n (10)^m \in \{uu^R : u \in (0+1)^*\}^*$ if and only if $n = m$. Like in the previous case, it is easy to infer from this that $\{uu^R : u \in (0+1)^*\}^*$ is not a regular language. ∎

Solution to Problem 25

(1) Note that a word w contains a non-trivial palindrome as a prefix if and only if it has a prefix in $01^*0 + 10^*1$. The set of such words is obviously regular.

(2) The set of words containing a non-trivial palindrome of even length as a prefix is not regular. The reasoning is similar to that showing non-regularity of $\{uu^R : u \in (0+1)^*\}^*$ in Problem 24: a word of the form $(01)^n(10)^m$ contains a non-trivial palindrome of even length as a prefix if and only if $0 < n \leq m$, and the language $\{(01)^n(10)^m : 0 < n \leq m\}$ is not regular.

(3) This language, say L, is not regular either. Notice that a word from the language $0\big((0+1)1\big)^*(0+1)0$ belongs to L if and only if the whole word is a palindrome. Therefore, if L were regular, the set of palindromes would also be regular, as it is the pre-image of $\big(0^{-1}L0^{-1}\big)1$ under the homomorphism $0 \mapsto 01$ and $1 \mapsto 11$. ∎

Solution to Problem 26

Consider the set of finite infixes of the Thue–Morse word, defined in Problem 7. By definition, this set is closed under infixes. It is infinite, because it contains arbitrarily long words. Assume that it contains an infinite regular language L. Since L is infinite, it contains arbitrarily long words. Hence, by the pumping lemma, there is a word $uvw \in L$ such that $v \neq \varepsilon$ and $uv^*w \subseteq L$. Consequently, the Thue–Morse word contains v^3 as an infix, which contradicts the fact that it is cube-free as proved in Problem 7. ∎

Solution to Problem 27

The set of binary representations of prime numbers is not a regular language. By contradiction, suppose that it is. Let N be the constant from the pumping lemma. Take a prime number $p > 2^N$ and let w be its binary representation. Since $|w| \geq N$, by the pumping lemma there exists a factorization $w = xyz$ where $|xy| \leq N$, $|y| \geq 1$, and for every $i \in \mathbb{N}$, the word xy^iz is the binary representation of a prime number. The word xy^iz represents the number

$$[z]_2 + [y]_2 \cdots 2^{|z|} + \cdots + [y]_2 \cdot 2^{|z|+(i-1)|y|} + [x]_2 \cdot 2^{|z|+i|y|}$$

$$= [z]_2 + [y]_2 \cdot 2^{|z|} \cdot \frac{2^{i|y|} - 1}{2^{|y|} - 1} + [x]_2 \cdot 2^{|z|+i|y|}.$$

Let us take $i = p$. By Fermat's little theorem $2^p \equiv 2 \mod p$, so

$$[x]_2 \cdot 2^{|z|+p|y|} \equiv [x]_2 \cdot 2^{|z|+|y|} \mod p.$$

Moreover, $2^{p\lfloor y \rfloor} - 1 \equiv 2^{\lfloor y \rfloor} - 1 \mod p$. Since $p > 2^{\lfloor y \rfloor} - 1 > 0$ and p is prime, the numbers $2^{\lfloor y \rfloor} - 1$ and p are co-prime. It follows that

$$\frac{2^{p\lfloor y \rfloor} - 1}{2^{\lfloor y \rfloor} - 1} \equiv 1 \mod p.$$

Therefore, we get $[xy^p z]_2 \equiv [xyz]_2 \mod p$. But since w has no leading 0's, $[xy^p z]_2 > [xyz]_2 = p$. Therefore $[xy^p z]_2$ is greater than p and divisible by p, which contradicts the fact that it is prime. ∎

Solution to Problem 28
First of all we notice that Pump(ab) is just $a(a + b)^*b$. Indeed, when pumping we do not change the first and the last letter, so Pump(ab) $\subseteq a(a + b)^*b$. Conversely, each word from $a(a + b)^*b$ can be factorized as $u_1 u_2 \ldots u_n$ for some $n \in \mathbb{N}$ and some $u_1, u_2, \ldots, u_n \in a^+ b^+$. This word belongs to Pump(ab), because it can be obtained by first pumping the whole word ab to get $(ab)^n$, and then pumping the ith occurrences of a and b until u_i is formed.

On the other hand the language Pump(abc) is not regular. We present an argument by Jakub Bujak. Let us first see that for each $u \in \{a, b, c\}^*$ there exists $v \in \{a, b, c\}^*$ such that $abc \cdot u \cdot v \in$ Pump(abc). This is easy to prove by induction on the length of u. For instance, if we want to obtain $abcu'v' \in$ Pump(abc) for $u' = ub$, by the induction hypothesis we have $abcuv \in$ Pump(abc) and we can take $a(bcu)^2 v = abcubcuv$ and let $v' = cuv$.

Towards a contradiction, assume that Pump(abc) is recognized by an automaton with n states. From the solution of Problem 7 it follows that there exist arbitrarily long square-free words over the alphabet $\{a, b, c\}$ that begin with abc. Let $abc \cdot u$ be a square-free word of length at least $3 \cdot 2^{n+1}$. By the initial observation, there is a word v such that $abc \cdot u \cdot v \in$ Pump(abc). A simple pumping argument shows that because Pump(abc) is recognized by an automaton with n states, we can choose v of length at most n. The following claim then leads to the desired contradiction.

Claim. If the longest square-free prefix of a word $w \in$ Pump(abc) has length k, then $k \leq 3 \cdot 2^{|w|-k}$.

Indeed, because the longest square-free prefix of $abc \cdot u \cdot v$ has length at least $|abc \cdot u| \geq 3 \cdot 2^{n+1}$, the claim implies that the length of the remaining suffix needs to be at least $n + 1$. However, it cannot be greater than $|v| \leq n$.

We prove the claim by structural induction. For $w = abc$ the claim holds with $k = 3$ and $|w| - k = 0$. Assume that the claim holds for a word $xyz \in$ Pump(abc) with non-empty y, and consider the word $xyyz$. Let k and k' be the lengths of the longest square-free prefixes of xyz and $xyyz$, respectively. Because xyy is not square-free, we have $k' < |xyy|$. If $k \geq |xy|$, then

$$k' < |xyy| \leq 2 \cdot |xy| \leq 2k.$$

If $k < |xy|$, then the prefix of xy of length $k + 1$ is not square-free, and consequently neither is any prefix of $xyyz$ of length at least $k + 1$. Hence, $k' = k$ and thus again $k' < 2k$ because $k \geq 1$. Moreover, in both cases $k' < k + |y|$ and therefore

$$|xyz| - k = |xyyz| - k - |y| < |xyyz| - k'.$$

By combining this with the claim for xyz we obtain the claim for $xyyz$:

$$k' \leq 2k \leq 2 \cdot 3 \cdot 2^{|xyz|-k} \leq 3 \cdot 2^{|xyz|-k+1} \leq 3 \cdot 2^{|xyyz|-k'}. \qquad \blacksquare$$

Solution to Problem 29. CONCATENATION

(1) Yes. Let $L \subseteq \{a\}^*$ be the set of words whose lengths are not odd prime numbers. This is not a regular language (see Problem 15). However, as L contains all words of even length as well as the word of length one, we have that $L^2 = \{a\}^*$, which means that L^2 is regular.

(2) We claim that the complement of L^2 is the set K defined by the regular expression $a(ba)^* + b(ab)^*$. Indeed, if $uv \in a(ba)^*$, then either $u \in (ab)^*$ or $v \in (ba)^*$. Similarly for $uv \in b(ab)^*$. Hence, K is contained in the complement of L^2. To prove the converse, take $w \notin K$. If w has even length, we can factorize it into two words of odd length, and all words of odd length are in L. Assume that w has odd length. Then w must be of the form $uaav$ or $ubbv$ for some words u and v. Since w has odd length, the lengths of u and v have different parities. This leads to four entirely analogous cases. Let us consider the case when $w = uaav$, u has even length, and v has odd length. We have either $u \in L$ or $uaa \in L$. Having odd length, both aav and v belong to L. Hence, in both subcases we obtain a factorization of $uaav$ into two words from L. $\qquad \blacksquare$

Solution to Problem 30

Let $\mathcal{A}$ be a finite automaton recognizing L (either deterministic or non-deterministic). Consider the non-deterministic automaton $\mathcal{B}$ obtained from $\mathcal{A}$ by:

- taking as the initial states of $\mathcal{B}$ the set of accepting states of $\mathcal{A}$,
- taking as the accepting state of $\mathcal{B}$ the initial state of $\mathcal{A}$, and
- reversing all transitions of $\mathcal{A}$: if $\mathcal{A}$ has a transition $p \xrightarrow{a} q$ then $\mathcal{B}$ has a transition $q \xrightarrow{a} p$.

It is easy to prove that $\mathcal{A}$ accepts w if and only if $\mathcal{B}$ accepts w^R. ∎

Solution to Problem 31

We start by proving that $X^{-1}L$ is regular. Consider a deterministic finite automaton $\mathcal{A}$ recognizing L. Let Q be the set of states of $\mathcal{A}$ and assume that $Y \subseteq Q$ are the states of $\mathcal{A}$ that can be reached by $\mathcal{A}$ when reading words from X. Let $\mathcal{B}$ be a non-deterministic automaton obtained from $\mathcal{A}$ by taking Y as the set of initial states, and keeping the transitions and accepting states. It is easy to prove that $\mathcal{B}$ recognizes $X^{-1}L$.

The fact that LX^{-1} is regular can be proved analogously, by changing the set of accepting states of $\mathcal{A}$. Alternatively, we can observe that $LX^{-1} = ((X^R)^{-1}L^R)^R$ and conclude using the already proved claim and the fact that regular languages are closed under reverse (Problem 30). ∎

Solution to Problem 32

This is true. Let $\mathcal{A}$ be a finite automaton recognizing L. Let Q be the set of all states of $\mathcal{A}$ and F the set of accepting states of $\mathcal{A}$. Each word w induces a function $f_w \colon \mathcal{P}(Q) \to \mathcal{P}(Q)$ defined as follows:

- $f_\varepsilon(X) = X$;
- $f_{wa}(X) = f_w(\{p \colon \exists q \in X.\, p \xrightarrow{a} q \text{ is a transition of } \mathcal{A}\})$.

Notice that the map $w \mapsto f_w$ is compositional (or homomorphic); that is, $f_{uv} = f_u \circ f_v$. Observe that for every word w, the language Lw^{-1} is recognized by the automaton $\mathcal{A}$ with the set of accepting states changed to $f_w(F)$. Since there are only finitely many functions from $\mathcal{P}(Q)$ to $\mathcal{P}(Q)$, there must be two distinct non-empty words u and v such that $f_u = f_v = f$. In that case both the languages $L\{uv\}^{-1}$ and $L\{vu\}^{-1}$ are recognized by $\mathcal{A}$ with the set of states changed to $f^2(F)$. ∎

Solution to Problem 33. CYCLIC SHIFT

Assume that $\mathcal{A}$ is a deterministic finite automaton recognizing L and let Q be the set of states of $\mathcal{A}$. We shall construct an automaton $\mathcal{B}$ that guesses the state p of $\mathcal{A}$ that is reached from the initial state by reading the word u. Then it simulates the behaviour of $\mathcal{A}$ as it reads v starting from state p. Whenever an accepting state is reached, $\mathcal{B}$ starts a new simulation of $\mathcal{A}$ from its initial state, trying to reach p.

Let the set of states of $\mathcal{B}$ be $Q \times \{0, 1\} \times Q$. The initial states of $\mathcal{B}$ are of the form $(p, 0, p)$. Given a state (p, i, q), when reading a letter a, the automaton $\mathcal{B}$ can move to a state (p, i, q') if $\mathcal{A}$ has a transition $q \xrightarrow{a} q'$. Additionally, for every accepting state q of $\mathcal{A}$ the automaton $\mathcal{B}$ can perform an ε-transition (see Problem 54) from a state $(p, 0, q)$ to the state $(p, 1, q_0)$ where q_0 is the initial state of $\mathcal{A}$. The accepting states of $\mathcal{B}$ are those of the form $(p, 1, p)$. It is easy to check that $\mathcal{B}$ recognizes Cycle(L).

There are non-regular languages L ,such that Cycle(L) is regular. For instance, consider the language

$$L = \{a^n b a^n : n \in \mathbb{N}\}.$$

A straightforward application of the pumping lemma shows that L is non-regular. However, Cycle(L) is the set of words $w \in \{a, b\}^*$ such that the length of w is odd and w contains exactly one letter b. Hence, Cycle(L) is regular. ∎

Solution to Problem 34

Let $\mathcal{A}$ be a finite deterministic automaton recognizing L and let Q be the set of states of $\mathcal{A}$. We shall construct a finite non-deterministic automaton recognizing the language K of words that are lexicographically greater (strictly) than some word of the same length in L. Since $L_{\min} = L - K$, it will follow that $L_{\min}$ is regular by the closure of the class of regular languages under difference.

To recognize K we shall construct a non-deterministic automaton $\mathcal{B}$ which guesses a word lexicographically smaller than the input word and verifies that the guessed word is in L by simulating the automaton $\mathcal{A}$ on it. The set of states of the automaton $\mathcal{B}$ is $\{=, <\} \times Q$. The initial state is $(=, q_0)$, where q_0 is the initial state of $\mathcal{A}$. For each $p \in Q$ and $a \in \{0, 1\}$, the automaton $\mathcal{B}$ can perform the following transitions:

- $(=, p) \xrightarrow{a} (=, q)$ if $p \xrightarrow{a} q$ is a transition of $\mathcal{A}$;
- $(=, p) \xrightarrow{a} (<, q)$ if $a = 1$ and $p \xrightarrow{0} q$ is a transition of $\mathcal{A}$; and
- $(<, p) \xrightarrow{a} (<, q)$ if $p \xrightarrow{b} q$ is a transition of $\mathcal{A}$ for some $b \in \{0, 1\}$.

The accepting states of $\mathcal{B}$ are those of the form $(<, q)$, where q is an accepting state of $\mathcal{A}$.

Consider a run of $\mathcal{B}$ over a word w that starts in the initial state $(=, q_0)$ and reaches an accepting state $(<, q)$. By the construction of $\mathcal{B}$, this run corresponds to a run of $\mathcal{A}$, starting in q_0 and reaching q, over some word of length $|w|$ but lexicographically smaller than w. Thus, $\mathcal{B}$ accepts w if and only if $w \in K$. ∎

Solution to Problem 35

Assume that $\mathcal{A}$ is a finite automaton recognizing L and Q is the set of states of $\mathcal{A}$. Let $\mathcal{R}$ be the set of binary relations over Q; that is, $\mathcal{R} = \mathcal{P}(Q \times Q)$. Notice that each letter $a \in \Sigma$ induces a relation $R_a \in \mathcal{R}$ defined as

$$R_a = \left\{ (p,q) \ : \ p \xrightarrow{a} q \text{ is a transition of } \mathcal{A} \right\}.$$

We call R_a the *effect relation* of a. We define the effect relation R_w for $w \in \Sigma^*$ analogously.

Let the set of states of $\mathcal{B}$ be $Q \times \mathcal{R}$. The initial state is (q_0, I) where q_0 is the initial state of $\mathcal{A}$ and I is the identity relation $I = \{(q,q) \ : \ q \in Q\}$. The automaton $\mathcal{B}$ has a transition

$$(p, R) \xrightarrow{a} \left(q, R \cdot \left(\bigcup_{b \in \Sigma} R_b \right) \right)$$

for each $R \in \mathcal{R}$ and each transition $p \xrightarrow{a} q$ of the automaton $\mathcal{A}$; the symbol $\cdot$ denotes the usual (left) composition of relations. The set of accepting states of $\mathcal{B}$ contains (p, R) if $(p, q) \in R$ for some accepting state q of $\mathcal{A}$.

Notice that if $\mathcal{B}$ reads a word w and reaches a state (p, R), then:

- $\mathcal{A}$ reaches p by reading w from the initial state; and
- R contains a pair (p, q) if and only if $\mathcal{A}$ can reach q by reading some word of length $|w|$ starting from the state p.

Therefore, w is accepted by $\mathcal{B}$ if and only if $w \in \frac{1}{2}L$.

The argument for $\sqrt{L}$ is similar, except that the transitions are

$$(p, R) \xrightarrow{a} (q, R \cdot R_a).$$

The second coordinate of the automaton $\mathcal{B}$ that computes effect relations is useful in a number of other problems. ∎

Solution to Problem 36

Let us fix for the remainder of the solution a finite automaton $\mathcal{A}$ with set of states Q, recognizing the language L. For each of the four languages we shall construct a recognizing automaton based on $\mathcal{A}$. The constructions will be similar to that in Problem 35, relying on computing effect relations.

We begin with Root(L). The set of states of the automaton recognizing Root(L) is the set $\mathcal{R}$ of all binary relations over Q; the initial state is the identity relation I. Given a letter a and a state R, the automaton moves to the state $R \cdot R_a$, where $R_a = \{(p,q): p \xrightarrow{a} q \text{ is a transition of } \mathcal{A}\}$, as in Problem 35. A state R is accepting if there exists $n \in \mathbb{N}$ and an accepting state q of $\mathcal{A}$ such that $(q_0, q) \in R^n$ for the initial state q_0 of $\mathcal{A}$. Clearly the automaton accepts w if and only if $w^n \in L$.

We now move to Sqrt(L). For $n \geq 0$, let

$$R_n = \{(p,q) \ : \ \mathcal{A} \text{ reaches } q \text{ from } p \text{ over some word of length } n\}.$$

Let the set of states of the automaton recognizing Sqrt(L) be $Q \times \mathcal{R} \times \mathcal{R}$. After reading a word w, the automaton should reach the state $(q, R_{2 \cdot |w|+1}, R_{|w|^2})$, where q is the state reached by $\mathcal{A}$ when reading w from the initial state. This invariant can easily be preserved. A state (p, P, R) is accepting if $(p, q) \in R$ for some accepting state q of $\mathcal{A}$.

The constructions for Log(L) and Fib(L) are similar, except that after reading w the automaton should be in states $(q, R_{2^{|w|}}, R_{2^{|w|}-1})$ and $(q, R_{F_{|w|}}, R_{F_{|w|}-1})$, respectively. ∎

Solution to Problem 37

Let $\mathcal{A}$ be a finite automaton recognizing L. One can construct a non-deterministic automaton $\mathcal{B}$ for the language $K = \{w : w^{|w|} \in L\}$, relying on effect relations introduced in the solution to Problem 35. The set of states of $\mathcal{B}$ is $\mathcal{R} \times \mathcal{R} \times \mathcal{R}$, where $\mathcal{R}$ is the set of binary relations over the set of states of $\mathcal{A}$. The automaton $\mathcal{B}$ initially guesses a relation $R \in \mathcal{R}$ and then maintains the invariant that after reading the word w the state reached is $(R, R_w, R^{|w|})$, where R^n is the n-fold composition of the relation R with itself. The automaton accepts w if $R = R_w$ (that is, the initial guess was correct) and $R^{|w|}$ contains a pair (q_0, q) with q_0 initial and q accepting in $\mathcal{A}$; that is, the accepting states of $\mathcal{B}$ are of the form (R, R, P) such that P contains a pair (q_0, q) with q_0 initial and q accepting in $\mathcal{A}$. ∎

Solution to Problem 38. SUBSTITUTION

(1) Consider a regular expression α generating L, and regular expressions α_a generating $f(a)$ for all $a \in \Sigma$. A regular expression for $f(L)$ can be obtained by substituting each letter a in α with α_a. This shows that $f(L)$ is a regular language. However, if $f(a)$ is not regular for some a, for $L = \{a\}$ we get $f(L) = f(a)$, so $f(L)$ is not regular either.

(2) Let $\mathcal{A}$ be a *deterministic* finite automaton recognizing K. We shall use the notions defined in the solution to Problem 35. Notice that for a deterministic automaton $\mathcal{A}$ the effect relations R_w are functional: for each state p of $\mathcal{A}$ there is exactly one state q of $\mathcal{A}$ such that $(p, q) \in R_w$. For a language $X \subseteq \Gamma^*$ we define the relation

$$R_X = \{(p, q) : \exists u \in X. \; \mathcal{A} \text{ reaches } q \text{ by reading } u \text{ from } p\}.$$

Let q_0 be the initial state of $\mathcal{A}$. We call a relation $R \in \mathcal{R}$ *good* if for each pair $(q_0, q) \in R$, the state q is accepting in $\mathcal{A}$. Notice that

- $R_{X \cdot X'} = R_X \cdot R_{X'}$ and
- $X \subseteq L$ if and only if R_X is good.

Using the above observations, it is easy to prove that $f^{-1}(K)$ can be recognized by a finite automaton. The set of states of this automaton is $\mathcal{R}$, the initial state is the identity relation I, and the accepting states are the good relations; when reading a letter a in a state R, the automaton moves to the state $R \cdot R_{f(a)}$.   ∎

Solution to Problem 39

Let $\mathcal{A}$ be a finite automaton recognizing L. The constructions for the first three languages are similar to those from Problem 35 and rely on the effect relations as well.

(1) The states of the automaton for L_{+--} are of the form (q, R), where q is a state of $\mathcal{A}$ and R is a binary relation over the states of $\mathcal{A}$. Reading a letter a in a state (q, R), the automaton moves to the state $(q', R \cdot T \cdot T)$ such that $q \xrightarrow{a} q'$ is a transition of $\mathcal{A}$ and

$$T = \left\{ (r, s) \ : \ \exists b.\, r \xrightarrow{b} s \text{ is a transition in } \mathcal{A} \right\}.$$

The initial state is (q_0, I), where q_0 is the initial state of $\mathcal{A}$ and I is the identity relation. The accepting states are the pairs (p, R) such that for some accepting state q, (p, q) belongs to R.

(2) For L_{++-} the construction is similar, except that the automaton moves to the state $(q', R \cdot T)$ at even positions of the input word and the state (q', R) at odd positions, and a state (p, R) is accepting if $(p, q) \in R$ for some accepting state q and the length of the word read is even. To determine the parity, the automaton additionally maintains in the states a counter modulo 2.

(3) For L_{-+-} the states have an additional component, storing a state guessed in the beginning and never changed: all states of the form (p, p, I) are initial, the automaton moves from state (p, q, R) to state $(p, q', R \cdot T)$, and accepts in states (p, q, R) such that $(q_0, p) \in R$ and $(q, q') \in R$ for some accepting q'.

(4) Finally, for $L = a^* b^* c^*$ we have

$$L_{+-+} \cap a^* c^* = \left\{ a^n c^n \ : \ n \in \mathbb{N} \right\},$$

and therefore L_{+-+} is not regular.   ∎

Solution to Problem 40

Let $\mathcal{A}$ be a finite deterministic automaton recognizing L and let Q be the set of states of $\mathcal{A}$. We construct a non-deterministic automaton $\mathcal{B}$ with the set of states $Q \times \{0, \ldots, k\}$. The initial state of $\mathcal{B}$ is $(q_0, 0)$ where q_0 is the initial state of $\mathcal{A}$. The transitions of $\mathcal{B}$ are of two forms:

- $(p, i) \xrightarrow{a} (q, i)$ if $p \xrightarrow{a} q$ is a transition of $\mathcal{A}$, and
- $(p, i) \xrightarrow{a} (q, i + 1)$ if $p \xrightarrow{b} q$ is a transition of $\mathcal{A}$ for some b and $i < k$.

A state (q, i) is accepting if q is an accepting state of $\mathcal{A}$. Clearly, $\mathcal{B}$ accepts a word w if and only if there is a word u accepted by $\mathcal{A}$ that has the same length as w and its Hamming distance from w is at most k. ∎

Solution to Problem 41

Let $\mathcal{A}$ and $\mathcal{B}$ be deterministic automata recognizing L and M, respectively. Let Q be the set of states of $\mathcal{A}$ and P be the set of states of $\mathcal{B}$. We shall build a non-deterministic automaton $\mathcal{C}$ recognizing $L \parallel M$ using the *asynchronous product* construction. The automaton will guess a split of the input word into two words and check that the words belong to L and M, respectively, by simulating the runs of $\mathcal{A}$ and $\mathcal{B}$. The set of states of $\mathcal{C}$ is $Q \times P$ and the initial state is the pair (q_0, p_0) of the initial states of $\mathcal{A}$ and $\mathcal{B}$. Given a state (q, p) of $\mathcal{C}$ and a letter a, the automaton can perform two transitions:

- to (q', p) where $q \xrightarrow{a} q'$ is a transition of $\mathcal{A}$;
- to (q, p') where $p \xrightarrow{a} p'$ is a transition of $\mathcal{B}$.

A state (q, p) of $\mathcal{C}$ is accepting if both p and q are accepting. Clearly a run of $\mathcal{C}$ over a word w corresponds to a split of w into two sub-sequences u and v. Such a run is accepting if and only if u is accepted by $\mathcal{A}$ and v is accepted by $\mathcal{B}$. Therefore, $\mathcal{C}$ accepts w if and only if $w \in L \parallel M$. ∎

Solution to Problem 42

Let us fix the alphabet $\{(,)\}$ and let $L = \{()\}$; that is, L contains only a single word, which has length two. Notice that $L^\sharp$ contains the word $(^n)^m$ if and only if $n = m$. Therefore, $L^\sharp$ is not regular. In fact, $L^\sharp$ is the set of balanced sequences of parentheses (see Problem 2). ∎

Solution to Problem 43

(1) No. If $\Sigma = \{a\}$, this family contains only finite and co-finite languages, which does not include the regular language $(aa)^*$. Indeed, the complement of a finite language is co-finite, and vice versa; the union of two finite languages is finite; the union of a co-finite language and any other language is co-finite; and the concatenation of two finite languages is finite. The concatenation of two co-finite languages is co-finite, because if all words of length at least n belong to both languages, then all words of length at least $2n$ belong to the concatenation. Finally, over a one-letter alphabet, the concatenation of a finite non-empty language and a co-finite language is co-finite, because if the finite language contains a word of length n and the co-finite language contains all words of length at least m, then the concatenation contains all words of length at least $n + m$.

(2) Still no. Over a one-letter alphabet there is only one homomorphism that preserves length: the identity.   ■

Solution to Problem 44

The Myhill–Nerode equivalence for L partitions $\{a, b\}^*$ into seven equivalence classes:

- $A = \{a^i \ : \ i \text{ is even}\}$;
- $B = \{a^i \ : \ i \text{ is odd}\}$;
- $C = \{a^i b^n \ : \ n > 0, i \text{ is even}\}$;
- $D = \{a^i b^n \ : \ n > 0, i \text{ is odd}\}$;
- $E = \{a^i b^n a^j \ : \ n > 0, j > 0 \text{ and } i + j \text{ is odd}\}$;
- $F = \{a^i b^n a^j \ : \ n > 0, j > 0 \text{ and } i + j \text{ is even}\}$;
- $\perp$ contains all other words.

Indeed, for a fixed word w, to check whether a word vw belongs to L it is enough to check to which class v belongs. For example, for $w = baa$, we have $vw \in L$ if and only if v is in A or C. On the other hand, for every v and v' coming from different classes there exists a word w such that one of the words vw and $v'w$ belongs to L and the other one does not. For example, if $v \in A$ and $v' \in D$ then $vb \in L$ but $v'b \notin L$.

As is always the case with Myhill–Nerode equivalence classes, adding single letters at the end of words is a well-defined function on the classes. For example, if $v \in A$ then $va \in B$ and $vb \in C$, and if $v \in \perp$ then $va \in \perp$ and $vb \in \perp$. This defines the following deterministic automaton with the classes as states:

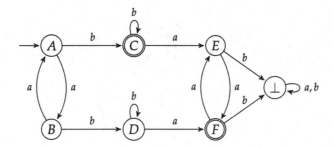

The initial state is A, since the empty word belongs to the class A. States C and F are accepting, since the corresponding classes are contained in the language L.

It is easy to prove by induction on the length of the word that on every word v, this automaton moves from the initial state A to the state whose corresponding class contains v. This is, again, a general feature of Myhill–Nerode equivalence classes. As a result, due to the way accepting states were defined, the automaton recognizes the language L.

Alternatively, if we came up with this automaton in some other way, we could verify that it is reachable and observable. In this case, reachability is obvious and observability is easy to check case by case. For example, the word ba is accepted from the state D but rejected from E, so from these two states different languages are recognized. ∎

Solution to Problem 45
Notice that every word v determines a set of letters that are permitted in a word w for vw to have a chance of being in L: a letter a is permitted after v if and only if $va \in L$. It is easy to update the set of permitted letters with each subsequent letter read: if the read letter is a then the current set should be intersected with the interval $\{a-2, \ldots, a+2\}$. Initially all letters are permitted, and a word should be rejected if and only if at some point a letter is read that is not permitted.

Not every set of permitted letters is reachable in this manner. Indeed, permitted letters always form an interval of size at least two (or zero, if the word can no longer belong to L). The reachable sets are states of the following automaton (with the non-accepting sink state $\emptyset$ omitted):
This automaton recognizes the correct language. It is also obviously minimal: from any two distinct sets of permitted letters the automaton recognizes different languages; indeed, the states can be distinguished by one-letter words. ∎

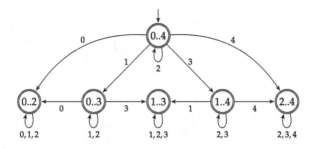

Solution to Problem 46

For $n = 1$ the answer is three, since NPal_1 contains only the empty word and the one-letter word 0. For $n = 2$ we have

$$\mathrm{NPal}_2 = \{\varepsilon, 0, 1, 01, 10\}$$

and to recognize it five states are necessary (and sufficient).

For $n > 2$, notice that a word contains no non-trivial palindromes if and only if each letter in it is different from the two preceding letters. Indeed, if this is not the case, then the word contains a palindrome of the form aa or aba. Conversely, if a word contains a non-trivial palindrome, then it contains a short palindrome; that is, a palindrome of the length two or three.

With this characterization, it is easy to see that the minimal automaton for NPal_n has:

- an initial state,
- a rejecting sink state,
- n states reachable after reading a single letter, and
- $n(n-1)$ states to remember the last two letters read, provided that those letters are distinct.

In total the automaton has $n(n-1) + n + 2 = n^2 + 2$ states.   ∎

Solution to Problem 47

Below we see a simple deterministic automaton accepting L, with a non-accepting sink state omitted. It is easy to see that none of the maximal paths can be extended to remain in L. The number of words in L is equal to the number of states, that is, 27.

Obviously this automaton is not minimal. An acyclic automaton like this can be minimized by a simple inductive procedure: one can progressively merge those states that (both accept or both reject and) make the same transitions to previously merged states.

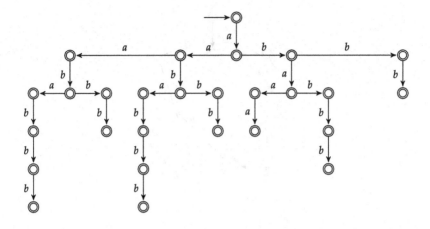

In this case, in the first step we merge all leaves in the tree (we mark them with a label 1), since they all make no transitions except to the sink state (omitted in the picture). Then we can merge all those states that only make *b*-transitions to states labelled with 1 (we label these with 2), and so on, resulting in the following labelling:

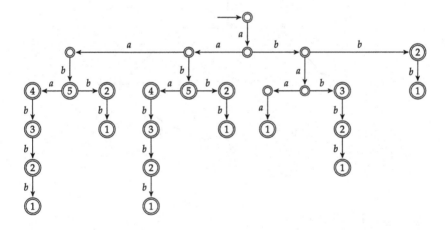

Merging states marked with the same labels we obtain a minimal automaton:

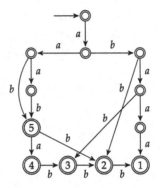

Solution to Problem 48

All words of length at most two obviously belong to L. Among words of length three only 000, 111, 010, and 101 are in L, and the latter two cannot be extended to words in L since 0101 and 1010 are both antipalindromes. Altogether we get

$$L = 0^* + 1^* + 010 + 101.$$

It is easy to see that the automaton below is minimal for this language.

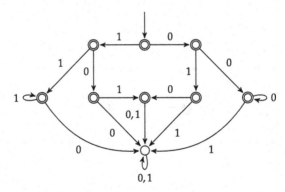

Solution to Problem 49

The key observation is that, regardless of k, every word w in L_k has a period of k; that is, the $(i+k)$th letter of w is the same one as the ith one. This is because the number of 1's in the infix $w[i..(i+k-1)]$ must be the same as in the infix $w[(i+1)..(i+k)]$. In particular, once the first k letters have been read, each consecutive letter is uniquely determined by the previous ones. Consequently, a word of length at least k belongs to L_k if and only if it has a period of k and its first k letters contain exactly two 1's; a word of length less than k belongs to L_k if and only if it contains at most two 1's.

With this insight, consider first the case of $k = 3$. The first three letters can form any one of the words 110, 101, or 011. Note that, up to cyclic shift, these are the same word. Therefore, after the first three letters every word in L_3 repeats the pattern of two 1's followed by a 0, and repeating this pattern is sufficient to fall into L_3. Here is an automaton that recognizes this (with a non-accepting sink state omitted), where each state is labelled with a member of its corresponding Myhill–Nerode equivalence class:

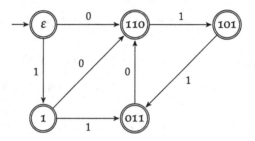

For the case of $k = 4$, the picture is a bit more complicated but similar. Every word in L_4, after the first few letters, enters one of the two cyclic patterns:

$$\ldots 010101010101 \ldots \qquad \text{or} \qquad \ldots 001100110011 \ldots .$$

An automaton that recognizes this, with each state labelled with a member of the corresponding Myhill–Nerode class of L_4 (and with a non-accepting sink state omitted as before), looks as follows:

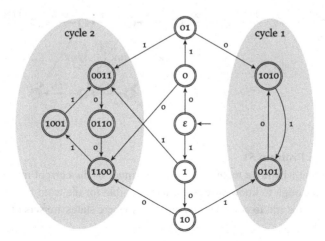

Again, it is straightforward to check that this automaton recognizes L_4 and that it recognizes a different language from each state. ■

Solution to Problem 50

First we construct a deterministic automaton that recognizes the language, faithfully simulating the behaviour of the machine (with rejecting sink state omitted):

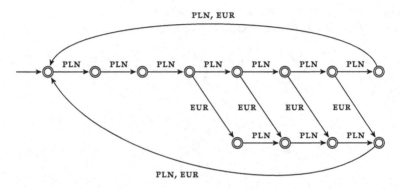

In the states from the top row the machine only contains PLN coins, and in the states from the bottom row it contains one EUR coin.

This automaton recognizes the correct language, but it is not minimal. Indeed, the two right-most states (7 PLN versus 1 EUR + 3 PLN) accept the same words and can be merged. The resulting automaton is minimal:

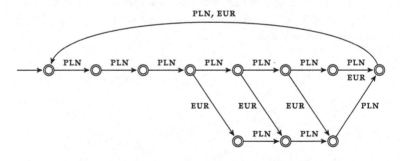

■

Solution to Problem 51

To determine whether a team is a possible winner of the current match, obviously it is enough to know whether it was possible for the team to participate in it. So it is natural to consider an automaton where states are sets of possible match-ups.

In the initial state, all three match-ups are possible. If it turns out that the first match was won by A, then the match was either AB or AC, so the next match is going to be either AC or AB. So when reading A from the initial state, the automaton moves to a state $A?$, meaning 'either AC or AB'. This state has a self-loop on the letter A. If the automaton reads B while it is in the state $A?$, then we know that the next match is going to be BC. Once the current match is unambiguously known, the automaton simply updates the current match according to the winner that it reads, and it goes into a rejecting sink state if it reads a team that could not participate in the current match. Here is the automaton, with the sink state omitted:

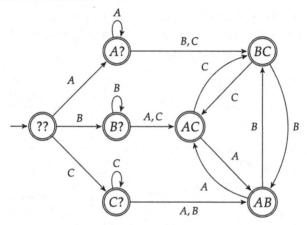

From the above reasoning it is clear that the automaton recognizes the correct language. To see that it is minimal, one has to check case by case that from every two distinct states different languages are recognized. For instance, from the state $A?$ the two-letter word AB is accepted but from the state $B?$ it is rejected. ∎

Solution to Problem 52

Regularity is easy, since Mr. X's decision whether to sell a stock depends only on the current stock ranking and on the rankings on the previous two days. It is easy to store that information in states of a finite automaton.

Actually, for any word w, the only information about a word v that is needed to determine if $vw \in L$, is

- whether v belongs to L, and if yes then
- the highest-valued stock on the last day, and
- the stock that dropped from the first to the second position on the last day, if any.

This results in an automaton of 11 states:

- an initial state 0;
- three states A, B, and C, indicating that the highest-priced stock was A (respectively B, C), and no stock dropped from the first to the second place on the last day;
- six states AB, AC, etc., indicating that the highest-priced stock was A (respectively A, etc.), and B (respectively C, etc.) dropped from the first to the second place on the last day;
- a rejecting sink state $\perp$.

Transitions of the automaton follow directly from the intuition. Here is a fragment of the automaton with all transitions outgoing from A and BA (states 0, AC, BC, and CB are not shown at all):

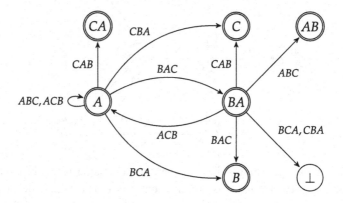

The automaton is obviously reachable and accepts L. It is also not difficult to check that every two distinct states recognize different languages, so the automaton is minimal.   ■

Solution to Problem 53

To decide if Mr. X could work on any given day, it is enough to know when he worked on the previous six days. The language of valid calendars is therefore regular, and it is easy to find an automaton with 58 states that recognizes it (there are $2^6 - 1 - 6 = 57$ ways to distribute at most four 1's among six positions, and an additional sink state is needed to reject invalid calendars).

However, that automaton is not minimal, since some histories of length six allow the same calendar continuations. For example, calendars 000000 and 111000 are Myhill–Nerode equivalent, since every calendar w that is itself valid completes both of them to valid calendars.

To understand this equivalence, notice that every calendar v of length six determines a sequence of numbers, which we call a *trace* of v,

$$a_1 a_2 a_3 a_4 a_5 a_6,$$

defined so that a_i is the maximal number of 1's in the next i positions that does not invalidate the calendar. For example,

- 000000 and 111000 both yield 123444,
- 101011 yields 011223, and
- 001111 yields 000123.

Every trace is a non-decreasing sextuple of digits between 0 and 4, starting with 0 or 1, incrementing by at most one with each position, and ending with 3 or 4. There are 35 such sextuples, starting from 000123 and ending with 123444.

It is not difficult to see that two calendars of length six that yield the same trace are Myhill–Nerode equivalent. We may define an automaton with traces as states, with the following transition relation. From a state $a_1 a_2 a_3 a_4 a_5 a_6$:

- if the current letter is 1 and $a_1 = 0$, move to the rejecting sink state;
- if the current letter is 1 and $a_1 = 1$, move to

$$(a_2 - 1)(a_3 - 1)(a_4 - 1)(a_5 - 1)(a_6 - 1)3;$$

- if the current letter is 0, move to

$$\min(1, a_2) \min(2, a_3) \min(3, a_4) \min(4, a_5) \min(5, a_6)4.$$

The sink state included; this gives an automaton with 36 states. The initial state is 123444, and all states except the sink are accepting.

This automaton accepts the language of valid calendars. To prove minimality, consider two distinct traces

$$a_1 a_2 a_3 a_4 a_5 a_6 \quad \text{and} \quad b_1 b_2 b_3 b_4 b_5 b_6.$$

Let the first difference between them be at position i, and assume without loss of generality that $a_i > b_i$. Then consider the unique calendar w of length i such that the number of 1's in the first j positions is exactly a_j, for $j \leq i$. The calendar w is accepted from the state corresponding to the trace $a_1 \ldots a_6$, but not from the one corresponding to $b_1 \ldots b_6$.

Alternatively, one can analyse calendars of length seven and show that any calendar with less than four 1's is equivalent to a calendar with exactly four 1's obtained by updating the necessary number of the earliest 0's. The argument is similar to that in the solution above. There are $\binom{7}{4} = 35$ calendars with exactly four 1's, which are moreover pairwise non-equivalent in the sense of the Myhill–Nerode relation. On the other hand, one can easily see that any calendar is equivalent to some calendar of seven days. ∎

Solution to Problem 54

Let $\mathcal{A} = (\Sigma, Q, I, \delta, F)$ be an automaton with ε-transitions. Let us write $p \xRightarrow{w} q$ if there is a run from p to q such that labels from $\Sigma \cup \{\varepsilon\}$ on the transitions constituting the run give the word w. Note that while $p \xrightarrow{a} q$ means that there is a single transition labelled with $a \in \Sigma \cup \{\varepsilon\}$, $p \xRightarrow{a} q$ means that there is a sequence of ε-transitions, followed by an a-transition, followed by yet another sequence of ε-transitions, together constitute a run from p to q. This is precisely why we introduce a separate symbol $\Longrightarrow$, rather than overloading the symbol $\rightarrow$ like for automata without ε-transitions. Consider $\mathcal{A}' = (\Sigma, Q, I', \delta', F')$ with

$$I' = \{q' \in Q \colon \exists q \in I.\, q \xRightarrow{\varepsilon} q'\},$$

$$F' = \{q' \in Q \colon \exists q \in F.\, q' \xRightarrow{\varepsilon} q\},$$

$$\delta' = \{(p, a, q) \in Q \times \Sigma \times Q \colon p \xRightarrow{a} q\}.$$

Clearly the automaton $\mathcal{A}'$ does not have ε-transitions. Let us see that it recognizes the same language as $\mathcal{A}$. A word $w = a_1 \ldots a_n$ is accepted by $\mathcal{A}'$ if and only if there is a run

$$I' \ni q_0 \xrightarrow{a_1} q_1 \xrightarrow{a_2} q_2 \xrightarrow{a_3} \cdots \xrightarrow{a_n} q_n \in F'.$$

By the definition of $\mathcal{A}'$, this happens if and only if

$$q_I \xRightarrow{\varepsilon} q_0 \xRightarrow{a_1} q_1 \xRightarrow{a_2} q_2 \xRightarrow{a_3} \cdots \xRightarrow{a_n} q_n \xRightarrow{\varepsilon} q_F$$

for some $q_I \in I$ and $q_F \in F$. The latter is equivalent to

$$q_I \xRightarrow{w} q_F,$$

which means exactly that w is accepted by $\mathcal{A}$. ∎

Solution to Problem 55

The function that flips the first letter does the job. It can be realized by the Mealy machine with states $Q = \{0, 1\}$ where 0 is the initial state, the transitions are $i \xrightarrow{x} 1$ for all $i \in Q$ and $x \in \{a, b\}$, and the output function is $\gamma(0, b) = a$, $\gamma(0, a) = b$, and $\gamma(1, x) = x$ for $x \in \{a, b\}$. ∎

Solution to Problem 56

(1) The construction for the composition is reminiscent of the one for the intersection of two regular languages (see Problem 62). For $i = 1, 2$, consider a Mealy machine $\mathcal{A}_i = (\Sigma, Q_i, q_I^i, \delta_i)$ with output function $\gamma_i \colon Q_i \times \Sigma_i \to \Sigma_{i+1}$ such that $\widehat{\gamma}_i = f_i$. Consider the product machine $\mathcal{A}$ defined as follows:

- the state space is $Q_1 \times Q_2$ with the initial state (q_I^1, q_I^2);
- transitions are determined component-wise, by letting the second automaton read the symbol output by the first one,

$$(q_1, q_2) \xrightarrow{a} (\delta_1(q_1, a), \delta_2(q_2, \gamma_1(q_1, a)));$$

- the output function γ is constructed by composing γ_1 with γ_2,

$$\gamma((q_1, q_2), a) = \gamma_2(q_2, \gamma_1(q_1, a)).$$

One can show by induction on the length of the word that $\widehat{\gamma} = \widehat{\gamma_2} \circ \widehat{\gamma_1}$.

(2) Let $\mathcal{A} = (\Sigma, P, p_I, \delta, F)$ be a deterministic automaton recognizing the language L and let us consider a Mealy machine $\mathcal{B} = (\Sigma, Q, q_I, \eta)$ with output function $\gamma \colon Q \times \Sigma \to \Delta$ such that $\widehat{\gamma} = f$. We construct a non-deterministic automaton $\mathcal{C}$ recognizing $\widehat{\gamma}(L)$ by a simple product construction. The set of states is $P \times Q$ with the initial state (p_I, q_I) and accepting states $F \times Q$. The transitions are

$$(p, q) \xrightarrow{\gamma(q,a)} (\delta(p, a), \eta(q, a))$$

for all $p \in P$, $q \in Q$, and $a \in \Sigma$. One can show by induction on the length of the word that $\mathcal{C}$ recognizes the language $\widehat{\gamma}(L)$.

(3) The construction for the pre-image is analogous to that for the image in item (2), except that the product automaton $\mathcal{C}$ runs over the alphabet Σ and it has transitions

$$(p, q) \xrightarrow{a} (\delta(p, \gamma(q, a)), \eta(q, a))$$

for all $p \in P$, $q \in Q$, and $a \in \Sigma$. ∎

Solution to Problem 57

Intuitively, when a Moore machine reads a symbol a in a state q, it executes a transition by moving to the successor state $\delta(q', a)$ and then outputs $\gamma(q')$, while a Mealy machine does things the other way around: it first outputs $\gamma(q, a)$ and then moves to the successor state $\delta(q, a)$.

It is straightforward to construct a Mealy machine equivalent to a given Moore machine: take the underlying deterministic automaton and define the output function as $\gamma'(q, a) = \gamma(\delta(q, a))$.

The other direction is less straightforward. After performing the transition to $\delta(q, a)$, we should output $\gamma(q, a)$, but we no longer have access to q and a. This can be amended by remembering the symbol to output. To this end, we change the set of states of the underlying automaton to $Q \times \Delta$ and define $\delta'((q, a), b) = (\delta(q, b), \gamma(q, b))$, and $\gamma'(q, a) = a$. For the initial state we can take (q_I, a_0) for an arbitrarily chosen symbol $a_0 \in \Delta$.   ∎

Solution to Problem 58

(1) To determine if a word over the alphabet $\{a, b, c\}$ is in L_k, we factorize it into blocks of letters a and b, separated by letters c; in the kth block the kth symbol from the end is supposed to be a. Let K be the language given by $c^{k-1}(a + b)^k$. It contains 2^k words, all of them of the same length. It suffices to show that no two words from K are Myhill–Nerode equivalent. If $u, v \in K$ are different, then the ith symbol from the end is different in u and v for some $i \in \{1, 2, \ldots, k\}$. Consequently, exactly one of the words $ub^{k-i}c$ and $vb^{k-i}c$ belongs to L_k.

For $(L_k)^R$ the argument is similar, but it uses the language K given by $\left(ca^{k-1}(a + b)\right)^k$. If $u, v \in K$ are different, then their ith blocks counting from the end are different for some $i \in \{1, 2, \ldots, k\}$. It follows that exactly one of the words uc^{k-i} and vc^{k-i} belongs to $(L_k)^R$.

(2) The automaton works in two phases. In the first phase, it identifies the kth symbol c. It uses states $q_0, \ldots, q_k$ with q_0 initial and transitions $\delta(q_i, a) = \delta(q_i, b) = (q_i, \to)$ and $\delta(q_i, c) = (q_{i+1}, \to)$ for $i \in \{0, 1, \ldots, k-1\}$. Upon reaching q_k the automaton moves to the second phase, in which it identifies the kth symbol from the end in the block just before the identified c, and verifies that it is a. It uses additional states $q_{k+1}, q_{k+2}, \ldots, q_{2k}$ and transitions $\delta(q_i, a) = \delta(q_i, b) = (q_{i+1}, \leftarrow)$ for $i \in \{k, k + 1, \ldots, 2k - 1\}$ and $\delta(q_{2k}, a) = (f, \leftarrow)$, where f is the unique accepting state.   ∎

Solution to Problem 59

Let $\mathcal{A} = (\Sigma, Q, I, \delta, F)$ be a two-way automaton. We can assume without loss of generality that before moving to an accepting state the automaton proceeds to $\lhd$, and that it has a transition $(q, \lhd, \to, q)$ for each state q. Such transitions cannot be used in an ordinary run, but they will make our construction more concise. We shall simulate $\mathcal{A}$ with an ordinary deterministic automaton $\mathcal{B}$ whose states will be pairs (h, P) such that $h \subseteq Q \times Q$ and $P \subseteq Q$. We call these pairs *macrostates*; we shall see that they represent precisely the information about the prefix read so far that the automaton $\mathcal{B}$ needs. In particular, P resembles the set of reachable states in the powerset construction and it is used to determine whether to accept or not, and h is used to update P properly.

After reading a prefix u of the input word w, the automaton $\mathcal{B}$ will be in the macrostate (h, P), where P is the set of states that the two-way automaton can reach when it exits u to the right for the first time during a run on $\triangleright w \triangleleft$, and h is a two-way variant of the effect relation and contains pairs of states (p, q) such that when starting in the right-most letter of the word u in state p, the two-way automaton can exit u to the right in state q.

For a word $u \in \Sigma^*$ and configurations $c \in Q \times \{1, 2, \ldots, |\triangleright u|\}$ and $d \in Q \times \{|\triangleright u| + 1\}$, a u-*trace from* c *to* d is a sequence of configurations $c = c_0, c_1, \ldots, c_k = d$ such that $c_1, c_2, \ldots, c_{k-1} \in Q \times \{1, 2, \ldots, |\triangleright u|\}$ and for all $i < k$ the automaton can move from c_i to c_{i+1}; that is, d is the first configuration during a run of the automaton starting in c when it moves past $\triangleright u$ (necessarily, via a move to the right). Notice that the number k of steps can be greater than $|\triangleright u|$.

The *characteristic macrostate* of the word u is (h_u, P_u) where

$$h_u = \{(p, q) \in Q \times Q : \text{there is a } u\text{-trace from } (p, |\triangleright u|) \text{ to } (q, |\triangleright u| + 1)\},$$
$$P_u = \{q \in Q : \text{there is } p \in I \text{ and a } u\text{-trace from } (p, 1) \text{ to } (q, |\triangleright u| + 1)\}.$$

Let $\overleftarrow{a} = \{(p, q) : (p, a, \leftarrow, q) \in \delta\}$ and $\overrightarrow{a} = \{(p, q) : (p, a, \rightarrow, q) \in \delta\}$ for $a \in \Sigma \cup \{\triangleright, \triangleleft\}$. It follows that

$$h_{ua} = \left(\overleftarrow{a} \cdot h_u\right)^* \cdot \overrightarrow{a} \quad \text{and} \quad P_{ua} = h_{ua}(P_u), \tag{$\diamond$}$$

where $h_{ua}(P_u) = \{q \in Q : (p, q) \in h_{ua} \text{ for some } p \in P_u\}$ is the image of the set P_u under the relation h_{ua}. In particular, the next macrostate (h_{ua}, P_{ua}) depends only on the letter a and the previous macrostate (h_u, P_u).

Hence, we can define the automaton $\mathcal{B}$ as follows:

- the initial macrostate is $(h_\varepsilon, P_\varepsilon)$;
- the transitions are $(h, P) \xrightarrow{a} \left(h^a, h^a(P)\right)$ for $h \subseteq Q \times Q, P \subseteq Q$, and $a \in \Sigma$;
- a macrostate (h, P) is accepting if $h^\triangleright(P) \cap F \neq \emptyset$.

Here $h^a = \left(\overleftarrow{a} \cdot h\right)^* \cdot \overrightarrow{a}$ for $h \subseteq Q \times Q$ and $a \in \Sigma \cup \{\triangleright, \triangleleft\}$. It follows from ($\diamond$) that upon reading a word u the automaton reaches the macrostate (h_u, P_u). This directly implies that the construction is correct. $\blacksquare$

Solution to Problem 60. DETERMINIZATION
First we prove both upper bounds. It is known that determinization can be performed using the *powerset construction*. Let us recall it here for completeness.

Let $\mathcal{A} = (\Sigma, Q, I, \delta, F)$ be a non-deterministic finite automaton. We construct a deterministic finite automaton $\mathcal{B}$ that tracks the set of states of $\mathcal{A}$ that are reachable from an initial state of $\mathcal{A}$ via the processed prefix of the input word. The states of $\mathcal{B}$ are subsets of Q and the initial state is the set I of the initial states of $\mathcal{A}$. When reading letter a in state S the automaton $\mathcal{B}$ moves to the state collecting all states of $\mathcal{A}$ that can be reached by firing a transition over a from a state in S; that is, $S \xrightarrow{a} \{q \in Q : \exists p \in S.p \xrightarrow{a} q\}$ for all $S \in \mathcal{P}(Q)$ and $a \in \Sigma$. By routine induction on the length of w we obtain $I \xrightarrow{w} \{q \in Q : \exists p \in I.p \xrightarrow{w} q\}$. We let state $S \in \mathcal{P}(Q)$ be accepting if and only if $S \cap F \neq \emptyset$. It follows immediately that $L(\mathcal{A}) = L(\mathcal{B})$.

Thus, for a non-deterministic automaton with n states, the powerset construction yields an equivalent deterministic automaton with 2^n states. As $\mathcal{B}_n$ has n states, this immediately gives a deterministic automaton recognizing $L(\mathcal{B}_n)$ with 2^n states. In the case of $L(\mathcal{A}_n)$, observe additionally that in the powerset construction only sets that contain state q_1 are reachable. The other sets can be removed from the powerset automaton, and therefore the number of states in the minimal deterministic automaton recognizing $L(\mathcal{A}_n)$ is at most 2^{n-1}.

Let us move on to the lower bounds. Observe that $L(\mathcal{A}_n)$ is the set of words in which the $(n-1)$th letter from the end equals a. It suffices to show that the Myhill–Nerode equivalence relation of $L(\mathcal{A}_n)$ has at least 2^{n-1} equivalence classes. To this end, we prove that any two different words $u, v \in \{a, b\}^*$ of length $n-1$ are not equivalent. As u and v are different, there exists some $1 \leq i \leq n-1$ such that $u[i] \neq v[i]$; assume without loss of generality that $u[i] = a$ and $v[i] = b$. Then, $ua^{i-1} \in L(\mathcal{A}_n)$, whereas $va^{i-1} \notin L(\mathcal{A}_n)$.

Now let us consider automaton $\mathcal{B}_n$. We show that its Myhill–Nerode equivalence relation has at least 2^n equivalence classes. Recall that q_1 is the initial state of $\mathcal{B}_n$. For each set S of states of $\mathcal{B}_n$ we shall define a word w_S such that $q_1 \xrightarrow{w_S} q$ if and only if $q \in S$. Then we shall show that for any two different sets $S_1, S_2 \subseteq Q = \{q_1, \ldots, q_n\}$, words w_{S_1} and w_{S_2} are not equivalent. This will finish the proof, as there are 2^n subsets of Q.

Fix a set $S \subseteq Q$ and let

$$w_S = a^{n-1} v_n v_{n-1} \ldots v_1,$$

where $v_i = a$ if $q_i \in S$ and $v_i = ab$ if $q_i \notin S$. Note that if we start in q_1, then after processing a^{n-1} all states in Q are reachable. In order to conclude that $q_1 \xrightarrow{w_S} q$ if and only if $q \in S$, we shall prove that if $q_i \in S$ then $q_i \xrightarrow{v_n v_{n-1} \ldots v_1} q_i$, and if $q_i \xrightarrow{v_n v_{n-1} \ldots v_1} q_j$ then $q_j \in S$.

Let $i > 1$. If we start processing $v_n v_{n-1} \ldots v_1$ in q_i, we arrive in q_1 after processing the first letter of v_i. If $q_i \notin S$, the next letter to process is b, which is impossible in q_1. Hence, we cannot process $v_n v_{n-1} \ldots v_1$ starting in $q_i \notin S$. Assuming we start in $q_i \in S$, we can loop in q_1 processing $v_{i-1}, v_{i-2}, \ldots$ as long as these words are equal to a, which translates to the corresponding states $q_{i-1}, q_{i-2}, \ldots$ being from S. Let v_j be the last word processed without leaving q_1 (possibly, $j = i$). Then, after consuming the remaining words $v_{j-1} v_{j-2} \ldots v_1$ we end up in q_j. This shows that, for $i > 1$, if $q_i \in S$ then $q_i \xrightarrow{v_n v_{n-1} \ldots v_1} q_i$, and if $q_i \xrightarrow{v_n v_{n-1} \ldots v_1} q_j$ then $q_j \in S$.

It remains to see what happens if we start processing $v_n v_{n-1} \ldots v_1$ in q_1. If we move to q_2 processing the first letter, then the reasoning is exactly like above: we arrive again in q_1 after reading the first letter of the word v_1, and either finish in q_1 if $q_1 \in S$, or cannot process the last letter if $q_1 \notin S$. The other possibility is that we loop in q_1 when processing the first letter. Again, we can loop in q_1 processing $v_n, v_{n-1}, \ldots$ as long as these words are equal to a, which translates to the corresponding states $q_n, q_{n-1}, \ldots$ being from S. Let v_j be the last word processed without leaving q_1 (since we loop at least once, $j \leq n$). Then, after consuming the remaining words $v_{j-1} v_{j-2} \ldots v_1$ we end up in q_j. Hence, if $q_1 \in S$ then $q_1 \xrightarrow{v_n v_{n-1} \ldots v_1} q_1$, and if $q_1 \xrightarrow{v_n v_{n-1} \ldots v_1} q_j$ then $q_j \in S$. This concludes the proof that $q_1 \xrightarrow{w_S} q$ if and only if $q \in S$.

Let us now fix some $S_1 \neq S_2$. Then, there is some $q_i \in Q$, which belongs to exactly one of S_1 or S_2; without loss of generality assume that $q_i \in S_1$ and $q_i \notin S_2$. If $i = 1$ then w_{S_1} and w_{S_2} are clearly not equivalent, as $w_{S_1} \in L$ and $w_{S_2} \notin L$. Otherwise, observe that state q_1 is reachable by the word $(ba)^{n+1-i}$ only from the state q_i. Therefore, $w_{S_1}(ba)^{n+1-i} \in L$ while $w_{S_2}(ba)^{n+1-i} \notin L$, which finishes the proof. ∎

Solution to Problem 61 Let $\mathcal{B}_n$ be the automaton $\mathcal{A}_n$ with all its transitions reversed. Notice that $L(\mathcal{B}_n)$ is the reverse of $L(\mathcal{A}_n)$, as the initial state and the unique accepting state are the same. The automaton $\mathcal{B}_n$ is not deterministic, but this is not directly relevant at this moment. Let $Q = \{q_1, q_2, \ldots, q_n\}$ be the set of states of $\mathcal{B}_n$ and let $L = L(\mathcal{B}_n)$. Notice that state q_1 is the unique accepting state of $\mathcal{B}_n$.

In order to show that every deterministic automaton recognizing L has at least 2^n states, it is enough to find 2^n words that are pairwise not Myhill–Nerode equivalent. To this end, we first prove that for every $S \subseteq Q$ there exists a word u_S such that S contains exactly these states q for which $q_1 \xrightarrow{u_S} q$.

Observe that in $\mathcal{B}_n$ the effect relations $R_a, R_c \subseteq Q \times Q$ (defined in the solution to Problem 35) are permutations of Q: R_a is a single cycle shifting all states by one, and R_c is a transposition that swaps q_1 and q_2 and fixes all other states. That is, R_a and R_c, understood as permutations of Q, have exactly the properties given in the hint. It follows that for every permutation σ of Q, there exists a word $u_\sigma \in \{a, c\}^*$ such that the effect relation R_{u_σ} is precisely the permutation σ.

We can now define u_S. For $S = \emptyset$ take $u_S = b$. For a non-empty set $S \subseteq Q$, take an arbitrary permutation π that maps $\{q_1, q_2, \ldots, q_{|S|}\}$ onto S and define

$$u_S = (ab)^{|S|-1} u_\pi .$$

It is easy to check that $q_1 \xrightarrow{(ab)^{k-1}} q$ if and only if $q \in \{q_1, q_2, \ldots, q_k\}$ for $k \leq n$. Then, the transition over u_π maps $\{q_1, q_2, \ldots, q_{|S|}\}$ onto S, and hence indeed S consists of exactly these states q for which $q_1 \xrightarrow{u_S} q$.

Now, if S_i and S_j are two different subsets of Q, some state q_ℓ belongs to exactly one of them, say $q_\ell \in S_i$ and $q_\ell \notin S_j$. Then $u_{S_i} a^{n-\ell} \in L$ and $u_{S_j} a^{n-\ell} \notin L$. That is, u_{S_i} and u_{S_j} are not Myhill–Nerode equivalent. As there are 2^n subsets of Q, this concludes the proof. ∎

Solution to Problem 62. INTERSECTION

The standard product construction gives an automaton of the required size. Let us recall it here. The states of the product automaton are pairs (p, q) where p is a state of $\mathcal{A}$ and q is a state of $\mathcal{B}$. A state (p, q) is initial if p is initial in $\mathcal{A}$ and q is initial in $\mathcal{B}$. Transitions are made synchronously in both components; that is, $(p, q) \xrightarrow{a} (p', q')$ if and only if $p \xrightarrow{a} p'$ in $\mathcal{A}$ and $q \xrightarrow{a} q'$ in $\mathcal{B}$. A pair of states (p, q) is accepting if p is accepting in $\mathcal{A}$ and q is accepting in $\mathcal{B}$. It is routine to show by induction on the length of w that $(p, q) \xrightarrow{w} (p', q')$ if and only if $p \xrightarrow{w} p'$ and $q \xrightarrow{w} q'$. It follows immediately from the choice of initial and accepting states that the product automaton recognizes $L(\mathcal{A}) \cap L(\mathcal{B})$. If both $\mathcal{A}$ and $\mathcal{B}$ have n states, then the product automaton has n^2 states.

The bound is asymptotically tight. Indeed, the languages generated by $(a^*b)^{n-1}$ and $(a^{n-1}b)^*$ can be recognized by finite automata with n states, but the only word in the intersection of these two languages is $(a^{n-1}b)^{n-1}$, whose length is $n(n - 1)$. Consequently, in each non-deterministic automaton recognizing the intersection, each path from an initial state to an accepting state has length $n^2 - n$ which implies that the automaton has at least $n^2 - n + 1$ states. ∎

Solution to Problem 63 We have $L_k = K_1 \cap K_2 \cap \cdots \cap K_k$ for

$$K_i = \left\{ u\$v : u, v \in \{a, b\}^{\geq i} \wedge u[i] = v[i] \right\} .$$

Each K_i can be easily recognized by a deterministic automaton with $\mathcal{O}(i)$ states. The complement of L_k is the union of the complements of $K_1, K_2, \ldots, K_k$, so it can be recognized by a non-deterministic automaton that guesses i and verifies that the input word does not belong to K_i. This automaton has $\mathcal{O}(k^2)$ states as it can be obtained by putting together k automata, each with $\mathcal{O}(k)$ states.

For the lower bound on the number of states in a non-deterministic automaton recognizing L_k we use a variant of the fooling method (see Section 2.2) suitable for non-deterministic automata. Let $\mathcal{A}$ be a non-deterministic automaton recognizing L_k. For $w \in \{a, b\}^k$, let X_w be the set of states of $\mathcal{A}$ that are reachable from an initial state by the word w and from which an accepting state is reachable by the word $\$w$. For every $w \in \{a, b\}^k$ we have $X_w \neq \emptyset$, because $w\$w \in L_k$. On the other hand, for all distinct $w, w' \in \{a, b\}^k$ we have $X_w \cap X_{w'} = \emptyset$, because $w\$w' \notin L_k$. Therefore, the union of all the sets X_w is of size at least 2^k, so $\mathcal{A}$ has at least 2^k states.

The above argument is a special case of a more general *fooling set method*. A *fooling set* for a language L over Σ is a set $\{(u_1, v_1), (u_2, v_2), \ldots, (u_n, v_n)\}$ of pairs of words over Σ such that $u_i v_i \in L$ for all i, but either $u_i v_j \notin L$ or $u_j v_i \notin L$ for all $i \neq j$. Arguing like above one shows that if L has a fooling set of size n, then each non-deterministic finite automaton recognizing L has at least n states. ∎

Solution to Problem 64

(1) We use a fixed alphabet $\Sigma = \{0, 1, \$\}$. We build a regular expression recognizing mistakes in a binary counter (which we can easily turn into an automaton). Let n be a positive integer. For $0 \le i < 2^n$ let $u_i \in \{0, 1\}^n$ be the binary representation of the natural number i with the least significant bit first, padded on the right with 0's. Consider the word

$$w_n = \$u_0 \$u_1 \$ \ldots \$u_{2^n - 1} \$.$$

For instance, $w_3 = \$000\$100\$010\$110\$001\$101\$011\$111\$$. We build a regular expression α of polynomial size recognizing precisely $\Sigma^* - \{w_n\}$. The expression checks whether the word has some mistake. The first group is syntactic mistakes:

- The word does not either start or end with $\$$: $\alpha_1 = \{0, 1\}\Sigma^* + \Sigma^*\{0, 1\}$.
- The word contains only one $\$$: $\alpha_2 = \{0, 1\}^*\$\{0, 1\}^*$.
- One block is too long or too short: $\alpha_3 = \Sigma^*\$ (\{0, 1\}^{<n} + \{0, 1\}^{>n}) \$\Sigma^*$.

The second group is arithmetic mistakes:

- The counter does not start with $00 \ldots 0$ or does not end with $11 \ldots 1$: $\alpha_4 = \$\{0, 1\}^*1\{0, 1\}^*\$\Sigma^* + \Sigma^*\$\{0, 1\}^*0\{0, 1\}^*\$$.
- Some 1 in a prefix of 1's is not turned into a 0 in its corresponding position in the next block: $\alpha_5 = \bigcup_{i=0}^{n-1} \Sigma^*\$1^i1\{0, 1\}^*\$0^i1\{0, 1\}^*\Sigma^*$.

- The first occurring 0 is not turned into a 1 in its corresponding position in the next block: $\alpha_6 = \bigcup_{i=0}^{n-1} \Sigma^* \$ 1^i 0 \{0,1\}^* \$ 1^i 0 \{0,1\}^* \Sigma^*$.
- Some bit x after 1^*0 is not copied correctly in its corresponding position in the next block: $\alpha_7 = \bigcup_{x \in \{0,1\}} \bigcup_{i=0}^{n-2} \Sigma^* \$ 1^* 0 \{0,1\}^i x \{0,1\}^*$ $\$ 0^* 1 \{0,1\}^i \bar{x} \Sigma^*$, where $\bar{0} = 1$ and $\bar{1} = 0$.

Putting all cases together, the sought expression is $\alpha = \alpha_1 + \cdots + \alpha_7$.

(2) Fix a positive integer n, and let $\Sigma_n = \{a_1, \ldots, a_n\}$. Let K_n consist of all words w over Σ_n that contain the letter a_n and for all $i \in \{1, 2, \ldots, n-1\}$ contain an occurrence of letter a_i:

- before the first occurrence of a letter from $\{a_{i+1}, \ldots, a_n\}$;
- between every two consecutive occurrences of letters from $\{a_{i+1}, \ldots, a_n\}$; and
- after the last occurrence of a letter from $\{a_{i+1}, \ldots, a_n\}$.

We prove by induction on n that every word in K_n has length at least $2^n - 1$. This is obvious for $n = 1$, as $\varepsilon \notin K_n$. For $n > 1$, take $w \in K_n$. Then w contains at least one letter a_n. If w contains exactly $k \geq 1$ letters a_n, then w contains $k + 1$ maximal infixes not containing a_n, sandwiched between the occurrences of a_n, as well as the beginning and the end of w. By definition, each of these maximal infixes belongs to K_{n-1}. By the induction hypothesis, each of these maximal infixes has length at least $2^{n-1} - 1$. Hence, the length of w is at least $k + (k+1) \cdot (2^{n-1} - 1)$, which is at least $2^n - 1$ for $k \geq 1$, as required.

Finally, we verify that the *complement of K_n* can be recognized by a non-deterministic automaton with $\mathcal{O}(n)$ states. With $\emptyset^* = \{\varepsilon\}$, we have that $w \notin K_n$ if and only if either w does not contain a_n or for some $i \in \{1, 2, \ldots, n-1\}$, w contains a (possibly empty) infix $u \in \{a_1, a_2, \ldots, a_{i-1}\}^*$ sandwiched between letters from $\{a_{i+1}, \ldots, a_n\}$ or the beginning or the end of w. Both the first condition and the second condition for a fixed i can be checked by a deterministic automaton with a constant number of states. The complement of K_n can be recognized by a non-deterministic automaton that first guesses which condition fails and then performs the corresponding check. This automaton has $\mathcal{O}(n)$ states, as it can be obtained by putting together n automata of constant size. ∎

Solution to Problem 65 Examine the language K_n described in the solution of Problem 64. As explained there, the complement of K_n can be expressed as the union of n languages recognized by deterministic automata with a constant number of states. Consequently, K_n is the intersection of n such languages. It was also shown that the shortest word in K_n has length at least $2^n - 1$. This implies that the shortest path from the initial state to an accepting state in every non-deterministic automaton recognizing K_n needs to have length at least $2^n - 1$, which requires at least 2^n states. ∎

Solution to Problem 66 We prove that for every pair of non-negative integers $m < n$, there exists an integer $k = \mathcal{O}(\log n)$ such that $n \not\equiv m \mod k$. This is enough to conclude: assuming $m = |u|$ and $n = |v|$, the automaton counting the length of the input word modulo k and accepting if it equals $m \mod k$, satisfies all the requirements.

Assume that $n \equiv m \mod k$ for all $k \in \{1, \ldots, \lceil 1+\log n\rceil\}$. Then it holds that $\mathrm{lcm}(1, \ldots, \lceil 1 + \log n\rceil)$ divides $n - m$. For $n \geq 128 = 2^7$ we have $\lceil \log n\rceil \geq 7$, so by Nair's theorem,

$$\mathrm{lcm}(1, \ldots, \lceil 1 + \log n\rceil) > 2^{\lceil 1+\log n\rceil} > n.$$

This contradicts the fact that $\mathrm{lcm}(1, \ldots, \lceil 1 + \log n\rceil)$ divides $n - m$. Therefore, for all $m < n$ where $n \geq 128$, there exists $k \leq 1 + \lceil \log n\rceil = \mathcal{O}(\log n)$ such that $m \not\equiv n \mod k$. When $n < 128$ both n and m are bounded by a constant, so in this case we can simply take $k = n$. ∎

Solution to Problem 67 Consider a descending sequence of equivalence relations

$$R_0 \supseteq R_1 \supseteq R_2 \supseteq \cdots$$

over states, defined as follows: $(p, q) \in R_i$ if states p and q are indistinguishable by words of length at most i. We shall see that if p and q are distinguishable, then $(p, q) \notin R_n$.

We first show that if $R_i = R_{i+1}$ for some i, then $R_i = R_j$ for all $j > i$. For a state p and a letter a, by p_a we denote the unique state such that $p \xrightarrow{a} p_a$. Observe that $(p, q) \in R_{i+1}$ if and only if for all $a \in \Sigma$ we have $(p_a, q_a) \in R_i$. Assume $R_i = R_{i+1}$. Then $(p, q) \in R_{i+1}$ if and only if for all $a \in \Sigma$ we have $(p_a, q_a) \in R_i$, and $(p, q) \in R_{i+2}$ if and only if for all $a \in \Sigma$ we have $(p_a, q_a) \in R_{i+1} = R_i$. Hence, $R_{i+1} = R_{i+2}$. This implies that $R_i = R_j$ for every $j > i$ by a straightforward induction.

By the assertion above, indices i such that $R_i \neq R_{i+1}$ form an initial segment of natural numbers. Moreover, there are at most $n - 1$ such indices, as an inclusion chain of different equivalence relations over n elements cannot be longer than n. Consequently, $R_n = R_{n+1}$ and hence $R_n = R_m$ for every $m > n$. But as p and q are distinguished by some word w, we have that $(p, q) \notin R_m$ for all $m \geq |w|$. It follows that $(p, q) \notin R_n$, as required. ∎

Solution to Problem 68 No, a regular language cannot have this property. Consider a non-deterministic automaton $\mathcal{A}$ with N states. Without loss of generality we can assume that all states in $\mathcal{A}$ are reachable from the initial state, and that some accepting state can be reached from each state. If there is a state p such that $p \xrightarrow{u} p$ and $p \xrightarrow{v} p$ for some distinct words u and v of the same length $k > 0$, then the growth is obviously exponential: if the shortest path from the initial state to p has length ℓ, and the shortest path from p to some accepting state has length m, then the number of words of length $\ell + k \cdot i + m$ in $L(\mathcal{A})$ is at least 2^i.

Assume that for each state p, for each $k \in \mathbb{N}$ there is at most one word u of length k such that $p \xrightarrow{u} p$. We show by induction on i that for every two states p and q there are at most $|\Sigma|^{i-1} \cdot n^{i-1}$ words w of length $n > 0$ such that $p \xrightarrow{w} q$ via a run visiting at most i states. As the growth is the number of words w of length n over which an accepting state is reached from the initial state, it will follow that the growth is bounded by $N \cdot |\Sigma|^{N-1} \cdot n^{N-1}$, which is a polynomial in n.

If $i = 1$ or $p = q$, the claim holds by our main assumption. Let us consider words w of length n such that $p \xrightarrow{w} q \neq p$ via a run using at most $i > 1$ states. Suppose that a run on w returns to p for the last time after reading the prefix of length $k < n$. By our main assumption, for each of the n choices of k, there is at most one possible choice for the length-k prefix of w. Next, there are at most $|\Sigma|$ choices of the $(k+1)$th letter of w (some transitions may be missing); this moves the run to some state p'. If $k + 1 = n$, it must hold that $p' = q$, so not all these choices are available; in this case the word w is complete. Otherwise, only $i - 1$ states can be used in the remaining part of the run on w, so by the induction hypothesis we can bound the number of possible suffixes by $|\Sigma|^{i-2} \cdot (n - k - 1)^{i-2} \leq |\Sigma|^{i-2} \cdot n^{i-2}$. Altogether we bound the number of words w by $|\Sigma| + (n - 1) \cdot |\Sigma| \cdot |\Sigma|^{i-2} \cdot n^{i-2} \leq |\Sigma|^{i-1} \cdot n^{i-1}$. ∎

Solution to Problem 69

(1) We present only one of many ways of obtaining this result. Consider the notion of an *extended automaton*, where transitions can be labelled by regular expressions, instead of just letters or ε. The behaviour of the automaton is defined in the natural way: if it fires a transition $q \xrightarrow{\alpha} q'$ it must read a sequence of consecutive letters of the input word that forms a word from $L(\alpha)$. For a given extended automaton $\mathcal{A}$ we shall construct a regular expression α such that $L(\alpha) = L(\mathcal{A})$ by iteratively simplifying the automaton while complicating the regular expressions it uses.

First, by a simple preprocessing we ensure that:

- the initial state has no incoming transitions;
- there is exactly one accepting state and it has no outgoing transitions;
- there is at most one transition between any two states.

We shall now iteratively eliminate states in such a way that the language recognized by the automaton stays invariant, and the above properties are maintained.

Let q be any remaining state that is neither initial nor accepting. To construct the new automaton we remove q from the state space and for each pair q_1, q_2 of remaining states we define the transitions as follows: If the old automaton has transitions

$$q_1 \xrightarrow{\alpha_1} q, \quad q \xrightarrow{\alpha} q, \quad q \xrightarrow{\alpha_2} q_2, \quad q_1 \xrightarrow{\alpha_{1,2}} q_2,$$

the new automaton has transition

$$q_1 \xrightarrow{\alpha_1 \alpha^* \alpha_2 + \alpha_{1,2}} q_2 \,;$$

if in the old automaton some of these transitions are missing, we adjust the definition of the new transition accordingly. One can easily see that this modification does not change the language recognized by the automaton.

During each elimination, regular expressions used in the automaton grow at most six times, so after eliminating all states except the unique initial state and the unique accepting state, the only regular expression appearing in the automaton has size at most $6^{n-2} = 2^{O(n)}$. This expression is equivalent to the original automaton.

(2) We sketch a solution by Andrzej Ehrenfeucht and Paul Zeiger.[1] Consider the alphabet $\Sigma_n = \{a_{(i,j)} : 1 \le i, j \le n\}$. Let $\mathcal{A}$ be the automaton with states $\{1, \ldots, n\}$ over alphabet Σ_n, where for all pairs (i,j) such that $i, j \in \{1, 2, \ldots, n\}$, we put a transition from state i to state j with label $a_{(i,j)}$. Let $L_{i,j}$ be the language recognized by the automaton $\mathcal{A}$ with the initial state set to i and the set of accepting states set to $\{j\}$. Clearly, each $L_{i,j}$ is recognized by an automaton with n states. Our goal is to show that each regular expression generating $L_{1,1}$ has length at least 2^{n-1}.

By a *cycle* in $\mathcal{A}$ we understand a sequence of transitions such that the target state of each transition is the source state of the next one, and the target state of the last transition is the source state of the first one. Because each transition in $\mathcal{A}$ has a different label, each cycle in $\mathcal{A}$ is uniquely determined by the word obtained by reading the labels from the sequence of transitions. We shall blur the distinction between the cycle and the

[1] A. Ehrenfeucht and P. Zeiger. Complexity measures for regular expressions. *Journal of Computer and System Sciences*, 12(2):134–146, 1976.

corresponding word, and treat the cycle as if it were a word. We say that a regular expression α *covers* a cycle C in $\mathcal{A}$ if $uCv \in L(\alpha)$ for some words u and v. By $I_C(\alpha)$ we denote the maximum number m such that α covers C^m, provided such an m exists. Otherwise, we say that α is *C-infinite* and we put $I_C(\alpha) = \infty$.

We claim that if α is not C-infinite, then $I_C(\alpha) < 2 \cdot |\alpha|$, where the length $|\alpha|$ of expression α is the total number of symbols it uses, including parentheses, stars, etc. Indeed, using the standard method one can turn α into an equivalent (non-deterministic) automaton $\mathcal{A}_\alpha$ with at most $2 \cdot |\alpha|$ states (see Problem 79). Assume that $uC^k v \in L(\alpha)$ for some $k > 2 \cdot |\alpha|$. Then, there is a corresponding accepting run of $\mathcal{A}_\alpha$. Since $k > 2 \cdot |\alpha|$, the automaton $\mathcal{A}_\alpha$ is in the same state after processing some two different copies of C and by pumping we obtain an accepting run over $uC^m v$ for an arbitrarily large m. Hence, $I_C(\alpha) = \infty$. This completes the proof of the claim.

The *start point of a word w over Σ_n* is the index $i \in \{1, \ldots, n\}$ such that the first letter of w is equal to $a_{(i,j)}$ for some j. Similarly, the *end point of w* is such index i that the last letter of w is equal to $a_{(j,i)}$ for some j. The *start point of a regular expression α over Σ_n* is an index i such that i is the start point of every $w \in L(\alpha)$. Similarly we define the *end point of a regular expression*. Observe that every non-empty word over Σ_n has a start point and an end point, but the same is not true for regular expressions; for example, $\alpha = a_{(1,2)} + a_{(2,3)}$ has no start point and no end point. A regular expression α will be called *normal* if every subexpression α' of α has a start point as well as an end point and additionally if $\alpha' = (\beta')^*$ then its start point and end point are equal.

We claim that for all $i, j \in \{1, \ldots, n\}$, every expression α with $L(\alpha) \subseteq L_{i,j}$ is normal. Indeed, suppose that some subexpression α' of α has no start point. Then there exist words $w, w' \in L(\alpha)$ such that $w = xyz$, $w' = xy'z$, and the start points of y and y' are different. This, however, is impossible because if $x \neq \varepsilon$ then the start points of both y and y' must be equal to the end point of x and if $x = \varepsilon$ then they must be equal to i. Hence, each subexpression of α has a start point. Analogously, each subexpression of α has an end point. Finally, consider a subexpression $\alpha' = (\beta')^*$ of α and suppose that the start point and the end point of α' are different. Then, the same is true of β'. But this means that there exists a word $w \in L(\alpha)$ such that $w = xyy'z$ and the end point of y is different from the start point y', which is again impossible by the observation made previously. This completes the proof that α must be normal.

We will show that there exists a cycle C passing through state 1 such that every normal expression α covering C satisfies $|\alpha| \geq 2^{n-1}$. This will finish the proof, as every regular expression recognizing the language $L_{1,1}$ has to be normal and has to cover C. We prove this claim by induction on n. For $n = 1$, we can take the cycle associated to the word $a_{(1,1)}$. Now let us show the induction step. By applying the induction hypothesis to the sub-automaton obtained by removing state n, there is a cycle C_1 which passes through state 1, avoids state n, and every normal expression covering C_1 has size at least 2^{n-2}. For $k = 2, 3, \ldots, n$, let C_k be the cycle obtained from C_1 by cyclically shifting the states so that C_k passes through k and avoids $k - 1$. Obviously, again, every normal expression covering C_k has size at least 2^{n-2}.

Let us define the cycle C as follows:

$$C = C_1^m a_{(1,2)} C_2^m a_{(2,3)} \ldots a_{(n-1,n)} C_n^m a_{(n,1)},$$

where $m = 2^n$. Suppose α is a regular expression covering C. By the definition of C we have $I_{C_k}(\alpha) \geq m = 2^n$ for each $k = 1, 2, \ldots, n$. So either $|\alpha| \geq 2^{n-1}$ and we are done, or α is C_k-infinite for all k. Let us focus on the second case.

For each k, let us consider a minimal (with respect to the relation 'subexpression of') subexpression α_k of α that is C_k-infinite. By minimality, for each k we have $\alpha_k = (\beta_k)^*$ for some subexpression β_k. Since α is normal, all subexpressions α_k and β_k are also normal. Let β_i be the shortest expression among $\beta_1, \beta_2, \ldots, \beta_n$. Since α_i is C_i-infinite, it covers C_i in particular, and hence by the induction hypothesis we have $|\alpha_i| \geq 2^{n-2}$.

Observe that the start point of α_i is equal to its end point, as α_i is a normal star expression. Denote this common start and end point of α_i as j. Consider now $\alpha_{j+1} = (\beta_{j+1})^*$; it covers C_{j+1} by assumption, so by the induction hypothesis we have that $|\alpha_{j+1}| \geq 2^{n-2}$. Since α_i is a star expression, and moreover it is the shortest among the star expressions α_k, for $k = 1, 2, \ldots, n$, we either have that subexpressions α_i and α_{j+1} are disjoint (as subexpressions of α), or α_i is a subexpression of α_{j+1} (possibly $\alpha_i = \alpha_{j+1}$). In the first case we are already done, since then $|\alpha| \geq |\alpha_i| + |\alpha_{j+1}| \geq 2^{n-2} + 2^{n-2} = 2^{n-1}$. Hence, from now on we consider only the case when α_i is a subexpression of α_{j+1}.

First, observe that $\alpha_i \neq \alpha_{j+1}$. Let us fix a word u witnessing that α_{j+1} covers C_{j+1}. By the minimality of α_{j+1}, C_{j+1} overlaps with at least two consecutive factors from $L(\beta_{j+1})$ in u. Consequently, C_{j+1} visits the start and end point of β_{j+1}. Since β_i has the start and end point equal to j, and C_{j+1} avoids j, we conclude that $\alpha_i \neq \alpha_{j+1}$.

Define $\alpha'_{j+1} = (\beta'_{j+1})^*$ as α_{j+1} with the subexpression α_i substituted with ε (one can then easily remove the usage of ε in a regular expression, and this modification only reduces its size). Using again the facts that α_{j+1} is a minimal subexpression covering p_{j+1}, the start and end point of α_i is j, and C_{j+1} avoids j, we derive that α'_{j+1} still covers C_{j+1}. Therefore, by the induction hypothesis we have $|\alpha'_{j+1}| \geq 2^{n-2}$. We conclude that

$$|\alpha| \geq |\alpha'_{j+1}| + |\alpha_i| \geq 2^{n-2} + 2^{n-2} = 2^{n-1},$$

and we are done.   ∎

Solution to Problem 70 Let $\mathcal{A} = (\Sigma, Q, q_I, \delta, F)$. The main observation is that we do not need to determinize $\mathcal{A}$. Starting from $i = 0$ and proceeding towards larger i, we compute the set S_i consisting of those states of $\mathcal{A}$ that are reachable from q_I by the word $w[1..i]$:

$$S_i = \left\{ q \in Q : q_I \xrightarrow{w[1..i]} q \right\} \subseteq Q.$$

The algorithm represents each S_i as a binary vector of length $|Q|$, where for each $q \in Q$ we store whether $q \in S_i$.

Clearly, we have $S_0 = \{q_I\}$, while the problem solved by the algorithm is equivalent to asking whether $S_{|w|}$ contains any accepting state. In order to compute S_{i+1} from S_i we iterate through all the states $p \in S_i$ and check for which states $q \in Q$ we have $p \xrightarrow{w[i+1]} q$. The set S_{i+1} contains all such states q. Note that to compute S_{i+1} from S_i we need at most $\mathcal{O}(|Q| + |\delta|)$ operations, so in total the algorithm runs in time $\mathcal{O}((|Q| + |\delta|) \cdot |w|) = \mathcal{O}(\|\mathcal{A}\| \cdot |w|)$, which finishes the proof.   ∎

Solution to Problem 71 For convenience, assume that $|w| = 2^k$; if $|w|$ is not a power of 2 we can pad w to the nearest power of 2 using a fresh blank letter and modify $\mathcal{A}$ by adding looping transitions over this letter.

The data structure is a binary tree t of depth k, where every node corresponds to some infix of the word w. The root corresponds to the whole word, $w[1..2^k]$. If an inner node corresponds to $w[i..j]$ then its left child corresponds to the first half of this infix, $w[i..\lfloor(i+j)/2\rfloor]$, and its right child corresponds to the second half of this infix, $w[(\lfloor(i+j)/2\rfloor + 1)..j]$. Thus, leaves correspond to infixes of length one. Let Q be the set of states of $\mathcal{A}$. In a node corresponding to infix v we store the effect relation $R_v \subseteq Q \times Q$, defined in the solution to Problem 35.

There are $2 \cdot 2^k - 1 = 2|w| - 1$ nodes in t. For the leaves the effect relations can be read directly from the transition relation of the automaton $\mathcal{A}$. Knowing the effect relations for two siblings, we easily compute the effect relation for their parent, because $R_{uv} = R_u \cdot R_v$. Hence, constructing each node takes constant time (recall that $\mathcal{A}$ is fixed). Thus, building the whole tree takes time $\mathcal{O}(|w|)$. It remains to show that we can perform the two operations within the specified time. One can check in time $\mathcal{O}(1)$ whether the whole word belongs to $L(\mathcal{A})$ by simply checking if the effect relation stored in the root relates an initial state to an accepting state. Let us focus on letter changes. If the letter at position i is changed, we need to update the information about all represented infixes containing this letter. These infixes correspond exactly to the nodes on the path from the root to the leaf corresponding to the infix $w[i..i]$. We recompute the effect relations for these nodes bottom-up, just like when the tree was originally constructed: we read the effect relation for the affected leaf from the transition relation, and then follow the path to the root, computing for each internal node the composition of the effect relations in its children. The whole update takes time proportional to the depth of the tree, that is, $\mathcal{O}(\log|w|)$. ∎

Solution to Problem 72 We use the data structure described in the solution of Problem 71. As argued there, it can be computed in time $\mathcal{O}(|w|)$. It remains to show that for given positions $i \leq j$ one can answer whether $w[i..j] \in L(\mathcal{A})$ in time $\mathcal{O}(\log|w|)$. Let $u = w[i..j]$. We shall compute the effect relation R_u and check whether it relates an initial state to an accepting state.

The effect relation R_u can be computed by composing effect relations of the factors in any factorization of u, as long as all factors are represented in the data structure. For instance, one could take $u = w[i..i] \ldots w[j..j]$, but this would take time linear in the length of u, which can be as long as the whole word. We show that it is possible to factorize u into $\mathcal{O}(\log|w|)$ factors, all represented in our data structure. Indeed, for each pair of consecutive positions $2p + 1$ and $2p + 2$, the effect relation is already stored in the data structure. Similarly, two consecutive length-two infixes beginning at positions $4p + 1$ and $4p + 3$ form an infix represented in the data structure, and so on. This way we can indeed factorize u into at most $2\log|w|$ factors, all of them represented in the data structure. Given i and j, these factors can be identified in the data structure as follows. Assume first that $1 < i < j < |w|$. Let x and y be the leaves corresponding to positions $i - 1$ and $j + 1$, and let π_x and π_y be the paths from x and y up to the children x' and y' of the lowest common ancestor of x and y, with x' and y' excluded. The factors in question are represented in the siblings of the nodes on π_x that are left children, taken in the bottom-up order, followed by the siblings of the nodes on π_y that are right children, in the top-down order. If $i = 1$, look only at the path π_y from the leaf y to the root (excluding the root), and dually if $j = |w|$. If $i = 1$ and $j = |w|$, then u equals w, which is represented in the root.   ∎

Solution to Problem 73 Let $\mathcal{A}_1 = (\Sigma, Q_1, q_1, \delta_1, F_1)$ and $\mathcal{A}_2 = (\Sigma, Q_2, q_2, \delta_2, F_2)$ be the input automata. We show how to construct an automaton recognizing $L(\mathcal{A}_1) - L(\mathcal{A}_2)$; one can symmetrically construct an automaton recognizing $L(\mathcal{A}_2) - L(\mathcal{A}_1)$. To test if $L(\mathcal{A}_1) = L(\mathcal{A}_2)$ it suffices to check that both constructed automata recognize the empty language, which can be easily done in time linear in their sizes. The construction of an automaton recognizing $L(\mathcal{A}_1) - L(\mathcal{A}_2)$ is similar to the standard product construction for the intersection of regular languages. That is, the automaton is $(\Sigma, Q, q, \delta, F)$, where

$$Q = Q_1 \times Q_2, q = (q_1, q_2), F = F_1 \times (Q_2 - F_2), \text{ and}$$
$$\delta = \left\{ ((p_1, p_2), a, (r_1, r_2)) \ : \ (p_1, a, r_1) \in \delta_1, \ (p_2, a, r_2) \in \delta_2 \right\}.$$

As the size of this automaton is proportional to the product of the sizes of $\mathcal{A}_1$ and $\mathcal{A}_2$, the claimed time complexity of the algorithm follows.   ∎

Solution to Problem 74 Let $Q = \{q_1, \ldots, q_s\}$ be the state space of $\mathcal{A}$ and q_1 be its initial state. For states $p, q \in Q$ and a number $0 \le i \le n$, let $N_{p,q,i}$ be the number of words w of length i such that $p \xrightarrow{w} q$. To solve the task it is sufficient to compute numbers $N_{q_1,q,n}$ for all $q \in Q$. Let M be an $s \times s$ matrix such that $M[i,j] = N_{q_i,q_j,1}$ for $i,j \in \{1, 2, \ldots, s\}$. The crucial observation is that for $m \ge 1$, $M^m[i,j] = N_{q_i,q_j,m}$, where M^m is the mth power of M.

We show this by induction on m. For $m = 1$ the claim holds by the definition of M. For the induction step, we have

$$M^{m+1}[i,j] = \sum_{k=1}^{s} M[i,k] \cdot M^m[k,j] = \sum_{k=1}^{s} N_{q_i,q_k,1} \cdot N_{q_k,q_j,m} = N_{q_i,q_j,m+1},$$

where the first equation follows from the definition of matrix multiplication, the second from the induction hypothesis, and the third holds because the number of words w of length $m + 1$ such that $q_i \xrightarrow{w} q_j$ and additionally $q_i \xrightarrow{w[1]} q_k$, equals exactly $N_{q_i,q_k,1} \cdot N_{q_k,q_j,m}$.

Therefore, in order to calculate $N_{q_1,q,n}$ for $q \in Q$ it is enough to compute M^n. This can be done using $\mathcal{O}(\log n)$ arithmetic operations using the standard binary power algorithm for logarithmic-time exponentiation. We briefly recall it here. Let the binary representation of n be $b_\ell b_{\ell-1} \ldots b_1 b_0$, where ℓ is the largest integer such that $2^\ell \le n$. Thus, we have

$$M^n = M^{2^\ell \cdot b_\ell} \cdot M^{2^{\ell-1} \cdot b_{\ell-1}} \cdot \ \cdots \ \cdot M^{2^1 \cdot b_1} \cdot M^{2^0 \cdot b_0}.$$

One can iteratively compute all the M^{2^i} for $i \leq \ell$ using $\mathcal{O}(\ell)$ arithmetic operations using the fact that $M^{2^i} = M^{2^{i-1}} \cdot M^{2^{i-1}}$. Note that each multiplication of these matrices uses $\mathcal{O}(s^3)$ arithmetic operations, which is considered constant for a fixed $\mathcal{A}$. Then we multiply all matrices M^{2^i} for which $b_i = 1$, which again requires $\mathcal{O}(\log n)$ arithmetic operations. ∎

Solution to Problem 75 We construct an automaton $\mathcal{A}$ that accepts exactly those words that have at least two different factorizations with respect to C, in which moreover the first factors are different. Note that C is a code if and only if no such word exists, so we reduce the problem to checking the emptiness of the language recognized by $\mathcal{A}$. The set Q of states of $\mathcal{A}$ consists of the initial state q_0 and the set $P \times P$, where

$$P = \{(u,j) \: : \: u \in C, \: 0 < j \leq |u|\}.$$

The intuition is that the automaton is in the state $((u_1,j_1),(u_2,j_2))$ if the first factorization of the input word is currently after reading the prefix of length j_1 of u_1, whereas the second factorization is after reading the prefix of length j_2 of u_2. The set F of accepting states is $P_F \times P_F$, where

$$P_F = \{(u,|u|) \: : \: u \in C\}.$$

The automaton $\mathcal{A}$ has two types of transitions. Transitions of the first type are of the form

$$(q_0, a, ((u_1, 1), (u_2, 1))),$$

where $a \in \Sigma$, $u_1 \neq u_2$, and $u_1[1] = u_2[1] = a$. Such transitions correspond to choosing the first factors in both factorizations; this is why we require $u_1 \neq u_2$. Transitions of the second type are of the form

$$(((u_1,j_1),(u_2,j_2)), a, ((u'_1,j'_1),(u'_2,j'_2))),$$

where for $i = 1, 2$ we have $u'[j'_i] = a$ and either $j'_i = j_i + 1 \leq |u_i|$ and $u'_i = u_i$ or $j_i = |u_i|$ and $j'_i = 1$. This corresponds to reading another letter of the current factor, or leaving the current factor and reading the first letter of the next factor.

The described construction can be realized effectively in polynomial time. Therefore, one can also check in polynomial time if the language recognized by $\mathcal{A}$ is empty, which is equivalent to verifying whether C is a code. ∎

Solution to Problem 76 We first present some auxiliary definitions and observations that will be useful for both items.

A *path* P in the automaton is a sequence of transitions

$$q_1 \xrightarrow{c_1} q_2, \: q_2 \xrightarrow{c_2} q_3, \: \ldots, \: q_n \xrightarrow{c_n} q_{n+1}.$$

We say that the *labelling* of P is $\text{lab}(P) = c_1 c_2 \ldots c_n$. A path is *simple* if the states $q_1, \ldots, q_{n+1}$ are pairwise different. A path is a *cycle* if $q_1 = q_{n+1}$ and it is a *simple cycle* if moreover the states $q_1, \ldots, q_n$ are different. A path is *accepting* if q_1 is the initial state and q_{n+1} is an accepting state. We say that two paths are *incident* if there is a state traversed by both of them. Of course, there are finitely many simple accepting paths in the automaton, as the length of every simple path is bounded by the number of states in the automaton. Similarly, there are only finitely many simple cycles in the automaton. In the sequel, we therefore assume that we may iterate through all simple accepting paths and simple cycles.

Every accepting path P can be partitioned into simple cycles and pieces, where each piece is a simple path and all pieces concatenated together in the order in which they appear on P form a simple accepting path. Indeed, imagine parsing an accepting path from the beginning to the end and cutting off a simple cycle whenever we meet a state that has been visited before. In this manner, at the end of the parsing we obtain a collection of simple cycles together with a simple accepting path. (Note that the obtained simple cycles do not need to appear contiguously on the path P.) The simple accepting path resulting from this process shall be called the *skeleton* of the original path P.

We consider the directed graph of transitions of the automaton; the key point of the reasoning will be the analysis of its strongly connected components. We say a path *crosses* a strongly connected component if it traverses any of its states. Note that each cycle resides entirely in one strongly connected component. We say that a path is *connected* to a cycle if it crosses the strongly connected component in which the cycle lies.

The (a, b)-*image* of path P is the pair $\big(\#_a(\text{lab}(P)), \#_b(\text{lab}(P))\big) \in \mathbb{N}^2$. A path P is called *fair* if a and b appear in $\text{lab}(P)$ the same number of times; that is, the (a, b)-image of $\text{lab}(P)$ is (m, m) for some $m \in \mathbb{N}$.

(1) If the condition is to be satisfied, then in particular every simple accepting path must be fair. Moreover, every cycle incident to a simple accepting path must be fair, since otherwise inserting this cycle into the accepting path would yield an accepting path with unequal numbers of occurrences of symbols.

   We claim that also every cycle connected (in the sense defined above) to an accepting path must be fair. Indeed, let q be any state on a cycle C, let p be any state on the simple accepting path P that belongs to the strongly connected component in which C lies, and let P_1 and P_2 be paths within this component leading from p to q and from q to p, respectively. The concatenation of P_1 and P_2 forms a cycle incident to P, thus $P_1 \cdot P_2$

must be fair. Similarly, the concatenation of P_1, C, and P_2 forms a cycle incident to P, hence also $P_1 \cdot C \cdot P_2$ must be fair. It follows that also C must be fair.

Thus, we have a necessary condition: all simple accepting paths as well as all simple cycles connected to any simple accepting path have to be fair. This condition can obviously be checked by an algorithm.

We claim that this condition is also sufficient. Indeed, take any accepting path P and decompose it into its skeleton and a collection of simple cycles. Observe that each of these cycles is connected to P. Therefore, provided that the condition from the previous paragraph holds, both the skeleton of P and all the simple cycles in the decomposition are fair. It follows that P itself is also fair.

(2) As each automaton has only finitely many runs on each input word, there are infinitely many accepted words w satisfying the assertion if and only if there are infinitely many accepting paths with this property. Thus, we can work with paths in $\mathcal{A}$, like in the previous item.

Here we need a more sophisticated notion than just a skeleton; we call it an *extended skeleton*. Given an accepting path P, we obtain an extended skeleton in a similar way as the skeleton, by cutting out simple cycles. This time, however, we can cut a cycle out only if *all* states on the cycle are visited elsewhere. By cutting out such cycles until there are none remaining, the path P is decomposed into an extended skeleton and a collection of simple cycles. Each of these cycles uses only states traversed by the extended skeleton, so in particular they are all incident to the extended skeleton. The construction ensures that the extended skeleton has the same set of visited states as the original path, but it may not be a simple path. Nevertheless, if the automaton has n states, then the extended skeleton visits each state q at most n times, because between every two consecutive visits in q we must see a state that is not visited elsewhere. This gives an n^2 upper bound on the length of the obtained extended skeleton. Therefore, there are only finitely many extended skeletons and we can iterate through them all in our algorithm.

Another consequence of this is that if there are infinitely many accepting paths P satisfying $\#_a(\text{lab}(P)) = \#_b(\text{lab}(P))$, then infinitely many among them have the same extended skeleton. Therefore, it suffices to check the condition for a fixed extended skeleton S.

Let $C_1, C_2, \ldots, C_k$ be the simple cycles incident to the fixed extended skeleton S. Let $(x^a, x^b) \in \mathbb{N}^2$ be the (a, b)-image of $\text{lab}(S)$, and let $(x_i^a, x_i^b) \in \mathbb{N}^2$ be the (a, b)-image of $\text{lab}(C_i)$ for $i = 1, 2, \ldots, k$. Then, the

(a, b)-images of the labels of accepting paths whose extended skeleton is S constitute the set

$$\left\{ (x^a, x^b) + \alpha_1(x_1^a, x_1^b) + \cdots + \alpha_k(x_k^a, x_k^b) \; : \; \alpha_1, \ldots, \alpha_k \in \mathbb{N} \right\},$$

where α_i indicates how many times C_i occurs in the decomposition of the accepting path. Note that each tuple $(\alpha_1, \alpha_2, \ldots, \alpha_k)$ can be realized by an accepting path, because all C_i are incident to S. Moreover, each $(\alpha_1, \alpha_2, \ldots, \alpha_k)$ can be realized by only finitely many different accepting paths. Consequently, it suffices to check whether infinitely many tuples $(\alpha_1, \alpha_2, \ldots, \alpha_k)$ yield a pair of the form (m, m) in the set above.

Let $y = x^a - x^b$, and let $y_k = x_k^a - x_k^b$ for $i = 1, 2, \ldots, k$. Then, our problem amounts to finding infinitely many solutions of the equation

$$y + \alpha_1 y_1 + \alpha_2 y_2 + \cdots + \alpha_k y_k = 0,$$

within non-negative integers $\alpha_1, \ldots, \alpha_k$.

If all y_i's are positive or all y_i's are negative, there are only finitely many solutions. Suppose then, without loss of generality, that $y_1 \leq 0$ and $y_2 \geq 0$. Observe now that if we have any solution $(\alpha_1, \alpha_2, \ldots, \alpha_k)$, then we have infinitely many solutions. Indeed, if $y_1 = 0$ then $(\ell, \alpha_2, \ldots, \alpha_k)$ is a solution for all $\ell \in \mathbb{N}$, if $y_2 = 0$ then $(\alpha_1, \ell, \ldots, \alpha_k)$ is a solution for all $\ell \in \mathbb{N}$, and otherwise $(\alpha_1 + \ell y_2, \alpha_2 - \ell y_1, \ldots, \alpha_k)$ is a solution for all $\ell \in \mathbb{N}$. Therefore, we are left with verifying whether the equation has any solutions at all.

We claim that if there is a solution, then there is also a solution where all the numbers α_i are bounded in terms of the absolute values of y_i's. Let $(\alpha_1, \ldots, \alpha_k)$ be a solution that minimizes $\sum_{j=1}^{k} \alpha_j$. Obviously, whenever $y_i = 0$, also $\alpha_i = 0$, because setting α_i to 0 preserves being a solution and can only decrease $\sum_{j=1}^{k} \alpha_j$. Next, let $M = \max_{j=1,\ldots,k} |y_j|$, and suppose there exist indices i and i' such that $\alpha_i, \alpha_{i'} > M$, $y_i < 0$, and $y_{i'} > 0$. Then, substituting α_i and $\alpha_{i'}$ respectively with $\alpha_i - y_{i'}$ and $\alpha_{i'} + y_i$ would yield a solution with strictly smaller $\sum_{j=1}^{k} \alpha_j$, which is a contradiction. Consequently, we have $\alpha_i \leq M$ either for all i such that $y_i < 0$, or for all i such that $y_i > 0$. Without loss of generality assume the former; the proof for the other case is symmetric. It follows that in the sum $y + \alpha_1 y_1 + \alpha_2 y_2 + \cdots + \alpha_k y_k$, the contribution from all summands with negative y_i's is not smaller than $-M \cdot \sum_{j=1}^{k} |y_j|$. Therefore, any α_i standing by a positive coefficient y_i cannot be larger than $|y| + M \cdot \sum_{j=1}^{k} |y_j|$, for otherwise the whole sum would be positive. We conclude that all the numbers α_i are bounded by $|y| + M \cdot \sum_{j=1}^{k} |y_j|$. Hence, the algorithm may search for any solution by scanning through all tuples $(\alpha_1, \ldots, \alpha_k)$ with $\alpha_i \leq |y| + M \cdot \sum_{j=1}^{k} |y_j|$.

We remark that the first part of the reasoning above can be simplified by using Parikh's theorem (see Problem 155). ∎

Solution to Problem 77 The algorithm constructs a two-dimensional table T indexed with pairs of states, with the following intended meaning: entry $T[p, q]$ contains a word w that synchronizes states p and q; that is, $p \xrightarrow{w} r$ and $q \xrightarrow{w} r$ for some state r. If no such word exists, $T[p, q]$ contains a marker $\bot$. The algorithm fills this table using dynamic programming. We first initialize entries of the form $T[p, p]$ to ε and the remaining entries to $\bot$. Then, we repeat the following until no new entries are filled: for every pair of states (p, q), for every letter a, if $T[p, q] = \bot$, $p \xrightarrow{a} p'$, $q \xrightarrow{a} q'$, and $T[p', q'] = w \neq \bot$, set $T[p, q] = aw$.

Note that if we set $T[p, q]$ to some word, then it is indeed a synchronizing word for p and q. We now verify that if there exists a word that synchronizes p and q, then the presented algorithm will find some synchronizing word and set it as the entry $T[p, q]$. For every pair of states (p, q) that has a synchronizing word, let $w_{p,q}$ be such a synchronizing word of minimum possible length. Assume that there is a pair of states that is *problematic* in the sense that (p, q) has a synchronizing word, but $T[p, q] = \bot$ at the end of the algorithm. Choose a problematic pair (p, q) such that $w_{p,q}$ is the shortest among problematic pairs. Clearly $w_{p,q} \neq \varepsilon$, so let $w_{p,q} = aw'_{p,q}$ for some symbol a. Let p' and q' be such that $p \xrightarrow{a} p'$ and $q \xrightarrow{a} q'$. Then $w'_{p,q}$ is a synchronizing word for p' and q', so by the minimality of $w_{p,q}$, the entry $T[p', q']$ is filled by the algorithm with some synchronizing word. But then in the next iteration of the loop the algorithm fills the entry $T[p, q]$, which is a contradiction.

Since each iteration of the loop fills an empty entry and there are $n^2 - n$ empty entries in the beginning, we infer that there are at most $n^2 - n$ iterations. Each iteration adds at most one to the maximum length of words contained in the table, so at the end all words in the table are of length at most $n^2 - n$.

A synchronizing word for the automaton exists if and only if $T[p, q] \neq \bot$ for all p and q. One implication is trivial: if some pair of states cannot be synchronized, there is no synchronizing word for all states. For the other direction, assume that $T[p, q] \neq \bot$ for all p and q. We construct a synchronizing word for the automaton as follows. We start from the word $w_0 = \varepsilon$ and inductively construct words $w_1, w_2, \ldots$ such that the cardinalities of the sets

$$Q_i = \left\{ p : q \xrightarrow{w_i} p \text{ for some } q \in Q \right\}$$

are strictly decreasing; the construction stops once $|Q_i| = 1$. To define w_i take any pair (p, q) of different states from Q_{i-1} and let

$$w_i = w_{i-1} \cdot T[p, q].$$

Note that $|Q_i| < |Q_{i-1}|$, because transition over w maps Q_{i-1} onto Q_i, and p and q have the same image. The procedure eventually constructs a word w_i for which $|Q_i| = 1$, which means that w_i is synchronizing. As the cardinalities of Q_i are strictly decreasing, there are at most $n - 1$ iterations of the procedure. In each iteration we append a word of length at most $n(n - 1)$, so we output a word of length at most $n(n - 1)^2 = \mathcal{O}(n^3)$.   ∎

Solution to Problem 78

(1) We claim that $w = b(a^{n-1}b)^{n-2}$ is a synchronizing word. To prove this, we show by induction that for all $i \in \{0, \ldots, n-2\}$, after reading the word $b(a^{n-1}b)^i$ the automaton is in one of the states $\{0, \ldots, n-2-i\}$, regardless of the starting state. Note that for $i = n - 2$ the assertion implies that w is a synchronizing word. For $i = 0$ indeed the automaton is in one of the states $\{0, \ldots, n - 2\}$. Assume that after reading the word $b(a^{n-1}b)^i$ for some $i < n - 2$ the automaton is in one of the states $\{0, \ldots, n - 2 - i\}$. Then after reading additionally a^{n-1}, the automaton is in one of the states $\{n - 1, 0, 1, \ldots, n - 2 - (i + 1)\}$. Finally, after reading b the automaton is in one of the states $\{0, 1, \ldots, n - 2 - (i + 1)\}$, which concludes the proof.

(2) Let w be any synchronizing word for the automaton. Denote $|w| = m$; we need to prove that $m \geq (n-1)^2$. Consider a sequence $Q_0, Q_1, \ldots, Q_m \subseteq Q$ such that $Q_0 = Q$, $Q_i = \{p : q \xrightarrow{w[i]} p$ for some $q \in Q_{i-1}\}$, and $|Q_m| = 1$. That is, Q_i contains states p such that for some $q \in Q$ we have $q \xrightarrow{w[1..i]} p$.

Let us analyse how the sets Q_i change in the sequence $Q_0, Q_1, \ldots, Q_m$. Place the states $0, 1, \ldots, n - 1$ on a circle, clockwise. If $w[i] = a$, then Q_i is simply Q_{i-1} shifted cyclically by one in the clockwise direction. If $w[i] = b$, then Q_i is equal to Q_{i-1}, except for the state $n - 1$ which, in case it belongs to Q_{i-1}, gets mapped to 0. That is,

$$Q_i = \begin{cases} Q_{i-1} & \text{if } (n - 1) \notin Q_{i-1}, \\ (Q_{i-1} - \{n - 1\}) \cup \{0\} & \text{if } (n - 1) \in Q_{i-1}. \end{cases}$$

Transformations of sets Q_i corresponding to transitions over a and b, as described above, will be called the *a-transformation* and the *b-transformation*, respectively.

For a set Q_i, a *gap* is a maximal subset of $Q - Q_i$ that is contiguous in the cyclic order of states on the circle. Observe that Q_0 has no gaps, and

Q_m has one gap of size $n-1$. The a-transformation only shifts all the gaps by one in the clockwise direction, thus preserving their sizes. Under the b-transformation, at most one gap gets extended by at most one state (or a new gap of size one can appear), while other gaps are either preserved, or possibly shrunk by one state. In particular, under a- and b-transformations there is a naturally defined correspondence between gaps before and after the transformation. We can identify gaps appearing in different sets Q_i via this correspondence, and treat them as one gap that gets modified by the consecutive transformations.

We now trace back the gap of size $n - 1$ that appears in Q_m. Let $i_1, i_2, \ldots, i_{n-1}$ be the indices such that i_j corresponds to the first moment when this gap had size j. Define the *clockwise end of the gap* at moment (index) i to be the first element of Q_i after the gap in the clockwise direction. Observe that since at each moment i_j the gap was extended by one element (or appeared for the first time when $j = 1$), at these moments its clockwise end was positioned at 0. On the other hand, for $j > 1$, the clockwise end of the gap had to be positioned at $n-1$ at moment $i_j - 1$, in order for the gap to be extended. However, in order to move the clockwise end point of the gap from 0 to $n - 1$ between moments i_{j-1} and $i_j - 1$, one needs to perform at least $n - 1$ a-transformations. We conclude that the whole sequence of transformations leading to creating a gap of size $n - 1$ had to consist of at least $n - 1$ b-transformations for extending the gap, and at least $(n - 2) \cdot (n - 1)$ a-transformations for shifting the clockwise end point of the gap to the position where the gap could be extended. In total these are $(n - 1)^2$ transformations, which implies the same lower bound on the length of w. ∎

Solution to Problem 79

(1) We first recall the standard construction of a non-deterministic automaton equivalent to a given regular expression β. We proceed by induction on the structure of β; that is, we show how to construct the corresponding automaton for larger and larger subexpressions α of β, finally obtaining an automaton for β itself. For atomic expressions a and $\emptyset$ one easily obtains corresponding automata of constant size. Now we perform a case distinction depending on the form of subexpression α; in each case we assume that we have already constructed automata for smaller subexpressions. For subexpression γ, let $\mathcal{A}_\gamma$ be the corresponding automaton.

When $\alpha = \alpha_1 + \alpha_2$, we take the disjoint union of $\mathcal{A}_{\alpha_1}$ and $\mathcal{A}_{\alpha_2}$ and we add a new initial state. The new initial state inherits transitions from both old initial states: if a state q is reachable via a letter a either from the initial state of $\mathcal{A}_{\alpha_1}$ or from the initial state of $\mathcal{A}_{\alpha_2}$, then we add a transition over a from the new initial state to q.

When $\alpha = \alpha_1\alpha_2$, we also take the disjoint union of $\mathcal{A}_{\alpha_1}$ and $\mathcal{A}_{\alpha_2}$, but now for every $a \in \Sigma$ we add new transitions from accepting states of $\mathcal{A}_{\alpha_1}$ to the states reachable by a transition over the letter a from the initial state of $\mathcal{A}_{\alpha_2}$. New accepting states are the accepting states of $\mathcal{A}_{\alpha_2}$, while the new initial state is the initial state of $\mathcal{A}_{\alpha_1}$.

Finally, when $\alpha = \alpha_1^*$ we proceed in a similar way. We take $\mathcal{A}_{\alpha_1}$ and add a new initial state q, which for all $a \in \Sigma$ has an outgoing transition labelled by a to every state reachable by a from the initial state of $\mathcal{A}_{\alpha_1}$. Similarly, for every $a \in \Sigma$ we add new transitions from accepting states of $\mathcal{A}_{\alpha_1}$ to the states reachable by a transition over the letter a from the initial state of $\mathcal{A}_{\alpha_1}$. The state q becomes the new initial state, whereas the new accepting states are q plus all the accepting states of $\mathcal{A}_{\alpha_1}$.

In this way we finally obtain $\mathcal{A}_\beta$, which recognizes the same language as β and has the number of states linear in the size of β. It is straightforward to implement each step of the construction in time $\mathcal{O}(|\Sigma| \cdot |\beta|)$. As there are at most $|\beta|$ steps, we conclude that $\mathcal{A}_\beta$ can be constructed in time $\mathcal{O}(|\Sigma| \cdot |\beta|^2)$, and hence its size is also $\mathcal{O}(|\Sigma| \cdot |\beta|^2)$. Now it suffices to apply the algorithm described in Problem 70 to $\mathcal{A}_\beta$ and w, which takes time $\mathcal{O}(|\mathcal{A}_\beta| \cdot |w|) = \mathcal{O}(|\Sigma| \cdot |\beta|^2 \cdot |w|)$.

(2) As in item (1), we first build an automaton recognizing $L(\beta)$ and then check whether it recognizes w. However, we optimize both procedures by performing them a bit differently than before.

We first construct an automaton $\mathcal{A}_\beta$ with ε-transitions that recognizes $L(\beta)$, such that the number of states in $\mathcal{A}_\beta$ is linear in $|\beta|$ and in every state of $\mathcal{A}_\beta$ there are at most two outgoing transitions. We construct it by induction on the structure of β, and to facilitate the induction we add one more invariant that will be maintained: there has to be exactly one initial state and one accepting state in the automaton, and the accepting state cannot have any outgoing transitions. For atomic expressions a and $\emptyset$ it is easy to obtain such automata of constant size. (In the automaton for $\emptyset$ the accepting state is not reachable from the initial state.) When $\alpha = \alpha_1 + \alpha_2$, we add a new initial state with two outgoing ε-transitions reaching initial states of $\mathcal{A}_{\alpha_1}$ and $\mathcal{A}_{\alpha_2}$. We also add a new state, which is the only accepting state, and two incoming ε-transitions from the accepting states of $\mathcal{A}_{\alpha_1}$ and $\mathcal{A}_{\alpha_2}$. When $\alpha = \alpha_1\alpha_2$, we add an ε-transition from the accepting state of $\mathcal{A}_{\alpha_1}$ to the initial state of $\mathcal{A}_{\alpha_2}$. The new initial state is the initial state of $\mathcal{A}_{\alpha_1}$ and the new accepting state is the accepting state of $\mathcal{A}_{\alpha_2}$. Finally, when $\alpha = \alpha_1^*$, we add an ε-transition from the accepting state of $\mathcal{A}_{\alpha_1}$ to the initial state of $\mathcal{A}_{\alpha_1}$. We add also a new initial state q_I and a new accepting state q_F. Then we add the following ε-transitions: from q_I to q_F, from q_I to the initial state of $\mathcal{A}_{\alpha_1}$, and from the accepting state of $\mathcal{A}_{\alpha_1}$ to q_F. By construction, in all the cases the constructed automata indeed satisfy the requirements and recognize languages which they are supposed to recognize. Moreover, during every step in the construction we add a constant number of states and transitions, so $\mathcal{A}_\beta$ can be constructed in time $\mathcal{O}(|\beta|)$ and has total size $\mathcal{O}(|\beta|)$.

Now it suffices to show that for automata with ε-transitions one can still design an algorithm working in time $\mathcal{O}(\|\mathcal{A}\| \cdot |w|)$ that determines whether $\mathcal{A}$ accepts w. Just like in the solution to Problem 70, for every $i \in \{0, \ldots, |w|\}$, we shall compute the set S_i of states reachable from the initial state by $w[1..i]$.

Let Q be the set of states of $\mathcal{A}$. Observe that for every set $S \subseteq Q$ it is possible to compute in time $\mathcal{O}(\|\mathcal{A}\|)$ the set of states reachable from S by any number of ε-transitions. Indeed, this can be done by taking the directed graph on Q induced by ε-transitions in $\mathcal{A}$, adding an additional source vertex s with an outgoing edge to every element of S, and finding states reachable from s using breadth-first search. As the graph has size $\mathcal{O}(\|\mathcal{A}\|)$, the algorithm runs in time $\mathcal{O}(\|\mathcal{A}\|)$.

Thus, we can compute in time $\mathcal{O}(\|\mathcal{A}\|)$ the set S_0 of states reachable from the initial state by the word $w[1..0] = \varepsilon$. To compute S_{i+1} from S_i in time $\mathcal{O}(\|\mathcal{A}\|)$, we first compute the set T_i of states reachable from S_i by a single transition over the letter $w[i + 1]$ (like before), and then use the algorithm above to compute all states reachable from T_i by ε-transitions, which is exactly S_{i+1}. ∎

Solution to Problem 80 Note first that a naive way of solving this problem, namely constructing an equivalent automaton for the expression β by induction on the structure of β, will not directly work. This is because handling each occurrence of $\cap$ or $-$ requires taking a product of two automata. As there may be linearly many occurrences of these operations in the expression, the size of the computed automaton can be exponential. In fact, Problem 65 shows that this exponential blow-up is unavoidable.

Instead, we apply the technique of dynamic programming. For all indices i, j with $0 \le i \le j \le |w|$, and every subexpression α of the input expression β, we will compute the boolean value $T[i, j, \alpha]$ defined as follows:

$$T[i, j, \alpha] = \big(w[(i + 1)..j] \in L(\alpha)\big).$$

That is, $T[i,j,\alpha]$ is the boolean value of the condition that the infix between positions $i+1$ and j belongs to the language recognized by α. Note that the answer to the whole task is the value $T[0,|w|,\beta]$. We now explain how the values $T[i,j,\alpha]$ are computed.

For atomic subexpressions, we put $T[i,j,\emptyset] = false$ for all i,j, and $T[i,i+1,a] = true$ if and only if $w[i+1] = a$. For non-atomic subexpressions we proceed from shorter subexpressions to longer, and from shorter infixes to longer. Thus, when we compute $T[i,j,\alpha]$, we can assume that we know all the values for subexpressions of α, as well as all the values $T[i',j',\alpha]$ for $j'-i' < j-i$. We make a case distinction depending on the form of α:

- if $\alpha = \alpha_1 + \alpha_2$, then $T[i,j,\alpha] = T[i,j,\alpha_1] \vee T[i,j,\alpha_2]$;
- if $\alpha = \alpha_1 \cap \alpha_2$, then $T[i,j,\alpha] = T[i,j,\alpha_1] \wedge T[i,j,\alpha_2]$;
- if $\alpha = \alpha_1 - \alpha_2$, then $T[i,j,\alpha] = T[i,j,\alpha_1] \wedge \neg T[i,j,\alpha_2]$;
- if $\alpha = \alpha_1\alpha_2$, then $T[i,j,\alpha] = \bigvee_{i \leq k \leq j} T[i,k,\alpha_1] \wedge T[k,j,\alpha_2]$;
- if $\alpha = \gamma^*$, then $T[i,j,\alpha] = (i=j) \vee \bigvee_{i \leq k < j} T[i,k,\alpha] \wedge T[k,j,\gamma]$.

One can easily see that in each case, the value of $T[i,j,\alpha]$ can be computed in time $\mathcal{O}(|w|)$. As there are $\mathcal{O}(|w|^2 \cdot |\beta|)$ values to compute, the whole algorithm works in time $\mathcal{O}(|w|^3 \cdot |\beta|)$. ∎

Solution to Problem 81 The set of states Q is the set of prefixes of words $w_1, w_2, \ldots, w_n$. The initial state is the empty word ε. A state is accepting if it has some w_i as a suffix. The transitions are defined in such a way that the current state is the longest word in Q that is a suffix of the currently read portion of the input word. ∎

Solution to Problem 82

(1) We show that for the special case of a single word the construction given in the solution for Problem 81 gives the minimal automaton. Recall that the set of states of the automaton is the set of all $n+1$ prefixes of the word w, the initial state is ε, the only accepting state is w, and the transitions are $u \overset{a}{\to} v$, where v is the longest prefix of w that is a suffix of ua.

It remains to see that there is no smaller automaton. To do this we prove that the Myhill–Nerode equivalence relation (see Section 2.4) for the language $\Sigma^* w$ has at least $n+1$ equivalence classes. We claim that all $n+1$ prefixes of w are pairwise inequivalent. Let u and v be two different prefixes of w, such that $|u| < |v|$. Since v is a prefix of w there is some v' such that $vv' = w$ and therefore $vv' \in \Sigma^* w$. Furthermore, because

v is longer than u, it follows that uv' is shorter than w and thus $uv' \notin \Sigma^*w$. Therefore v' witnesses the fact that u and v are not Myhill–Nerode equivalent.

(2) Recall that in $\mathcal{A}$ transitions are of the form $u \xrightarrow{a} v$ where v is the longest prefix of w that is a suffix of ua. Let us distinguish *forward transitions*, where $|u| < |v|$, and *backward transitions*, where $|u| \geq |v|$.

Note that for forward transitions it must hold that $v = ua$. Since both u and ua are prefixes of w, there are exactly n forward transitions in the automaton.

We shall call a backward transition *non-trivial* if $v \neq \varepsilon$. We need to show that there are at most n non-trivial backward transitions. We will show that for every number k there is at most one non-trivial backward transition such that $|ua| - |v| = k$.

Let $u \xrightarrow{a} v$ be a non-trivial backward transition and let $k = |ua| - |v|$. Then, for $x = u[1..k] = w[1..k]$ we have $xv = ua$.

By definition, both u and v are prefixes of w. Hence, v is a prefix of $xv = ua$. Therefore, $v[i] = v[i + k]$ for $i = 1, 2, \ldots, |v| - k$. It follows that $v = x^m y$, where $y = x[1..r]$, $|v| = m \cdot k + r$, and $r < k$.

As $ua = xv$, we conclude that $ua = x^{m+1}y$. It follows that every prefix of u, or equivalently, every prefix of w of length at most $|u|$, is of the form $x^{m'}y'$ for some m' and some prefix y' of x.

Recall that ua is not a prefix of w. Let b be a letter such that ub is a prefix of w. Then, ub is the shortest prefix of w not of the form $x^{m'}y'$. Equivalently, u is the longest prefix of w of this form. For a given w and k this uniquely determines u, and consequently also v and a. As $1 \leq k \leq n$, there are at most n non-trivial backward transitions.

(3) As shown in item (2), there are only $\mathcal{O}(n)$ non-trivial transitions, that is, transitions whose target state is not ε. It suffices to compute these non-trivial transitions in time $\mathcal{O}(n)$. This boils down to formalizing the preprocessing phase of the Knuth–Morris–Pratt pattern matching algorithm as a construction of a deterministic automaton.

We say that a word u is a *border* of a word v if u is both a proper prefix and a proper suffix of u. First, we compute the table T such that $T[0] = 0$ and for all $0 < i \leq n$ the value $T[i]$ is the length of the longest border of $w[1..i]$. Clearly $T[1] = 0$. For $i > 1$ we proceed as follows. Assume we have already computed $T[i]$. Observe first that word $w[1..(j + 1)]$ is the longest border of $w[1..(i + 1)]$ if and only if j is the highest index such that the following two conditions hold: $w[1..j]$ is the border of $w[1..i]$, and $w[j + 1] = w[i + 1]$. Therefore, looking for $T[i + 1]$ boils down to searching through the borders $w[1..j]$ of $w[1..i]$ from the longest to the shortest, and checking when the condition $w[j + 1] = w[i + 1]$ holds for the first time. Observe now that the structure of the borders of $w[1..i]$ is very easy to read from the table T. Of course the longest one is $w[1..T[i]]$. Note now that being a border of $w[1..T[i]]$ is equivalent to being a border of $w[1..i]$ shorter than $T[i]$. Thus the second longest border of $w[1..i]$ is $w[1..T[T[i]]]$, the third is $w[1..T[T[T[i]]]]$, etc. It is now clear how to compute $T[i + 1]$. We set $j = T[i]$ and check the condition $w[j + 1] = w[i + 1]$. In the positive case we set $T[i + 1] = j + 1$, and in the negative case we assign $j := T[j]$ in the loop until the condition is satisfied. If we obtain $j = 0$ and the condition is still not satisfied, we set $T[i + 1] = 0$.

We need to argue that the algorithm for computing T described above runs in time $\mathcal{O}(n)$. To this end, we will use the standard amortized analysis of time complexity. Consider the following potential function: after the ith iteration, the potential is equal to $T[i]$. Observe that the work performed when computing $T[i + 1]$ is proportional to the number of times we are in the negative case and we assign $j := T[j]$. This loop is performed until we find j for which we have $w[j + 1] = w[i + 1]$, which is when we break the loop and set $T[i + 1] = j + 1$. Observe that in each iteration of the loop, the value of j decreases by at least one. Therefore, the number of iterations is at most $T[i] - T[i + 1] + 1$. By summing up these inequalities from $i = 0$ to $n - 1$, we obtain that the total number of iterations of the loops for all i's is at most $n + T[0] - T[n]$. Since $T[n] \geq T[0]$, we infer that the total number of iterations of all the loops does not exceed n. Hence, the running time of the algorithm for computing T is $\mathcal{O}(n)$.

Having constructed the table T, we are ready to compute transitions of the automaton:

- let $\delta(\varepsilon, w[1]) = w[1]$ and $\delta(\varepsilon, a) = \varepsilon$ for $a \neq w[1]$;
- for $i = 1, 2, \ldots, n - 1$, let $\delta(w[1..i], w[i + 1]) = w[1..i + 1]$ and $\delta(w[1..i], a) = \delta(w[1..T[i]], a)$ for $a \neq w[i + 1]$.

One can easily show that these definitions are correct using the same arguments as for the construction of table T. Moreover, if we store only non-trivial transitions, then the transition function can be computed in time $\mathcal{O}(n)$ as follows. We compute the non-trivial transitions from $w[1..i]$ for $i = 0, 1, 2, 3, \ldots$, starting with $i = 0$, where there is only one non-trivial value to compute. When computing the values $\delta(w[1..i], \cdot)$, we first fill the value $\delta(w[1..i], w[i + 1])$ in constant time. Then, we iterate through the set of non-trivial transitions of the form $\delta(w[1..T[i]], a)$ for $a \in \Sigma - \{w[i + 1]\}$, which we have computed before. Each such transition gives rise to one non-trivial transition from $w[1..i]$. Hence, to compute the non-trivial transitions from $w[1..i]$ we spend time proportional to their number, plus a constant. As shown in item (2), there are only $O(n)$ non-trivial transitions in total, hence the whole running time is $O(n)$. ∎

Solution to Problem 83. RECOGNIZING SUBWORDS

(1) For a word $u \in \Sigma^*$, define

$$\underline{u} = \{i \in \{0, 1, \ldots, n\} : u \text{ is a suffix of } w[1..i]\},$$

where $w[1..0] = \varepsilon$. We describe an automaton for the language in the problem. The states are

$$Q = \{\underline{u} : u \in \Sigma^*\}.$$

The initial state is $\underline{\varepsilon} = \{0, 1, \ldots, n\}$. After reading a word u, the automaton stores the set $\underline{u}$. The transition function is not hard to define: if the current state is a set $X \subseteq \{0, \ldots, n\}$ and the input letter is a, then the new state is those positions i such that the ith letter is a and $i - 1$ is in X. The accepting states are the sets that contain n.

To see that this automaton is minimal (which will be needed in the following items), we prove that for each two different states there is a distinguishing word accepted from exactly one of them. Take $\underline{u} \neq \underline{v}$ and assume that $i \in \underline{u} - \underline{v}$. Then $w[(i + 1)..n]$ is accepted from $\underline{u}$, but not from $\underline{v}$.

We now show that Q has size at most $2n + 1$; in particular the minimal automaton will have at most $2n + 1$ states. To prove this we show that Q is what is called a *laminar family* of sets, which is a family of sets such that

$$X \cap Y = \emptyset \quad \text{or} \quad X \subseteq Y \quad \text{or} \quad Y \subseteq X \quad \text{for all } X, Y \in Q.$$

Indeed, suppose that $u, v \in \Sigma^*$ are such that the intersection $\underline{u} \cap \underline{v}$ is non-empty. It follows that either u is a suffix of v, or the other way round, and therefore either $\underline{v} \subseteq \underline{u}$ or $\underline{u} \subseteq \underline{v}$. This shows that Q is laminar.

We claim that every non-empty laminar family Δ of non-empty subsets of a set X has size at most $2|X| - 1$. In particular every laminar family of possibly empty subsets has size at most $2|X|$; this solves the problem because $Q - \{\underline{\varepsilon}\}$ is a laminar family of subsets of $\{1, 2, \ldots, n\}$.

We prove the claim by induction on $|X|$. If Δ contains only X then we are done. Otherwise, let $X_1, \ldots, X_k$ be the sets in $\Delta - \{X\}$ that are maximal with respect to inclusion; they are pairwise disjoint. Define $\Delta_i \subseteq \Delta$ to be the sets of Δ that are contained in X_i. Because Δ is laminar and does not contain the empty set, every element of Δ is either X itself or belongs to some Δ_i. Using this observation and the induction hypothesis we get

$$|\Delta| \leq 1 + \sum_{j=1}^{k} |\Delta_j| \leq 1 + \sum_{j=1}^{k} (2|X_j| - 1).$$

We show that the right-hand sum above is at most $2|X| - 1$. If $k \geq 2$ then this is because the sets $X_1, \ldots, X_k$ are disjoint; otherwise $k = 1$ and it follows from $|X_1| < |X|$.

(2) We know that $\mathcal{A}$ is the minimal deterministic automaton for a language consisting of exactly $n+1$ words. By item (1), it has at most $2n+1$ states. We show the claim by proving that for each finite language $L \subseteq \Sigma^*$, the minimal deterministic automaton $\mathcal{B}$ for L has at most $|L| + |Q| - 2$ transitions that do not lead to the sink state, Q being the set of states of the automaton $\mathcal{B}$.

We can associate with $\mathcal{B}$ a directed graph with edges labelled with elements of Σ: its vertices are the states of $\mathcal{B}$ and its edges are defined according to the transition relation of $\mathcal{B}$. Because $\mathcal{B}$ recognizes a finite language, it has the sink state. Moreover, the graph G obtained by removing the sink state from the graph above is a directed acyclic graph, whose unique source vertex is the initial state q_0 of $\mathcal{B}$.

Consider a spanning tree t of the graph G, whose root is q_0; it has exactly $|Q| - 2$ edges (we have removed the sink state). Let S be the set of edges in G that are not in t. It remains to see that $|S| \leq |L|$. We claim that $\mathcal{B}$ has at least $|S|$ different accepting runs. Indeed, for each transition $q \xrightarrow{a} p$ in S consider the run that traces the unique path from q_0 to q in the spanning tree, takes the transition $q \xrightarrow{a} p$, and then continues to some accepting state of $\mathcal{B}$; note that by minimality of $\mathcal{B}$ an accepting state is reachable from each state except the sink state. All the obtained runs differ by the first transition in S. Because $\mathcal{B}$ is deterministic, it has exactly $|L|$ accepting runs. Therefore, $|S| \leq |L|$.

(3) For the word *barbara* the construction gives the following automaton:

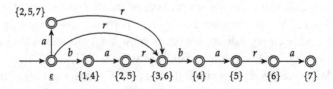

We omit the sink state $\emptyset$ in the picture. It is easy to see that the states $\{2, 5\}$ and $\{2, 5, 7\}$ are equivalent. A shorter example is *baa*. ∎

Solution to Problem 84 The minimal automata $\mathcal{A}_{inf}$ and $\mathcal{A}_{suf}$ recognizing, respectively, the infixes and the suffixes of the word *abbababa* are depicted below:

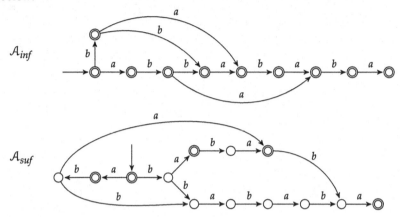

It is straightforward to check that they are minimal.

The construction for infixes easily generalizes to $w_n = ab(ba)^n$: one simply extends (or shortens) the main path of the automaton to spell out the whole word w_n; in the case of shortening, the transitions leading to the removed states are redirected to the sink state. Including the sink state, this gives $2n + 5$ states for the word w_n.

For suffixes we can see this in terms of the sets $\underline{u}$ defined in the solution of Problem 83. For $0 \le i \le n - 1$, $1 \le j \le n - 1$, and $2 \le k \le n - 1$, we have

$$
\begin{aligned}
\underline{abb(ab)^i a} &= \underline{bb(ab)^i a} &= \{2i + 4\}, \\
\underline{abb(ab)^i} &= \underline{bb(ab)^i} &= \{2i + 3\}, \\
\underline{b(ab)^j a} &= \underline{(ab)^j a} &= \{2j + 4, 2j + 6, \ldots, 2n + 2\}, \\
\underline{b(ab)^k} &= \underline{(ab)^k} &= \{2k + 3, 2k + 5, \ldots, 2n + 1\}, \\
\underline{b(ab)} & &= \{5, 7, \ldots, 2n + 1\}, \\
\underline{(ab)} & &= \{5, 7, \ldots, 2n + 1\} \cup \{2\}, \\
\underline{ba} & &= \{4, 6, \ldots, 2n + 2\}, \\
\underline{a} & &= \{4, 6, \ldots, 2n + 2\} \cup \{1\}, \\
\underline{b} & &= \{3, 5, \ldots, 2n + 1\} \cup \{2\}.
\end{aligned}
$$

For $n \ge 2$ all sets in the right column are different, except that for $i = j = k = n - 1$, the sets in lines 1 and 3 are both equal to $\{2n + 2\}$, and the sets in lines 2 and 4 are both equal to $\{2n + 1\}$. This gives $n + n + (n - 1) + (n - 2) + 5 - 2 = 4n$ states; including the initial state $\underline{\varepsilon}$, and the sink state, we get $4n + 2$ states. For $n = 1$ we get seven states, and for $n = 0$ only four states. ∎

7

Context-Free Languages

Solution to Problem 85 Suppose for the sake of notation that the palindromes are over the alphabet $\{a, b\}$. A context-free grammar generating the set of palindromes is

$$S \to aSa \mid bSb \mid a \mid b \mid \varepsilon.$$

It can be proven by induction on the size of derivations that all words generated from S are palindromes. Moreover, one can prove that S generates all palindromes by induction on the length of the word.

The following grammar generates the set of words that are not palindromes:

$$S \to aSa \mid bSb \mid X,$$
$$X \to aYb \mid bYa,$$
$$Y \to aY \mid bY \mid \varepsilon.$$

The non-terminal Y generates all the words. From X we can generate all the words that are not palindromes because the first and the last letters are different. We then claim that S generates all words that are not palindromes. Suppose that a word w of length n is not a palindrome. Hence, there is $1 \leq i \leq \lfloor n/2 \rfloor$ such that $w[i] \neq w[n - i + 1]$. Take the smallest such i. Then, using our standard notation for subwords, w has the form $vw[i..(n-i+1)]v^{\mathrm{R}}$, for $v = w[1..(i-1)]$. By our choice of i, $w[i..(n - i + 1)]$ is generated from X. By induction on the length of v it can be shown that S generates w. ∎

Solution to Problem 86 Let the grammars be

$$\mathcal{G} = (\Sigma_\mathcal{G}, \mathcal{N}_\mathcal{G}, S_\mathcal{G}, \mathcal{R}_\mathcal{G}) \quad \text{and} \quad \mathcal{H} = (\Sigma_\mathcal{H}, \mathcal{N}_\mathcal{H}, S_\mathcal{H}, \mathcal{R}_\mathcal{H}),$$

with $L(\mathcal{G}) = L$ and $L(\mathcal{H}) = K$. Without loss of generality we can assume that the sets of non-terminals $\mathcal{N}_\mathcal{G}$ and $\mathcal{N}_\mathcal{H}$ are disjoint. The grammar for $L \cup K$ is obtained by putting the two grammars together, and adding a fresh start symbol S with the rule $S \to S_\mathcal{G} \mid S_\mathcal{H}$; that is, the grammar is

$$\left(\Sigma_\mathcal{G} \cup \Sigma_\mathcal{H}, \mathcal{N}_\mathcal{G} \cup \mathcal{N}_\mathcal{H} \cup \{S\}, S, \mathcal{R}_\mathcal{G} \cup \mathcal{R}_\mathcal{H} \cup \{S \to S_\mathcal{G} \mid S_\mathcal{H}\} \right).$$

Similarly for LK, but this time the new rule is $S \to S_\mathcal{G} S_\mathcal{H}$. For L^*, we take $\mathcal{G}$ and add a new rule $S \to S_\mathcal{G} S \mid \varepsilon$. Finally, for L^R we reverse the right-hand side of every rule: a rule $X \to w$ becomes $X \to w^R$. The correctness of this construction can be proved by induction on the length of the derivation. ∎

Solution to Problem 87

(1) This language is the union of four languages:

$$\{a^i b^j c^k : i > j\} \cup \{a^i b^j c^k : i < j\} \cup \{a^i b^j c^k : j > k\} \cup \{a^i b^j c^k : j < k\}.$$

A context-free grammar for the union of finitely many context-free languages can be constructed easily from the context-free grammars for these languages (see Problem 86). We provide a context-free grammar for the first language, the remaining three being analogous. Consider the following grammar:

$$S \to Sc \mid X,$$
$$X \to aXb \mid Y,$$
$$Y \to aY \mid a.$$

The non-terminal Y generates all words of the form a^p with $p > 0$. Then, X generates all words of the form $a^q a^p b^q$ with $p > 0$; that is, all words of the form $a^i b^j$ with $i > j$. Finally, S generates all words of the form $a^i b^j c^k$ with $i > j$; that is, precisely the first language.

(2) The definition of the language can be rewritten as

$$\{a^i b^j a^k : i + k = j\} = \{a^i b^i \cdot b^k a^k : i, k \in \mathbb{N}\} = L^2,$$

where $L = \{a^i b^i : i \in \mathbb{N}\}$. A context-free grammar for the concatenation of two languages can be constructed from context-free grammars for the two languages (see Problem 86). In our case it suffices to give a context-free grammar for L:

$$S \to \varepsilon \mid aSb.$$

(3) This language can be rewritten as the union of two languages:

$$\{a^p a^q b^r c^r c^q d^p : p, q, r \geq 0\} \cup \{a^p b^q b^r c^r d^q d^p : p, q, r \geq 0\}.$$

Consider the grammar

$$S \to aSd \mid X_1 \mid X_2,$$
$$X_1 \to aX_1c \mid Y,$$
$$X_2 \to bX_2d \mid Y,$$
$$Y \to bYc \mid \varepsilon.$$

The non-terminal Y generates all words of the form $b^r c^r$. The non-terminals X_1 and X_2 generate all words of the form $a^q b^r c^r c^q$ and $b^q b^r c^r d^q$, respectively. The starting symbol S generates the whole language.

(4) This language is generated by the grammar

$$S \to aSb \mid aSbb \mid aabbb.$$

This follows from the fact that $0 \le i < j < 2i$ if and only if there exist numbers p and q such that $0 \le p \le q \le 2p$ and $i = p + 2, j = q + 3$.

(5) We can rewrite this language as

$$L = \{a^{2p} \cdot aa \cdot b^q \cdot b \cdot b^p : q{>}0 \wedge p{\ge}0\} \cup \{a^{2p} \cdot a \cdot b^q \cdot b \cdot b^p : q{>}0 \wedge p{\ge}0\}.$$

Consider the grammar

$$S \to aaSb \mid aaXb \mid aXb,$$
$$X \to bX \mid b.$$

The non-terminal X generates a non-empty block of b's. Derivations starting in S and using the transition $S \to aaXb$ generate exactly the first language above, and those using $S \to aXb$ generate exactly the second one. ∎

Solution to Problem 88

(1) Consider the grammar

$$S \to aSb \mid bSa \mid SS \mid \varepsilon.$$

We claim that the set of words generated by S is the set of words containing the same number of a's and b's.

By induction on the length of the derivation one can immediately verify that every generated word has the same number of a's and b's.

For the other inclusion we take a word $w \in \{a, b\}^*$ with the same number of a's and b's and we construct a derivation of this word. We proceed by induction on the length of w.

If w is the empty word then we use the rule $S \to \varepsilon$.

Suppose that w can be factorized as uv with both u and v non-empty and u having the same number of a's and b's. Then also v has the same number of a's and b's. Since both u and v are shorter than w, by the induction hypothesis we have derivations of u and v from S. We obtain a derivation of w by applying the rule $S \to SS$, and then using the derivations of u and v.

The last case is when w is not empty and cannot be factorized as in the previous paragraph. Suppose that w starts with a; the case when w starts with b is analogous. By the assumption, for every proper prefix v of w, the number of a's in v is greater than the number of b's in v. Since the numbers of a's and b's in w are the same, w must end with b. Thus w is of the form aub with u having the same number of a's and b's. By the induction hypothesis there is a derivation of u from S. We obtain a derivation of w using the rule $S \to aSb$.

(2) Consider the grammar

$$S \to SS \mid aSbSa \mid aaSb \mid bSaa \mid \varepsilon.$$

It is clear that S generates only words with twice as many a's as b's. We need to show that every such word can be generated. The proof is by induction on the length of w. If w has length zero then w is the empty word so it is generated by S. Below we only consider non-empty words w in the language.

Recall that $w[i..j]$ is the subword of w starting at position i and ending at position j; in particular, $w[1..0]$ is the empty word. We write $\#_a(w[i..j])$ for the number of occurrences of a in $w[i..j]$.

For a word w, let $rank(w, i)$ be the function measuring how far $w[1..i]$ is from being a word in the language, namely:

$$rank(w, i) = \#_a(w[1..i]) - 2 \cdot \#_b(w[1..i]).$$

So $rank(w, i+1) = rank(w, i) + 1$ if $w[i+1..i+1]$ is a and $rank(w, i+1) = rank(w, i) - 2$ if it is b. We also have $rank(w, 0) = rank(w, n) = 0$ since $w[1..0]$ is the empty word, and $w[1..n] = w$ has twice as many a's as b's.

We perform a case analysis based on the values taken by the function $rank$. The easiest case is when there exists $i \in \{1, \ldots, n-1\}$ such that $rank(w, i) = 0$. Then $w[1..i]$ as well as $w[i+1..n]$ have twice as many a's as b's. Because the two words are shorter than w, by the induction hypothesis we can derive both of them from S. Consequently, we can derive w from S using the rule $S \to SS$.

Now suppose the first case does not hold, $rank(w, 1) = 1$, and there exists $i \in \{1, \ldots, n - 1\}$ for which $rank(w, i)$ is negative. Let us suppose also that i is the smallest such index. We thus have $rank(w, 1) = 1$, $rank(w, i) = -1$, and in consequence $rank(w, i - 1) = 1$, so the word $w[2..i - 1]$ has twice as many a's as b's. By assumption the rank is never zero for $j \in \{1, \ldots, n - 1\}$, so $rank(w, j) < 0$ for all $j \in \{i + 1, \ldots, n - 1\}$. It means that $rank(w, n - 1) = -1$, because $rank(w, n) = 0$. From this we deduce that $w[i + 1..n - 1]$ has twice as many a's as b's. Summing up, the word w is of the form $a \cdot w[2..i - 1] \cdot b \cdot w[i + 1..n - 1] \cdot a$. By the induction hypothesis we can derive $w[2..i - 1]$ and $w[i + 1..n - 1]$ from S. Consequently, we can derive w from S using the rule $S \to aSbSa$.

The remaining two cases are when $rank(w, i)$ is strictly positive for all $i \in \{1, \ldots, n - 1\}$, or strictly negative. They are covered by similar reasonings.

(3) Consider the grammar

$$S \to \varepsilon \mid SS \mid aa \mid bb \mid abSba \mid baSab.$$

We show that the start symbol S generates the language L of words of even length with the same number of b's in odd and even positions.

By induction on the length of the derivation it can be easily shown that every word derived from S is in L. In the remainder we prove that every word $w \in L$ can be derived from S. The proof is by induction on the length of w. If w has length zero or two, then it clearly is derivable from S.

Next, suppose that w has a proper prefix u in L. In this case $w = uv$ for some word $v \in L$. By the induction hypothesis, u and v can be derived from S. Consequently, w can be derived as well using the rule $S \to SS$.

The remaining case is when $w \in L$ has length at least four and does not have a proper prefix in L. We see that either in every proper even-length prefix of w the number of b's in even positions is greater than the number of b's in odd positions, or in every such prefix the number of b's in even positions is smaller than the number of b's in odd positions. This is because the difference between the number of b's in even and odd positions may change by at most one, when we move from one prefix of w of even length to the next such prefix. In the first possibility above, $w = abvba$ for some $v \in L$; and in the second possibility, $w = bavab$ for some $v \in L$. By the induction hypothesis v can be derived from S. Hence, w can be derived using $S \to abSba$ or $S \to baSab$. ∎

Solution to Problem 89

(1) The language is generated by the grammar

$$X \to p \mid true \mid false \mid (X) \mid (X \wedge X) \mid (X \vee X) \mid (\neg X).$$

(2) Consider the grammar

$$X_1 \to true \mid (\neg X_0) \mid (X_1 \vee X) \mid (X_1 \wedge X_1) \mid (X_p \vee X_{\neg p}),$$
$$X_0 \to false \mid (\neg X_1) \mid (X_0 \wedge X) \mid (X_0 \vee X_0) \mid (X_p \wedge X_{\neg p}),$$
$$X_p \to p \mid (X_p \vee X_p) \mid (X_p \vee X_0) \mid (X_p \wedge X_1) \mid (X_p \wedge X_p) \mid (\neg X_{\neg p}),$$
$$X_{\neg p} \to \neg p \mid (X_{\neg p} \vee X_{\neg p}) \mid (X_{\neg p} \vee X_0) \mid (X_{\neg p} \wedge X_1) \mid (X_{\neg p} \wedge X_{\neg p}) \mid (\neg X_p).$$

The non-terminal X_1 generates all formulas that evaluate to *true* independently of the value of p. Similarly, X_0 generates all formulas that evaluate to *false*. The non-terminal X_p generates all formulas that are logically equivalent to p; analogously, $X_{\neg p}$ generates all formulas equivalent to $\neg p$. ∎

Solution to Problem 90

(1) Consider the grammar

$$S \to X_2,$$
$$X \to 0 \mid 1 \mid (X) \mid (X + X) \mid (X \cdot X),$$
$$X_0 \to 0 \mid (X_0) \mid (X_0 + X_0) \mid (X_0 \cdot X) \mid (X \cdot X_0),$$
$$X_1 \to 1 \mid (X_1) \mid (X_0 + X_1) \mid (X_1 + X_0) \mid (X_1 \cdot X_1),$$
$$X_2 \to (X_2) \mid (X_0 + X_2) \mid (X_2 + X_0) \mid (X_1 + X_1) \mid (X_1 \cdot X_2) \mid (X_2 \cdot X_1).$$

The non-terminal X generates all fully parenthesized expressions, and X_0, X_1, and X_2 generate those that evaluate, respectively, to 0, 1, and 2.

(2) Consider the grammar

$$S \to X_4,$$
$$X \to 0 \mid 1 \mid XX + \mid XX \cdot,$$
$$X_0 \to 0 \mid X_0 X_0 + \mid XX_0 \cdot \mid X_0 X \cdot,$$
$$X_1 \to 1 \mid X_0 X_1 + \mid X_1 X_0 + \mid X_1 X_1 \cdot,$$
$$X_n \to X_i X_j + \mid X_k X_l \cdot,$$

for $i + j = n$, $k \cdot l = n$, and $n = 2, 3, 4$. The non-terminal X generates all expressions, and the non-terminal X_n generates expressions that evaluate to n. ∎

Solution to Problem 91

(1) Let L be the language of balanced sequences of parentheses. Consider the grammar

$$E \to EE \mid OO \mid (O) \mid \varepsilon,$$
$$O \to EO \mid OE \mid (E).$$

We claim that E generates precisely words from L with an even number of opening parentheses, while O generates precisely words from L with an odd number of opening parentheses. To show that all such words are generated one can use induction on the length of the word. To show that only these words are generated one can employ induction on the length of the derivation.

(2) Consider the grammar

$$S \to \varepsilon \mid () \mid Y,$$
$$Y \to (Y) \mid ()() \mid ()Y \mid Y() \mid YY.$$

We say that a word is *clean* if it does not contain a subword $(())$. Our goal is to show that S generates precisely clean words from L. It is clear that the grammar generates only words from L. Moreover Y cannot generate $()$, so every word generated by the grammar is clean. Next, we prove that every clean word from L can be generated from S, and if it has length at least four, then also from Y. We proceed by induction on the length of the word. Short clean words from L are ε and $()$. Other clean words from L have one of two forms: (w) or $u_1 u_2$, where w, u_1, and u_2 are non-empty words from L. Observe that w should be a clean word other than $()$. So the case of a word of the form (w) is handled by the rule $Y \to (Y)$ and the induction hypothesis. For the case $u_1 u_2$, each of the two words must be clean, be it short or not. These cases are handled by the other rules for Y. ∎

Solution to Problem 92 Let $L \subseteq \{(,)\}^*$ be the language of balanced sequences of parentheses. One possible grammar generating this language is

$$S \to (S) \mid SS \mid \varepsilon.$$

This grammar is ambiguous because $()()()$ has two derivations; after using $S \to SS$ we have two choices: from the first S we can derive either $()$ or $()()$.

An unambiguous grammar exploits the property that every opening parenthesis has exactly one matching closing parenthesis. We claim that the following is an unambiguous grammar for the language L:

$$X \to (X)X \mid \varepsilon.$$

It is easy to show that all derived words are in L by induction on the length of the derivation.

We show that every word w from L has a unique derivation tree from X. Recall that by the characterization of L from Problem 2 a word is in L if: (i) it has the same number of ('s and)'s, and (ii) every prefix of the word has at least as many ('s as)'s.

If w is the empty word then the claim is clear. Otherwise w starts with an opening parenthesis, $w = (u$. So u is not well parenthesized as it has one spare closing parenthesis. Let $v)$ be the shortest prefix of u that has more closing parentheses than opening parentheses. By the characterization we have recalled above, v is well parenthesized. So $w = (v)u$ and v can be derived from X, as well as u. We need to show that this is the unique choice. Using once again the characterization, $v)$ cannot be derived from X, nor any longer word v' such that (v') is a prefix of w. Indeed, (v') can be represented as $(v)v'')$, and since the number of opening and closing parentheses in (v) is the same, the number of opening parentheses in $v)$ is smaller than the number of closing parentheses. Thus there is a unique way to derive w from X, since the first X in the rule should be matched with v that is uniquely determined.   ∎

Solution to Problem 93 Consider the grammar

$$Z \rightarrow aZ_+bZ \mid bZ_-aZ \mid \varepsilon,$$
$$Z_+ \rightarrow aZ_+bZ_+ \mid \varepsilon,$$
$$Z_- \rightarrow bZ_-aZ_- \mid \varepsilon.$$

Notice the similarity between the rules for Z_+ and Problem 92.

It is clear that the grammar generates only words with the same number of occurrences of a and b.

For the other direction we first consider non-terminal Z_+. An easy induction on the length of the derivation shows that words derived from Z_+ have the same number of occurrences of a and b; moreover in every prefix the number of occurrences of a is not smaller than the number of occurrences of b. An argument very similar to that from Problem 92 shows that all such words are derivable from Z_+ in a unique way. By the same argument Z_- generates precisely the words w with $\#_a(w) = \#_b(w)$ and $\#_a(w') \leq \#_b(w')$ for every prefix w' of w.

Now consider a word w with the same number of occurrences of a and b. Suppose that it begins with a. Let v be the shortest word such that avb is a prefix of w and $\#_a(avb) = \#_b(avb)$. Then $\#_a(v) = \#_b(v)$, and for every prefix v' of v, $\#_a(v') \geq \#_b(v')$. So v is derivable from Z_+. By definition of v there is no shorter word with these properties. Suppose then that there is a longer word u

with these properties. Then, $aub = avbv''b$ for some v'', but because $\#_a(v) = \#_b(v)$, we have that $\#_a(vb) < \#_b(vb)$, making vbv'' not derivable from Z_+. Thus, if w begins with a, then there is a unique way one can apply the rule $Z \to aZ_+bZ$ to derive w. The symmetric property holds when w begins with b. ∎

Solution to Problem 94 Suppose L is regular. Let $\mathcal{A}$ be a finite automaton recognizing L. We construct a grammar simulating the automaton $\mathcal{A}$. The grammar has a non-terminal X_p for every state p of $\mathcal{A}$ and rules:

$$X_p \to aX_q \quad \text{for all transitions } p \xrightarrow{a} q \text{ in } \mathcal{A},$$

$$X_p \to \varepsilon \quad \text{for all accepting states } p \text{ of } \mathcal{A}.$$

The start symbol of the grammar is X_{q_0} where q_0 is the initial state of $\mathcal{A}$. To show that X_{q_0} generates L it suffices to observe that there is a one-to-one correspondence between accepting runs

$$q_0 \xrightarrow{a_1} q_1 \xrightarrow{a_2} \cdots \xrightarrow{a_n} q_n$$

and derivations

$$X_{q_0} \to a_1 X_{q_1} \to \cdots \to a_1 \dots a_n X_{q_n} \to a_1 \dots a_n.$$

This shows the implication from (a) to (b).

For the implication from (b) to (a), we construct an automaton with a state q_X for each non-terminal X of the grammar, and transitions $q_X \xrightarrow{a} q_Y$ for every rule $X \to aY$ and $q_X \xrightarrow{\varepsilon} q_Y$ for every rule $X \to Y$. (In Problem 54 we show how to eliminate ε-transitions.) We make q_X accepting if there is a rule $X \to \varepsilon$. The initial state is q_S, where S is the start symbol of the grammar. That this automaton recognizes the language of words generated from S follows immediately by the one-to-one correspondence between derivations

$$S \to a_1 X_1 \to a_1 a_2 X_2 \to \cdots \to a_1 \dots a_n X_n \to a_1 \dots a_n$$

and accepting runs

$$q_S \xrightarrow{a_1} q_{X_1} \xrightarrow{a_2} q_{X_2} \to \cdots \xrightarrow{a_n} q_{X_n}.$$

For the equivalence between (b) and (c) observe that every grammar as in (b) is right-linear. Hence, it suffices to prove that every right-linear grammar is equivalent to one in the restricted form described in (b). For every rule $X \to u$ we take new a non-terminal T_w for each suffix w of u and we replace $X \to u$ with rules

$$X \to T_u,$$

$$T_{aw} \to aT_w,$$

$$T_\varepsilon \to \varepsilon,$$

for each suffix aw of u. Similarly, for every rule $X \to vY$ we take a new non-terminal T_{wY} for each suffix w of v, and we replace $X \to vY$ with rules

$$X \to T_{vY},$$
$$T_{awY} \to aT_{wY},$$
$$T_Y \to Y,$$

for each suffix aw of v. The obtained grammar is in the restricted form described in (b) and it generates the same language as the initial grammar.

For the equivalence between (a) and (d) we use the solution of Problem 86 which shows that the grammar obtained by reversing the right-hand side of every rule generates the reverse of the language generated by the original grammar. Reversing the right-hand sides of all rules in a left-linear grammar gives a right-linear grammar, and vice versa. In the light of the equivalence between (a) and (c), this means that left-linear grammars generate precisely reverses of all regular languages. Since regular languages are closed under reverse, we conclude that left-linear grammars actually generate precisely all regular languages.   ∎

Solution to Problem 95 Consider the grammar

$$A \to aB \mid \varepsilon,$$
$$B \to Ab.$$

The words generated from A are $a^n b^n$ for $n \in \mathbb{N}$.

Grammars of the considered form generate only *linear* context-free languages (in fact, all of them). A typical context-free language that is not linear is

$$L = \left\{ a^i b^i c^j d^j \ : \ i, j \in \mathbb{N} \right\}.$$

One can prove that this language is not linear using the pumping lemma for linear context-free languages (see Problem 120). Here we give a direct proof. Suppose that there is a grammar of the required form that generates this language; that is, all rules are of the form $X \to \varepsilon, X \to Y, X \to wY$, or $X \to Yw$ with $w \in \Sigma^*$. Arguing like in the implication from (a) to (b) in Problem 94, one can show that without loss of generality w in these rules can be assumed to be a single letter. Let n be the number of non-terminals in the grammar; consider a derivation of the word $a^i b^i c^j d^j$ with $i, j > n$. Because i and j are greater than the number of non-terminals, some non-terminal X repeats before any b or c is generated; that is, the derivation has the form

$$S \to^* a^k X d^l \to^* a^k a^{k'} X d^{l'} d^l \to^* a^i b^i c^j d^j$$

for some X and k, l, k', l' with either $k' > 0$ or $l' > 0$. But this implies that $X \to^* a^{i-(k+k')} b^i c^j d^{j-(l+l')}$ and consequently $S \to^* a^k X d^l \to^* a^{i-k'} b^i c^j d^{j-l'}$. This is a contradiction because the latter word does not belong to L. ∎

Solution to Problem 96

Let $\mathcal{G}$ be a grammar without self-loops. Consider the following *dependency graph* associated with $\mathcal{G}$: its nodes are the non-terminals of $\mathcal{G}$ and there is a directed edge from X to Y if there is a rule $X \to \alpha$ with Y appearing in α.

Recall that a *strongly connected component* of a directed graph is a set of nodes such that every node in the set is reachable via a directed path from every other node in the set, and it is a maximal set with this property. A strongly connected component is *bottom* if no other component can be reached from it (via directed paths). The *height* of a strongly connected component is the largest number of distinct strongly connected components that one can traverse (via directed paths) before a bottom component is reached. Thus, each bottom component has height 0, and from each component one can go only to components of smaller height.

We are now ready to show that each non-terminal of $\mathcal{G}$ generates a regular language. We proceed by induction on the height of the strongly connected component of the dependency graph of $\mathcal{G}$ that contains the non-terminal.

Consider a strongly connected component, and suppose that it contains two non-terminals X and Y with rules $X \to \alpha_X A \beta_X$ and $Y \to \alpha_Y B \beta_Y$, where α_X and β_Y are both non-empty, and A and B are two non-terminals in the considered component (possibly X or Y). The latter assumption implies that there are derivations $A \to^* \alpha_A Y \beta_A$ and $B \to^* \alpha_B X \beta_B$; this time all four $\alpha_A, \beta_A, \alpha_B$, and β_B may be empty. Putting them together we get a derivation

$$X \to^* \alpha_X \alpha_A Y \beta_A \beta_X \to^* \alpha_X \alpha_A \alpha_Y \alpha_B X \beta_B \beta_Y \beta_A \beta_X.$$

Since α_X and β_Y are not empty, we obtain a self-loop. Since we have assumed that there are no self-loops, there are two symmetric possibilities. The first possibility is that all rules for non-terminals in the strongly connected component are of the form $X \to \alpha A$ or $X \to \alpha$, where α is a sequence of terminals and non-terminals from strongly connected components of strictly smaller height and A is a non-terminal symbol from this component. The second possibility is that all these rules are of the form $X \to A\alpha$ or $X \to \alpha$ with α and A as above. In either case, Problem 94 tells us that every non-terminal X in the strongly connected component generates a regular language R_X over the alphabet of terminals and non-terminals from components of strictly smaller height. The language (over the alphabet of terminals) generated by X can be obtained from R_X by substituting each non-terminal Y occurring in R_X with the language R_Y. Because Y belongs to a component of strictly smaller height, R_Y is a regular language by the induction hypothesis. We conclude by the closure of regular languages by substitution.   ∎

Solution to Problem 97

Let us first see that the stated bound is tight. Consider a grammar with non-terminals $X_1, \ldots, X_m$ and rules

$$X_i \rightarrow \underbrace{X_{i+1} \ldots X_{i+1}}_{l} \qquad \text{for } i \in \{1, \ldots, m-1\},$$

$$X_m \rightarrow \varepsilon.$$

The unique derivation tree from the non-terminal X_1 is a tree of height m with every internal node having l children. Written in linear form, it gives a derivation of length $1 + l + l^2 + \cdots + l^{m-1}$.

Now we show that this is indeed an upper bound on the shortest derivation of ε. For every symbol X, let d_X be the length of the smallest derivation of ε from X. (We put $d_X = \infty$ if there is no such derivation.) For example, if there is a rule $X \rightarrow \varepsilon$, then $d_X = 1$. Now, let us take a symbol Y and a shortest derivation of ε from Y. This derivation should start with a rule $Y \rightarrow \alpha$ where all non-terminals in α have strictly shorter derivations of ε. So $d_Y \leq 1 + l \cdot d$ where $d = \max \{d_X : X \text{ occurs in } \alpha\}$. Since there are m non-terminals, we get the desired estimation $d_S \leq 1 + l + l^2 + \cdots + l^{m-1}$, where S is the start symbol of the grammar.   ∎

Solution to Problem 98

For every non-terminal X from which it is possible to derive ε, let us fix one such derivation tree t_X. Let D be the maximal size of t_X among all non-terminals X. Let t be a derivation tree of w. Let us replace each maximal subtree of t that yields ε with t_X, where X is the non-terminal in the root of this maximal subtree. Let t' be the resulting derivation tree.

Mark a node of t' green if its subtree yields a non-empty word and grey if its subtree yields ε. Then, every green internal node has at least one green child. Suppose that in t' there is a green node n_1 with only one green child n_2, and n_2 has only one green child n_3, and so on up to n_{m+1}, where m is the number of non-terminals in $\mathcal{G}$. Then, two of these nodes, say n_i and n_j with $i < j$, are labelled by the same non-terminal. We can make the derivation tree smaller by unpumping the segment between n_i and n_j; that is, by plugging the subtree rooted at n_j instead of the subtree rooted at n_i. Let t'' be the tree obtained by sequentially applying such unpumpings as long as possible.

We claim that in t'' there are at most $(2|w| - 1)m$ green nodes. Indeed, there are $|w|$ green leaves and at most $|w| - 1$ nodes with at least two green children. Every node of either of these two types can be preceded by at most $m - 1$ nodes with one green child. Let l be the maximal length of the right-hand side of a rule in $\mathcal{G}$. Then, every internal green node in t'' has at most $l - 1$ grey children. The subtrees rooted at these children yield ε and, by the definition of t', their size is at most D. Hence, the size of t'' is at most $(2|w| - 1)m(1 + D(l - 1))$; this proves the claim for $C = 2m(1 + D(l - 1))$. ∎

Solution to Problem 99

Let $\mathcal{G}$ be the input grammar. For every non-terminal X of $\mathcal{G}$ one can determine whether X generates the empty word, and whether X generates a non-empty word. Based on this we normalize $\mathcal{G}$ as follows. First, we eliminate all non-terminals that generate no words and remove all rules involving such non-terminals. Next, we eliminate all non-terminals that generate only ε and we remove them from the right-hand side of every rule. If the start symbol gets removed, we can immediately answer that $L(\mathcal{G})$ is finite. Otherwise, we call the resulting grammar $\mathcal{G}'$. Clearly $L(\mathcal{G}) = L(\mathcal{G}')$.

Let S be the start symbol of $\mathcal{G}'$. Suppose that $\mathcal{G}'$ has m non-terminal symbols and the right-hand sides of its rules have length at most l. We show that $\mathcal{G}'$ generates infinitely many words if and only if there is a non-terminal X and two derivations $S \to^* \alpha' X \beta'$ and $X \to^* \alpha X \beta$ of length at most m with $\alpha\beta \neq \varepsilon$ where α, β, α', and β' are sequences of terminal and non-terminal symbols. Notice that the latter condition is easy to check.

To see that the condition is sufficient, note that using such two derivations we can get $S \to^* \alpha' \alpha^n X \beta^n \beta'$. Thus we can derive infinitely many words, because $\alpha\beta \neq \varepsilon$ and every non-terminal in $\mathcal{G}'$ generates a non-empty word.

It remains to prove that the condition is necessary. Suppose that $L(\mathcal{G}')$ is infinite. Take a word in $L(\mathcal{G}')$ of length strictly greater than l^m and let t be the smallest derivation tree of this word. A derivation tree of height at most m can only yield words of length at most l^m; thus t is of height strictly greater than m. This implies that on some branch of t some non-terminal X appears twice among nodes at the topmost $m + 1$ levels. This gives derivations $S \to^* \alpha' X \beta'$ and $X \to^* \alpha X \beta$ of length at most m. Moreover $\alpha\beta \neq \varepsilon$, as otherwise we would get a smaller derivation tree for the same word by unpumping the part of t between the two occurrences of X. ∎

Solution to Problem 100

Take a context-free grammar $\mathcal{G}$ generating an infinite language. Let Y be a non-terminal of $\mathcal{G}$ generating finitely many words. Because the start symbol generates infinitely many words, Y is not the start symbol. Remove Y from the grammar and replace every rule $X \to \alpha$ by rules $X \to \alpha_1 \mid \ldots \mid \alpha_n$ where $\alpha_1, \ldots, \alpha_n$ are the results of replacing occurrences of Y in α by words generated by Y, in every possible way. For example, if $\alpha = YZY$ and Y generates $\{a, b\}$, then we get $\alpha_1 = aZa$, $\alpha_2 = aZb$, $\alpha_3 = bZa$, and $\alpha_4 = bZb$. With this operation we have eliminated Y and the resulting grammar generates the same set of words as the original one. Proceeding in the same way we can eliminate every non-terminal generating only a finite set of words, without changing the generated language. Notice that by Problem 99 this construction is effective.   ∎

Solution to Problem 101

Let $L = \{a^i b^j a^i b^j : i, j \geq 1\}$. By way of contradiction, suppose that L is context-free, and let N be the constant from the pumping lemma. Let $w = a^N b^N a^N b^N$. Since $w \in L$, w has a factorization as in the lemma. Suppose that the letter a appears in *left* or *right*; in the symmetric case when the letter b appears in *left* or *right* we proceed similarly. Since $|left \cdot infix \cdot right| \leq N$, it is impossible for *left* and *right* to span both blocks of a's. Hence in w_2 one block of a's has more letters than in the respective block in w, and the other has not. Thus, $w_2 \notin L$, and we get a contradiction.

Let us now see that the complement of L is context-free. Let $\Sigma = \{a, b\}$ and $M = \Sigma^* - (a^+ b^+ a^+ b^+)$. A word belongs to $\Sigma^* - L$ if and only if either it is in M, or it is not in M, and either the number of a's in the first block is different from the number of a's in the second block, or the same condition holds for the b's. Thus, if we let

$$N_a = \bigcup_{m \neq n} a^m b^+ a^n b^+ \quad \text{and} \quad N_b = \bigcup_{m \neq n} a^+ b^m a^+ b^n,$$

we have $\Sigma^* - L = M \cup N_a \cup N_b$. Since context-free languages are closed under union, it suffices to show that N_a and N_b are context-free. The language N_a is generated by the following context-free grammar:

$$S \to AXB \mid XAB,$$
$$A \to Aa \mid a,$$
$$B \to Bb \mid b,$$
$$X \to aXa \mid B.$$

Indeed, A generates the language a^+, B generates the language b^+, and X generates precisely the words of the form $a^n b^+ a^n$ for $n \geq 0$; it follows immediately that S generates N_a. The grammar for N_b is analogous. ∎

Solution to Problem 102

(1) Towards a contradiction, suppose that the language is context-free. Let N be the constant from the pumping lemma for context-free languages. Consider the word $w = a^N b^N a^N$ and the factorization $w = prefix \cdot left \cdot infix \cdot right \cdot suffix$ guaranteed by the pumping lemma. For $k \in \mathbb{N}$, let $w_k = prefix \cdot left^k \cdot infix \cdot right^k \cdot suffix$. Since the combined length of $left \cdot infix \cdot right$ is at most N, we have that this subword cannot span both blocks of a's. There are several cases to consider, all being quite similar. For example, if $left$ contains a letter a from the first block of a's and $right$ contains a letter b from the block of b's, then $w_0 = a^K b^M a^N$ for some $K, M < N$, proving that w_0 is not in the language. The other cases are similar and in every case we reach a contradiction. Hence, the language is not context-free.

(2) Notice that the classical pumping lemma for context-free languages is insufficient for this language, since a factorization of a word $a^i b^i c^k$ with $k \neq i$ as in the pumping lemma might have $left \cdot infix \cdot right$ consisting only of c's, which might allow pumping without leaving the language. Therefore, we use Ogden's lemma instead. Let N be the constant from Ogden's lemma, and consider the word $w = a^N b^N c^{N+N!}$ where we mark the a's and the b's. By Ogden's lemma, w can be factorized as $w = prefix \cdot left \cdot infix \cdot right \cdot suffix$, where $left \cdot right$ contains an a or a b, and $left \cdot infix \cdot right$ has at most N occurrences of a and b in total. Consequently, $left \cdot infix \cdot right$ cannot simultaneously contain a's, b's, and c's, and cannot consist only of c's. Assume that it does not contain c's. If $left \cdot right$ does not contain the same number of a's and b's, then w_2 cannot be of the form $a^i b^i c^*$, so it does not belong to the language. Otherwise, suppose $left \cdot right$ contains exactly k occurrences of a and k occurrences of b, for some $k \leq N$. Then, for $\ell = (N!+k)/k$, the word w_ℓ contains $N+(\ell-1)\cdot k = N+N!$ occurrences of a, and the same for b, thus $w_\ell = a^{N+N!} b^{N+N!} c^{N+N!}$, so w_ℓ does not belong to the language. Finally, assume that $left \cdot infix \cdot right$ contains no a's. Then, it must contain at least one b, and then clearly w_2 has more b's than a's, so w_2 does not belong to the language. In each case we reached a contradiction; thus the language is not context-free.

(3) We use Ogden's lemma again. Assume that the language is context-free, and let N be the number from this lemma. Consider the word

$w = a^{N!}b^{2N!}c^{3N!}$ from the language and mark all positions in w with letter a. Consider the factorization as in the lemma. Since w_2 must belong to $a^*b^*c^*$, it follows that *left, right* $\in a^* + b^* + c^*$. Recall that at least one of *left*, and *right* contains a marked letter, so exactly one of the three following possibilities must occur:

$$left, right \in a^* \quad \text{or} \quad left \in a^+, right \in b^+ \quad \text{or} \quad left \in a^+, right \in c^+.$$

Suppose the second case holds; the other cases are similar. We claim that there is a number k such that the word w_k has the same number of a's as c's. Indeed, if $\ell = |left|$ then $\#_a(w_k) = N! - \ell + k \cdot \ell$, so it suffices to take $k = 2N!/\ell + 1$; here we use the fact that *left* has at most N marked positions, so $|left| \le N \le 2N!$. But then w_k does not belong to the language. ∎

Solution to Problem 103

(1) Let $L = \{a^n b^n c^n : n \ge 1\}$. Suppose $K \subseteq L$ is an infinite context-free language contained in L. Let N be the constant from the pumping lemma for context-free languages. Since K is infinite, it contains some word w of the form $a^n b^n c^n$ of length at least N. Consider the factorization $w = prefix \cdot left \cdot infix \cdot right \cdot suffix$ guaranteed by the pumping lemma. Then, $w_k = prefix \cdot left^k \cdot infix \cdot right^k \cdot suffix$ belongs to $K \subseteq L \subseteq a^*b^*c^*$ for all $k \in \mathbb{N}$. It follows that *left, right* $\in a^* + b^* + c^*$ (otherwise w_2 would not belong to $a^*b^*c^*$). Hence, some letter $x \in \{a, b, c\}$ appears neither in *left* nor in *right*, and some other letter $y \in \{a, b, c\}$ does appear either in *left* or in *right*. Consequently, the word w_2 has fewer occurrences of x than occurrences of y. That means that $w_2 \notin L$, which is a contradiction.

Let us now move to the complement of L. Observe that a word $w \in \{a, b, c\}^*$ does not belong to L if either it is not of the form $a^*b^*c^*$, or $\#_a(w) \ne \#_b(w)$, or $\#_b(w) \ne \#_c(w)$. It follows that the complement of L is equal to

$$\left(\{a, b, c\}^* - a^*b^*c^*\right) \cup L_{a<b} \cup L_{b<a} \cup L_{b<c} \cup L_{c<b},$$

where $L_{x<y} = \left\{w \in a^*b^*c^* : \#_x(w) < \#_y(w)\right\}$ for $x, y \in \{a, b, c\}$. The first component of the above union is regular, so it is also context-free. Because context-free languages are closed under finite unions, it suffices to show that the remaining components are context-free.

The language $L_{a<b}$ is generated by the following grammar:

$$S \to XbBC,$$

$$X \to \varepsilon \mid aXb,$$

$$B \rightarrow \varepsilon \mid bB,$$
$$C \rightarrow \varepsilon \mid cC.$$

Indeed, the symbol B generates the language b^*, C generates c^*, and X generates $\{a^n b^n : n \geq 0\}$. Hence, the symbol S generates precisely the language $\{a^n b^n bb^k c^l : k, n, l \geq 0\}$, which is equal to $L_{a<b}$. Grammars for the languages $L_{b<a}$, $L_{b<c}$, and $L_{c<b}$ are analogous.

(2) The argument is similar. Let $L = \{(a^n b^n)^n : n \geq 1\}$. Suppose that $K \subseteq L$ is an infinite context-free language. Let N be the constant from the pumping lemma for context-free languages. Because K is infinite, it contains $w = (a^n b^n)^n$ for some $n \geq \max(N, 2)$. Let $w = prefix \cdot left \cdot infix \cdot right \cdot suffix$ be the factorization guaranteed by the pumping lemma. Because $|left \cdot infix \cdot right| \leq N \leq n$, either the first block of a's is contained in *prefix* or the last block of b's is contained in *suffix*. Either way, when *left* and *right* are pumped, at least one block does not change its length. But since *left* and *right* are not both empty, the length of the whole word grows. It follows easily that $w_k \notin L$ for $k > 1$. Hence, L is not context-free.

The complement of L is context-free. A word does not belong to L if and only if it is of (at least) one of the following forms:

- $(a + b)^* a + b(a + b)^*$;
- $(a^+ b^+)^* a^n b^m (a^+ b^+)^*$ for some $m \neq n$;
- $(a^+ b^+)^* a^+ b^m a^n b^+ (a^+ b^+)^*$ for some $m \neq n$;
- $a^n (b^+ a^+)^m b^+$ for some $m \neq n - 1$.

Each case gives rise to a context-free language; the arguments are similar to the one used in item (1). ∎

Solution to Problem 104

(1) This language is not context-free. Towards a contradiction, assume that it is and let N be the constant obtained by applying the pumping lemma for context-free languages. Consider the word $w = a^N b^N c^{N^2}$, which belongs to the language, and its factorization

$$w = prefix \cdot left \cdot infix \cdot right \cdot suffix$$

guaranteed by the pumping lemma. We will refer to the subwords a^N, b^N, and c^{N^2} as blocks. Since the length of $left \cdot infix \cdot right$ is at most N, we have that this subword cannot contain all three blocks (since each block has length at least N). If this subword spanned only one block, then

$$w_2 = prefix \cdot left^2 \cdot infix \cdot right^2 \cdot suffix$$

would not be in the language, since we have modified one block without changing the others. Therefore, the word *left* · *infix* · *right* spans two consecutive blocks. Assume that these blocks are a^N and b^N. Then, *left* $= a^K$ and *right* $= b^M$ for some $K, M > 0$. Consequently, $w_2 = a^{N+K} b^{N+M} c^{N^2}$ with $K, M > 0$, so w_2 is not in the language. Finally, assume that the spanned blocks are b^N and c^{N^2}. Then *left* $= b^K$, and *right* $= c^M$ for some $K, M > 0$, and $w_2 = a^N b^{N+K} c^{N^2+M}$. Note also that $K + M \leq N$. In order to have $N \cdot (N + K) = N^2 + M$, we need $NK = M$, which is impossible since $NK \geq N \geq K + M > M$.

(2)   This language is not context-free, because its homomorphic image under the homomorphism mapping d to c and leaving the remaining letters a, b, and c unchanged is the language $\{a^i b^j c^k : i, j > 0, k > 1, i \cdot j = k\}$, whose union with $\{abc\}$ is the language in item (1), which is not context-free.   ∎

Solution to Problem 105

Not always. The set of palindromes in $L = \{a^n b^n a^m : m, n \in \mathbb{N}\}$ is $\{a^n b^n a^n : n \in \mathbb{N}\}$, which is not context-free (see Problem 103(1)).   ∎

Solution to Problem 106

If $\Sigma = \{a\}$, then $L = \{a^{2^n} : n \in \mathbb{N}\}$, which is not only context-free, but also regular. For the converse implication, assume that a and b are two distinct letters in Σ. The intersection of L with the regular language $a^+ b^+ a^+ b^+$ is equal to

$$\{a^n b^m a^n b^m : n, m \geq 1\},$$

which is not context-free (see Problem 101). Since context-free languages are closed under intersections with regular languages, this implies that L is not context-free either.

We now show that the complement of L is context-free. First, all words of odd length belong to the complement of L. Second, observe that if a word w has even length, then it belongs to the complement of L if and only if two matching positions in w in the word carry a different letter; that is, $w \in \Sigma^m a \Sigma^n \Sigma^m b \Sigma^n$ for two distinct symbols $a, b \in \Sigma$ and some $m, n \geq 0$. The latter can be rewritten as

$$w \in \Sigma^m a \Sigma^m \Sigma^n b \Sigma^n \qquad \text{for some } m, n \geq 0.$$

Let U be the set of words of the latter form. Then, the complement of L is the union of the (regular) set of words of odd length, and the language U. As context-free languages are closed under union, it remains to show that U is context-free. Consider the grammar with rules

$$S \to R_x R_y \qquad \text{for all distinct } x, y \in \Sigma,$$
$$R_x \to y R_x z \mid x \qquad \text{for all } x, y, z \in \Sigma.$$

Clearly, R_x generates words of the form $\Sigma^n x \Sigma^n$ for $n \in \mathbb{N}$, and S generates the language U. ∎

Solution to Problem 107

We reuse the idea from the solution to Problem 106. Assume $k \geq 2$. Observe that a word does not belong to L_k if either its length is not a multiple of k, or it is, and it is of the form $uavbw$, where a and b are two distinct letters from Σ and $u, v, w \in \Sigma^*$ are such that $|u| + |w| + 1 = (k-1) \cdot (|v|+1)$. It is not difficult to check that the words satisfying the latter condition are precisely those of the form

$$\Sigma^{(k-1)m+\mu} \, a \, \Sigma^m \Sigma^n \, b \, \Sigma^{(k-1)n+v} \tag{$\diamond$}$$

for some $m, n, \mu, v \geq 0$ such that $\mu + v = k - 2$. To see this, one can verify that for $u, v, w \in \Sigma^*$ satisfying $|u| + |w| + 1 = (k - 1) \cdot (|v| + 1)$, choosing the following values for m, n, μ, and v in the expression ($\diamond$) yields a language which contains the word $uavbw$:

$$m = |u| \div (k - 1),$$
$$\mu = |u| \bmod (k - 1),$$
$$n = |w| \div (k - 1),$$
$$v = |w| \bmod (k - 1),$$

with $\div$ denoting the integer division. For fixed $a, b \in \Sigma$ and $\mu, v \geq 0$ satisfying $\mu + v = k - 2$, the set of words ($\diamond$) is generated by the following context-free grammar:

$$S \to L_a^{\mu} R_b^{v},$$
$$L_a^{\mu} \to \Sigma^{k-1} L_a^{\mu} \Sigma^1 \mid \Sigma^{\mu} a,$$
$$R_b^{v} \to \Sigma^1 R_b^{v} \Sigma^{k-1} \mid b \Sigma^{v},$$
$$\Sigma^l \to a_1 \ldots a_l \qquad \text{for all } 1 \leq l \leq k - 1, a_1, \ldots, a_l \in \Sigma.$$

Therefore, the grammar for the complement of the language L_k can be obtained by taking the set of all rules as above, for all distinct $a, b \in \Sigma$ and all $\mu, v \geq 0$ satisfying $\mu + v = k - 2$. ∎

Solution to Problem 108

Recall that context-free languages are closed under homomorphic images. Consider the homomorphism $f : \{a, b, \$\}^* \rightarrow \{a, b\}^*$ that erases the letter $\$$; that is, $a \mapsto a$, $b \mapsto b$, and $\$ \mapsto \varepsilon$. The image of L under this homomorphism is equal to $\{ww : w \in \{a, b\}^*\}$, which is not context-free as shown in Problem 106. Hence L is not context-free.

More directly, if L were generated by a context-free grammar, then erasing each occurrence of $\$$ in this grammar would result in a context-free grammar generating the language $\{ww : w \in \{a, b\}^*\}$, a contradiction.

Let us now move to the complement of L. Observe that a word w belongs to $\{a, b, \$\}^* - L$ if, and only if, it satisfies at least one of the following conditions:

- w contains either zero or at least two occurrences of the letter $\$$;
- w is of the form $u\$v$, for $u, v \in \{a, b\}^*$ such that $|u| \neq |v|$;
- w is of the form $uau'\$vbv'$, where $u, u', v, v' \in \{a, b\}^*$ and $|u'| = |v'|$;
- w is of the form $ubu'\$vav'$, where $u, u', v, v' \in \{a, b\}^*$ and $|u'| = |v'|$.

Note that the above cases are not disjoint: for example, the word $ab\$a$ is of both the second form and the third form. In the third and fourth conditions we purposely omitted the conditions $|u| = |v|$; adding it would also give valid conditions, but the argument that follows would no longer work.

From the above observation it follows that the complement of L is a union of four (non-disjoint) languages, described by the above conditions. Clearly, the first condition describes a regular language. The second condition describes a context-free language which can be generated by the start symbol S in the following grammar:

$$S \rightarrow XY \mid YX,$$
$$X \rightarrow \$ \mid aXa \mid aXb \mid bXa \mid bXb,$$
$$Y \rightarrow a \mid b \mid aY \mid bY.$$

Also the language described by the third condition is context-free, and it is generated by the start symbol S in the following grammar:

$$S \rightarrow YaX,$$
$$X \rightarrow aXa \mid aXb \mid bXa \mid bXb \mid \$Yb,$$
$$Y \rightarrow \varepsilon \mid aY \mid bY.$$

The non-terminal X produces words of the form $u'\$vbv'$ where $u', v, v' \in \{a, b\}^*$ and $|u'| = |v'|$. Hence, S produces all words satisfying the third condition. Finally, the fourth condition is analogous. As context-free languages are closed under unions, this proves that $\{a, b, \$\}^* - L$ is context-free. ∎

Solution to Problem 109

(1) Let K be the regular language ba^*ba^*b. Observe that if $u, v \in K$, then u is an infix of v if, and only if, $u = v$. It follows that

$$L \cap K\$K = \left\{ ba^i ba^j b\$ba^i ba^j b \ : \ i, j \in \mathbb{N} \right\}.$$

Using an argument analogous to that in Problem 101, one shows that this language is not context-free. As $K\$K$ is regular and context-free languages are closed under intersections with regular languages, L is not context-free.

The complement of L is not context-free either, because

$$(\{a, b, \$\}^* - L) \cap K\$ba^*b = \left\{ ba^m ba^n b\$ba^r b \ : \ m, n, r \in \mathbb{N}, r \neq m \wedge r \neq n \right\}$$

is not context-free, which is shown similarly as in Problem 102(3).

(2) L is generated by the following context-free grammar:

$$S \to YX,$$
$$X \to aXa \mid bXb \mid Y\$,$$
$$Y \to aY \mid bY \mid \varepsilon.$$

Indeed, the symbol X generates the set of words of the form $v(a+b)^*\$v^R$, and the symbol S generates the set of words of the form $(a+b)^* v(a+b)^*\$v^R$, which is equal to L.

On the other hand, the complement of L is not context-free, and the argument is the same as in item (1). ∎

Solution to Problem 110

L is not context-free, because

$$L \cap ba^*ba^*b\$ba^*b = \left\{ ba^n ba^n b\$ba^n b \ : \ n \in \mathbb{N} \right\}$$

is not context-free, which can be shown as in Problem 103(1).

On the other hand, the complement of L is context-free. It is the union of the complement of $(a + b)^*\$(a + b)^*$, and the following two languages:

$$L_1 = \left\{ w\$v^R \ : \ w, v \in \{a, b\}^*, \ v \text{ is not a prefix of } w \right\},$$
$$L_2 = \left\{ w\$v^R \ : \ w, v \in \{a, b\}^*, \ v \text{ is not a suffix of } w \right\}.$$

We show that L_1 is context-free, the argument for L_2 being analogous. This will imply that the complement of L is context-free, as a union of three context-free languages.

By definition of L_1, a word $w\$v^R$ belongs to L_1 if, and only if, for some $u \in \{a, b\}^*$ one of the following three conditions holds:

- $w \in ua(a + b)^*$ and $v \in ub(a + b)^*$;
- $w \in ub(a + b)^*$ and $v \in ua(a + b)^*$;
- $w = u$ and $v \in u(a + b)^+$.

Accordingly, L_1 can be generated by the start symbol S in the following context-free grammar:

$$S \to aSa \mid bSb \mid X,$$
$$X \to aY\$Yb \mid bY\$Ya \mid \$Ya \mid \$Yb,$$
$$Y \to aY \mid bY \mid \varepsilon.$$

Indeed, Y generates $(a + b)^*$ and X generates all words of the forms

$$a(a + b)^*\$(a + b)^*b, \quad b(a + b)^*\$(a + b)^*a, \quad \text{and} \quad \$(a + b)^+.$$

From S we derive precisely uXu^R for $u \in \{a, b\}^*$, which turns the three forms into the three conditions listed above.   ■

Solution to Problem 111

Let $M = L \cap ba^*bba^*bba^*b = \{ba^nbba^nbba^nb : n \in \mathbb{N}\}$. If L were context-free, then so would M be, as an intersection of a context-free and a regular language. It can be shown that M is not context-free, similarly as in Problem 103(1).

We now show that the complement of L is context-free. Let $\Sigma = \{a, b\}$. A word $w \in \Sigma^*$ is not in L if, and only if, one of the following holds:

- The length of w is not divisible by 3. The language of all words with this property is the regular language $L_1 = (\Sigma^3)^*(\Sigma^1 + \Sigma^2)$.
- The word w can be split into three parts w_1, w_2, and w_3 of equal lengths, but $w_1 \neq w_2^R$. This happens precisely when the length of w is $3n$ for some $n \in \mathbb{N}$, and its ith symbol (where $1 \leq i \leq n$) differs from its $(2n + 1 - i)$th symbol. By substituting $j = n - i$ and $k = i - 1$, we have that the language of all words with this property can be written as

$$L_2 = \left\{uavbw : u \in \Sigma^k, v \in \Sigma^{2j}, w \in \Sigma^{j+2k+1}, j, k \in \mathbb{N}\right\} \cup$$
$$\left\{ubvaw : u \in \Sigma^k, v \in \Sigma^{2j}, w \in \Sigma^{j+2k+1}, j, k \in \mathbb{N}\right\}.$$

The first ingredient of the union is generated by the following grammar:

$$S \rightarrow XSXX \mid aRX,$$
$$R \rightarrow XXRX \mid b,$$
$$X \rightarrow a \mid b.$$

Indeed, R produces all words of the form $\Sigma^{2j} b \Sigma^j$, and S produces all words of the form $\Sigma^k a (\Sigma^{2j} b \Sigma^j) \Sigma^{2k+1}$. The grammar for the second ingredient is obtained by swapping a and b.

- The last case is when the word can be split into three parts w_1, w_2, and w_3 of equal lengths, but $w_2 \neq w_3^R$. This is symmetric to the previous case: the language L_3 of such words equals L_2^R, which is also context-free since context-free languages are closed under reverse.

The complement of L equals $L_1 \cup L_2 \cup L_3$, hence it is also context-free. ∎

Solution to Problem 112

(1) If this language were context-free, so would be its intersection with the regular language $10^*10^*10\$10^*10^*11$, which is equal to

$$\left\{ 10^i 10^j 10\$10^i 10^j 11 \ : \ i,j \in \mathbb{N} \right\}.$$

It can be shown, as in Problem 101, that the latter language is not context-free.

(2) There is a minor technical difficulty due to the fact that the binary representation of a number may contain leading 0's. For instance the language contains words of the form $0^m 01\#(0^n 10)^R$ for every $m, n \in \mathbb{N}$. To circumvent this, we first consider the following related language which forbids leading 0's:

$$M = \left\{ x\$y^R \ : \ x = 1^n, y = 10^n, n \in \mathbb{N} \right\} \cup$$
$$\left\{ x\$y^R \ : \ x = 1w01^n, y = 1w10^n, w \in \{0,1\}^*, n \in \mathbb{N} \right\}.$$

The language M is generated by the following grammar:

$$S \rightarrow Y1 \mid 1X1,$$
$$X \rightarrow 0X0 \mid 1X1 \mid 0Y1,$$
$$Y \rightarrow 1Y0 \mid \$.$$

The language from the statement equals $0^* M 0^*$, so it is also context-free by the closure of context-free languages under concatenation. ∎

Solution to Problem 113

(1) Consider the language $L_1 \cap 1^+0^+\$1^+0^+ = \{1^i0^j\$1^i0^{j+1} : i,j \geq 1\}$. It can be shown as in Problem 101 that this language is not context-free.

(2) L_2 is not context-free. Let $M = L_2 \cap \{10^+1\$10^+10^+1\}$. If $w \in M$, then w must be of the form $\mathrm{bin}(n)\$\mathrm{bin}(n^2)$ where $n = 2^i + 1$ for some $i \geq 1$. For such n, we have $n^2 = 2^{2i}+2^{i+1}+1$. It follows that M is the language of all words of the form $10^{i-1}1\$10^i10^{i-2}1$, where $i \geq 3$. This language is not context-free, which can be shown as in Problem 103(1).   ■

Solution to Problem 114

(1) This language is not context-free. For $n \geq 1$, we have $n \leq m$ if, and only if, one of the following conditions holds:

- $\mathrm{bin}(n) = \mathrm{bin}(m)$, or
- $|\mathrm{bin}(n)| < |\mathrm{bin}(m)|$, or
- there exist words $u, v, w \in \{0, 1\}^*$ such that

$$\mathrm{bin}(n) = 1w0u,$$
$$\mathrm{bin}(m) = 1w1v,$$

and $|u| = |v|$ (and thus $|\mathrm{bin}(n)| = |\mathrm{bin}(m)|$).

Let L denote the considered language. By way of contradiction, assume that L is context-free. Let N be the constant from the pumping lemma, and consider the word $w = 1^N0^N \$ 1^N0^N$ consisting of four blocks of digits of the same length N. Clearly, $w \in L$. Let

$$w = \mathit{prefix} \cdot \mathit{left} \cdot \mathit{infix} \cdot \mathit{right} \cdot \mathit{suffix}$$

as in the statement of the pumping lemma, and define

$$w_k = \mathit{prefix} \cdot \mathit{left}^k \cdot \mathit{infix} \cdot \mathit{right}^k \cdot \mathit{suffix}$$

for every $k \in \mathbb{N}$. Since $\mathit{left}\cdot\mathit{infix}\cdot\mathit{right}$ has length at most N, it cannot span three consecutive blocks of digits. If it spans only the left part, before the separator \$, then $w_2 \notin L$ because the left part becomes longer than the right one. Similarly, if it spans only the right part, then $w_0 \notin L$ for the same reason. Thus, it remains to consider the case when it spans both parts. Notice that the separator \$ necessarily belongs to infix, because otherwise w_2 would have more than one separator, and thus it would not be in L. Thus, assume that $\mathit{left} = 0^i$ is on the left of the separator, and $\mathit{right} = 1^j$ is on the right of the separator. These two words are not both empty; that is, either $i > 0$ or $j > 0$ (or both). If $i < j$ (and thus $j > 0$), then w_0 is not in L since the right part is shorter than the left one.

Similarly, if $i > j$ (and thus $i > 0$), then $w_2 \notin L$. Finally, if $i = j > 0$, then $w_0 = 1^N 0^{N-i} \$ 1^{N-i} 0^N \notin L$. In every case we reach a contradiction; thus L is not context-free.

(2) This language is context-free. We can express it as the union of three languages, corresponding to the three cases of the characterization in the previous item. The first language is

$$\left\{ u \$ u^R \ : \ u \in 1(0+1)^* \right\},$$

which is essentially the language of palindromes, and thus is context-free. The second language is

$$\left\{ 1u \$ v1 \ : \ u, v \in \{0, 1\}^*, |u| < |v| \right\},$$

which is clearly context-free. The third and last language is

$$\left\{ 1w0u \$ v1w^R1 \ : \ u, v, w \in \{0, 1\}^*, |u| = |v| \right\},$$

which is generated by the following grammar:

$$S \rightarrow 1T1,$$
$$T \rightarrow 0T0 \,|\, 1T1 \,|\, 0U1,$$
$$U \rightarrow 0U0 \,|\, 0U1 \,|\, 1U0 \,|\, 1U1 \,|\, \$.$$

Indeed, U generates words of the form $\{0, 1\}^n \$ \{0, 1\}^n$, and thus S generates the required language. ∎

Solution to Problem 115

(1) This language is context-free. Note that $\mathbf{D_1}$ can be generated by the grammar

$$S \rightarrow SS \,|\, (S) \,|\, \varepsilon,$$

and its reverse $\mathbf{D_1^R}$ by the grammar

$$S \rightarrow SS \,|\,)S(\,|\, \varepsilon.$$

When we split a word $w \in \mathbf{D_1}$ into two parts, $w = uv$, certain parentheses opened in u are dangling, and they are later closed in v. If u has n dangling parentheses, then

$$u = u_0(u_1(\ldots u_{n-1}(u_n \quad \text{with } u_0, \ldots, u_n \in \mathbf{D_1},$$
$$v = v_0)v_1)\ldots v_{n-1})v_n \quad \text{with } v_0, \ldots, v_n \in \mathbf{D_1}.$$

Therefore, $v^R = v_n^R)v_{n-1}^R)\ldots v_1^R)v_0^R$. We claim that the grammar below generates the required language from the start symbol S:

$$S \to X(S)Y \mid XY,$$
$$X \to XX \mid (X) \mid \varepsilon,$$
$$Y \to YY \mid)Y(\mid \varepsilon.$$

We have that X generates $\mathbf{D_1}$, and Y generates $\mathbf{D_1^R}$. It follows from the analysis above that S produces the required language.

(2) This language is not context-free. First notice that $\mathbf{D_2}$ can be generated from the grammar

$$S \to SS \mid (S) \mid [S] \mid \varepsilon.$$

Unlike in the previous case, in order to split a word $w \in \mathbf{D_2}$ into two parts $w = uv$, when reading uv^R we have to count separately *two* different kinds of parentheses, which is something context-free grammars cannot do. Indeed, the intersection of the considered language with the regular language $(^*[^*)^*]^*$ equals $\{(^i[^j)^i]^j : i,j \in \mathbb{N}\}$, and thus it is not context-free (see Problem 101). ∎

Solution to Problem 116

Each finite language is context-free, so it suffices to show that each infinite set L of square-free words is not context-free. This can be proved by a direct application of the pumping lemma.

By way of contradiction, assume that L is context-free and let N be the constant from the pumping lemma. Because L is infinite, it contains a word w of length at least N. Then, w can be factorized as

$$w = prefix \cdot left \cdot infix \cdot right \cdot suffix$$

with *left* and *right* not both empty, and thus by the pumping lemma also

$$w_2 = prefix \cdot left^2 \cdot infix \cdot right^2 \cdot suffix$$

belongs to L. But this is a contradiction, because w_2 contains $left^2$ and $right^2$, and at least one of them is non-empty. ∎

Solution to Problem 117

Let $L \subseteq \{0, 1\}^*$ be the set of all finite prefixes of the Thue–Morse word. This language is cube-free, as shown in Problem 7. We show that the complement of L is context-free.

It follows from the third characterization in Problem 7 that L contains precisely the words $w = t_0 t_1 \ldots t_{n-1}$ for which $t_0 = 0$, $t_{2k} = t_k$ for $2k < n$, and

$t_{2k+1} = 1 - t_k$ for $2k < n - 1$. Therefore, a word w is in the complement of L if, and only if, one of the following conditions holds:

- w begins with 1, or
- $w = x0y1z$ with $|y| = |x| - 1$, or
- $w = x1y0z$ with $|y| = |x| - 1$, or
- $w = x0y0z$ with $|y| = |x|$, or
- $w = x1y1z$ with $|y| = |x|$.

Since context-free languages are closed under finite unions, it is enough to show that the five sets of words defined by the conditions above are context-free. For example, the language of words satisfying the second condition is generated by the following grammar:

$$S \rightarrow S0 \mid S1 \mid 0T1 \mid 1T1,$$
$$T \rightarrow 0 \mid 0T0 \mid 1T1 \mid 1T0 \mid 0T1.$$

Clearly, the symbol T generates all words of the form

$$(0 + 1)^n 0(0 + 1)^n$$

for $n \in \mathbb{N}$, and the symbol S generates all words of the form

$$(0 + 1)^{n+1} 0(0 + 1)^n 1(0 + 1)^*,$$

which are precisely the words satisfying the second condition. Grammars for the remaining conditions can be constructed similarly. ∎

Solution to Problem 118

Consider the set L of Lyndon words of the form $0^* 1 0^* 1 0^* 1$. Using Ogden's lemma we show that L is not context-free, thus proving that the set of all Lyndon words is not context-free either.

Let N be the constant from Ogden's lemma applied to L, and consider the word $w = 0^{N+1} 1 0^N 1 0^N 1$ in L with the middle block of 0's marked. Consider the factorization $w = prefix \cdot left \cdot infix \cdot right \cdot suffix$ guaranteed by Ogden's lemma. Since words in L contain precisely three 1's, *left* and *right* consist of 0's only. There are the following two cases.

- The factor *left* is a non-empty infix of the left block 0^{N+1}. Then *right* is contained in the middle block, because it must contain a marked position. Then w_0 is of the form $0^i 1 0^j 1 0^N 1$ with $i \leq N, j < N$, and thus not in L because $0^N 1 0^i 1 0^j 1$ is lexicographically smaller.

- The factor *left* is not a non-empty infix of the left block 0^{N+1}. Then either *left* or *right* is a non-empty infix of the middle block of 0's. Hence, for sufficiently large n, the word w_n is of the form $0^{N+1}10^j10^k1$ with $j > N + 1$, $k \geq N$, and thus not in L because $0^j10^k10^{N+1}1$ is lexicographically smaller.

This shows that L is not context-free.   ∎

Solution to Problem 119

(1) Let 2^V be the set of all valuations of variables, that is, functions from V to {*false, true*}. A propositional formula φ clearly induces a boolean function $\widehat{\varphi}$ mapping each valuation in 2^V to {*false, true*} in the natural way: for $val \in 2^V$, $\widehat{\varphi}(val)$ is the value of the formula φ when each predicate $v \in V$ is replaced by $val(v)$. For example, φ is a tautology if and only if $\widehat{\varphi}(val) = true$ for each $val \in 2^V$. Let Φ be the set of all such boolean functions; that is, functions from 2^V to {*false, true*}. Note that Φ is finite, and contains $2^{2^{|V|}}$ elements. Our grammar contains a non-terminal F_ρ for each $\rho \in \Phi$ generating exactly those formulas φ that induce the boolean function ρ; that is, $\rho = \widehat{\varphi}$. Since we are interested in tautologies, $F_{\widehat{true}}$ is the starting non-terminal. The rules are as follows:

$$clF_{\widehat{true}} \to true,$$
$$F_{\widehat{false}} \to false,$$
$$F_{\widehat{v}} \to v \qquad\qquad \text{for each } v \in V,$$
$$F_{\neg\rho} \to (\neg F_\rho) \qquad\qquad \text{for each } \rho \in \Phi,$$
$$F_{\rho_1 \vee \rho_2} \to (F_{\rho_1} \vee F_{\rho_2}) \qquad\qquad \text{for each } \rho_1, \rho_2 \in \Phi,$$
$$F_{\rho_1 \wedge \rho_2} \to (F_{\rho_1} \wedge F_{\rho_2}) \qquad\qquad \text{for each } \rho_1, \rho_2 \in \Phi.$$

Here, for two given boolean functions $\rho_1, \rho_2 \in \Phi$, we write $\rho_1 \vee \rho_2$ for the boolean function $\rho \in \Phi$ such that for every valuation $val \in 2^V$, $\rho(val) = \rho_1(val) \vee \rho_2(val)$, and similarly for $\neg\rho$ and $\rho_1 \wedge \rho_2$.

It remains to prove that $F_{\widehat{true}}$ generates precisely the tautologies. We actually prove something stronger. For a non-terminal F_ρ, let $L(F_\rho)$ be the set of formulas it generates. We prove that, for every $\rho \in \Phi$,

$$L(F_\rho) = \{\varphi : \widehat{\varphi} = \rho\}.$$

We proceed by proving two inclusions.

The '$\subseteq$' inclusion says that the grammar rules are *sound*; that is, they generate only correct formulas. It can be proved by induction on the length of derivations. Let $\varphi \in L(F_\rho)$. The base cases when φ equals *true*, *false*, or a variable v from V are clear. For the inductive step, let $\varphi = (\varphi_1 \vee \varphi_2)$ (the other cases are similar). Then, φ is generated by applying the rule $F_\rho \to (F_{\rho_1} \vee F_{\rho_2})$ for some ρ_1 and ρ_2 satisfying $\rho = \rho_1 \vee \rho_2$, and thus $\varphi_1 \in L(F_{\rho_1})$ and $\varphi_2 \in L(F_{\rho_2})$. Then, by the inductive hypothesis, $\widehat{\varphi_1} = \rho_1$ and $\widehat{\varphi_2} = \rho_2$. Therefore, by the definition of $\vee$,

$$\widehat{\varphi} = \widehat{\varphi_1} \vee \widehat{\varphi_2} = \rho_1 \vee \rho_2 = \rho$$

as required.

The '$\supseteq$' inclusion says that the grammar rules are *complete*; that is, they generate all correct formulas. It can be proved by induction on the length of the formula. Consider a formula φ. The base cases when φ equals *true*, *false*, or a variable v from V are clear. For the inductive step, let $\varphi = (\varphi_1 \vee \varphi_2)$ (the other cases are similar). Then, by the induction hypothesis for the two subformulas φ_1 and φ_2, we have that $\varphi_1 \in L(F_{\widehat{\varphi_1}})$ and $\varphi_2 \in L(F_{\widehat{\varphi_2}})$. Note that $\widehat{\varphi} = \widehat{\varphi_1} \vee \widehat{\varphi_2}$ by the definition of $\vee$. Thus, by applying the rule $F_{\widehat{\varphi}} \to (F_{\widehat{\varphi_1}} \vee F_{\widehat{\varphi_1}})$ we immediately get $\varphi \in L(F_{\widehat{\varphi}})$, as required.

(2) Let T be the set of all tautologies, and let U be the set of words of the form $(xu_1 \vee (\neg xu_2))$ with $u_1, u_2 \in 1(0+1)^*$. Notice that a word $(xu_1 \vee (\neg xu_2)) \in U$ represents a tautology if, and only if, $u_1 = u_2$. Hence

$$T \cap U = \left\{ (xu \vee (\neg xu)) : u \in 1(0+1)^* \right\}.$$

It can be shown that this language is not context-free in the same way as in Problem 106. Since context-free languages are closed under intersection with regular languages, T is not context-free either.

Note that the solution above would not work if we represented indices in unary. In this case, $T \cap U$ would turn out to be context-free. However, we could then take, for example,

$$U = \left\{ ((x1^{i_1} \vee x1^{i_2}) \vee (\neg(x1^{j_1} \vee x1^{j_2}))) : i_1, i_2, j_1, j_2 > 0 \right\};$$

then $T \cap U$ would consist of words as above such that either $i_1 = j_1$ and $i_2 = j_2$ or $i_1 = j_2$ and $i_2 = j_1$. One can show that this language is not context-free by an argument similar to the one in Problem 101. ∎

Solution to Problem 120

Let $\mathcal{G}$ be a linear context-free grammar generating the language $L \subseteq \Sigma^*$. Without loss of generality we can assume that $\mathcal{G}$ has no rules of the form $Y \to Z$. Let n be the number of non-terminals in $\mathcal{G}$. Consider a derivation

$$S = \alpha_0 \to \alpha_1 \to \cdots \to \alpha_m = w \in L(\mathcal{G})$$

with $m > n$. Because $\mathcal{G}$ is linear, each of $\alpha_0, \alpha_1, \ldots, \alpha_{m-1}$ contains exactly one non-terminal. By the pigeonhole principle, for some $i < j \leq n$, the words α_i and α_j contain the same non-terminal X. That is, the derivation has the form

$$S \rightarrow^* \alpha_i = prefix \cdot X \cdot suffix$$
$$\rightarrow^* \alpha_j = prefix \cdot left \cdot X \cdot right \cdot suffix$$
$$\rightarrow^* \alpha_m = prefix \cdot left \cdot infix \cdot right \cdot suffix = w.$$

Because $\mathcal{G}$ has no rules of the form $Y \rightarrow Z$, it follows that $left \cdot right \neq \varepsilon$. Moreover, $|prefix \cdot left| \leq n\ell$ and $|right \cdot suffix| \leq n\ell$, where ℓ is the maximal length of the right-hand side of a rule in $\mathcal{G}$. By skipping the derivation steps leading from α_i to α_j we get

$$S \rightarrow^* prefix \cdot X \cdot suffix \rightarrow^*$$
$$\rightarrow^* prefix \cdot infix \cdot suffix = w_0,$$

and by repeating these steps k times we get

$$S \rightarrow^* prefix \cdot X \cdot suffix \rightarrow^*$$
$$\rightarrow^* prefix \cdot left \cdot X \cdot right \cdot suffix \rightarrow^*$$
$$\vdots$$
$$\rightarrow^* prefix \cdot left^k \cdot X \cdot right^k \cdot suffix \rightarrow^*$$
$$\rightarrow^* prefix \cdot left^k \cdot infix \cdot right^k \cdot suffix = w_k.$$

Because a derivation with m steps yields a word of length at most $m\ell$, each word $w \in L(\mathcal{G})$ of length at least $n\ell + 1$ has a derivation with at least $n + 1$ steps. Thus, the claim holds with $N = n\ell + 1$. ∎

Solution to Problem 121
Let N be the constant from Problem 120 and consider the word $w = a^N b^N c^N d^N \in L$. We have $w = prefix \cdot left \cdot infix \cdot right \cdot suffix$ with $left \cdot right \neq \varepsilon$, $|prefix \cdot left| \leq N$, and $|right \cdot suffix| \leq N$. Consequently, *left* consists only of a's, and *right* consists only of d's. Therefore, in the word $w_2 = prefix \cdot left^2 \cdot infix \cdot right^2 \cdot suffix$ there are either too many a's or too many d's, and thus $w_2 \notin L$, which is a contradiction. ∎

Solution to Problem 122
Let N be the constant from Problem 120 and consider the word $w = a^N b^{2N} a^N \in L$. We have $w = prefix \cdot left \cdot infix \cdot right \cdot suffix$ with $left \cdot right \neq \varepsilon$, $|prefix \cdot left| \leq N$, and $|right \cdot suffix| \leq N$. Consequently, *left* is contained in the first block of a's and *right* is contained in the second block of a's. Therefore,

in $w_2 = prefix \cdot left^2 \cdot infix \cdot right^2 \cdot suffix$ there are more a's than b's, and thus $w_2 \notin L$, which is a contradiction. ∎

Solution to Problem 123

(1) The pushdown automaton recognizing the language of palindromes works in two phases: in the first phase it reads a prefix of the input word and stores it on the stack; in the second phase it reads the remaining suffix of the input word and compares it with the contents of the stack.

Let us now define the automaton formally. As stack symbols we use the input symbols, plus an initial stack symbol; that is, $\Gamma = \Sigma \cup \{Z_I\}$. We need three states: $Q = \{q_1, q_2, q_F\}$. The state q_1 is initial. It is used in the first phase, where we have transitions

$$q_1, a, Z \to q_1, aZ \quad \text{for } a \in \Sigma \text{ and } Z \in \Gamma.$$

At any point the automaton can guess that the first half of the input word has been already read, and change its state to q_2:

$$q_1, a, Z \to q_2, Z \quad \text{for } a \in \Sigma \cup \{\varepsilon\} \text{ and } Z \in \Gamma.$$

Above, we let the automaton read a single letter in the middle, to allow palindromes of an odd length. Then the automaton can read only the letter that is on the top of the stack (and it must remove it from the stack):

$$q_2, a, a \to q_2, \varepsilon \quad \text{for } a \in \Sigma.$$

Finally, when only the initial symbol remains on the stack, the automaton can change its state to the accepting state q_F:

$$q_2, \varepsilon, Z_I \to q_F, Z_I.$$

From the accepting state q_F there are no transitions, so if the input word is not read yet, the automaton will be stuck. It is not difficult to check that the constructed automaton indeed recognizes the language of palindromes.

(2) To recognize the language of balanced sequences of parentheses it is enough to remember on the stack the number of currently open parentheses. Thus we need only two stack symbols, $\Gamma = \{Z_I, \square\}$, and only two states, $Q = \{q_1, q_F\}$, where q_1 is initial and q_F is accepting. An opening parenthesis can always be read, resulting in one $\square$ stored on the stack:

$$q_1, (, Z \to q_1, \square Z \quad \text{for } Z \in \Gamma.$$

A closing parenthesis can be read only when the number of currently open parentheses is not zero:

$$q_1,), \square \rightarrow q_1, \varepsilon.$$

The automaton can accept when all opening parentheses are closed; that is, when the stack is empty (not counting the initial symbol):

$$q_1, \varepsilon, Z_I \rightarrow q_F, Z_I.$$

(3) The automaton will keep on the stack the difference between the number of a's and twice the number of b's; we shall call it the *balance*. There is a small difficulty to overcome: the balance need not be positive, and thus we have to encode negative numbers in the stack height that has to be non-negative. Because of this we use two different stack symbols: the stack consists of a's if the balance is positive (too many a's), and it consists of b's if the balance is negative (too many b's).

Thus, we take $\Gamma = \{Z_I, a, b\}$ and $Q = \{q_1, q_2, q_F\}$, where q_1 is the initial state, and q_F is accepting. When a is read, the balance increases; that is, either the number of b's decreases, or, if there are no b's on the stack, the number of a's increases:

$$q_1, a, b \rightarrow q_1, \varepsilon,$$
$$q_1, a, Z \rightarrow q_1, aZ \quad \text{for } Z \in \{a, Z_I\}.$$

When b is read we proceed dually, except that the balance is changed by two:

$$q_1, b, Z \rightarrow q_1, bbZ \quad \text{for } Z \in \{b, Z_I\}.$$

To pop two a's from the stack, we need to use an auxiliary state q_2:

$$q_1, b, a \rightarrow q_2, \varepsilon,$$
$$q_2, \varepsilon, a \rightarrow q_1, \varepsilon.$$

It is also possible that the stack contains only one a; in this case, after popping this a we want to push b:

$$q_2, \varepsilon, Z_I \rightarrow q_1, bZ_I.$$

As in previous automata, we accept when the stack is empty:

$$q_1, \varepsilon, Z_I \rightarrow q_F, Z_I.$$

(4) The construction is based on the observation that a word over Σ is not of the form ww if and only if it is of odd length, or it belongs to $\Sigma^k a \Sigma^l \Sigma^k b \Sigma^l$ for some $k, l \in \mathbb{N}$ and $a, b \in \Sigma$ with $a \neq b$; that is, there

is a position in the first half such that on the corresponding position in the second half there is a different letter. At first glance this may look hopeless, because a similar language $\{a^k b^l c^k d^l : k, l \in \mathbb{N}\}$ is not context-free. The trick is, however, that $\Sigma^l \Sigma^k = \Sigma^k \Sigma^l$, and it is not difficult to recognize the union of $\Sigma^k a \Sigma^k \Sigma^l b \Sigma^l$ over all k and l.

We take $\Gamma = \{Z_I, \square\}$ and $Q = \{q_1, q_4, q_F, q_e, q_o\} \cup \{q_{2,a}, q_{3,a} : a \in \Sigma\}$. The state q_1 is initial, and states q_F and q_o are accepting. The automaton can decide to check that the word is of odd length. From q_1 it goes to q_o, and then it alternates between q_o and q_e, accepting if the input finishes when it is in q_o:

$$q, a, Z_I \rightarrow q_o, Z_I \quad \text{for } q \in \{q_1, q_e\}, a \in \Sigma,$$
$$q_o, a, Z_I \rightarrow q_e, Z_I \quad \text{for } a \in \Sigma.$$

Otherwise, it first reads a word in Σ^k, putting k symbols on the stack:

$$q_1, a, Z \rightarrow q_1, \square Z \quad \text{for } a \in \Sigma, Z \in \Gamma.$$

Then it reads a letter and stores it in its state:

$$q_1, a, Z \rightarrow q_{2,a}, Z \quad \text{for } a \in \Sigma, Z \in \Gamma.$$

Next, the automaton removes all k symbols from the stack, and simultaneously it reads a word in Σ^k; when the stack becomes empty, the automaton reads a word in Σ^l, putting l symbols on the stack:

$$
\begin{aligned}
q_{2,b}, a, \square &\rightarrow q_{2,b}, \varepsilon && \text{for } a, b \in \Sigma, \\
q_{2,b}, \varepsilon, Z_I &\rightarrow q_{3,b}, Z_I && \text{for } b \in \Sigma, \\
q_{3,b}, a, Z &\rightarrow q_{3,b}, \square Z && \text{for } a, b \in \Sigma, Z \in \Gamma.
\end{aligned}
$$

Then, the automaton can decide that it has read l symbols, and now it has to read a symbol different from the one stored in its state:

$$q_{3,b}, a, Z \rightarrow q_4, Z \quad \text{for } a, b \in \Sigma \text{ with } a \neq b, Z \in \Gamma.$$

Finally, the automaton removes all l symbols from the stack, reading simultaneously a word in Σ^l, and it accepts when the stack becomes empty:

$$
\begin{aligned}
q_4, a, \square &\rightarrow q_4, \varepsilon && \text{for } a \in \Sigma, \\
q_4, \varepsilon, Z_I &\rightarrow q_F, Z_I.
\end{aligned}
$$ ∎

Solution to Problem 124

The pushdown automaton will first read the part of the word before \$, that is, $\text{bin}(n)$, and store it on the stack; this reverses the word, so we have $\text{bin}(n)^R$ on the stack, reading top-down. Then the automaton will read simultaneously corresponding letters of $\mathrm{bin}(n)^R$ from the stack and $\mathrm{bin}(n+1)^R$ from the input, and ensure that these are really representations of two consecutive natural numbers.

Let us see how $\mathrm{bin}(n)^R$ and $\mathrm{bin}(n+1)^R$ are related. Since the numbers are reversed, the most significant bit is on the right. The general scheme is

$$\mathrm{bin}(n)^R = 1^k 0 w \qquad \text{and} \qquad \mathrm{bin}(n+1)^R = 0^k 1 w,$$

for some $k \in \mathbb{N}$ and $w \in \{0,1\}^*$. However, we have to remember that binary representations of numbers do not contain leading 0's (except $\mathrm{bin}(0) = 0$), so w must not end with 0. Moreover, if w is empty and $k > 0$, then $\mathrm{bin}(n)^R$ equals just 1^k, not $1^k 0$.

We now implement this formally in a pushdown automaton $\mathcal{A}$. We take $Q = \{q_1, q_2, q_2', q_3, q_{4,0}, q_{4,1}, q_F\}$ and $\Gamma = \{Z_I, 0, 1\}$. The state q_1 is initial, and the state q_F is accepting. The automaton begins by storing on the stack the part of the input until $\$$:

$$q_1, a, Z \rightarrow q_1, aZ \quad \text{for } a \in \{0,1\}, Z \in \Gamma,$$
$$q_1, \$, Z \rightarrow q_2, Z \quad \text{for } Z \in \Gamma.$$

Now, by popping symbols from the stack, we can read the first part of the word, reversed. We expect a prefix 1^k on the stack, and a prefix 0^k on the input:

$$q, 0, 1 \rightarrow q_3, \varepsilon \quad \text{for } q \in \{q_2, q_3\}.$$

Notice that the automaton stays in q_2 if $k = 0$, and moves to q_3 if $k > 0$.

Now we have three possibilities. If the prefix was empty, we might be left with a single 1 on the input, and a single 0 on the stack. Then the represented numbers are 0 and 1:

$$q_2, 1, 0 \rightarrow q_2', \varepsilon,$$
$$q_2', \varepsilon, Z_I \rightarrow q_F, Z_I.$$

We had to pass through an auxiliary state q_2' in order to ensure that the stack became empty. Another special case is a single 1 on the input, and empty stack:

$$q_3, 1, Z_I \rightarrow q_F, \varepsilon.$$

The remaining (generic) case is that we have 1 on the input and 0 on the stack, both followed by the same suffix:

$$q, 1, 0 \rightarrow q_{4,0}, \varepsilon \quad \text{for } q \in \{q_2, q_3\},$$
$$q, 0, 0 \rightarrow q_{4,0}, \varepsilon \quad \text{for } q \in \{q_{4,0}, q_{4,1}\},$$
$$q, 1, 1 \rightarrow q_{4,1}, \varepsilon \quad \text{for } q \in \{q_{4,0}, q_{4,1}\}.$$

We accept if both words end simultaneously, and their last digits were 1's:

$$q_{4,1}, \varepsilon, Z_I \rightarrow q_F, Z_I. \qquad \blacksquare$$

Solution to Problem 125

We multiply n by 3 using an algorithm similar to long multiplication. The difference is that instead of multiplying the first number (digit by digit) by subsequent digits of the second number, and summing up appropriately shifted results, we multiply it (bit by bit) directly by the second number, relying on the fact that the second number is constant.

Indeed, when the suffix of $\text{bin}(n)$ is multiplied by 3, the carry can be at most 2. Let us take

$$Q = \{q_1, q_2, q_2'\} \cup \{p_{c,a} \,:\, c \in \{0,1,2\}, a \in \{0,1\}\} \cup \{r_c : c \in \{0,1,2\}\}$$

and $\Gamma = \{Z_I, 0, 1\}$. The state q_1 is initial, and the state r_0 is accepting. As in Problem 124, the automaton begins by storing on the stack the part of the input until \$:

$$\begin{aligned} q_1, a, Z &\rightarrow q_1, aZ \quad \text{for } a \in \{0,1\}, Z \in \Gamma, \\ q_1, \$, Z &\rightarrow q_2, Z \quad \text{for } Z \in \Gamma. \end{aligned}$$

We have a special case when this part of the input represents 0:

$$\begin{aligned} q_2, 0, 0 &\rightarrow q_2', \varepsilon, \\ q_2', \varepsilon, Z_I &\rightarrow r_0, Z_I. \end{aligned}$$

In the general situation, we multiply consecutive digits by 3; when the carry is c and the last digit was a, the state becomes $p_{c,a}$:

$$\begin{aligned} q_2, \varepsilon, Z &\rightarrow p_{0,0}, \varepsilon \quad \text{for } Z \in \Gamma, \\ p_{c,a}, e, b &\rightarrow p_{d,b}, \varepsilon \quad \text{for } a, b \in \{0,1\}, c \in \{0,1,2\}, \\ & e = (3b + c \bmod 2), \text{ and } d = \left\lfloor \frac{3b+c}{2} \right\rfloor. \end{aligned}$$

When the stack becomes empty, the smaller number has ended. Then the a subscript of the current state $p_{c,a}$ is the most significant digit of the representation; we have to ensure that it is not 0, because leading 0's are forbidden ($a = 0$ also when the representation is empty, which is forbidden as well). The remaining part of the larger number should contain the carry:

$$\begin{aligned} p_{c,1}, \varepsilon, Z_I &\rightarrow r_c, Z_I \quad \text{for } c \in \{0,1,2\}, \\ r_c, e, Z_I &\rightarrow r_d, Z_I \quad \text{for } c \in \{1,2\}, e = (c \bmod 2), \text{ and } d = \left\lfloor \frac{c}{2} \right\rfloor. \end{aligned}$$

Recall that the state r_0 is accepting.

The construction can be easily generalized to the language

$$\left\{ \operatorname{rep}_k(n) \,\$\, \operatorname{rep}_k(l \cdot n)^{\mathrm{R}} \,:\, n \in \mathbb{N} \right\}$$

for any fixed natural numbers $k, l \geq 2$, where $\operatorname{rep}_k(n)$ denotes the representation of n in base k. ∎

Solution to Problem 126

The idea is to store the current state in the topmost stack symbol. If we did just that, the state could be easily updated when the stack grows or when its size remains unchanged. But when the height of the stack decreases, there is no way to update the state: on the right-hand side of the transition we have an empty sequence, and we cannot modify the stack symbol that now becomes the topmost one. The solution is that already while pushing a symbol we guess the state in which the automaton will be when this symbol is popped. Recall here that according to our definition of pushdown automata, if a symbol becomes topmost, it is popped in the next transition (and possibly immediately pushed back). To keep the guesses consistent, we also include in each symbol the state in which the automaton will pop the symbol directly below it (we shall see that this information can be maintained). The only reason why we need two states is that accepting and non-accepting states need to be distinguished.

Let us fix a pushdown automaton $\mathcal{A}$. Without loss of generality we can assume that the initial state of $\mathcal{A}$ is not accepting. Let us also assume that no transition of $\mathcal{A}$ removes the initial symbol from the stack; this can be easily ensured by adding a new initial symbol, and treating the original initial symbol as an ordinary symbol that is put in the first step on top of the new initial symbol. The equivalent two-state automaton $\mathcal{A}'$ has states $\{p_1, p_F\}$, where p_1 is initial and p_F is accepting. For a state q of $\mathcal{A}$ we let $\bar{q} = p_F$ if q is accepting, and $\bar{q} = p_1$ otherwise. The new stack alphabet is $Q \times \Gamma \times Q$, where Q and Γ are the set of states and the stack alphabet of $\mathcal{A}$. The new initial stack symbol is (q_I, Z_I, q_I), where q_I and Z_I are the initial state and the initial stack symbol of $\mathcal{A}$ (the third component is irrelevant, since there is nothing below the initial symbol). As explained before, the new stack symbol (q_c, Z, q_r) enriches the original stack symbol Z with two states: q_c is the state in which this symbol is popped (that is, if the symbol is currently topmost, it should be the current state), and q_r is the state in which the symbol directly below is popped. If this stack symbol is never to become topmost, or is never to be removed, q_c and q_r, respectively, can be arbitrary states.

The transitions of the new automaton are defined based on the transitions of $\mathcal{A}$: for each transition $q, a, Z \rightarrow q_0, Z_1 Z_2 \ldots Z_k$ in $\mathcal{A}$ with $k > 0$ and each choice of $q_1, \ldots, q_k$, we add in $\mathcal{A}'$

$$\bar{q}, a, (q, Z, q_k) \rightarrow \overline{q_0}, (q_0, Z_1, q_1)(q_1, Z_2, q_2) \ldots (q_{k-1}, Z_k, q_k);$$

and for each transition $q, a, Z \rightarrow q_0, \varepsilon$ in $\mathcal{A}$, we add in $\mathcal{A}'$

$$\bar{q}, a, (q, Z, q_0) \rightarrow \overline{q_0}, \varepsilon.$$

Let us analyse the correspondence between configurations of the two automata. We say that a configuration of $\mathcal{A}'$ is *well formed* if it is of the form $(\overline{q_0}, w, (q_0, Z_1, q_1)(q_1, Z_2, q_2) \ldots (q_{m-1}, Z_m, q_m))$, where $m \geq 1$ and $q_m = q_l$. The *projection* of this configuration is the configuration $(q_0, w, Z_1 Z_2 \ldots Z_m)$ of $\mathcal{A}$.

In order to prove that $L(\mathcal{A}') \subseteq L(\mathcal{A})$, take a word in $L(\mathcal{A}')$, and an accepting run of $\mathcal{A}'$ on that word. Tracing the transitions of $\mathcal{A}'$ it is easy to see that every configuration of that run is well formed, and that $\mathcal{A}$ can transit between the projections of these configurations; the resulting sequence of projections forms an accepting run of $\mathcal{A}$.

For the other inclusion, take a word in $L(\mathcal{A})$, and an accepting run of $\mathcal{A}$ on that word. In order to get a run of $\mathcal{A}'$, we need to add pairs of states to stack symbols in configurations of this run. We begin from the end: we replace the last configuration c of the run by any well-formed configuration of $\mathcal{A}'$ whose projection is c. Then we proceed backwards: we observe that if $c \vdash_\mathcal{A} d$ and d is the projection of a well-formed configuration d', then $c' \vdash_{\mathcal{A}'} d'$ for some well-formed configuration c' whose projection is c. This gives us an accepting run of $\mathcal{A}'$ on the same word, proving that $L(\mathcal{A}') \supseteq L(\mathcal{A})$. ∎

Solution to Problem 127

We will say that a transition

$$q, a, Z \rightarrow q', \alpha$$

is *short* if $|\alpha| \leq 2$. We claim that each transition can be replaced by a sequence of short transitions, without introducing new states. To ensure that the sequence of transitions is executed correctly, we introduce new stack symbols. Take a transition

$$q, a, Z \rightarrow q', Z_1 Z_2 \ldots Z_k.$$

Extend the stack alphabet with fresh stack symbols $Y_0, Y_1, \ldots, Y_k$ (specific for this transition only); the intuition is that Y_i stands for $Z_1 Z_2 \ldots Z_i$. Replace the original transition by the following transitions:

$$q, a, Z \to q', Y_k,$$
$$q', \varepsilon, Y_i \to q', Y_{i-1} Z_i \quad \text{for } i \in \{1, \ldots, k\},$$
$$q', \varepsilon, Y_0 \to q', \varepsilon. \qquad \blacksquare$$

Solution to Problem 128

Let us fix a pushdown automaton $\mathcal{A}$. Suppose first that we do not aim at reducing the number of states. As explained in Problem 126, we can assume without loss of generality that no transition of $\mathcal{A}$ removes the initial symbol from the stack. Each transition replaces the topmost stack symbol Z with symbols $Z_1 Z_2 \ldots Z_n$. Equally well we can do that with a sequence of transitions: the first transition pops Z, and the following transitions push symbols $Z_n, Z_{n-1}, \ldots, Z_1$. Unlike in Problem 127, we use fresh states (not fresh stack symbols) to ensure that the new transitions are executed as intended. To replace the transition

$$q, a, Z \to q', Z_1 \ldots Z_k,$$

we take fresh states $p_1, \ldots, p_k$ (specific for this transition only), let $p_0 = q'$, and introduce the following new transitions:

$$q, a, Z \to p_k, \varepsilon,$$
$$p_i, \varepsilon, Y \to p_{i-1}, Z_i Y \quad \text{for } i \in \{1, \ldots, k\}, Y \in \Gamma.$$

If we want to limit the number of states, the task becomes harder. Notice that the construction described in Problem 126 replaces push transitions with non-push transitions: the new transitions not only push a new symbol, but also replace the previously topmost symbol. Below we present a construction yielding a four-state automaton with only push and pop transitions.

By the simple construction described above we may assume that $\mathcal{A}$ has only push and pop transitions, and never removes the initial stack symbol. We first construct an equivalent pushdown automaton $\mathcal{A}'$ such that each word it accepts can also be accepted by a run in which each pushed stack symbol is topmost in at most three configurations; that is, by a run

$$(q_0, w_0, \gamma_0), (q_1, w_1, \gamma_1), \ldots, (q_m, w_m, \gamma_m)$$

that has no four indices $0 \le k < l < r < s \le m$ such that $\gamma_k = \gamma_l = \gamma_r = \gamma_s$, and γ_k is a suffix of γ_i for all $i \in \{k, k+1, \ldots, s\}$. We say that such run has the ≤ 3 property.

In order to ensure this property, we allow the automaton to copy every stack symbol arbitrarily many times. When $\mathcal{A}'$ sees a (particular copy) of a stack symbol at the top of the stack for the second time, it duplicates it. Since the new copy is now seen as the topmost stack symbol for the first time, we can continue. The third time is reserved for popping the symbol. A single pop of the original automaton is implemented by a sequence of pops of all the copies of the original symbol; to indicate when the sequence should end, we mark the original symbol. Thus, the new stack alphabet is $\Gamma' = \Gamma \times \{0, 1\}$, where Γ is the stack alphabet of $\mathcal{A}$; stack symbol $(Z, 0)$ denotes the original of the symbol Z, and $(Z, 1)$ denotes an additional copy of that symbol. The new initial stack symbol is $(Z_I, 0)$ where Z_I is the initial stack symbol of $\mathcal{A}$. The set of states remains unchanged. For every push transition $q, a, Z \to q', YZ$ of $\mathcal{A}$, and every $i \in \{0, 1\}$, we add to $\mathcal{A}'$ the transition

$$q, a, (Z, i) \to q', (Y, 0)(Z, i).$$

For every pop transition $q, a, Z \to q', \varepsilon$ of $\mathcal{A}$ we add to $\mathcal{A}'$ the transition

$$q, a, (Z, 0) \to q', \varepsilon.$$

Additionally, for every $q \in Q$, $Z \in \Gamma$, and $i \in \{0, 1\}$, we add to $\mathcal{A}'$ the transitions that allow one to add and remove copies of the topmost symbol:

$$q, \varepsilon, (Z, i) \to q, (Z, 1)(Z, i),$$
$$q, \varepsilon, (Z, 1) \to q, \varepsilon.$$

It is easy to see that $L(\mathcal{A}') = L(\mathcal{A})$. Moreover, every word of $L(\mathcal{A}')$ can be accepted by a run having the ≤ 3 property thanks to the already mentioned strategy: whenever we see some stack symbol as the topmost one for the second time, and we are not going to pop it, then we create a new copy of this symbol.

Next, we transform $\mathcal{A}'$ to an equivalent four-state automaton $\mathcal{A}''$ with only push and pop transitions. The construction is based on that in Problem 126. The difference is that having access only to push and pop operations, we cannot modify the current state written in the topmost stack symbol. But thanks to the ≤ 3 property, every symbol is topmost only in three configurations; we can guess all three states of these configurations already when creating this symbol. To remember which of these three states is the current one, we shall use the states of $\mathcal{A}''$.

Thus, the automaton $\mathcal{A}''$ has states $\{p_1, p_2, p_3, p_F\}$, where p_1 is initial and p_F is accepting. The new stack alphabet is $Q^3 \times \Gamma' \times Q \times \{2, 3\}$, where Q and Γ' are the set of states and the stack alphabet of $\mathcal{A}'$. The new initial stack symbol is $(q_I, q_I, q_I, Z'_I, q_I, 2)$, where q_I and Z'_I are the initial state and the initial stack symbol of $\mathcal{A}'$ (only the first and fourth coordinates are relevant). A stack symbol $(q_1, q_2, q_3, Z, q_r, i)$ enriches the original stack symbol Z with four states and an index. The states q_1, q_2, and q_3 are three states in which the symbol will be topmost during the run. The state q_r is the state in which this symbol is popped. When this happens, the symbol below becomes topmost; consequently, q_r must appear among the first three states of the symbol below. Since the first of these states is the one in which the symbol below gets pushed, q_r is either the second or the third; this is indicated by i.

Let us now describe the transitions of $\mathcal{A}''$. We add a push transition

$$p_i, a, (q_1, q_2, q_3, Z, q_r, j) \rightarrow p_1, (q_1', q_2', q_3', Y, q_{i+1}, i+1)(q_1, q_2, q_3, Z, q_r, j)$$

whenever there is a transition $q_i, a, Z \rightarrow q_1', YZ$ in $\mathcal{A}'$ for $i \in \{1, 2\}$, and a pop transition

$$p_i, a, (q_1, q_2, q_3, Z, q_r, j) \rightarrow p_j, \varepsilon$$

whenever there is a transition $q_i, a, Z \rightarrow q_r, \varepsilon$ in $\mathcal{A}'$ for $i \in \{1, 2, 3\}$. We also add a transition that allows the automaton $\mathcal{A}$ to accept whenever the state of $\mathcal{A}'$ is accepting:

$$p_i, a, (q_1, q_2, q_3, Z, q_r, j) \rightarrow p_F, \varepsilon$$

whenever q_i is accepting in $\mathcal{A}'$.

Consider a configuration c of the automaton $\mathcal{A}''$, given as

$$c = (p_i, w, (q_{1,1}, q_{1,2}, q_{1,3}, Z_1, q_{1,r}, j_1) \ldots (q_{m,1}, q_{m,2}, q_{m,3}, Z_m, q_{m,r}, j_m)).$$

We say that c is *well formed* if $m \geq 1$ and $q_{k,r} = q_{k+1, j_k}$ for all $1 \leq k < m$. The *projection* of c is the configuration $(q_{1,i}, w, Z_1 Z_2 \ldots Z_m)$ of $\mathcal{A}'$.

The proof that $L(\mathcal{A}'') \subseteq L(\mathcal{A}')$ is straightforward: we see that every reachable configuration of $\mathcal{A}''$ (except accepting configurations with state p_F) is well formed, and that transitions of $\mathcal{A}''$ project to transitions of $\mathcal{A}'$.

In order to prove that $L(\mathcal{A}'') \supseteq L(\mathcal{A}')$, for every word in $L(\mathcal{A}')$ we have to consider a run of $\mathcal{A}'$ on that word that has the ≤ 3 property; such a run exists by the definition of $\mathcal{A}'$. Then, while creating a stack symbol, we have to annotate it by the three states in which it will be seen as the topmost stack symbol, and by the state in which it will be popped; if the stack symbol will be topmost fewer than three times, or will never be popped, we can put arbitrary states in the corresponding positions. It is not difficult to show that this leads to an accepting run of $\mathcal{A}''$.

Is it possible to reduce further the number of states? We conjecture that the language

$$\{a^k \$ a^l \$ a^l \$ a^m \$ a^m \$ a^k \$: k, l, m \in \mathbb{N}\}$$

cannot be recognized by a three-state pushdown automaton with push and pop transitions only. ∎

Solution to Problem 129

Let us fix a pushdown automaton $\mathcal{A} = (\Sigma, \Gamma, Q, q_I, Z_I, \delta, F)$ recognizing the language L.

(1) A first idea might be to make every state accepting. This is incorrect, because such an automaton accepts any word for which there exists a run, without checking if this run can be extended to reach an accepting state. Instead, the automaton should guess a suitable extension of the input word and check that it leads to acceptance. The automaton works in two phases. In the first phase, it processes the input word just like the original automaton $\mathcal{A}$, but at any moment it can move to the second phase. In the second phase, the automaton behaves almost like $\mathcal{A}$, but instead of reading letters from the input, it guesses them. Thus, the new set of states is $Q \times \{1, 2\}$, the initial state is $(q_I, 1)$, and the set of accepting states is $F \times \{2\}$; the stack alphabet remains unchanged. For every transition $q, a, Z \to q', \gamma$ of $\mathcal{A}$, the constructed automaton has two transitions:

$$(q, 1), a, Z \to (q', 1), \gamma,$$
$$(q, 2), \varepsilon, Z \to (q', 2), \gamma.$$

Additionally, for all $q \in Q$ and $Z \in \Gamma$ we include the transition

$$(q, 1), \varepsilon, Z \to (q, 2), Z,$$

which corresponds to moving from the first phase to the second phase.

(2) The solution is obtained by swapping the two phases described in item (1): in the first phase the letters are guessed, and in the second phase they are read from the input.

(3) Here we use three phases: in the first and third phase letters are guessed, and in the second phase they are read from the input. ∎

Solution to Problem 130

(1) The language $L = \{a^n b^n : n \in \mathbb{N}\}$ is context-free and not regular. The set of infixes of words from L is simply $a^* b^*$.

(2) The language $L = \{ca^n b^n c : n \in \mathbb{N}\}$ is also context-free and not regular. But the set of infixes of words from L is not regular, because its intersection with the regular language $ca^* b^* c$ is equal to L itself. ∎

Solution to Problem 131

Let us fix a pushdown automaton $\mathcal{A} = (\Sigma, \Gamma, Q, q_I, Z_I, \delta, F)$ recognizing the language L. The idea is very simple: we just run $\mathcal{A}$ backwards. The only difficulty is that the definition of a pushdown automaton is not symmetric, so we have to work out some details. Without loss of generality we can assume that in the pushdown automaton $\mathcal{A}$ recognizing L every transition is a push or a pop transition, and none of them adds or removes the initial stack symbol (see Problem 128). Additionally, we assume that $\mathcal{A}$ accepts only in configurations in which the stack consists solely of the initial stack symbol. In order to obtain that, we add two new states q_{erase} and q_F; the state q_F becomes the only accepting state. From any state that was accepting previously, we add an ε-transition to the state q_{erase}. In this state the automaton pops from the stack every symbol other than the initial one. When only the initial stack symbol remains, the automaton moves to the state q_F and accepts.

In the sequel we assume that the pushdown automaton $\mathcal{A}$ recognizing L satisfies these assumptions. As the set of states of the pushdown automaton recognizing L^R we take $Q \cup \{q_I'\}$, where q_I' is a fresh initial state. We make q_I the unique accepting state. The stack alphabet is $\Gamma \times \Gamma$, with (Z_I, Z_I) being the initial symbol. In a stack symbol $(Z, Z') \in \Gamma \times \Gamma$ we remember not only the current stack symbol Z, but also the symbol Z' just below. From the new initial state q_I' we can transit to any accepting state of $\mathcal{A}$:

$$q_I', \varepsilon, (Z_I, Z_I) \rightarrow q, (Z_I, Z_I) \quad \text{if } q \in F.$$

Then, for every push transition $q, a, Z \rightarrow q', YZ$ of $\mathcal{A}$ we create the transition

$$q', a, (Y, Z) \rightarrow q, \varepsilon,$$

and for every pop transition $q, a, Z \rightarrow q', \varepsilon$ of $\mathcal{A}$ and every $(Y, Y') \in \Gamma \times \Gamma$ we create the transition

$$q', a, (Y, Y') \rightarrow q, (Z, Y)(Y, Y').$$

Notice that the stack of every reachable configuration of the resulting automaton is of the form $(Z_1, Z_2)(Z_2, Z_3)(Z_3, Z_4) \ldots (Z_{k-1}, Z_k)$. Knowing this, it is easy to prove that the resulting automaton simulates accepting runs of $\mathcal{A}$ backwards.   ∎

Solution to Problem 132

Let us fix a pushdown automaton $\mathcal{A} = (\Sigma, \Gamma, Q, q_I, Z_I, \delta, F)$ recognizing the language L. In order to find words vw such that wv is accepted by $\mathcal{A}$, we should take some configuration (q, v, γ), run $\mathcal{A}$ from that configuration until it accepts v, then run $\mathcal{A}$ on w from the initial configuration (q_I, w, Z_I), and check that it indeed ends in the configuration (q, ε, γ). The key difficulty is to ensure that the initial stack contents equals the final stack contents. The idea is to generate and record the initial stack contents γ on the fly. We imagine that the automaton starts with γ on the stack, but in reality we have on the stack nothing but two copies of the topmost symbol of γ: one for the automaton to consume, and one for the record. Then, whenever $\mathcal{A}$ makes the stack empty (except for the copies kept for the record), we guess the next symbol of γ, and we put it on the stack, along with its copy for the record just below. Assuming that the original automaton $\mathcal{A}$ always empties its stack before accepting, when the simulated run of $\mathcal{A}$ accepts v, on the stack we have the original stack contents γ, reversed. In the second phase we proceed symmetrically: when we run $\mathcal{A}$ on w from the initial configuration, and it wants to push a symbol, we guess whether this symbol will be popped while processing w or not. As long as we guess that it will be popped before w ends, we just push it. Assume that at some point we guess for the first time that the symbol will not be popped. That is, it forms part of γ. Notice that such a choice makes sense only if the stack contains no symbols that will be popped. That means that the stack contains only the reversed copy of γ. In particular, the topmost symbol on the stack is the initial symbol of $\mathcal{A}$ and the one below is the first symbol pushed by $\mathcal{A}$ that is not popped while processing w. This is exactly the symbol that $\mathcal{A}$ wants to push just now. We can update our copy of γ by popping one symbol. This way we maintain the invariant that the topmost remaining symbol of the copy of γ is the most recently pushed symbol never to be popped.

To simplify the details of the construction, we assume the following:

- every transition of $\mathcal{A}$ is a push or a pop transition;
- no transition of $\mathcal{A}$ adds or removes the initial stack symbol; and
- in all reachable accepting configurations of $\mathcal{A}$, the stack contains only the initial symbol.

The new stack alphabet is $(\Gamma \times \{\uparrow, \downarrow\}) \cup \{Z'_I\}$, where Z'_I is the new initial stack symbol. For each Z, the stack symbol $(Z, \uparrow)$ is used to represent the actual stack of $\mathcal{A}$, while $(Z, \downarrow)$ is used to indicate recorded copies of guessed symbols Z. The set of states is

$$\{q'_I, q_{F,1}, q_{F,2}\} \cup (Q \times \{1, 2\} \times Q) \cup (Q \times Q \times \Gamma),$$

where q'_I is initial and $q_{F,2}$ is accepting. A state (p, i, q) represents a situation when $\mathcal{A}$ was started from state p (and thus it should end in that state), its current state is q, and we are in phase i. The remaining states are auxiliary.

In the beginning, we guess the state and the topmost stack symbol of the configuration in which $\mathcal{A}$ will start:

$$q'_I, \varepsilon, Z'_I \to (q, 1, q), (Z, \uparrow)(Z, \downarrow)Z'_I \quad \text{for } q \in Q, Z \in \Gamma.$$

In both phases, transitions directly simulating transitions of $\mathcal{A}$ are available: for every pop transition $q, a, Z \to q', \varepsilon$ of $\mathcal{A}$ we have transitions

$$(p, i, q), a, (Z, \uparrow) \to (p, i, q'), \varepsilon \quad \text{for } p \in Q, i \in \{1, 2\};$$

for every push transition $q, a, Z \to q', Z'Z$ of $\mathcal{A}$ we have transitions

$$(p, i, q), a, (Z, \uparrow) \to (p, i, q'), (Z', \uparrow)(Z, \uparrow) \quad \text{for } p \in Q, i \in \{1, 2\}$$

and additionally

$$(p, 2, q), a, (Z, \downarrow) \to (p, 2, q'), (Z', \uparrow)(Z, \downarrow) \quad \text{for } p \in Q,$$

in the second phase, to give access to the most recent symbol pushed by $\mathcal{A}$ that will never be popped again (initially, Z_I).

In the first phase, whenever $\mathcal{A}$ uses up the stack symbols guessed so far, we may guess one more stack symbol:

$$(p, 1, q), \varepsilon, (Z, \downarrow) \to (p, 1, q), (Y, \uparrow)(Y, \downarrow)(Z, \downarrow) \quad \text{for } p, q \in Q, Y, Z \in \Gamma.$$

In the second phase we proceed dually: whenever we see the topmost symbol Z of the reversed copy of γ, instead of pushing Y we can pop $(Z, \downarrow)$ and check if the uncovered symbol is $(Y, \downarrow)$. That is, for every push transition $q, a, Z \to q', YZ$ of $\mathcal{A}$ we create transitions

$$
\begin{aligned}
(p, 2, q), a, (Z, \downarrow) &\to (p, q', Y), \varepsilon & \text{for } p \in Q, \\
(p, q', Y), \varepsilon, (Y, \downarrow) &\to (p, 2, q'), (Y, \downarrow) & \text{for } p \in Q, Y \in \Gamma.
\end{aligned}
$$

We transit from the first phase to the second phase when the state is accepting, and we see $(Z_I, \uparrow)$ on the top of the stack. Since Z_I is never pushed or popped by $\mathcal{A}$, we may be sure that there are no more stack symbols with $\uparrow$ below $(Z_I, \uparrow)$. We then pop $(Z_I, \uparrow)$ to uncover the topmost symbol of the reversed copy of γ and continue from the initial state of $\mathcal{A}$:

$$(p, 1, q), \varepsilon, (Z_I, \uparrow) \to (p, 2, q_I), \varepsilon \quad \text{for } p \in Q, q \in F.$$

We can finish the second phase and accept if the state is the same as in the beginning, and if we have used up the reversed copy of γ:

$$
\begin{aligned}
(q, 1, q), \varepsilon, (Z, \downarrow) &\to q_{F,1}, \varepsilon \quad \text{for } q \in Q, Z \in \Gamma, \\
q_{F,1}, \varepsilon, Z_I' &\to q_{F,2}, Z_I'.
\end{aligned}
$$

It is not difficult to check that the resulting pushdown automaton indeed recognizes $\text{Cycle}(L)$. ∎

Solution to Problem 133

Let $\mathcal{A} = (\Sigma, \Gamma, P, p_I, Z_I, \delta, E)$ be the pushdown automaton recognizing L, and let $\mathcal{B} = (\Sigma, Q, q_I, \eta, F)$ be the finite automaton recognizing K.

(1) The automaton recognizing $L \cap K$, while reading an input word, has to simultaneously trace the configuration of $\mathcal{A}$ and the state of $\mathcal{B}$. This is achieved by the product construction. The set of states is $P \times Q$, with initial state (p_I, q_I) and the set of final states $E \times F$. Let $p, a, Z \rightarrow p', \gamma$ be a transition of $\mathcal{A}$. If $a = \varepsilon$, the state of $\mathcal{B}$ remains unchanged; that is, for every state q of $\mathcal{B}$ we create the transition

$$(p, q), \varepsilon, Z \rightarrow (p', q), \gamma .$$

If $a \in \Sigma$, for every transition $q \xrightarrow{a} q'$ of $\mathcal{B}$ we create the transition

$$(p, q), a, Z \rightarrow (p', q'), \gamma .$$

Since both $\mathcal{A}$ and $\mathcal{B}$ have to (independently) accept the input word, the constructed automaton indeed recognizes $L \cap K$.

Context-free languages are not closed under intersection, for instance,

$$\left\{ a^n b^n c^k : n, k \in \mathbb{N} \right\} \cap \left\{ a^k b^n c^n : n, k \in \mathbb{N} \right\} = \left\{ a^n b^n c^n : n \in \mathbb{N} \right\},$$

which is not a context-free language by Problem 103.

(2) Here we have to combine the above construction with Problem 129(1). The pushdown automaton proceeds in two phases. In the first phase it faithfully simulates $\mathcal{A}$, but at an arbitrary moment it can move to the second phase. In the second phase it guesses an extension of the input word, letter by letter, and checks that it is accepted by $\mathcal{B}$ from the initial state and by $\mathcal{A}$ from the last configuration of the first phase; that is, the automaton no longer reads symbols from the input, but it guesses them and simulates both $\mathcal{A}$ and $\mathcal{B}$ on the guessed symbols, using the product construction.

As the set of states we take $P \cup (P \times Q)$ with initial state p_I and the set of final states $E \times F$. Let $p, a, Z \rightarrow p', \gamma$ be a transition of $\mathcal{A}$. Then, we have the same transition in the constructed automaton for the first phase:

$$p, a, Z \rightarrow p', \gamma.$$

We also create transitions of the second phase: if $a = \varepsilon$, for every $q \in Q$ we create the transition

$$(p, q), \varepsilon, Z \rightarrow (p', q), \gamma ,$$

and if $a \in \Sigma$, for every transition $q \xrightarrow{a} q'$ of $\mathcal{B}$ we create the transition

$$(p, q), \varepsilon, Z \rightarrow (p', q'), \gamma .$$

Additionally, for all $p \in P$ and $Z \in \Gamma$ we allow the automaton to change the phase:

$$p, \varepsilon, Z \to (p, q_I), Z.$$

For the case when K is context-free, see item (3).

(3)   The construction is entirely analogous to that in item (2), except that in the first phase the letters are guessed and fed to $\mathcal{A}$ and $\mathcal{B}$, and in the second phase they are read and fed to $\mathcal{A}$.

Now suppose K is assumed to be only context-free, instead of regular. Consider the languages

$$L = \left\{ a^n b a^{2n} b \colon n \in \mathbb{N} \right\}^* \left\{ a^n b b a^{2n} \colon n \in \mathbb{N} \right\}$$

and

$$K = ab \left\{ a^n b a^n b \ \colon \ n \in \mathbb{N} \right\}^* b.$$

Then, $K^{-1}L = \left\{ a^{2^n} \ \colon \ n \geq 1 \right\}$, which is not context-free.

Notice that $K^{-1}L = (L^R(K^R)^{-1})^R$. Since context-free languages are closed under reverse, it follows that item (2) fails as well when K is only assumed to be context-free.   ∎

Solution to Problem 134

(1)   This language is regular. What we have to remember after reading a prefix w is the triple

$$(\#_a(w) - min(w), \quad \#_b(w) - min(w), \quad \#_c(w) - min(w)).$$

Note that one of the three coordinates is always 0. The numbers in this triple can be easily updated after reading a single letter. Moreover a word u should be rejected if after reading some prefix of it some coordinate in the triple exceeds 2017. In this case, we no longer have to keep the triple; we can simply reject the word immediately. Hence, we can take $\{0, \ldots, 2017\}^3$ as the set of states of the finite automaton.

(2)   This language is not regular. The reason is that the condition

$$max(w) - med(w) \leq 2017$$

does not limit the differences between $\#_a(w)$, $\#_b(w)$, and $\#_c(w)$. It may be the case that the number of c's is initially very small, but later we have so many c's that the number of c's actually matters for the inequality. Consider for instance the intersection of the discussed language with the regular language $(ab)^*c^*$. The resulting language $\{(ab)^m c^n \ \colon \ n \leq 2017 + m\}$ is clearly not regular, and it should be if the original were.

On the other hand, the discussed language is context-free. For a prefix w it is enough to remember the pair

$$(max(w) - med(w), \quad med(w) - min(w)),$$

along with the information about which of $\#_a(w)$, $\#_b(w)$, and $\#_c(w)$ is the smallest and which is the greatest. Whenever $max(w) - med(w)$ exceeds 2017 we can immediately reject, so this component can be stored in the state. The second component, $med(w) - min(w)$, can grow arbitrarily, but we can store it on the stack in unary, as the number of copies of a fixed stack symbol. It is easy to update the described information when a letter is read from the input. ∎

Solution to Problem 135

First, let us modify $\mathcal{A}$ into a pushdown automaton $\mathcal{A}'$ that reads at each step the transition used in that step. More precisely, every transition $r = (q, a, Z \rightarrow q', \gamma)$ of $\mathcal{A}$ is replaced by the transition $q, r, Z \rightarrow q', \gamma$ in $\mathcal{A}'$. Let L' be the language recognized by $\mathcal{A}'$. For $u \in L'$, let $\pi(u)$ be the corresponding word read by $\mathcal{A}$; that is, if u is $r_1 \ldots r_k$ with $r_i = (q_i, a_i, Z_i \rightarrow q'_i, \gamma_i)$ then $\pi(u)$ is $a_1 \ldots a_k$; notice that some of the a_i's may be ε. We have that $L(\mathcal{A}) = \{\pi(u) : u \in L'\}$. We want to exhibit a constant C such that for every non-empty word $w \in L(\mathcal{A})$ there is a word $u \in L'$ of length at most $C \cdot |w|$ such that $\pi(u) = w$.

To achieve this we pass to context-free grammars, which allows us to use the bound on the length of derivations from Problem 98. Let $\mathcal{G}'$ be a context-free grammar generating the language L'. The set of terminals of $\mathcal{G}'$ is precisely the set of transitions of the automaton $\mathcal{A}$. Let $\mathcal{G}$ be a context-free grammar obtained from $\mathcal{G}'$ by turning each terminal symbol $r = (q, a, Z \rightarrow q', \gamma)$ into a non-terminal and adding rule $r \rightarrow a$; the set of terminals of $\mathcal{G}$ is the input alphabet of $\mathcal{A}$. Clearly, $\mathcal{G}$ generates $L(\mathcal{A})$. By Problem 98, there exists a constant C_1 such that for each non-empty w generated by $\mathcal{G}$ there is a derivation of length at most $C_1 \cdot |w|$. Let l be the maximal length of the right-hand side of a rule in $\mathcal{G}$. We will show that for every non-empty word $w \in L(\mathcal{G})$ there exists a word $u \in L(\mathcal{G}')$ of length at most $l \cdot C_1 \cdot |w|$ such that $\pi(u) = w$.

Consider a non-empty word $w \in L(\mathcal{G})$ and a derivation of w of length at most $C_1 \cdot |w|$. This derivation can be presented as a derivation tree D. Each step of the derivation produces at most l new nodes in D; accounting for the root we infer that the size of D is at most $l \cdot C_1 \cdot |w| + 1$. By the construction of $\mathcal{G}$, each node in D that is labelled with a transition $r = (q, a, Z \rightarrow q', \gamma)$ has a unique child: a leaf with label a. Let D' be obtained from D by cutting off the unique children of all nodes labelled with transitions of $\mathcal{A}$. It follows easily from the way $\mathcal{G}$ was constructed that D' is a derivation tree of $\mathcal{G}'$ and that it yields a word

u such that $\pi(u) = w$. Because D' was obtained from D by cutting off nodes, the size of D' is also bounded by $l \cdot C_1 \cdot |w| + 1$. As each leaf of D' yields at most one letter of u and the root of D' is not a leaf, we obtain $|u| \leq l \cdot C_1 \cdot |w|$. ∎

Solution to Problem 136

Basically, we have to trace the automaton $\mathcal{A}$ and see what stack contents it can create while reaching some configuration c. When $\mathcal{A}$ pushes something on the stack, there are two possibilities. One possibility is that the pushed symbols will be still present on the stack in the considered configuration c. Then the finite automaton we are going to create can simply read these stack symbols from the input. Another possibility is that the pushed symbols will be removed before reaching the configuration c. In this case we are not interested in the part of the run between pushing these symbols and removing them again; we only need to know in which state the pushdown automaton will be after removing those symbols, so that we can continue the run. Fortunately, the set of possible resulting states does not depend on the stack contents below the currently topmost symbol, so it is a finite amount of information.

Let us describe the construction of the finite automaton. A sequence of configurations $(q_0, w_0, \gamma_0), (q_1, w_1, \gamma_1), \ldots, (q_m, w_m, \gamma_m)$ is called a *partial run* of $\mathcal{A}$ if $(q_i, w_i, \gamma_i) \vdash_{\mathcal{A}} (q_{i+1}, w_{i+1}, \gamma_{i+1})$ for all $i < m$ (it differs from a run in that (q_0, w_0, γ_0) need not be an initial configuration). For $\gamma \in \Gamma^*$, we say that this partial run *stays over* γ if γ is a proper suffix of γ_i for all $i < m$ (it follows that γ is a suffix of γ_m, possibly not proper). We define the set $R \subseteq Q \times \Gamma \times Q$ of *returns*: we have $(p, Z, q) \in R$ if $(p, w, Z) \vdash_{\mathcal{A}}^* (q, v, \varepsilon)$ for some $w, v \in \Sigma^*$. For every stack contents $\gamma \in \Gamma^*$ we have the key property that $(p, Z, q) \in R$ if and only if for some $w, v \in \Sigma^*$ there is a partial run from $(p, w, Z\gamma)$ to (q, v, γ) that stays over γ.

Let L_1 be the language of words that are the possible contents of the stack of $\mathcal{A}$. We now define a finite automaton $\mathcal{B}$ recognizing L_1^R; that is, $\mathcal{B}$ reads the stack contents from the bottom, not from the top. This suffices to show that L_1 is regular. We let the automaton have words on transitions, but it can be easily turned into a standard finite automaton by introducing intermediate states and eliminating ε-transitions. As the set of states of $\mathcal{B}$ we take $(Q \times \Gamma) \cup \{q_F\}$, with (q_I, Z_I) being the initial state and q_F being accepting. Consider a transition $q, a, Z \to q_1, Z_1 \ldots Z_k$ of $\mathcal{A}$. For all $j \in \{1, \ldots, k\}$ and all $q_2, \ldots, q_j \in Q$ such that $(q_i, Z_i, q_{i+1}) \in R$ for all $i \in \{1, \ldots, j-1\}$, we create the transition $((q, Z), Z_k Z_{k-1} \ldots Z_{j+1}, (q_j, Z_j))$ in $\mathcal{B}$. Notice that for $j = k$ the word $Z_k Z_{k-1} \ldots Z_{j+1}$ is empty; for $j = 1$ we have no additional states nor do we consider any returns, we just have $q_j = q_1$; finally, for $k = 0$ we create no transitions. Additionally, for all $q \in Q$ and $Z \in \Gamma$ we add the transition

$((q, Z), Z, q_F)$ that accepts after reading additionally the topmost stack symbol. It is straightforward to see that $\mathcal{B}$ indeed recognizes L_1^R.

Quite similarly we can recognize the languages L_2 of all stack contents (not necessarily reachable in a run) from which $\mathcal{A}$ can reach an accepting configuration. Besides returns, we also need to consider a set $S \subseteq Q \times \Gamma$ of accepting suffixes: we have $(p, Z) \in S$ if $(p, w, Z) \vdash^*_{\mathcal{A}} (q, \varepsilon, \gamma')$ for some $w \in \Sigma^*$, $\gamma' \in \Gamma^*$, and some accepting state $q \in F$. For each stack contents $\gamma \in \Gamma^*$ we have the property that $(p, Z) \in S$ if and only if for some $w \in \Sigma^*$, $\gamma' \in \Gamma^*$, and $q \in F$ there is a partial run from $(p, w, Z\gamma)$ to $(q, \varepsilon, \gamma'\gamma)$ that stays over γ.

This time we read the stack from the top, that is, we create a finite automaton $\mathcal{C}$ recognizing directly L_2. Its set of states is $Q \cup \{q_F\}$, with q_I remaining the initial state and q_F being accepting. For every return $(p, Z, q) \in R$ we create a transition (p, Z, q) that reads from input the next stack symbol and performs a return removing this symbol from the stack. Additionally, for every accepting suffix $(p, Z) \in S$ we create a transition (p, Z, q_F) that accepts after reading the next stack symbol. We also add a transition (q_F, Z, q_F) for every $Z \in \Gamma$, as we can have arbitrary stack symbols below the part actually analysed by $\mathcal{A}$.

Finally, consider the language of words that are possible stack contents in accepting runs of $\mathcal{A}$. It is clearly the intersection of the regular languages L_1 and L_2; hence, it is also regular. ∎

Solution to Problem 137

We present a solution given by a student, Adam Wilczyński. Let $\mathcal{A}$ be a deterministic pushdown automaton recognizing the language from the problem statement. We shall use it to construct a (deterministic) pushdown automaton $\mathcal{B}$ recognizing $\{a^n b^n a^n : n \in \mathbb{N}\}$, a language that is not context-free, thus reaching a contradiction. The automaton $\mathcal{B}$ simulates $\mathcal{A}$ in two phases. In the first phase directly, and in the second phase with the roles of a and b swapped. It moves from the first phase to the second phase when it first visits an accepting state of $\mathcal{A}$ after reading at least one letter from the input. It accepts when it first reaches an accepting state of $\mathcal{A}$ after reading at least one letter in the second phase.

More precisely, the set of states of $\mathcal{B}$ is $Q \times \{1, 2\} \times \{0, 1\}$, where the second component is the phase number and the third component indicates if the automaton has already read a letter from the input during the current phase. The initial state is $(q_I, 1, 0)$, where q_I is the initial state of $\mathcal{A}$. Let $q, \sigma, Z \to q', \gamma$ be a transition in $\mathcal{A}$. Then, in the first phase, $\mathcal{B}$ has transitions

$$(q, 1, j), \sigma, Z \to (q', 1, j'), \gamma,$$

where $j \in \{0, 1\}$, $j' = j$ if $\sigma = \varepsilon$, and $j' = 1$ if $\sigma \in \{a, b\}$. The only exception is when $j = 1$ and q' is accepting, because this is the moment to change phase:

$$(q, 1, 1), \sigma, Z \to (q', 2, 0), \gamma.$$

In the second phase we swap the roles of a and b: the transitions are

$$(q, 2, j), \sigma', Z \to (q', 2, j'), \gamma,$$

where j and j' are as before, and either $\{\sigma, \sigma'\} = \{a, b\}$ or $\sigma' = \sigma = \varepsilon$. This time there are no exceptions. As accepting states of $\mathcal{B}$ we take $(q, 2, 1)$ for all accepting states q of $\mathcal{A}$, as well as $(q_I, 1, 0)$ to ensure that the empty word is accepted.

We claim that $\mathcal{B}$ recognizes $\{a^n b^n a^n : n \in \mathbb{N}\}$. Consider an accepting run of $\mathcal{B}$. The prefix of the word at the moment of changing phases is accepted by $\mathcal{A}$, and no shorter non-empty prefix is accepted by $\mathcal{A}$, so this prefix must be of the form $a^n b^n$. The whole word, after swapping a and b in the second part, is longer and once again accepted by $\mathcal{A}$, so it must be of the form $a^n b^n b^n$. Then, the word accepted by $\mathcal{B}$ is of the form $a^n b^n a^n$. The converse implication follows straight from the construction.

It is essential for correctness that $\mathcal{A}$ is deterministic. Indeed, in an arbitrary pushdown automaton $\mathcal{A}$ an accepting run on $a^n b^{2n}$ need not pass through an accepting state after reading the prefix $a^n b^n$. However, because $\mathcal{A}$ is deterministic, the accepting run on $a^n b^n$ is necessarily a prefix of the accepting run on $a^n b^{2n}$. ∎

Solution to Problem 138

Let $\mathcal{A}$ be a deterministic pushdown automaton recognizing the language of palindromes over $\{a, b\}$. We shall construct a (deterministic) pushdown automaton $\mathcal{B}$ recognizing $L = \{ba^n ba^n ba^n ba^n b : n \geq 1\}$. In the state, $\mathcal{B}$ remembers the state of $\mathcal{A}$, the information whether $\mathcal{A}$ has passed through an accepting state after reading the last input symbol, and the state of a deterministic finite automaton $\mathcal{C}$ recognizing the regular language $ba^+ ba^+ ba^+ ba^+ b$. We basically run both $\mathcal{A}$ and $\mathcal{C}$ in parallel. However, after reading a word in $ba^+ ba^+ b$, we allow the next a to be read only if $\mathcal{A}$ has passed through an accepting state after reading the last input symbol. This means that at that moment we require that the prefix read so far was of the form $ba^n ba^n b$. At the end we accept if both $\mathcal{A}$ and $\mathcal{C}$ accept. Because $\mathcal{C}$ accepts, the word is of the form $ba^i ba^j ba^k ba^l b$. Because the first part was accepted by $\mathcal{A}$, we get $i = j$. And because the whole input word is also accepted by $\mathcal{A}$, it is also a palindrome, which gives $i = j = k = l$. This gives us a contradiction, since the language L is not context-free. ∎

Solution to Problem 139

Consider $L = \{a^n b^m c^m \$\$ d^{3n} : m, n \in \mathbb{N}\}$. It is easy to see that this is a context-free language: it is recognized by a pushdown automaton that pushes onto the stack three a's whenever it reads a and one b when it reads b, and then it pops one b when reading c and one a when reading d. We show that $\frac{1}{2}L$ is not context-free.

Towards a contradiction, suppose $\frac{1}{2}L$ is context-free. Let N be the constant from the pumping lemma and fix $n > N$. Then $a^n b^n c^n \$\$ d^{3n} \in L$ and hence

$$w = a^n b^n c^n \$ \in \tfrac{1}{2}L.$$

By the pumping lemma there is a factorization

$$w = \textit{prefix} \cdot \textit{left} \cdot \textit{infix} \cdot \textit{right} \cdot \textit{suffix}$$

such that $|\textit{left} \cdot \textit{infix} \cdot \textit{right}| \leq N$ and for every k,

$$w_k = \textit{prefix} \cdot \textit{left}^k \cdot \textit{infix} \cdot \textit{right}^k \cdot \textit{suffix} \in \tfrac{1}{2}L.$$

From the definition of L and $\frac{1}{2}L$ it follows that $\textit{left}, \textit{right} \in a^* + b^* + c^*$.

If $\textit{left} \cdot \textit{right}$ contains some b's but no c's, or vice versa, then w_2 has different numbers of b's and c's, which is a contradiction.

If $\textit{left} \cdot \textit{right}$ contains both b's and c's, it must hold that $\textit{left} = b^s$ and $\textit{right} = c^s$ for some $s > 0$. We have $w_2 = a^n b^{n+s} c^{n+s} \$ \in \frac{1}{2}L$. This can happen only when $w_2 \cdot \$ d^{3n+2s} \in L$. By the definition of L we have $3n = 3n + 2s$, which is a contradiction for $s > 0$.

If $\textit{left} \cdot \textit{right}$ contains neither b's nor c's, then $\textit{left} \cdot \textit{right} = a^s$ for some $s > 0$. We have $w_2 = a^{n+s} b^n c^n \$ \in \frac{1}{2}L$. This can happen only if $w_2 \cdot \$ d^{3n+s} \in L$. By the definition of L we have $3(n + s) = 3n + s$, which is a contradiction for $s > 0$. ∎

Solution to Problem 140

(1) Let L be a context-free language recognized by a pushdown automaton $\mathcal{A} = (\Sigma, \Gamma, Q, q_I, Z_I, \delta, F)$, and let M be a regular language recognized by a (non-deterministic) finite automaton $\mathcal{B} = (\Sigma, R, r_I, \gamma, G)$. The shuffle of L and M is recognized by the *asynchronous product* of $\mathcal{A}$ and $\mathcal{B}$; that is, the pushdown automaton

$$\mathcal{C} = (\Sigma, \Gamma, Q \times R, (q_I, r_I), Z_I, \beta, F \times G),$$

where the transitions in β are

$$(q, r), a, Z \to (q', r), \zeta \quad \text{and} \quad (q, r), a, Z \to (q, r'), Z$$

for all transitions $q, a, Z \to q', \zeta$ in $\mathcal{A}$ and $r \xrightarrow{a} r'$ in $\mathcal{B}$.

It is easy to prove by induction on the length of the run that

$$((q, r), w, \gamma) \vdash_{\mathcal{C}}^* ((q', r'), \varepsilon, \gamma')$$

if and only if there exist words u and v such that

$$(q, u, \gamma) \vdash_{\mathcal{A}}^* (q', \varepsilon, \gamma') \quad \text{and} \quad r \xrightarrow{v} r',$$

and w is a shuffle of u and v.

(2) Consider the languages:

$$L = \{a^n b^n : n \in \mathbb{N}\} \quad \text{and} \quad M = \{c^n d^n : n \in \mathbb{N}\}.$$

Intersecting $L \parallel M$ with the regular language $a^* c^* b^* d^*$ we obtain the language

$$\{a^i c^j b^i d^j : i, j \in \mathbb{N}\}.$$

Applying the homomorphism $a \mapsto a$, $c \mapsto b$, $b \mapsto a$, $d \mapsto b$, we obtain the language $\{a^i b^j a^i b^j : i, j \in \mathbb{N}\}$, proved not to be context-free in Problem 101. By the closure of context-free languages under intersection with regular languages and homomorphic images, it follows that $L \parallel M$ is not context-free either. ∎

Solution to Problem 141

Consider the language of all permutations of abc,

$$L = \{abc, acb, bac, bca, cab, cba\},$$

and let $M = \{w : \#_a(w) = \#_b(w) = \#_c(w) \wedge |w| > 0\}$. We claim that $L^\sharp = M$, and that M is not context-free.

To prove $L^\sharp = M$, for every $n \geq 1$ we define $L^{\parallel n}$ as follows: $L^{\parallel 1} = L$ and $L^{\parallel k+1} = L^{\parallel k} \parallel L$. It is clear that $L^\sharp = \bigcup_{n \geq 1} L^{\parallel n}$. Next, define

$$M_n = \{w : \#_a(w) = \#_b(w) = \#_c(w) = n\}.$$

We show that $L^{\parallel n} = M_n$ for all $n \geq 1$. The inclusion $\subseteq$ is obvious. We prove the converse inclusion by induction on n. The base case $n = 1$ holds by definition. Suppose the property holds for some n. Let $w \in M_{n+1}$. By removing three different letters from w we obtain $w' \in M_n = L^{\parallel n}$. By definition the removed word is an element of L, hence $w \in L^{\parallel n} \parallel L$. We conclude by observing that $M = \bigcup_{n \geq 1} M_n$.

To prove that M is not context-free, note that by intersecting it with the regular language $a^* b^* c^*$ we obtain $\{a^n b^n c^n : n \geq 1\}$, which is not context-free by Problem 103. ∎

Solution to Problem 142

Let us begin with a concrete example. Consider $K = b^*ab^*$ and $L = a^*ba^*$. Then $\bigcup_{i \in \mathbb{N}}(K^i \cap L^i)$ is the language of words in which the number of a's equals the number of b's. Hence, the language is not regular.

Now we come back to arbitrary regular K and L. Let $\mathcal{A} = (\Sigma, Q, q_I, \delta, F)$ and $\mathcal{B} = (\Sigma, Q', q_I', \delta', F')$ be the finite automata recognizing K and L, respectively. In the pushdown automaton $\mathcal{C}$ we are going to simulate $\mathcal{A}$ and $\mathcal{B}$ in parallel, using a variant of the product construction. At any moment if one of the two finite automata accepts, it can either continue or be restarted from the initial state. However, we have to make sure that $\mathcal{A}$ and $\mathcal{B}$ are restarted the same number of times. This can be easily done using the stack, on which we maintain the difference between the number of restarts of the two automata.

Formally, as the set of states we take $(Q \times Q') \cup \{q_F\}$ with (q_I, q_I') being initial and q_F being accepting. The stack alphabet is $\Gamma = \{Z_I, A, B\}$.

For every pair of transitions of the two automata reading the same letter, $(p, a, q) \in \delta$ and $(p', a, q') \in \delta'$, we create the transition

$$(p, p'), a, Z \rightarrow (q, q'), Z \quad \text{for } Z \in \Gamma.$$

We can restart each automaton if it accepts, recording information about this on the stack:

$$\begin{aligned}
(q, q'), \varepsilon, Z &\rightarrow (q_I, q'), AZ &&\text{for } q \in F, q' \in Q', Z \in \{A, Z_I\}, \\
(q, q'), \varepsilon, B &\rightarrow (q_I, q'), \varepsilon &&\text{for } q \in F, q' \in Q', \\
(q, q'), \varepsilon, Z &\rightarrow (q, q_I'), BZ &&\text{for } q \in Q, q' \in F', Z \in \{B, Z_I\}, \\
(q, q'), \varepsilon, A &\rightarrow (q, q_I'), \varepsilon &&\text{for } q \in Q, q' \in F'.
\end{aligned}$$

We accept if both automata accept, and they were restarted the same number of times:

$$(q, q'), \varepsilon, Z_I \rightarrow q_F, Z_I \text{for } q \in F, q' \in F'. \qquad \blacksquare$$

Solution to Problem 143

Consider the following languages over the alphabet $\{a, b, c\}$:

$$K = (b + c)^*a(b + c)^*, \quad L = (a + c)^*b(a + c)^*, \quad M = (a + b)^*c(a + b)^*.$$

Then, $K^n = \{w : \#_a(w) = n\}$, and similarly for L^n and M^n. Hence,

$$K^n \cap L^n \cap M^n = \{w : \#_a(w) = \#_b(w) = \#_c(w) = n\}$$

and

$$\bigcup_{n \in \mathbb{N}} K^n \cap L^n \cap M^n = \{w : \#_a(w) = \#_b(w) = \#_c(w)\}.$$

By intersecting with the regular language $a^*b^*c^*$ we obtain $\{a^nb^nc^n : n \in \mathbb{N}\}$, which is not context-free by Problem 103.   ∎

Solution to Problem 144
Let

$$L = \left\{a^mb^mc^id^jb^nc^n : m,n,i,j \geq 1\right\}.$$

L is context-free because it is the concatenation of the context-free languages $\{a^nb^n : n \geq 1\}$, c^+, a^+, and $\{b^nc^n : n \geq 1\}$. Moreover,

$$\sqrt{L} = \{w : ww \in L\} = \left\{a^nb^nc^n : n \geq 1\right\},$$

which is not context-free by Problem 103.   ∎

Solution to Problem 145
Let L be the language from the solution to Problem 144. It follows that

$$\text{Root}(L) = L \cup \left\{a^nb^nc^n : n \geq 1\right\}.$$

We show that $\text{Root}(L)$ is not context-free. Indeed, by intersecting $\text{Root}(L)$ with the regular language $a^*b^*c^*$ we obtain $\{a^nb^nc^n : n \geq 1\}$, which is not context-free by Problem 103.   ∎

Solution to Problem 146
Let $\mathcal{A} = (\Sigma, Q, q_I, \delta, F)$ be an automaton recognizing L. For every state $q \in Q$ we define two new automata $\mathcal{A}_{q_I \to q}$ and $\mathcal{A}_{q \to F}$. The automaton $\mathcal{A}_{q_I \to q}$ is the same as $\mathcal{A}$ but its only final state is q. Similarly, $\mathcal{A}_{q \to F}$ is the same as $\mathcal{A}$ but its initial state is q. Let $L_{q_I \to q}$ and $L_{q \to F}$ be the corresponding regular languages. By construction,

$$L = \bigcup_{q \in Q} L_{q_I \to q} \cdot L_{q \to F}.$$

By Problem 30, the reverse of a regular language is regular. Therefore, $(L_{q \to F})^R$ is regular for every q. Let $(\mathcal{A}_{q \to F})^R$ be the corresponding automaton. It is easy to define $\mathcal{A}_q$, an automaton recognizing $L_{q_I \to q} \cdot (L_{q \to F})^R$: take a copy of $\mathcal{A}_{q_I \to q}$ and a copy of $(\mathcal{A}_{q \to F})^R$ and add ε-transitions from q to all initial states of $(\mathcal{A}_{q \to F})^R$. The initial state is inherited from $\mathcal{A}_{q_I \to q}$ and the final states from $(\mathcal{A}_{q \to F})^R$. Thus we get that the language

$$\bigcup_{q \in Q} L_{q_I \to q} \cdot (L_{q \to F})^R = \left\{uv^R : uv \in L\right\}$$

is regular.

We define the pushdown automaton $\mathcal{B}_q$ by modifying $\mathcal{A}_q$. We shall need a special stack symbol \$ $\notin \Sigma$. In the copy of $\mathcal{A}_{q_I \to q}$ the states change like in the original, but additionally all letters read are pushed onto the stack. In the copy of $(\mathcal{A}_{q \to F})^R$ the states also change like before, but when the automaton reads a letter it also pops a letter from the stack and compares the two letters. If they are different or the stack is empty, then the automaton pushes \$ onto the stack and continues. Because \$ is not in Σ, from this moment on the symbol read from the input and the symbol on top of the stack will always be different, and \$ will be pushed back on the stack after reading each letter. Thus the word processed in the first copy is compared with the word processed in the second copy (in reverse order because we put the first part of the word on the stack). Notice that the stack is empty after processing the whole input if and only if the compared parts of the word are equal. The automaton $\mathcal{B}_q$ should accept if at the end it is in an accepting state of $\mathcal{A}_q$ and the stack is non-empty. Thus we get

$$\bigcup_{q \in Q} L(\mathcal{B}_q) = \left\{ uv^R : u^R \neq v^R,\ uv \in L \right\} = \left\{ uv^R : u \neq v,\ uv \in L \right\}. \quad \blacksquare$$

Solution to Problem 147
By Problem 94, there exists a right-linear grammar for L. One easily rewrites it using only rules of the form $X \to zY$ for $z \in \{a, b\}$ and $X \to \varepsilon$. To generate the desired language, replace each rule $X \to zY$ with $X \to h_1(z)Y(h_2(z))^R$. Clearly, the resulting grammar is linear context-free. Checking that it generates the desired language is straightforward. $\quad \blacksquare$

Solution to Problem 148
Intersecting with the regular language $a_1^* b_1^* a_2^* b_2^*$ and applying the homomorphism $a_1 \mapsto a$, $a_2 \mapsto a$, $b_1 \mapsto b$, $b_2 \mapsto b$ we obtain the language $\left\{ a^i b^j a^i b^j : i, j \in \mathbb{N} \right\}$, proved not to be context-free in Problem 101. $\quad \blacksquare$

Solution to Problem 149
Consider finite alphabets Σ_1, Σ_2, and Γ. Let $h_i : \Sigma_i \to \Gamma^*$ for $i = 1, 2$. Let k be the maximal length of words in $h_1(\Sigma_1)$ plus the maximal length of words in $h_2(\Sigma_2)$, and let I be the set of words in Γ^* of length at most k.

Consider the following grammar. The set of non-terminals is $\{S_v : v \in I\}$. The start symbol of the grammar is S_ε. For each $a \in \Sigma_1$ and $b \in \Sigma_2$ we have the rules

$$S_v \to aS_w \quad \text{for } w = v \cdot h_1(a),$$
$$S_w \to S_u b \quad \text{for } w = h_2(b) \cdot u,$$
$$S_\varepsilon \to \varepsilon.$$

Obviously this grammar is linear. To prove that the grammar generates the language $\{xy^R : h_1(x) = h_2(y)\}$, we show that for each v, the language generated from S_v is $\{xy^R : v \cdot h_1(x) = h_2(y)\}$.

We prove correctness by induction on the length of the derivation. The only derivation of length one is $S_\varepsilon \to \varepsilon$, which is correct. Assume that all derivations of length at most n are correct. Consider a derivation of length $n + 1$. Suppose that the first step is $S_v \to aS_w$. Then, by the induction hypothesis, after the remaining n steps we derive a word axy^R such that $w \cdot h_1(x) = h_2(y)$. Because $w = v \cdot h_1(a)$, we have

$$v \cdot h_1(ax) = v \cdot h_1(a) \cdot h_1(x) = w \cdot h_1(x) = h_2(y).$$

Suppose that the first step is $S_w \to S_u b$. Then, by the induction hypothesis, after the remaining n steps we derive a word $xy^R b$ such that $u \cdot h_1(x) = h_2(y)$. Because $w = h_2(b) \cdot u$, we have

$$w \cdot h_1(x) = h_2(b) \cdot u \cdot h_1(x) = h_2(b) \cdot h_2(y) = h_2(by).$$

We prove completeness by induction on the length of the word. The only word of length zero is ε, which can be derived using the rule $S_\varepsilon \to \varepsilon$. Assume that for each $v \in I$, all words z of length at most n such that $z = xy^R$ and $v \cdot h_1(x) = h_2(y)$ can be derived from the symbol S_v. Consider a word z of length $n + 1 > 0$ such that $z = xy^R$ and $v \cdot h_1(x) = h_2(y)$ for some $v \in I$. We have $y \neq \varepsilon$, because otherwise it would follow that $x = \varepsilon$, and z would be empty. Let $y^R = (y')^R b$ for some $b \in \Sigma_2$. We have $v \cdot h_1(x) = h_2(b) \cdot h_2(y')$. Hence, either $h_2(b)$ is a prefix of v, or vice versa. In the first case we have $v = h_2(b) \cdot u$ and $u \cdot h_1(x) = h_2(y')$ for some u. Because $|u| \leq |v|$, we have $u \in I$. Hence $S_v \to S_u b$, and $S_u \to^* x(y')^R$ by the induction hypothesis; that is, $S_v \to^* xy^R$. Assume now that v is a prefix of $h_2(b)$. It follows that x is non-empty. Let $x = ax'$. We have $v \cdot h_1(a) \cdot h_1(x') = h_2(y)$. Because $|v| \leq |h_2(b)|$, it holds that $|v \cdot h_1(a)| \leq k$, so $v \cdot h_1(a) \in I$. Thus, $S_v \to aS_w$ for $w = v \cdot h_1(a)$, and $S_w \to^* x'y^R$ by the induction hypothesis; that is, $S_v \to^* xy^R$. Hence, in both cases $z = xy^R$ can be derived from S_v.

We now modify the grammar above to generate $\{xy^R : h_1(x) \neq h_2(y)\}$. We remove the rule $S_\varepsilon \to \varepsilon$, introduce three new non-terminals L, R, and C, and add the following rules for all S_v and $b \in \Sigma_2$:

$S_v \to L$ if $v \neq \varepsilon$,

$S_v \to Rb$ if v is a strict prefix of $h_2(b)$,

$S_v \to Cb$ if v is not a prefix of $h_2(b)$, nor vice versa.

We also add as the following rules for all $a \in \Sigma_1$ and $b \in \Sigma_2$:

$$L \to aL \mid \varepsilon,$$
$$R \to Rb \mid \varepsilon,$$
$$C \to aC \mid Cb \mid \varepsilon.$$

The resulting grammar is obviously linear. The proof that it generates the desired language follows the same steps as for the first grammar. It relies on the observation that $h_1(x) \neq h_2(y)$ if and only if one of the words $h_1(x)$ and $h_2(y)$ is a *strict* prefix of the other, or neither is a prefix of the other. ∎

Solution to Problem 150

Let L be a linear context-free language, generated by a linear grammar $\mathcal{G} = (\Sigma, \mathcal{N}, S, \mathcal{R})$, and let M be a regular language, recognized by a deterministic finite automaton $\mathcal{A} = (\Sigma, Q, q_I, \delta, F)$ (without ε-transitions). We construct a new linear grammar $\mathcal{G}'$ that enriches $\mathcal{G}$ with the ability to simulate the automaton $\mathcal{A}$. The grammar $\mathcal{G}'$ has non-terminals $Q \times \mathcal{N} \times \mathcal{P}(Q)$, start symbol (q_I, S, F), and two types of rules: for every rule $X \to uYv$ in $\mathcal{G}$ we include the rule

$$(q, X, R) \to u\,(p, Y, T)\,v$$

where $q \xrightarrow{u} p$ and $T = \left\{ t \in Q \ : \ \exists r \in R.\, t \xrightarrow{v} r \right\}$, and for every rule $X \to v$ in $\mathcal{G}$ we include the rule

$$(q, X, R) \to v$$

if $q \xrightarrow{v} r$ for some $r \in R$.

By a straightforward induction one shows that for any natural number n, there is a derivation of length n,

$$(q_I, S, F) \to^* u\,(q, X, R)\,v,$$

if and only if the following hold:

- there is a derivation $S \to^* uXv$ of length n;
- $q_I \xrightarrow{u} q$; and
- $R = \{r \in Q : \exists f \in F.\, r \xrightarrow{v} f\}$.

Using this we easily show that $\mathcal{G}'$ generates $L \cap M$. Assume that w is generated by $\mathcal{G}'$. Then there exists a derivation $(q_I, S, F) \to^* w$. If the length of the derivation is one then there is a rule $(q_I, S, F) \rightarrow w$ in $\mathcal{G}'$, and the claim follows by the definition of $\mathcal{G}'$. Otherwise, there is a derivation

$$(q_I, S, F) \rightarrow^* u(q, X, R)v$$

and a rule $(q, X, R) \rightarrow t$ such that $utv = w$. We have proved that this implies the following: there is a derivation $S \rightarrow^* uXv$ in $\mathcal{G}$; $q_I \xrightarrow{u} q$; and $R = \{p \in Q : \exists f \in F. p \xrightarrow{v} f\}$. By the definition of $\mathcal{G}'$, there is a rule $X \rightarrow t$ in $\mathcal{G}$ and there exists $r \in R$ such that $q \xrightarrow{t} r$. Hence, we can piece together a derivation of w in $\mathcal{G}$ and an accepting run of $\mathcal{A}$ on w; that is, $w \in L \cap M$. The converse implication is equally simple. ∎

Solution to Problem 151

Let $\mathcal{A}$ be a deterministic pushdown automaton recognizing the language L. To recognize $\min(L)$ we modify $\mathcal{A}$ by removing each transition originating in an accepting state. The resulting automaton $\mathcal{B}$ is deterministic by construction. It also follows easily that it recognizes $\min(L)$.

Indeed, because $\mathcal{A}$ is deterministic, there is at most one run of $\mathcal{A}$ on each word. Moreover, if there is a run ρ on u and u' is a prefix of u, then there is also a run ρ' on u' which is a prefix of ρ. By the definition of $\mathcal{B}$, if $\mathcal{B}$ accepts u, then so does $\mathcal{A}$ and the run of $\mathcal{A}$ on u does not visit accepting states before reading all of u. Since the runs of $\mathcal{A}$ on prefixes of u are prefixes of the run on u, none of them ends in an accepting state. Hence, all strict prefixes of u are rejected. Conversely, if u is accepted by $\mathcal{A}$, but all its strict prefixes are rejected, the run of $\mathcal{A}$ on u will not visit accepting states before reading all of u. Hence, u will be also accepted by $\mathcal{B}$. ∎

Solution to Problem 152

By definition $\min(L) = \{a^i b^j c^k : k = \min(i,j)\}$. Suppose that $\min(L)$ is context-free. We apply Ogden's lemma to show a contradiction. Let N be the constant from Ogden's lemma applied to $\min(L)$, and consider the word $w = a^N b^{N+1} c^N \in \min(L)$ with all a's marked. Then there exists a factorization

$$w = prefix \cdot left \cdot infix \cdot right \cdot suffix$$

such that *left* or *right* contains a, and $w_k = prefix \cdot left^k \cdot infix \cdot right^k \cdot suffix$ belongs to $\min(L)$ for all $k \in \mathbb{N}$.

Because $\min(L) \subseteq a^* b^* c^*$, we have *left*, *right* $\in a^* + b^* + c^*$. Moreover, since either *left* or *right* contains an a, we have *left* $\in a^*$. There are two cases.

- If *right* $\in a^* + b^*$, then $w_2 \notin \min(L)$ because the number of c's is strictly smaller than the number of b's and the number of a's (recall that either *left* or *right* contains an a).

- If *right* $\in c^+$, then $w_3 \notin \min(L)$ because the number of c's is strictly greater than the number of b's, which is strictly smaller than the number of a's (*left* contains an a).

Thus $\min(L)$ is not context-free. ∎

Solution to Problem 153

Consider the context-free language

$$L = \left\{ a^m b^n c^m : m, n \in \mathbb{N} \right\} \cup \left\{ a^m b^n c^n : m, n \in \mathbb{N} \right\}.$$

We shall prove that $\max(L)$ is not context-free. From the definition of $\max(L)$ it follows that

$$\max(L) = \left\{ a^m b^n c^p : p = \max(m, n) \right\}.$$

Suppose that $\max(L)$ is context-free. We apply the pumping lemma to show a contradiction. Let N be the constant from the pumping lemma applied to $\max(L)$ and consider the word $w = a^{N+1} b^N c^{N+1} \in \max(L)$. There exists a factorization

$$w = prefix \cdot left \cdot infix \cdot right \cdot suffix$$

such that either *left* or *right* is non-empty, $|left \cdot infix \cdot right| \leq N$, and the words $w_k = prefix \cdot left^k \cdot infix \cdot right^k \cdot suffix$ belong to $\max(L)$ for all $k \in \mathbb{N}$.

Because $\max(L) \subseteq a^* b^* c^*$, we have that $left, right \in a^* + b^* + c^*$.

- If *right* $\in a^+ + b^+$, then *left* $\in a^* + b^*$ and $w_3 \notin \max(L)$ because the number of a's or the number of b's is strictly greater than the number of c's (depending on which letters occur in *left* and *right*).

- If *right* $\in c^+$, then *left* $\in b^* + c^*$. If $w_2 \in \max(L)$, then it easily follows that $|left| = |right| + 1$. But then $w_3 \notin \max(L)$.

- The remaining case is *right* $= \varepsilon$. For *left* $\in a^* + b^*$, we argue as in the first case. For *left* $\in c^+$ we have $w_2 \notin \max(L)$ because the number of c's is strictly greater than both the number of a's and the number of b's.

Therefore, $\max(L)$ is not context-free. ∎

Solution to Problem 154

For the first part, suppose L is generated by a finite automaton $\mathcal{A}$. We construct a pushdown automaton $\mathcal{B}$ recognizing the language M. The construction is similar to that in Problem 40: we simulate an accepting run of $\mathcal{A}$ on a word of the same length as the input word, but possibly differing on some positions. To guarantee the condition from the definition of M, we maintain the difference between the number of positions at which the words agreed and the number of positions at which they differed. For this purpose we use an integer counter, maintained in the stack in the usual way, using two stack symbols $\boxplus$ and $\boxminus$. The pushdown automaton $\mathcal{B}$ has the same states as $\mathcal{A}$ plus a fresh unique accepting state f. The initial state is also inherited from $\mathcal{A}$. The transition relation $\mathcal{B}$ contains three types of transitions. For every transition $q \xrightarrow{a} q'$ in $\mathcal{A}$ we add in $\mathcal{B}$ transitions simulating a step over a when the input letter is a,

$$q, a, Z_I \rightarrow q', \boxplus Z_I, \quad q, a, \boxplus \rightarrow, q', \boxplus\boxplus, \quad \text{and} \quad q, a, \boxminus \rightarrow q', \varepsilon,$$

and when the input letter is any letter $b \neq a$,

$$q, b, Z_I \rightarrow q', \boxminus Z_I, \quad q, b, \boxminus \rightarrow q', \boxminus\boxminus, \quad \text{and} \quad q, b, \boxplus \rightarrow q', \varepsilon.$$

To accept, for every accepting state q of $\mathcal{A}$ we add in $\mathcal{B}$ transitions

$$q, \varepsilon, Z_I \rightarrow f, Z_I \quad \text{and} \quad q, \varepsilon, \boxplus \rightarrow f, \boxplus.$$

Checking that $\mathcal{B}$ recognizes M is straightforward.

For the second part, we prove that M is not always regular due to a simple pumping argument. Consider the language $L = a^*$ over the alphabet $\{a, b\}$. Then M consists of words w such that $\#_b(w) \leq \#_a(w)$. Suppose M is regular and let p be the constant from the pumping lemma. Then $b^p a^p \in M$, and the pumping lemma gives a factorization $b^p a^p = xyz$ with $|xy| \leq p$ such that $xy^i z \in M$ for all $i \in \mathbb{N}$. This is a contradiction because $\#_b(xy^i z) > \#_a(xy^i z)$ for all $i > 1$. ∎

Solution to Problem 155. PARIKH'S THEOREM

A Let $\mathcal{G}$ be a grammar with non-terminals $\mathcal{N}$ and terminals Σ.

We shall allow non-terminals in the leaves of derivation trees. Thus, a derivation tree T with non-terminal X in the root corresponds to a derivation $X \rightarrow^* \alpha \in (\Sigma \cup \mathcal{N})^*$. A derivation tree is *trivial* if it has only one node. The *yield* of T, denoted by $y(T)$, is the word over Σ obtained from α by skipping all non-terminals. For a set $\mathcal{C}$ of derivation trees, we let $y(\mathcal{C}) = \{y(T) : T \in \mathcal{C}\}$. We write $\mathcal{N}_T$ for the set of non-terminals used in T and $T.x$ for the subtree of T rooted at a node x. A *ground* derivation tree is a derivation tree without non-terminals in leaves.

For $X \in \mathcal{N}$, an X-loop Δ is a non-trivial derivation tree corresponding to a derivation $X \rightarrow^+ \alpha X \beta$ for some $\alpha, \beta \in \Sigma^*$; that is, the root of Δ and one of its leaves have label X, and the remaining leaves have labels from $\Sigma \cup \{\varepsilon\}$. Consider a derivation tree T. To *inject* an X-loop Δ at an X-labelled node x of T means to replace the subtree $T.x$ in T with the derivation tree T' obtained by replacing the unique X-labelled leaf of Δ with $T.x$. Dually, if some X-labelled node x in T has an X-labelled descendant y, we can decompose T into two parts: a derivation tree T' obtained from T by replacing $T.x$ with $T.y$, and a derivation tree Δ obtained from $T.x$ by removing all descendants of y. If Δ is an X-loop, then we say that Δ was *contracted* in T to obtain T', and that T' is a *contraction* of T. (Note how injections and contractions correspond to pumping and unpumping.) We call a ground derivation tree *minimal* if all its contractions contain fewer distinct non-terminals. An X-loop is *minimal* if its only contraction is a trivial derivation tree.

With all the necessary notions explained, we now proceed to construct a regular language that has the same Parikh image as $L(\mathcal{G})$.

Claim 1. The set of minimal ground derivation trees is finite.

Suppose that T is a minimal ground derivation tree and let $X \in \mathcal{N}$. Fix a branch of T and let $x_1, \ldots, x_k$ be the X-labelled nodes on this branch, listed in top-down order. By the minimality of T, for all $i < k$, contracting the X-loop Δ_i corresponding to the part of T between x_i and x_{i+1} would remove all occurrences of some non-terminal. Hence, each Δ_i contains a non-terminal that does not occur outside of Δ_i. It follows that $k - 1 \leq |\mathcal{N} - \{X\}|$. Thus we have proved that X occurs at most $|\mathcal{N}|$ times on each branch of T. Because all internal nodes of T are labelled with elements of $\mathcal{N}$, each branch of T has length at most $|\mathcal{N}|^2 + 1$. In other words, the depth of minimal derivation trees is bounded. Since their branching is bounded by the maximal size of the rules, it follows that minimal derivation trees have bounded size. Consequently, there are only finitely many of them.

Claim 2. For all $X \in \mathcal{N}$, the set of minimal X-loops is finite.

Consider a minimal X-loop Δ. Suppose that some $Y \in \mathcal{N}$ is used in three nodes x_1, x_2, and x_3 lying on a single branch of Δ. Assume that these nodes are listed in top-down order. Consider the derivation trees Δ_i corresponding to the part of Δ between x_i and x_{i+1} for $i = 1, 2$. At least one of them does not contain the X-labelled leaf of Δ and, in consequence, is a Y-loop. This contradicts the minimality of Δ. Hence, each non-terminal occurs at most twice on each branch. Continuing like for Claim 1 we obtain Claim 2.

Let $\mathcal{D}$ be the set of all minimal ground derivation trees whose root is labelled with the start symbol of $\mathcal{G}$, and let $\mathcal{E}_X$ be the set of all minimal X-loops. By Claims 1 and 2, $\mathcal{D}$ and $\mathcal{E}_X$ are finite for all X.

Claim 3. $L(\mathcal{G})$ has the same Parikh image as the regular language

$$\bigcup_{U \in \mathcal{D}} \left(y(U) \cdot \left(\bigcup_{X \in \mathcal{N}_U} y(\mathcal{E}_X) \right)^* \right).$$

Take a word $w = y(U) \cdot y(\Delta_1).....y(\Delta_k)$, where $U \in \mathcal{D}$ and each Δ_i is an X-loop for some X occurring in U. Then, we can inject each Δ_i into U at some X-labelled node. By construction, the resulting derivation tree T yields a word w' with the same Parikh image as w. Because T is a ground derivation tree, it follows that $w' \in L(\mathcal{G})$.

Next, we prove by structural induction that for each ground derivation tree T whose root is labelled with the start symbol of $\mathcal{G}$, there exists $U \in \mathcal{D}$ such that $\mathcal{N}_U = \mathcal{N}_T$ and some word in $y(U) \cdot \left(\bigcup_{X \in \mathcal{N}_U} y(\mathcal{E}_X) \right)^*$ has the same Parikh image as $y(T)$. If T is minimal, we take $U = T$ and the word $y(T)$. Assume that T is not minimal and that the induction hypothesis holds for all contractions of T. Because T is not minimal, we can contract an X_0-loop Δ_0 in T without changing the set of non-terminals used. If Δ_0 is not minimal, we can contract a smaller X_1-loop Δ_1 in Δ_0. But then we can also contract Δ_1 in T without changing the set of non-terminals used, and so on. Proceeding this way we eventually identify a minimal X_k-loop Δ_k that can be contracted in T and the resulting contraction T' uses the same non-terminals as T. By the induction hypothesis there exist $U \in \mathcal{D}$ with $\mathcal{N}_U = \mathcal{N}_{T'}$ and a word $w \in y(U) \cdot \left(\bigcup_{X \in \mathcal{N}_U} y(\mathcal{E}_X) \right)^*$ with the same Parikh image as $y(T')$. Taking the same U and the word $w \cdot y(\Delta_k)$ we obtain the induction hypothesis for T. This completes the proof of Claim 3.   ∎

Solution to Problem 156

Let $L \subseteq \{a\}^*$. By Parikh's theorem (Problem 155), there is a regular language $M \subseteq \{a\}^*$ whose Parikh image is the same as that of L. Because two words from $\{a\}^*$ have the same Parikh image if and only if they are equal, it follows that $L = M$.   ∎

Solution to Problem 157

Let L be defined by a context-free grammar $\mathcal{G}$, and let Σ be the set of terminal symbols of $\mathcal{G}$. For every rule $X \to \alpha$ replace every $b \in \Sigma$ by a. This way we obtain a new grammar, call it $\mathcal{G}_a$, generating a language over $\{a\}$. Every derivation tree of $\mathcal{G}$ can be transformed into a derivation tree of $\mathcal{G}_a$ by changing every leaf labelled by $b \in \Sigma$ into a. So $a^{|w|}$ is derivable for every $w \in L$. Similarly, if a^n is derivable in $\mathcal{G}_a$, then there is $w \in L$ with $n = |w|$. Since $\mathcal{G}_a$ is a context-free grammar over a one-letter alphabet, the language it generates is regular by Problem 156. ∎

Solution to Problem 158

Let L be a context-free language with the prefix property, over an alphabet Σ. If L is finite, then it is regular, and we are done. We assume that L is infinite. Let N be the constant for L guaranteed by the pumping lemma for context-free languages. Let w be a word of length at least N. Then, there exists a factorization

$$w = prefix \cdot left \cdot infix \cdot right \cdot suffix$$

such that

$$prefix \cdot left^n \cdot infix \cdot right^n \cdot suffix \in L$$

for all $n \in \mathbb{N}$. We consider two cases.

If $|left| > 0$, then by the prefix property it follows that every $w \in L$ is a prefix of $prefix \cdot left^m$ for some $m \in \mathbb{N}$. Let M denote the language of all prefixes of words in $\{prefix \cdot left^m : m \in \mathbb{N}\}$. It is clear that M is a regular language, and that $L \subseteq M$.

If $|left| = 0$, then by the prefix property it follows that every $w \in L$ is a prefix of $prefix \cdot infix \cdot right^m$ for some $m \in \mathbb{N}$. Let M denote the language of all prefixes of words in $\{prefix \cdot infix \cdot right^m : m \in \mathbb{N}\}$. It is clear that M is regular and that $L \subseteq M$.

In both cases for every n the language M contains exactly one word of length n. Since $L \subseteq M$, it follows that

$$L = M \cap \{u \in \Sigma^* : \exists v \in L. |v| = |u|\}.$$

Because regular languages are closed under intersection, to see that L is regular it suffices to show that $\{u \in \Sigma^* : \exists v \in L. |v| = |u|\}$ is regular. But the latter language is the pre-image of $\{a^{|w|} : w \in L\}$ under the homomorphism mapping all letters to a. Hence, its regularity follows from the regularity of $\{a^{|w|} : w \in L\}$ (Problem 157) and the closure of regular languages under homomorphic pre-images. ∎

Solution to Problem 159

(1) Yes. Consider the complementary languages

$$L = \bigcup_{n \in \mathbb{N}} \left\{ a^n \; : \; 2^{2n} \leq n < 2^{2n+1} \right\},$$

$$M = \bigcup_{n \in \mathbb{N}} \left\{ a^n \; : \; 2^{2n+1} \leq n < 2^{2n+2} \right\}.$$

We prove that neither of them contains an infinite regular language. Suppose $L' \subseteq L$ is an infinite regular language. By the pumping lemma, for large enough n there exist k, l, and m such that $2^{2n} \leq k + l + m < 2^{2n+1}$, $l \geq 1$, and $a^k a^{l \cdot i} a^m \in L'$ for all $i \geq 0$. It follows that $l < 2^{2n+1}$ and thus there exists i such that $2^{2n+1} \leq k + l \cdot i + m < 2^{2n+2}$, which is a contradiction. Similarly, M does not contain an infinite regular language.

(2) No. Consider a context-free language L over a finite alphabet Σ, and let M be its complement. Fix $a \in \Sigma$ and consider the languages $L_a = L \cap a^*$ and $M_a = M \cap a^*$. By the closure of context-free languages under intersections with regular languages, L_a is context-free. Moreover, L_a is a language over a one-letter alphabet and thus by Problem 156 it is a regular language. From the definition of M_a it follows that $M_a = a^* - L_a$, which means that it is a regular language, too. Since a^* is infinite, it follows that either L_a or M_a is an infinite regular language. ∎

8

Theory of Computation

Solution to Problem 160

(1) The tape alphabet of the machine contains, besides the input symbols, the blank symbol and a symbol #. The overall idea is as follows. The machine starts by marking two symbols with #: the very first input symbol, and a non-deterministically chosen occurrence of the same symbol in the input word (using states $start_0$ and $start_1$ in the table). If the input word is of the form ww, the intention is to mark the first letters of both copies of w. Then the machine returns to the left # (using state ret, see the table), enters state go, and repeats a subroutine that marks with # two input symbols that are directly to the right of a #, at the same time checking that the two input symbols are equal (using states go_0, and go_1, go'_0, go'_1, ret, and ret'). Thus the machine maintains on its tape two increasingly long blocks of #'s. Finally, once the two blocks of #'s touch, the machine enters the state *check* with the aim of checking that all letters of the input word have already been marked.

The machine has 12 states; the initial state is *start*, and the only accepting state is *ok*. We encourage the reader to contemplate the table, showing the transition relation. The rows of the table correspond to states and the columns to tape symbols. The entry corresponding to a state q and a tape symbol a lists all the triples (p, b, t) such that (q, a, p, b, t) is a transition.

(2) A machine recognizing the set of palindromes can be defined similarly, except that the blocks of #'s grow in opposite directions from the two ends of the input word.

(3) We give a sketch of the solution, leaving the details to the reader. We use a four-tape machine to implement an algorithm that verifies if a given number is prime by trying to divide it by each smaller number. The first tape is the input tape and it remains unchanged throughout the computation. On the second tape we enumerate numbers smaller than the input number,

Table 8.1 *A Turing machine recognizing the language* $\{ww : w \in \{0,1\}^*\}$.

	0	1	B	#
start	$(\text{start}_0, \#, \rightarrow)$	$(\text{start}_1, \#, \rightarrow)$	$(\text{ok}, \text{B}, \circlearrowleft)$	
start_0	$(\text{start}_0, 0, \rightarrow)$ $(\text{ret}, \#, \leftarrow)$	$(\text{start}_0, 1, \rightarrow)$		
start_1	$(\text{start}_1, 0, \rightarrow)$	$(\text{start}_1, 1, \rightarrow)$ $(\text{ret}, \#, \leftarrow)$		
ret	$(\text{ret}, 0, \leftarrow)$	$(\text{ret}, 1, \leftarrow)$		$(\text{go}, \#, \rightarrow)$
go	$(\text{go}_0, \#, \rightarrow)$	$(\text{go}_1, \#, \rightarrow)$		$(\text{check}, \#, \circlearrowleft)$
go_0	$(\text{go}_0, 0, \rightarrow)$	$(\text{go}_0, 1, \rightarrow)$		$(\text{go}'_0, \#, \rightarrow)$
go_1	$(\text{go}_1, 0, \rightarrow)$	$(\text{go}_1, 1, \rightarrow)$		$(\text{go}'_1, \#, \rightarrow)$
go'_0	$(\text{ret}', \#, \leftarrow)$			$(\text{go}'_0, \#, \rightarrow)$
go'_1		$(\text{ret}', \#, \leftarrow)$		$(\text{go}'_1, \#, \rightarrow)$
ret'	$(\text{ret}, 0, \leftarrow)$	$(\text{ret}, 1, \leftarrow)$	$(\text{check}, \text{B}, \rightarrow)$	$(\text{ret}', \#, \leftarrow)$
check		$(\text{ok}, \text{B}, \circlearrowleft)$		$(\text{check}, \#, \rightarrow)$

starting from 2. For each number on the second tape, we simulate the long division algorithm using the two remaining tapes. One of them is intended to store the quotient (calculated digit by digit), while the other one stores the remainder to be divided at a given stage of the long division process. ∎

Solution to Problem 161

(1) We define a non-deterministic Turing machine $\mathcal{M}$ with three tapes. The input word is stored on the first tape, with the head initially over its first (left-most) letter. The two remaining heads are initially over the corresponding cells of the respective tapes. The input word correctly encodes a graph only if its length is n^2, for some $n \geq 1$. In this case, it consists of n *segments*, each segment of length n describing all edges outgoing from some vertex of the graph.

In its initial state q_0, the machine $\mathcal{M}$ copies the first n input symbols to the second tape, where n is chosen non-deterministically, and writes n symbols 0 on the third tape. This is made possible by the following transitions:

$$(q_0, b, \text{B}, \text{B}, q_0, b, b, 0, \rightarrow, \rightarrow, \rightarrow),$$
$$(q_0, b, \text{B}, \text{B}, q_1, b, b, 0, \rightarrow, \rightarrow, \rightarrow), \qquad \text{for } b \in \{0,1\}.$$

This first phase of the computation finishes when $\mathcal{M}$ enters state q_1.

In the second phase, $\mathcal{M}$ checks whether the length of the input is actually n^2. This can be done for instance by using both the second and the third tapes to count from 1 to n (by moving the heads), thus effectively counting from 1 to n^2.

In the third stage, $\mathcal{M}$ non-deterministically searches for a path from vertex 0 to vertex $n - 1$. The invariant to be maintained after each search step is that the second tape always stores a segment of the input word corresponding to a vertex that is accessible from vertex 0. Note that after the first phase the second tape contains the segment of vertex 0. In consequence, $\mathcal{M}$ can accept when the last (right-most) symbol on the second tape is 1.

To perform the search, the machine iteratively invokes a subroutine that moves along a single edge of the graph. The subroutine starts in state p_1, with all three heads placed over the first non-empty cell of the respective tapes. In state p_1, the subroutine has a non-deterministic choice: either change the state to p_2 without any activity of the heads,

$$(p_1, b_1, 1, b_3, p_2, b_1, 1, b_3, \circlearrowleft, \circlearrowleft, \circlearrowleft), \qquad \text{for } b_1, b_3 \in \{0, 1\},$$

but only if the current symbol on the second tape is 1; or do the following:
- move one cell to the right on the second tape;
- move n cells to the right on the first tape, using the third tape as a counter;
- stay in state p_1.

In the low-level Turing machine code (using auxiliary states p_1' and p_1''):

$$
\begin{aligned}
&(p_1, b_1, b_2, 0, p_1', b_1, b_2, 0, \circlearrowleft, \rightarrow, \circlearrowleft), \\
&(p_1', b_1, b_2, 0, p_1', b_1, b_2, 0, \rightarrow, \circlearrowleft, \rightarrow), \\
&(p_1', b_1, b_2, \text{B}, p_1'', b_1, b_2, \text{B}, \circlearrowleft, \circlearrowleft, \leftarrow), \qquad \text{for } b_1, b_2 \in \{0, 1\}. \\
&(p_1'', b_1, b_2, 0, p_1'', b_1, b_2, 0, \circlearrowleft, \circlearrowleft, \leftarrow), \\
&(p_1'', b_1, b_2, \text{B}, p_1, b_1, b_2, \text{B}, \circlearrowleft, \circlearrowleft, \rightarrow),
\end{aligned}
$$

In state p_2, the subroutine copies n symbols from the first tape to the second (again using the third tape as a counter), and moves all three heads back to the initial position.

(2) We only briefly sketch the major modifications needed to make the machine from item (1) deterministic. First, the value n cannot be guessed non-deterministically; instead, the machine deterministically considers all consecutive values $n = 1, 2, \ldots$, checking for each of them if the input word has length exactly n^2, until n is already too large for that to hold. Second, a path in the graph cannot be guessed non-deterministically; instead, a deterministic search strategy needs to be applied. One possible

strategy is depth-first search, which can be implemented by using the second tape to store a stack of vertex segments instead of just one segment. In fact, the depth of the stack can be bounded by n, which guarantees that the computation terminates.   ∎

Solution to Problem 162

(1) For simplicity assume $n > 0$. We construct a deterministic machine $\mathcal{M}$ with nine states and tape alphabet $\{a, b, b', \bar{b}, \text{B}\}$. The machine starts in the initial state q_0 with its head over the first (left-most) a. In its first steps, $\mathcal{M}$ writes one symbol b to the left of the input:

$$(q_0, a, q_0, a, \leftarrow),$$
$$(q_0, \text{B}, q_1, b, \rightarrow).$$

Then $\mathcal{M}$ iterates a subroutine that first rewrites the right-most a to B (thus decreasing the length of the a-block by one), and then doubles the length of the b-block. The subroutine starts in state q_1. The first task is realized by the following transitions:

$$(q_1, a, q_1, a, \rightarrow),$$
$$(q_1, \text{B}, q_2, \text{B}, \leftarrow),$$
$$(q_2, a, q_3, \text{B}, \leftarrow),$$
$$(q_3, a, q_3, a, \leftarrow).$$

The second task then starts in state q_3 with $\mathcal{M}$'s head over the right-most symbol b; for each b, the machine rewrites it to $\bar{b}$, and replaces the first blank symbol to the left of the current tape contents by b':

$$(q_3, b, q^{\leftarrow}, \bar{b}, \leftarrow),$$
$$(q^{\leftarrow}, x, q^{\leftarrow}, x, \leftarrow) \qquad \text{for } x \in \{b, b'\},$$
$$(q^{\leftarrow}, \text{B}, q^{\rightarrow}, b', \rightarrow),$$
$$(q^{\rightarrow}, x, q^{\rightarrow}, x, \rightarrow) \qquad \text{for } x \in \{b, b'\},$$
$$(q^{\rightarrow}, \bar{b}, q_3, \bar{b}, \leftarrow).$$

The second task finishes if a symbol b' is seen instead of b in state q_3; now it only remains to rewrite all symbols b' and $\bar{b}$ back to b, which is done in state q_4:

$$(q_3, b', q_3, b', \leftarrow),$$
$$(q_3, \text{B}, q_4, \text{B}, \rightarrow),$$
$$(q_4, x, q_4, b, \rightarrow) \qquad \text{for } x \in \{b', \bar{b}\},$$
$$(q_4, a, q_1, a, \circlearrowleft).$$

The subroutine ends as it begins: in state q_1, with $\mathcal{M}$'s head on the leftmost symbol a. However, if in state q_4 a blank symbol is seen instead of a, the machine rewrites all symbols b to a and ends in state q_f:

$$(q_4, \text{B}, q_5, \text{B}, \leftarrow),$$
$$(q_5, b, q_5, a, \leftarrow),$$
$$(q_5, \text{B}, q_f, \text{B}, \rightarrow).$$

(2) The solution is analogous to the one for item (1). ∎

Solution to Problem 163

(1) For deterministic one-tape Turing machines $\mathcal{M}_1$ and $\mathcal{M}_2$, we construct a deterministic two-tape Turing machine $\mathcal{M}$ recognizing $L(\mathcal{M}_1) \cup L(\mathcal{M}_2)$, using the product construction.

For $i = 1, 2$, let Q_i, q_i, and T_i be the state space, the initial state, and the tape alphabet of the machine $\mathcal{M}_i$. Suppose the input word of $\mathcal{M}$ is on the first tape. In the preprocessing phase, $\mathcal{M}$ copies the word to the second tape, places both heads on the first position of w, and enters the state (q_1, q_2). Then $\mathcal{M}$ simulates both $\mathcal{M}_1$ and $\mathcal{M}_2$ by executing their consecutive steps in parallel; the first tape is used to store the content of $\mathcal{M}_1$'s tape, and the second one to store the content of $\mathcal{M}_2$'s tape. To simplify the description of $\mathcal{M}$, we assume without loss of generality that both $\mathcal{M}_1$ and $\mathcal{M}_2$ can always make a move: this can be guaranteed by adding trivial loops in place of missing transitions. For every transition (p, a, p', a', s) of $\mathcal{M}_1$ and (q, b, q', b', t) of $\mathcal{M}_2$, the machine $\mathcal{M}$ has a transition

$$((p, q), (a, b), (p', q'), (a', b'), (s, t)).$$

Accepting states of $\mathcal{M}$ are pairs (p, q) with either p accepting in $\mathcal{M}_1$ or q accepting in $\mathcal{M}_2$. Thus, $\mathcal{M}$ accepts w if and only if one of $\mathcal{M}_1$, and $\mathcal{M}_2$ does.

(2) Intersection of languages can be recognized similarly to union, except that the accepting states are pairs (p, q) where both p and q are accepting.

(3) To recognize the concatenation of the languages recognized by $\mathcal{M}_1$ and $\mathcal{M}_2$, the machine $\mathcal{M}$ tests if there is a factorization uv of the input word w such that u is accepted by $\mathcal{M}_1$ and v is accepted by $\mathcal{M}_2$. A nondeterministic machine could simply guess a factorization uv and then simulate $\mathcal{M}_1$ on u and $\mathcal{M}_2$ on v on separate tapes, just like in item (1). However, $\mathcal{M}$ is required to be deterministic, so we need to check all factorizations. As machines $\mathcal{M}_1$ and $\mathcal{M}_2$ may run forever over some input words, we check all factorizations in parallel, advancing the simulated runs in a round-robin fashion. Note also that we cannot use a separate

tape for each of these simulated runs, because the number of tapes must be fixed and cannot depend on the length of the input word.

In the preprocessing phase, $\mathcal{M}$ writes all $n = |w| + 1$ factorizations on its tape, using fresh tape symbols # and $ to separate the factors and factorizations:

$$u_1 \# v_1 \$ u_2 \# v_2 \$ \ldots \$ u_n \# v_n.$$

Then $\mathcal{M}$ continues by executing $\mathcal{M}_1$ on inputs $u_1, \ldots, u_n$ and $\mathcal{M}_2$ on inputs $v_1, \ldots, v_n$. This is achieved by iteratively invoking a subroutine that performs, for $i = 1, \ldots, n$, the following actions:

- execute one step of $\mathcal{M}_1$ on u_i; if the new configuration takes one more cell, shift to the right the suffix of the tape content starting from the next # or $ (whichever comes first);
- execute one step of $\mathcal{M}_2$ on v_i; if necessary, make space like above.

The machine $\mathcal{M}$ accepts as soon as $\mathcal{M}_1$ accepts u_i and $\mathcal{M}_2$ accepts v_i for some i (like in item (2) we assume that $\mathcal{M}_1$ and $\mathcal{M}_2$ loop in accepting states).

(4) The construction of $\mathcal{M}$ is similar to the one in item (3). The machine $\mathcal{M}$ unconditionally accepts the empty input word. Given a non-empty input word w, the machine $\mathcal{M}$ enumerates all factorizations of w into arbitrarily many non-empty factors, using # and $ to separate factors and factorizations, respectively. Then $\mathcal{M}$ iteratively invokes a subroutine that simulates $\mathcal{M}_1$ on every factor in a round-robin fashion, and accepts as soon as $\mathcal{M}_1$ accepts all factors of some factorization. ∎

Solution to Problem 164

Consider an arbitrary Turing machine $\mathcal{M}$ with set of states Q, initial state q_0, and tape alphabet T. Assume that the head of $\mathcal{M}$ is initially placed on the first symbol of the input word. We faithfully simulate machine $\mathcal{M}$ by a machine $\mathcal{M}'$ that never goes to the left of the initial head position. The idea is to fold the infinite tape of $\mathcal{M}$ in two, and put it on the right-infinite tape of $\mathcal{M}'$. Thus, the tape alphabet T' of $\mathcal{M}'$ contains pairs $(a, b) \in T^2$ of tape symbols of $\mathcal{M}$, representing the contents of two tape cells at the same distance from the initial position of the head: a is the one to the right, and b is the one to the left. Additionally, the machine $\mathcal{M}'$ needs to remember in its state whether it currently visits the right, or the left half of $\mathcal{M}$'s tape; thus the state space Q' of $\mathcal{M}'$ contains pairs (q, RIGHT) and (q, LEFT), for $q \in Q$.

When visiting the right half of $\mathcal{M}$'s tape, the machine $\mathcal{M}'$ behaves just like $\mathcal{M}$: for every transition (q, a, p, a', t) of $\mathcal{M}$ and every $b \in T$, the machine $\mathcal{M}'$ contains the transition

$$((q, \text{RIGHT}), (a, b), (p, \text{RIGHT}), (a', b), t).$$

Note that the second component b of the tape symbol is not touched by this transition. On the other hand, when visiting the left half of $\mathcal{M}$'s tape, the direction t must be reversed. Define the reverse function:

$$\text{REV}(\rightarrow) = \leftarrow, \qquad \text{REV}(\leftarrow) = \rightarrow, \qquad \text{REV}(\circlearrowleft) = \circlearrowleft.$$

Then, for every transition (q, a, p, a', t) of $\mathcal{M}$ and every $b \in T$, the machine $\mathcal{M}'$ has the transition

$$((q, \text{LEFT}), (b, a), (p, \text{LEFT}), (b, a'), \text{REV}(t)).$$

This time the first component b is not touched by the transition.

The machine $\mathcal{M}'$ should be able to notice a transition from one half of the tape to the other. To this aim, in its first step $\mathcal{M}'$ marks the current tape position with a marker !, using the transition:

$$(q_0, a, (q_0, \text{RIGHT}), (!, a), \circlearrowleft).$$

As a result of this transition, $\mathcal{M}'$ enters the state (q_0, RIGHT) to indicate that it is currently visiting the right half of the tape (as will become clear below, $\mathcal{M}'$ could enter the state (q_0, LEFT) equally well). Thus the tape alphabet of $\mathcal{M}'$ is $T' = T \cup T^2 \cup (\{!\} \times T)$. The marker ! informs $\mathcal{M}'$ that it can move from one half of the tape to the other, which is achieved by the following transitions:

$$((q, \text{LEFT}), (!, a), (q, \text{RIGHT}), (!, a), \circlearrowleft),$$
$$((q, \text{RIGHT}), (!, a), (q, \text{LEFT}), (!, a), \circlearrowleft),$$

for every $q \in Q$ and $a \in T$. We apply the convention that the initial tape cell belongs both to the right and to the left half of the tape. Finally, we add the transitions applicable in the position marked by !, taking care to never go to the left:

$$
\begin{array}{ll}
((q, \text{RIGHT}), (!, a), (p, \text{RIGHT}), (!, b), \rightarrow) & \text{if } (q, a, p, b, \rightarrow) \in \delta, \\
((q, \text{LEFT}), (!, a), (p, \text{LEFT}), (!, b), \rightarrow) & \text{if } (q, a, p, b, \leftarrow) \in \delta, \\
((q, \text{RIGHT}), (!, a), (p, \text{RIGHT}), (!, b), \circlearrowleft) & \text{if } (q, a, p, b, \circlearrowleft) \in \delta.
\end{array}
$$

Thus, whenever $\mathcal{M}'$ finds itself in the initial position of the head, we require that a transition of $\mathcal{M}$ going right be simulated in the right half; and symmetrically for a transition of $\mathcal{M}$ going left. In the case of a transition staying in the same position, we arbitrarily choose the right half, but the simulation could equally well be carried out in the left half.

One minor issue still remains to be addressed. As the left half of $\mathcal{M}$'s tape initially contains only blanks, every symbol a of the input word (except for the first symbol) should be replaced at a suitable moment by the pair (a, B). Similarly, every blank symbol B visited by $\mathcal{M}'$ should be replaced by the pair (B, B). To this aim we add, for every $q \in Q$ and $a \in T$ (including $a = \text{B}$), the following transitions:

$$((q, \text{LEFT}), a, (q, \text{LEFT}), (a, \text{B}), \circlearrowleft),$$

$$((q, \text{RIGHT}), a, (q, \text{RIGHT}), (a, \text{B}), \circlearrowleft).$$

The accepting states of $\mathcal{M}'$ are the states of the form (q, LEFT) and (q, RIGHT) for q an accepting state of $\mathcal{M}$. ∎

Solution to Problem 165

Let $\mathcal{M}$ be a non-deterministic Turing machine. Define the *configuration graph* of $\mathcal{M}$ as follows: the vertices of the graph are all configurations of $\mathcal{M}$, and there is an edge from a configuration c to another configuration c' if $\mathcal{M}$ can reach c' from c in one step; that is, if $c \vdash_{\mathcal{M}} c'$.

Fix the initial configuration $c_0 = q_0 w$, where $q_0 \in Q$ is the initial state of $\mathcal{M}$. On input w, our deterministic machine $\mathcal{M}'$ equivalent to $\mathcal{M}$ performs a breadth-first search of the configuration graph of $\mathcal{M}$, starting from the node c_0. In other words, once all configurations at depth n are enumerated, $\mathcal{M}'$ starts enumerating configurations at depth $n + 1$. During its computation, the tape of $\mathcal{M}'$ stores all the configurations $c_0, c_1, c_2, \ldots$ that have already been enumerated, separated by a special fresh tape symbol \$. Furthermore, a different special symbol # is used to separate those configurations whose successors have all been already enumerated from the other configurations. For instance, if the content of the tape is

$$\$c_0 \$c_1 \$c_2 \$c_3 \#c_4 \$c_5 \$,$$

then the successors of the configurations c_4 and c_5 are still to be enumerated. Compared to the tape alphabet T of $\mathcal{M}$, the tape alphabet of $\mathcal{M}'$ contains the additional symbols \$ and #, as well as pairs $(a, q) \in T \times Q$ indicating the head position and state of $\mathcal{M}$. Each c_i represents a configuration and belongs to $T^* (T \times Q) T^*$; that is, c_i contains exactly one symbol from $T \times Q$.

In the preprocessing phase, $\mathcal{M}'$ marks the position of the head of $\mathcal{M}$, surrounds the input word $w_0 w_1 \ldots w_k$ with the two special symbols,

$$\#(w_0, q_0) w_1 \ldots w_k \$,$$

and places its head over the symbol #. Then, $\mathcal{M}'$ keeps repeating a subroutine generating all successor configurations of the configuration immediately on the right of the head's position, until an accepting configuration is enumerated or there are no configurations left to process. The subroutine consists of the following actions:

- go right and find the closest symbol $(a, q) \in T \times Q$;
- for every applicable transition of $\mathcal{M}$ (that is, for every transition of the form (q, a, p, b, t), for some p, b, t), copy the whole word between # and \$ to the closest blank cells on the right, taking into account the effect of applying the transition; append the symbol \$ after each newly generated configuration;
- go left to the symbol # and overwrite it with \$;
- go right to the first \$, overwrite it with #, and keep the head over it.

The machine $\mathcal{M}'$ accepts if an accepting configuration is found. ∎

Solution to Problem 166

Let $\mathcal{M}$ be a Turing machine over the alphabet $\{0, 1\}$, with states Q and transitions δ, that uses k tape symbols $\{a_1, \ldots, a_k\}$, including the blank symbol B. To construct the machine $\mathcal{M}'$ we encode tape symbols in unary: a_i is encoded as a k-bit word $w_i = 0^{i-1} 1 0^{k-i}$. Accordingly, the content of the tape of $\mathcal{M}$ is organized into *segments* of length k, each segment encoding one tape symbol of $\mathcal{M}$. The states of the machine $\mathcal{M}'$ are pairs (r, n), where $r \in \delta$ is a transition of $\mathcal{M}$, $1 \leq n \leq n_r$, and n_r depends on r as described below. The simulation of a transition r starts in state $(r, 1)$; we maintain an invariant asserting that the simulation starts and ends with the head of $\mathcal{M}'$ over the left-most cell of a segment. Consider the case when r goes right:

$$r = (q, a_i, p, a_j, \rightarrow),$$

for some $a_i \neq B$. To simulate this transition, the machine $\mathcal{M}'$ needs $k+1$ states; that is, $n_r = k + 1$ in this case. During the simulation, $\mathcal{M}'$ makes k steps to the right, in order to overwrite the word $w_i = c_1 c_2 \ldots c_k$ encoding a_i with the word $w_j = d_1 d_2 \ldots d_k$ encoding a_j, using transitions

$$((r, l), c_l, (r, l + 1), d_l, \rightarrow)$$

for $l = 1, 2, \ldots, k$. Thus $\mathcal{M}'$ moves through states $(r, 1), (r, 2), \ldots, (r, k + 1)$ checking that it really sees the encoding of a_i, and overwrites the segment with the encoding of a_j. In state $(r, k+1)$, the machine non-deterministically chooses the next transition to be simulated: for every $c \in \{0, 1, B\}$ and every transition r' of $\mathcal{M}$ that starts in the target state p of r, the machine $\mathcal{M}'$ has the transition

$$((r, k + 1), c, (r', 1), c, \circlearrowleft).$$

The simulation of a transition $r = (q, B, p, a_i, \rightarrow)$ that goes right but starts with the blank symbol is similar, except that we must be prepared for two different representations of B: either the bit-word encoding, or a segment of k blanks (never visited before). Therefore, we also include variants of the transitions above with $c_l = $ B for all l.

In the case when r stays in the same position, the machine $\mathcal{M}'$ needs $2k + 1$ states; that is, $n_r = 2k + 1$. The additional k states allow $\mathcal{M}'$ to make k moves to the left. Analogously, when r goes left, we need $n_r = 3k + 1$. The accepting states of $\mathcal{M}'$ are the states (r, n_r) for those transitions r of $\mathcal{M}$ whose target state p is accepting in $\mathcal{M}$ (without loss of generality we may assume that the initial state is not accepting).

The transitions of $\mathcal{M}'$ described above assume that the tape is organized into segments; and that $\mathcal{M}'$ starts in a state $(r, 1)$ for some r whose source state is the initial state of $\mathcal{M}$. Therefore $\mathcal{M}'$ needs an additional initialization phase, which is left to the reader.   ∎

Solution to Problem 167

Let $\mathcal{M}$ be a one-tape Turing machine with set of states Q and tape alphabet T. We construct an equivalent machine $\mathcal{M}'$ with four states

$$Q' = \{ini, fin, one, two\},$$

where *ini* is the initial state, and *fin* is the only accepting state.

Since $\mathcal{M}'$ is to have only four states, it will have to keep information about the current state of $\mathcal{M}$ on its tape. A first attempt might be to use the tape alphabet $T \cup (T \times Q)$. The challenge is that we need to move information about the state between adjacent cells as the head of the simulated machine $\mathcal{M}$ moves; this is not directly possible with any fixed number of states. Instead, we shall encode states in binary and move the encoding bit by bit. Without loss of generality we can assume that the states are n-bit numbers; that is, $Q \subseteq \{0, \ldots, 2^n - 1\}$. We define the tape alphabet of $\mathcal{M}'$ as

$$T' = T \cup (T \times \widehat{Q} \times C),$$

where $C = \{\text{START}, \text{COPYSRC}_{\rightarrow}, \text{COPYDST}_{\rightarrow}, \text{COPYSRC}_{\leftarrow}, \text{COPYDST}_{\leftarrow}\}$ is a set of *control modes*, and

$$\widehat{Q} = \left\{ \langle q, i \rangle : q \in \{0, \ldots, 2^n - 1\}, \ 0 \leq i \leq n \right\}.$$

Thus, during the simulation, the current tape position of $\mathcal{M}$ is *decorated* with additional markings: instead of storing just a tape symbol a and a state q, it stores $(a, \langle q, i \rangle, c)$; the role of i is to indicate the bit of q to be copied and the control mode c helps carry out the copying.

In its very first step, the machine $\mathcal{M}'$ initializes the simulation of $\mathcal{M}$ by decorating its current tape cell (in particular, $\mathcal{M}'$ writes to its tape the actual initial state q_0 of $\mathcal{M}$), using one of the following transitions:

$$(ini, a, one, (a, \langle q_0, 0 \rangle, \text{START}), \circlearrowleft) \qquad \text{for } a \in T.$$

(The choice of the target state *one* is irrelevant here, it could equally well be *two*.) The control mode START forces $\mathcal{M}'$ to start the simulation of the next step of $\mathcal{M}$. Every transition $(q, a, p, b, \circlearrowleft)$ of $\mathcal{M}$ that does not move $\mathcal{M}$'s head is easily simulated by $\mathcal{M}'$ using the following transition:

$$(one, (a, \langle q, 0 \rangle, \text{START}), one, (b, \langle p, 0 \rangle, \text{START}), \circlearrowleft).$$

The whole difficulty is to simulate $\mathcal{M}$'s transitions that do move the head: this is when $\mathcal{M}'$ has to move the information about the state to an adjacent cell.

Consider a transition $(q, a, p, b, \rightarrow)$ of $\mathcal{M}$ that moves right (the other direction is handled symmetrically). The simulation starts with the following transition:

$$(one, (a, \langle q, 0 \rangle, \text{START}), two, (b, \langle p, 0 \rangle, \text{COPYSRC}_\rightarrow), \rightarrow).$$

This time the choice of the destination state *two* is relevant, as it contains the information about the direction of copying: $one = \leftarrow, two = \rightarrow$. Note that the control mode of the source cell is set to COPYSRC$_\rightarrow$, and the head of $\mathcal{M}'$ is moved to the destination cell. Now $\mathcal{M}'$ decorates the destination cell by executing one of the following transitions:

$$(two, a, one, (a, \langle 0, 0 \rangle, \text{COPYDST}_\rightarrow), \leftarrow) \qquad \text{for } a \in T.$$

Note that the direction of the transition is $\leftarrow$, which is determined by the source state *two*. This time, the destination state *one* is again irrelevant. Once the destination cell is decorated, $\mathcal{M}'$ performs the actual copying using the following transitions in the source cell (for $a \in T, p \in Q$, and $0 \le i < n$):

$$(one, (a, \langle p, i \rangle, \text{COPYSRC}_\rightarrow), one, (a, \langle p, i{+}1 \rangle, \text{COPYSRC}_\rightarrow), \rightarrow) \quad \text{if } p[i] = 0,$$
$$(one, (a, \langle p, i \rangle, \text{COPYSRC}_\rightarrow), two, (a, \langle p, i{+}1 \rangle, \text{COPYSRC}_\rightarrow), \rightarrow) \quad \text{if } p[i] = 1,$$

where $p[i]$ stands for the ith bit of p. Note that this time the destination state is again relevant, as it contains the information about the copied bit. The above transitions are complemented by the following ones used in the destination cell (for $a \in T, p \in \{0, \ldots, 2^n - 1\}$, and $0 \le i < n$):

$$(one, (a, \langle p, i \rangle, \text{COPYDST}_\rightarrow), one, (a, \langle p, i{+}1 \rangle, \text{COPYDST}_\rightarrow), \leftarrow),$$
$$(two, (a, \langle p, i \rangle, \text{COPYDST}_\rightarrow), one, (a, \langle (p + 2^i), i{+}1 \rangle, \text{COPYDST}_\rightarrow), \leftarrow).$$

Again, the destination state *one* is irrelevant. In order to finish the copying, $\mathcal{M}'$ performs the following transitions:

$$(one, (a, \langle p, n \rangle, \text{COPYSRC}_\rightarrow), one, a, \rightarrow),$$

$$(one, (a, \langle p, n \rangle, \text{COPYDST}_{\rightarrow}), one, (a, \langle p, 0 \rangle, \text{START}), \circlearrowleft).$$

The first of the two transitions removes the decoration from the source cell, and the second one restores the control mode START in the destination cell in order to start the simulation of the next step of $\mathcal{M}$. The machine $\mathcal{M}'$ enters its accepting state *fin* once it sees a tape symbol of the form $(a, \langle q, 0 \rangle, \text{START})$ for an accepting state q of $\mathcal{M}$. ∎

Solution to Problem 168

(1) Fix a one-tape machine $\mathcal{M}$. To construct an equivalent two-tape write-once machine $\mathcal{M}'$, assume that the input of $\mathcal{M}'$ is given on the first tape. To simulate the first step of $\mathcal{M}$, the machine $\mathcal{M}'$ copies the whole content of the first tape to the second tape, taking into account the potential overwrite performed during the first step of $\mathcal{M}$. The copying is carried out by synchronously moving both heads of $\mathcal{M}'$ along the input word. While copying, $\mathcal{M}'$ also marks on the second tape the position of the head of $\mathcal{M}$. Once the copying is complete, $\mathcal{M}'$ writes a separator symbol $ on both tapes.

At this point, the entire configuration of $\mathcal{M}$ after its first step is represented on the second tape of $\mathcal{M}'$. Now $\mathcal{M}'$ moves the head of the second tape to the beginning of this representation and simulates the next step of $\mathcal{M}$, representing the resulting configuration on the first tape, and so on. Thus, the simulation lists the consecutive configurations of $\mathcal{M}$ on the first and the second tapes in an alternating fashion. $\mathcal{M}'$ accepts whenever $\mathcal{M}$ does.

(2) Fix a one-tape write-once machine $\mathcal{M}$ with state space Q and tape alphabet $T \cup \{\text{B}\}$, where $\text{B} \notin T$. Without loss of generality we may assume that $\mathcal{M}$ may only enter an accepting state if it sees a blank symbol. Furthermore, we may assume that every transition of $\mathcal{M}$ goes either left or right, but never stays in the same position.

We will use a variant of effect relations, similar to the one used for two-way automata in Problem 59. The key challenge is that, in contrast to two-way automata, even write-once Turing machines can write.

For a word $w \in T^*$, define the *left-to-right* relation $lr(w) \subseteq Q \times Q$ as follows: $(p, q) \in lr(w)$ if $\mathcal{M}$ has a run on w that starts in state p with the head on the first (left-most) letter of w, and ends in state q with the head on the first (blank) tape cell immediately after the last letter of w; moreover, the run stays within the word w until its last transition (as $\mathcal{M}$ is write-once, no letter is overwritten during the run). Intuitively speaking, the relation represents the transformation of a state p in which $\mathcal{M}$

enters the word w from the left into a state q in which $\mathcal{M}$ exits the word w to the right. Similarly, define the *right-to-left* relation $rl(w)$, the *left-to-left* relation $ll(w)$, and the *right-to-right* relation $rr(w)$.

We claim that the four relations can be computed by a finite automaton. More precisely, there is a deterministic finite automaton with the set of states $(\mathcal{P}(Q \times Q))^4$ which, after reading an input word $w \in T^*$, reaches the state

$$(lr(w), rl(w), ll(w), rr(w)).$$

To see this, note first that, as the machine never stays in the same position,

$$ll(a) = rl(a) = \{(p,q) \ : \ (p,a,q,a,\leftarrow) \in \delta\},$$
$$lr(a) = rr(a) = \{(p,q) \ : \ (p,a,q,a,\rightarrow) \in \delta\}.$$

Now assume that we know all four relations $lr(w), rl(w), ll(w)$, and $rr(w)$ and want to compute, say, $ll(wa)$ for some $a \in T$. Which pairs (p,q) are in $ll(wa)$? The machine $\mathcal{M}$ can enter w from the left and exit to the left (without reaching a). Therefore, we should include in $ll(wa)$ all pairs from $ll(w)$. But $\mathcal{M}$ can also enter w from the left, move to a, move back to w, and exit w to the left. This means that we need to include all pairs from $lr(w) \cdot ll(a) \cdot rl(w)$, where

$$r \cdot s = \{(x,z) \ : \ \exists y. \ (x,y) \in r \wedge (y,z) \in s\}$$

is the usual (left) composition of binary relations r and s. In general, the machine can move between w and a many times before exiting w to the left. The complete formula is

$$ll(wa) \ = \ ll(w) \ \cup \ lr(w) \cdot ll(a) \cdot \big(rr(w) \cdot ll(a)\big)^* \cdot rl(w). \tag{$\diamond$}$$

In a similar vein, the automaton computes the remaining three relations. The initial state of the automaton is the 4-tuple where the left-to-right and right-to-left relations are the identity relation, and the left-to-left and right-to-right relations are empty.

We now describe a non-deterministic finite automaton equivalent to $\mathcal{M}$. The automaton first reads the input word and computes $(lr(w), rl(w), ll(w), rr(w))$ as described above. Afterwards, the automaton performs only ε-transitions, non-deterministically choosing tape symbols to prepend or append to the current tape content, and updating the four relations. Additionally, the automaton maintains information on the last state of the non-deterministically chosen run of $\mathcal{M}$ that begins in q_0 with the head over the first symbol of w and ends when $\mathcal{M}$ first exits the current tape content (to the left or to the right). During the ε-transitions, the states of the automaton are 6-tuples from

$$(\mathcal{P}(Q \times Q))^4 \times Q \times \{\leftarrow, \rightarrow\}.$$

The last component indicates the direction in which $\mathcal{M}$ exits the current tape contents.

The first transition after reaching the end of the input word w non-deterministically chooses the state and direction of $\mathcal{M}$ when it first exits the word w:

$$(lr, rl, ll, rr) \xrightarrow{\varepsilon} (lr, rl, ll, rr, q, \leftarrow) \quad \text{whenever } (q_0, q) \in ll,$$

$$(lr, rl, ll, rr) \xrightarrow{\varepsilon} (lr, rl, ll, rr, q, \rightarrow) \quad \text{whenever } (q_0, q) \in lr.$$

The subsequent transitions non-deterministically choose the next tape symbol a written by $\mathcal{M}$, and update the four relations as well as the exit state and direction:

$$(lr(u), rl(u), ll(u), rr(u), p, \rightarrow) \xrightarrow{\varepsilon} (lr(ua), rl(ua), ll(ua), rr(ua), q_1, d_1),$$

$$(lr(u), rl(u), ll(u), rr(u), p, \leftarrow) \xrightarrow{\varepsilon} (lr(au), rl(au), ll(au), rr(au), q_2, d_2),$$

where $lr(au), rl(au), ll(au)$, and $rr(au)$ are computed by formulas analogous to ($\diamond$), and (q_1, d_1) and (q_2, d_2) range over possible states and directions of $\mathcal{M}$ upon exiting ua and au, respectively. The possible choices for (q_1, d_1) and (q_2, d_2) depend only on the old 6-tuple but not on the word u: (q_1, d_1) ranges over $(q, \leftarrow)$ such that

$$(p, q) \in \overleftarrow{a} \cdot \left(rr(u) \cdot ll(a)\right)^* \cdot rl(u)$$

and over $(q, \rightarrow)$ such that either $(p, \mathrm{B}, q, a, \rightarrow) \in \delta$, or

$$(p, q) \in \overleftarrow{a} \cdot \left(rr(u) \cdot ll(a)\right)^* \cdot rr(u) \cdot lr(a),$$

where $\overleftarrow{a} = \{(p', q') : (p', \mathrm{B}, q', a, \leftarrow) \in \delta\}$; the restrictions on (q_2, d_2) are entirely symmetric. Note how the relation $\overleftarrow{a}$ is used to overwrite B with a, and the relation $ll(a)$ is used to model all later visits of the head of $\mathcal{M}$ to the cell containing this a.

A state (lr, rl, ll, rr, q, d) is accepting if $\mathcal{M}$ can move from q to an accepting state when seeing B. $\blacksquare$

Solution to Problem 169

Let $\mathcal{M}$ be a deterministic one-tape Turing machine that recognizes a language L and makes $\mathcal{O}(n)$ steps on an input of length n. Let Q be the set of states of $\mathcal{M}$ and let $C \in \mathbb{N}$ be such that $\mathcal{M}$ makes at most Cn steps on inputs of length n.

The main idea of the proof is to show that the assumption about linear runtime in fact implies a stronger property, namely that the machine visits every tape cell only a bounded number of times.

For an integer i, we say that a run ρ *crosses the ith cut* at a given moment in time if at that moment the head moves either from the ith cell to the $(i + 1)$th or vice versa. Here, we assume that cells are indexed by integers and the input word is placed at positions 1 through n. We shall prove the following claim.

Claim 1. There exists an integer K such that for each run ρ and integer i, the run ρ crosses the ith cut at most K times.

Before we prove Claim 1, we show why it implies that L is regular. For each integer i, let the *ith crossing sequence* be the sequence $\chi_i = (q_1, q_2, \dots)$ of states from Q that consists of states in which the machine is when the run ρ crosses the ith cut for the first time, for the second time, etc. By Claim 1, the number of crossings is always bounded by K, hence $\chi_i \in Q^{\leq K} = \bigcup_{k=0}^{K} Q^k$ for each integer i.

To prove that L is regular, we describe an automaton recognizing the set L' of words of the form $B^* w B^*$ that are the initial tape contents of the segment of the tape used by $\mathcal{M}$ during the computation on $w \in L - \{\varepsilon\}$. To simplify the construction we assume that $\mathcal{M}$ begins its computation by entering from the left the first cell of this segment, and finishes by moving right from the last cell of the segment. If the original $\mathcal{M}$ does not have this property, we replace it by a machine that first marks the current cell as the left limit, then moves on to the input word, simulates the original $\mathcal{M}$ as long as it does not go beyond the left limit, and before finishing moves to the first cell on the right that has not been visited yet. Because of the last pass to the right, this modification may increase the bound on the length of crossing sequences by one. The modified machine accepts $w \in L - \{\varepsilon\}$ only if the initial position is far enough to the left, and it loops on ε. Still, we have that $L - \{\varepsilon\} = (B^*)^{-1} L' (B^*)^{-1} \cap \Sigma^*$ where Σ is the input alphabet of $\mathcal{M}$, so the regularity of L will follow by the closure properties of regular languages.

The automaton recognizing L' guesses crossing sequences from left to right, and verifies that they constitute a run of $\mathcal{M}$ over the input word. That is, the set of states is $Q^{\leq K}$. The initial crossing sequence consists solely of the initial state of $\mathcal{M}$, and each final crossing sequence consists of a single accepting state of $\mathcal{M}$. Given a crossing sequence $\chi = (q_1, q_2, \dots)$ and the next input symbol a, the automaton non-deterministically guesses the next consistent crossing sequence χ'. When is χ' consistent? Since $\mathcal{M}$ enters the tape segment from the left, it also enters each cell for the first time from the left, and this happens when $\mathcal{M}$ is in the state q_1 of χ. The state q_1 and the tape symbol a determine: which symbol a' will be written in the cell, whether $\mathcal{M}$ will leave the cell to the left or to the right, and what the new q' will be. If $\mathcal{M}$ leaves to the right, then q' should be equal to the first state of χ'; if $\mathcal{M}$ leaves to the left, then q' should be equal to the second state of χ. When the machine visits the position for the next time, the symbol written in the cell is a', and a similar consistency check must be performed. And so on, until all states of both crossing sequences are used (the last time the machine leaves the cell, it moves to the right). This describes the set of consistent triples $(\chi, a, \chi') \in Q^{\leq K} \times \Sigma \times Q^{\leq K}$, which is the transition relation of the automaton. It also completes the construction of the automaton for L'.

It remains to prove Claim 1. Fix an integer $i \in \{0, 1, \ldots, n\}$; that is, i corresponds to one of the cuts within the input word. The proof for the other cuts is essentially the same. We would like to show that the length of the crossing sequence χ_i is at most K, for some constant K to be defined later. The following simple unpumping statement will be crucial.

Claim 2. Suppose u can be factorized as $u = xyz$, where x, y, and z are non-empty words over Σ such that the crossing sequences at the cuts between x and y, and between y and z, coincide. Define $u' = xz$. Then $\mathcal{M}$ accepts u if and only if $\mathcal{M}$ accepts u'. Moreover, the ith crossing sequence of the run ρ' on u' is equal to the ith crossing sequence of ρ when $i \leq |x|$, and to the $(i + |y|)$th crossing sequence of ρ when $i \geq |x|$.

Claim 2 follows easily by observing that, after removing the infix y, the segments of the run before y and the segments after y can be glued together to form the run ρ' of $\mathcal{M}$ on u'. This is because the crossing sequences at the left and right ends of y are equal.

Recall that C is the multiplicative constant in the bound on the number of steps of $\mathcal{M}$. Call $i \in \mathbb{Z}$ *thin* if the crossing sequence χ_i is of length at most $2C$, and *thick* otherwise. Note that there are at most $|Q^{\leq 2C}|$ possible crossing sequences corresponding to thin positions. Let us examine the number of thin cuts in $\{1, 2, \ldots, i - 1\}$. If this number is larger than $|Q^{\leq 2C}|$, then there are two cuts $1 \leq j_1 < j_2 < i$ such that the crossing sequences at these cuts are equal. Consequently, we can factorize u as $u = xyz$, where y is the infix between cells j_1 (exclusive) and j_2 (inclusive) so that Claim 2 can be applied to this factorization. Thus, $\mathcal{M}$ accepts xz if and only if $\mathcal{M}$ accepts u, and the crossing sequence at cut $i - (j_2 - j_1)$ of the run of $\mathcal{M}$ on u' is equal to χ_i, which is the crossing sequence we want to bound.

We can apply a symmetric unpumping if the number of thin cuts in $\{i + 1, i + 2, \ldots, n - 1\}$ is larger than $|Q^{\leq 2C}|$. Let u' be a word obtained from u by applying both these kinds of unpumpings exhaustively, always keeping the initial crossing sequence χ_i intact. Then, supposing ρ' is the run of $\mathcal{M}$ on u' with crossing sequences $(\chi'_j)_{j\in\mathbb{Z}}$, we have the following:

- ρ' is accepting if and only if ρ was accepting;
- there is a cut $i' \in \{0, 1, \ldots, n'\}$ such that $\chi'_{i'} = \chi_i$, where n' is the length of u'; and
- there are at most $3 + 2|Q^{\leq 2C}|$ thin cuts in $\{0, 1, \ldots, n'\}$, i.e., at most $|Q^{\leq 2C}|$ between 1 and $i' - 1$, at most $|Q^{\leq 2C}|$ between $i' + 1$ and $n' - 1$, plus any of $\{0, i', n'\}$.

Now, we use the following straightforward observation that connects the length of the run with the total length of crossing sequences.

Claim 3. If ρ is a run of $\mathcal{M}$ with crossing sequences $(\chi_j)_{j\in\mathbb{Z}}$, then the length of ρ is equal to $\sum_{j\in\mathbb{Z}} |\chi_j|$.

From Claim 3 it immediately follows that in each run of $\mathcal{M}$ on an input word of length m, at most $m/2$ cuts in $\{0, 1, \ldots, m\}$ can be thick. Indeed, otherwise the total length of the run would be larger than $m/2 \cdot 2C = Cm$, contradicting the assumption about the upper bound on the runtime of the machine. Since in the run of $\mathcal{M}$ on u' we have at most $3 + 2|Q^{\leq 2C}|$ thin cuts in $\{0, 1, \ldots, n'\}$, we infer that u' has to be of constant length, more precisely, of length at most $6 + 4|Q^{\leq 2C}|$. Therefore, the run of $\mathcal{M}$ on u' must have length at most $C \cdot (6 + 4|Q^{\leq 2C}|)$, and consequently every crossing sequence of this run has at most this length. This in particular applies to the crossing sequence $\chi'_{i'}$, which is equal to the original crossing sequence χ_i in u. We infer that $|\chi_i| \leq C \cdot (6 + 4|Q^{\leq 2C}|)$ for all $i \in \{0, 1, \ldots, n\}$. For other i the argument is analogous, except that one performs unpumping in the whole word u without splitting it into two parts. Thus, we may take $K = C \cdot (6 + 4|Q^{\leq 2C}|)$. This concludes the proof of Claim 1. ∎

Solution to Problem 170

Transitions of an automaton with two stacks are 7-tuples of the form

$$(q, s_1, s_2, a, p, w_1, w_2) \in Q \times S_1 \times S_2 \times (\Sigma \cup \{\varepsilon\}) \times Q \times S_1^* \times S_2^*,$$

where Q is the set of states, Σ is the input alphabet, S_1 and S_2 are stack alphabets of the two stacks. The meaning is: in state $q \in Q$, if the topmost elements on the two stacks are $s_1 \in S_1$ and $s_2 \in S_2$, read a from the input, change the state to p, and replace s_1 with w_1 and s_2 with w_2. Just like for ordinary pushdown automata, we adopt the convention that the order of letters in w_1 and w_2

corresponds to the downward direction in the stacks. The automaton accepts by entering one of the distinguished accepting states.

In the simulation of a Turing machine $\mathcal{M}$ by an automaton with two stacks, the first stack stores the tape content to the left of $\mathcal{M}$'s head, and the second stack stores the tape content to the right of the head, including the current cell. (Thus both stack alphabets are equal to the tape alphabet of $\mathcal{M}$.) The tape symbol seen by the head of $\mathcal{M}$ is always the topmost element on the second stack.

In the preprocessing phase, the automaton pushes the input word onto the second stack, but in reverse order. This is achieved by first pushing the consecutive letters of the input word onto the first stack, and then popping symbols from the first stack one by one and pushing them onto the second stack, in a sequence of ε-transitions. The preprocessing phase uses two fresh states. In the proper simulation phase, the automaton uses the same states as the simulated machine $\mathcal{M}$. The simulation of a transition of $\mathcal{M}$ going right, say

$$(q, a, p, b, \rightarrow),$$

is performed using the following ε-transitions of the automaton:

$$(q, c, a, \varepsilon, p, bc, \varepsilon) \qquad \text{for } c \in S_1.$$

That is, the automaton checks if a is at the top of the second stack, pops it, and pushes b onto the first stack. In a similar vein one simulates the transitions that go left or stay in the same position. To ensure that the stored portion of the tape grows as $\mathcal{M}$ visits new cells, whenever a stack becomes empty during the simulation phase, the automaton pushes B.

For every k, an automaton with k stacks can be easily simulated by a Turing machine, and therefore also by an automaton with two stacks.   ∎

Solution to Problem 171

To make the definition of the simulating automaton compact, we use generalized put and get transitions operating on a non-empty word $w \in S^+$ rather than a single symbol $a \in S$:

$$(q, \text{get}(w), p), \qquad (q, \text{put}(w), p).$$

Both are easily simulated by sequences of ordinary transitions.

The simulation of a given Turing machine $\mathcal{M}$ starts with a preprocessing phase which adds all letters of the input to the queue. For convenience, let the automaton additionally add one blank symbol B at the beginning and one at the end of the input. Furthermore, assume that, instead of the very first input letter a, the pair (a, q_0) is added to the queue, where q_0 is the initial state of

$\mathcal{M}$. During the simulation there is always exactly one element of $T \times Q$ in the queue; as usual, T and Q are the tape alphabet and the set of states of $\mathcal{M}$. The queue alphabet is $T \cup T \times Q \cup \{!\}$, where ! is an additional special symbol.

The proper simulation is organized into *rounds*, each round corresponding to a single step of the machine. In each round the automaton scans all symbols in the queue (by removing them and adding them back to the queue), and accounts for the effect of one transition of $\mathcal{M}$. The simulation phase relies on two states, q_{start} and q_{round}. In order to recognize the end of a round, we introduce a starting transition

$$(q_{\text{start}}, \text{put}(\text{B}!\text{B}), q_{\text{round}})$$

that adds the symbol ! to the queue (sandwiched between two blank symbols for reasons to be explained later), and a corresponding ending transition

$$(q_{\text{round}}, \text{get}(!), q_{\text{start}})$$

that removes ! from the queue. In state q_{round} the automaton either scans the next symbol in the queue by executing a get transition followed by a put transition,

$$(q_{\text{round}}, \text{get}(a), q_a), \qquad (q_a, \text{put}(a), q_{\text{round}})$$

for $a \in T$ (auxiliary states q_a are used here); or accounts for the effect of the next transition of $\mathcal{M}$. The latter is done by removing three symbols from the queue, followed by adding three suitably modified symbols to the queue. For instance, if $\mathcal{M}$ has a transition

$$r = (q, a, p, b, \leftarrow),$$

the simulating automaton has the pair of (generalized) transitions

$$(q_{\text{round}}, \text{get}(c(a, q)d), q_{r,c,d}), \qquad (q_{r,c,d}, \text{put}((c, p)bd), q_{\text{round}})$$

for every $c, d \in T$ (again, auxiliary states $q_{r,c,d}$ are used here). Note that the automaton non-deterministically chooses between scanning letters and accounting for a transition of $\mathcal{M}$. Furthermore, note that possibly $c = \text{B}$, which corresponds to the head of $\mathcal{M}$ being placed at the left end of its working space; similarly, possibly $d = \text{B}$ when the head of $\mathcal{M}$ is at the right end of its working space. However, there is no risk of the simulating automaton running out of blank symbols in such situations, as every round starts with putting B!B in the queue, which extends the working space of the simulated machine with one blank symbol at both ends.

The automaton enters an accepting state after accounting for a transition r whose target state is accepting. ∎

Solution to Problem 172

Let $\mathcal{M}$ be a one-tape non-deterministic Turing machine over a one-letter input alphabet $\{1\}$. As explained in the statement of the problem, an input word $w \in \{1\}^*$ represents the natural number $n = |w|$ in unary.

We shall construct a three-counter automaton $\mathcal{A}$ equivalent to $\mathcal{M}$. By Problem 166, we can assume that the tape alphabet of $\mathcal{M}$ is $\{1, 2, \mathsf{B}\}$ and that $\mathcal{M}$ never writes B. As the automaton $\mathcal{A}$ can only manipulate numbers, we treat a tape content $w \in \{1, 2\}^*$ of $\mathcal{M}$ as the ternary encoding of a natural number (never using digit 0). Note that using tape alphabet $\{0, 1, \mathsf{B}\}$ and binary encoding would not work, as it would not distinguish words that differ only by leading 0's, for instance, 01 and 0000001. Our idea is similar to that in Problem 170: we want to maintain the invariant that two parts of the tape content, the one to the left of $\mathcal{M}$'s head and the one to the right of $\mathcal{M}$'s head including the cell scanned by the head, are stored in the two counters c_1 and c_2, respectively. We adopt the convention that the cells closest to the head correspond to the lowest bits.

By the definition of counter automata, initially counter c_1 stores $n = |w|$ and c_2 and c_3 are set to 0. In order to start satisfying our invariant, $\mathcal{A}$ needs to perform some preprocessing, after which the value of counter c_2 is the number whose ternary encoding is a word of 1's of length n (as all the tape symbols are initially to the right of $\mathcal{M}$'s head), and the value of counter c_1 is 0 (which corresponds to the empty word, as no tape symbols are initially to the left of $\mathcal{M}$'s head). This is achieved by iterating the following sequence of transitions as long as $c_1 > 0$: decrement c_1; multiply c_2 by 3; and increment c_2. The corresponding fragment of $\mathcal{A}$ can be depicted as follows:

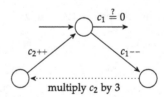

The dotted edge labelled with 'multiply c_2 by 3' is actually a macro that makes use of the third counter c_3; this edge stands for the following fragment of the automaton (we label transitions by sequences of operations, in order to avoid drawing auxiliary intermediate states):

$$c_2\text{--}; c_3\text{++}; c_3\text{++}; c_3\text{++} \qquad\qquad c_3\text{--}; c_2\text{++}$$

$$\longrightarrow \bigcirc \overset{\curvearrowright}{\underset{}{\qquad}} \xrightarrow{\quad c_2 \overset{?}{=} 0 \quad} \bigcirc \overset{\curvearrowright}{\underset{}{\qquad}} \xrightarrow{\quad c_3 \overset{?}{=} 0 \quad} \longrightarrow$$

Once the invariant is satisfied, the simulation of $\mathcal{M}$'s transitions is similar to that in Problem 170. First, $\mathcal{A}$ should read the tape symbol under $\mathcal{M}$'s head; in terms of numeric values stored in the counters, this amounts to computing the remainder of the division of c_2 by 3. This is achieved by the following fragment of the automaton:

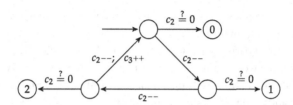

Note that after entering one of the states 0, 1, or 2, the value of counter c_3 is the integer part of the quotient of c_2 by 3. Now $\mathcal{A}$ recovers the original value of c_2, which can be easily done as in the 'multiply c_2 by 3' macro above. The automaton also stores in its state the current state of $\mathcal{M}$ (not depicted in the pictures above); thus $\mathcal{A}$ has enough information to choose a transition of $\mathcal{M}$ applicable in a given configuration. In effect, $\mathcal{A}$ changes the state of $\mathcal{M}$ and the tape symbol under $\mathcal{M}$'s head (this is achieved by one or two increments or decrements of c_2). Finally, $\mathcal{A}$ accounts for the move of $\mathcal{M}$'s head: for instance, to simulate a move to the left, the automaton: multiplies c_2 by 3 and increases it by the remainder of the division of c_1 by 3; and replaces the value of c_1 by the integer part of the division of c_1 by 3. In order to carry out these actions using only three counters, $\mathcal{A}$ first uses c_3 to divide c_1 by 3 and stores the remainder in its state; then it uses the same counter c_3 to multiply c_2 by 3; finally, c_2 is incremented by the remainder stored in the state. ∎

Solution to Problem 173

(a) $\Longleftrightarrow$ (b) Assume that $L \subseteq \Sigma^*$ is recursively enumerable; that is, $L = L(\mathcal{M})$ for some Turing machine $\mathcal{M}$ that may not halt on some input words. The machine $\mathcal{M}$ computes a partial function that, on a word w, returns the contents of $\mathcal{M}$'s tape in the accepting configuration if $\mathcal{M}$ accepts w, and is undefined otherwise. The domain of this function is L.

Conversely, if a partial function $f : \Sigma^* \rightharpoonup \Gamma^*$ is computed by a machine $\mathcal{M}$, then the language accepted by $\mathcal{M}$ is the domain of f.

(a) $\Longrightarrow$ (c) Assume that $L = L(\mathcal{M})$ for some Turing machine $\mathcal{M}$ that may not halt on some input words. Consider a machine that, given an input word w:

- puts a special marker $ after w and writes a copy of w after that marker;
- simulates $\mathcal{M}$ on the copied w, treating the marker $ as the beginning of the tape;
- if $\mathcal{M}$ halts and accepts, erases everything from the tape starting from the marker $ and accepts; and otherwise rejects.

This machine computes a partial identity function whose domain (and hence also image) coincides with $L(\mathcal{M})$.

(c) $\Longrightarrow$ (d) Let a partial function $f : \Sigma^* \rightharpoonup \Gamma^*$ be computed by a machine $\mathcal{M}$ that accepts some words, but may not halt on some input words. We construct a machine $\mathcal{M}'$ simulating machine $\mathcal{M}$ on all words of a limited length for a limited time and gradually extending the length and time allowed. The machine $\mathcal{M}'$ runs the following algorithm:

Input: a number n
count $\leftarrow 0$
for $k \leftarrow 1, 2, 3, 4, \ldots$ **do**
    for all words w of length at most k **do**
        simulate $\mathcal{M}$ on input w for at most k steps
        if $\mathcal{M}$ accepted **then**
            count $\leftarrow$ *count* $+ 1$
        if *count* $\geq n$ **then**
            halt and accept.

This machine halts and accepts on every input. This is because some word w is accepted by $\mathcal{M}$ in (say) m steps, so for each $k \geq \max(|w|, m)$ the variable *count* is incremented at least once, so eventually its value reaches any given n.

It is easy to modify $\mathcal{M}'$ so that, just before halting, it replaces the contents of its tape with the contents of the tape of the instance of $\mathcal{M}$ that has just been simulated, and erases all other information. The modified version of $\mathcal{M}'$ produces exactly those output words that are produced by accepting runs of $\mathcal{M}$.

(d) $\Longrightarrow$ (a) Assume that L is the set of output words produced by a machine $\mathcal{M}$ that halts on every input. Consider a machine $\mathcal{M}'$ that, given a word w, generates all inputs for $\mathcal{M}$ one by one and simulates $\mathcal{M}$ on each of them, halting and accepting whenever $\mathcal{M}$ produces w. If $w \in L$ then it will eventually be produced and accepted, since each simulated run of $\mathcal{M}$ terminates. If $w \notin L$ then it will never be produced and so $\mathcal{M}'$ will not halt. As a result, $L(\mathcal{M}') = L$. ∎

Solution to Problem 174

For the left-to-right implication, assume that L is accepted by a machine $\mathcal{M}$ that halts on all inputs. Consider a machine $\mathcal{M}'$ that, given a number $n \geq 0$, computes the $(n + 1)$th smallest number k that is accepted by $\mathcal{M}$. This can be achieved by running the following algorithm:

Input: a number n
$k \leftarrow 0$
count $\leftarrow 0$
while *count* $< n + 1$ **do**
    if $\mathcal{M}$ accepts k **then**
        count $\leftarrow$ *count* $+ 1$
    $k \leftarrow k + 1$
output $k - 1$ **and accept**.

If L is infinite then $\mathcal{M}'$ halts for all inputs, and it computes a strictly increasing function whose image is L.

For the right-to-left implication, every finite language is obviously decidable. Assume a strictly increasing function $f : \mathbb{N} \to \mathbb{N}$ computed by a machine $\mathcal{M}$. Consider a machine $\mathcal{M}'$ that, given a number n, computes $f(k)$ by simulating $\mathcal{M}$ on consecutive input numbers $k = 0, 1, 2, \ldots$, stops as soon as $f(k) \geq n$, and accepts if and only if $f(k) = n$. Since $\mathcal{M}$ halts on every input k and the function f is strictly increasing, $\mathcal{M}'$ halts for every n and accepts exactly those numbers that are in the image of f. ∎

Solution to Problem 175
Suppose that a language L is accepted by a machine $\mathcal{M}_1$, and its complement $\Sigma^* - L$ by a machine $\mathcal{M}_2$; both machines may not halt on some inputs. Consider a two-tape machine $\mathcal{M}$ that, on an input word w, copies w to a second tape and then simulates $\mathcal{M}_1$ on one tape and $\mathcal{M}_2$ on the other, in parallel, just like in Problem 163. Let $\mathcal{M}$ accept as soon as $\mathcal{M}_1$ accepts, and reject as soon as $\mathcal{M}_2$ accepts. Since every input word is accepted either by $\mathcal{M}_1$ or by $\mathcal{M}_2$, the machine $\mathcal{M}$ halts on every input and accepts the language L. Therefore, L is decidable and so is its complement. ∎

Solution to Problem 176
The following solution is due to Emil Post, who called such languages *simple*.

Consider an effective enumeration of all Turing machines over the alphabet $\Sigma = \{0, 1\}$; that is, an infinite non-repetitive sequence of machines

$$\mathcal{M}_1, \mathcal{M}_2, \mathcal{M}_3, \ldots$$

such that there exists a Turing machine that, given a number n, outputs $[\mathcal{M}_n]$, where $[\mathcal{M}]$ stands for the code of a machine $\mathcal{M}$ in some fixed encoding of Turing machines as words.

Furthermore, consider the language

$$L = \{([\mathcal{M}], w) \; : \; \mathcal{M} \text{ accepts } w\}.$$

L is recursively enumerable: given $[\mathcal{M}]$ and w, simply simulate $\mathcal{M}$ on w and accept if it accepts. By Problem 173, L is the image of some computable function from Γ^* to Σ^*, where Σ is the alphabet of L and Γ is some finite alphabet. The set Γ^* can be equipped with a computable total order; for example, for $\Gamma = \{0, 1\}^*$, there is

$$\varepsilon < 0 < 1 < 00 < 01 < 10 < 11 < 000 < 001 < \cdots.$$

This gives a computable function from $\mathbb{N}$ to Γ^*, and by composition a computable function

$$f \colon \mathbb{N} \to \Sigma^*$$

whose image is L.

Call a word $w \in \Sigma^*$ *good* if there are numbers $k, n \in \mathbb{N}$ such that:

- $f(k) = ([\mathcal{M}_n], w)$;
- $|w| > n$; and
- k is the least such number for n, that is, for all $k' < k$ such that $f(k') = ([\mathcal{M}_n], v)$, it holds that $|v| \le n$.

Define K to be the set of all good words. We shall show that K has all the required properties.

First, K is recursively enumerable. Indeed, given an input word w, compute $f(k)$ for increasing values of k, and whenever $f(k) = ([\mathcal{M}], w)$ for some machine $\mathcal{M}$, find n such that $\mathcal{M} = \mathcal{M}_n$ and check whether $|w| > n$. If the input word is in K, then it will eventually be detected.

Second, the complement of K is infinite. To see this, notice that each number n gives rise to at most one good word; therefore, for every m, there are at most m good words of length at most m.

Finally, to say that the complement of K does not contain any infinite recursively enumerable subset, we may equivalently say that K has a non-empty intersection with every infinite recursively enumerable language. To see this, consider any such language L and let $\mathcal{M}_n$ be the machine that accepts it. Since L is infinite, it contains some words w such that $|w| > n$. One of these words is good. ∎

Solution to Problem 177

First, consider a *universal* Turing machine U over some finite alphabet of size, say, k. Such a machine accepts exactly those words of the form $([\mathcal{M}], w)$ for which [$\mathcal{M}$] is a representation of a Turing machine $\mathcal{M}$ according to some fixed representation schema, w is a word over the input alphabet of $\mathcal{M}$, and $\mathcal{M}$ accepts w. It easily follows from the undecidability of the halting problem that, given an input word v, it is undecidable whether U accepts v.

Now consider a machine U^1 over a one-letter input alphabet which, on an input word w, first computes the base-k representation of the length of w, treats the resulting number as a word over the input alphabet of U, and then simulates U on it. Clearly, it is also undecidable whether U^1 accepts a given word.

Now from Problem 172 it follows that there exists a three-counter automaton with the desired property. (Indeed, take a three-counter automaton equivalent to U^1.) Call that automaton $A3$.

We shall construct a two-counter automaton A that will simulate the contents of the three counters of $A3$ (call them c_1, c_2, and c_3) on two counters (call them d_1, and d_2). The idea is that a configuration of $A3$ with numbers n_1, n_2, and n_3 stored in counters c_1, c_2, and c_3, respectively, is represented by a configuration of A with the number $2^{n_1} 3^{n_2} 5^{n_3}$ stored in the counter d_1, with the counter d_2 used for bookkeeping.

For example, whenever $A3$ wants to increment c_2, A will multiply the number stored in d_1 by 3. To this end, A first moves the contents of d_1 to d_2 by zeroing d_2, then repeatedly decrementing d_1 and incrementing d_2 until d_1 reaches zero. Then A repeatedly decrements d_2 and increments d_1 thrice, until d_2 reaches zero.

Similarly, decrementing counters of $A3$ is simulated by division, and zero tests are simulated by checking divisibility.

The automaton A is not equivalent to $A3$: it accepts a number 2^n whenever $A3$ accepts n. However, the problem of checking whether it accepts a given input number is clearly undecidable. ∎

Solution to Problem 178
First let us prove that, were the original Post correspondence problem decidable, the modified one would be decidable too. We shall do that by constructing a computable reduction from the modified problem to the original. For an instance P of the modified Post correspondence problem, consisting of

$$u_1, u_2, \ldots, u_n \in \Sigma^* \quad \text{and} \quad w_1, w_2, \ldots, w_n \in \Sigma^*,$$

consider the alphabet $\Sigma' = \Sigma \cup \{\triangleleft, \diamond, \triangleright\}$ extending Σ with three fresh letters, and an instance P' of the original Post correspondence problem consisting of

$$x_0, x_1, x_2, \ldots, x_n, x_{n+1} \in (\Sigma')^* \quad \text{and} \quad y_0, y_1, y_2, \ldots, y_n, y_{n+1} \in (\Sigma')^*$$

where:

- x_i for $i = 1, \ldots, n$ arises from u_i by replacing each letter $a \in \Sigma$ with $a\diamond$;
- y_i for $i = 1, \ldots, n$ arises from w_i by replacing each letter $a \in \Sigma$ with $\diamond a$;
- $x_0 = \triangleleft\diamond x_1$ and $y_0 = \triangleleft y_1$;
- $x_{n+1} = \triangleright$ and $y_{n+1} = \diamond\triangleright$.

Consider any solution $u_1 u_{i_2} \ldots u_{i_m} = w_1 w_{i_2} \ldots w_{i_m}$ for P. It is easy to see that

$$\triangleleft\diamond x_1 x_{i_2} \ldots x_{i_m} \triangleright = \triangleleft y_1 y_{i_2} \ldots y_{i_m} \diamond\triangleright,$$

and therefore

$$x_0 x_{i_2} \ldots x_{i_m} x_{n+1} = y_0 y_{i_2} \ldots y_{i_m} y_{n+1}$$

is a legal solution to P'.

On the other hand, consider any solution $x_{i_1} x_{i_2} \ldots x_{i_m} = y_{i_1} y_{i_2} \ldots y_{i_m}$ to P'. What can the first letter of this solution be? It cannot be $\diamond$, because no word among $x_0, \ldots, x_{n+1}$ begins with $\diamond$. It cannot be a letter from Σ or $\triangleright$, because no word among $y_0, \ldots, y_{n+1}$ begins with such a letter. The only remaining option is $\triangleleft$; therefore $i_1 = 0$ and the solution can be presented as

$$\triangleleft\diamond x_1 x_{i_2} \ldots x_{i_m} = \triangleleft y_1 y_{i_2} \ldots y_{i_m}.$$

Dropping all $\triangleleft$, $\diamond$, and $\triangleright$ from both sides, we obtain u_i from x_i and w_i from y_i for $i = 1, \ldots, n$, u_1 from each x_0, w_1 from each y_0, and the empty word ε from each x_{n+1} and y_{n+1}. As a result,

$$u_1 u_{i_2} \ldots u_{i_m} = w_1 w_{i_2} \ldots w_{i_m},$$

where only $i_j \in \{1, \ldots, n\}$ are included, is a solution to P.

Altogether, P' has a solution if and only if P has a solution of the form $u_1 \ldots = w_1 \ldots$. Since P' can be computed from P, if the original Post correspondence problem were decidable, then so would be the modified problem.

We shall now show that the modified Post correspondence problem is undecidable. It is convenient to present an instance of the Post correspondence problem as a set of tiles

$$\begin{bmatrix} u_1 \\ w_1 \end{bmatrix}, \quad \begin{bmatrix} u_2 \\ w_2 \end{bmatrix}, \quad \cdots \quad \begin{bmatrix} u_n \\ w_n \end{bmatrix}$$

and ask whether the tiles can be arranged horizontally, possibly with repetitions, so that the words above and below the horizontal lines concatenate to the same word.

We construct a computable reduction from the halting problem to the modified Post correspondence problem. Consider an instance $([\mathcal{M}], w)$ of the Turing machine halting problem. We shall construct an instance P of the modified Post correspondence problem such that P has a legal solution if and only if $\mathcal{M}$ accepts w. Assume that $\mathcal{M}$ only accepts by moving the head to the beginning of its tape and going into an accepting state q_A.

Consider the following set of tiles, over the alphabet $Q \cup \Gamma \cup \{\diamond\}$, where Q is the set of states, Γ is the working alphabet of $\mathcal{M}$, and $\diamond$ is a special separator symbol:

- $\begin{bmatrix} \diamond \\ \diamond q_0 w \diamond \end{bmatrix}$, where $q_0 \in Q$ is the initial state of $\mathcal{M}$; this will be the chosen initial tile for solutions of P;
- $\begin{bmatrix} qa \\ bq' \end{bmatrix}$ for each $q, q' \in Q$ and $a, b \in \Gamma$ such that $\mathcal{M}$ in state q, upon reading a on the tape, writes b, changes its state to q', and moves its head to the right;
- $\begin{bmatrix} q\diamond \\ bq'\diamond \end{bmatrix}$ for each $q, q' \in Q$ and $b \in \Gamma$ such that $\mathcal{M}$ in state q, upon reading the blank symbol on the tape, writes b, changes its state to q', and moves its head to the right;
- $\begin{bmatrix} cqa \\ q'cb \end{bmatrix}$ for each $q, q' \in Q$ and $a, b, c \in \Gamma$ such that $\mathcal{M}$ in state q, upon reading a on the tape, writes b, changes its state to q', and moves its head to the left;
- $\begin{bmatrix} cq\diamond \\ q'cb\diamond \end{bmatrix}$ for each $q, q' \in Q$ and $b, c \in \Gamma$ such that $\mathcal{M}$ in state q, upon reading the blank symbol on the tape, writes b, changes its state to q', and moves its head to the left;
- $\begin{bmatrix} \diamond \\ \diamond \end{bmatrix}$ and $\begin{bmatrix} a \\ a \end{bmatrix}$ for each $a \in \Gamma$.

We shall need some more tiles to complete the task, but for now let us see how one may begin to construct a solution from these tiles. For example, let $w = abd$ and let $\mathcal{M}$ in the initial state q_0, upon reading a, write c and move to the right in a state q_1. For the instance P given as above, a solution must begin with a sequence of tiles

$$\begin{bmatrix} \diamond \\ \diamond q_0 abd \diamond \end{bmatrix} \begin{bmatrix} q_0 a \\ cq_1 \end{bmatrix} \begin{bmatrix} b \\ b \end{bmatrix} \begin{bmatrix} d \\ d \end{bmatrix} \begin{bmatrix} \diamond \\ \diamond \end{bmatrix} \cdots$$

That is, any solution for P must begin with $\diamond q_0abd\diamond cq_1bd\diamond\ldots$ and, more generally, with an encoding of all of an initial segment of a run of $\mathcal{M}$ on w.

Note that no solution can actually be completed, as in all tiles $\left[\frac{v}{w}\right]$ considered so far there is $|v| \le |w|$. To allow complete solutions when $\mathcal{M}$ reaches an accepting state $q_A \in Q$ on w, we extend P with tiles

- $\left[\frac{aq_A}{q_A}\right]$ and $\left[\frac{q_Aa}{q_A}\right]$, for all $a \in \Gamma$, and
- $\left[\frac{\diamond q_A\diamond}{\diamond}\right]$.

For example, if $\mathcal{M}$ eventually reaches an accepting configuration bq_Add, then a partial solution constructed as above and ending with $\ldots\diamond bq_Add\diamond$ may be completed with

$$\ldots\frac{\cdots}{\diamond bq_Add}\left[\frac{\diamond}{\diamond}\right]\left[\frac{b}{b}\right]\left[\frac{q_Ad}{q_A}\right]\left[\frac{d}{d}\right]\left[\frac{\diamond}{\diamond}\right]\left[\frac{b}{b}\right]\left[\frac{q_Ad}{q_A}\right]\left[\frac{\diamond}{\diamond}\right]\left[\frac{bq_A}{q_A}\right]\left[\frac{\diamond q_A\diamond}{\diamond}\right].$$

In general, P has a solution if and only if $\mathcal{M}$ accepts w, which completes a reduction of the (undecidable) halting problem to the modified Post correspondence problem. ∎

Solution to Problem 179

For a Turing machine $\mathcal{M}$, a *successful run* is a sequence

$$\diamond c_0\diamond c_1\diamond\ldots\diamond c_n\diamond,$$

where the c_i are configurations of $\mathcal{M}$, c_0 is an initial configuration, c_n is an accepting configuration, $c_i \vdash_{\mathcal{M}} c_{i+1}$, and additionally $|c_0| = |c_1| = \cdots = |c_n|$. Clearly a machine accepts a non-empty language if and only if it admits a successful run, with some configurations padded with blank symbols as needed.

Let us take a moment to understand the step relation $\vdash_{\mathcal{M}}$ between configurations of a machine $\mathcal{M}$. For simplicity, assume without loss of generality that $\mathcal{M}$ moves its head at each step. If $\mathcal{M}$, upon seeing a letter a in a state q, writes b, goes into state q', and moves the head to the right, we have

$$cqa \vdash_{\mathcal{M}} cbq'$$

for every letter c. If in a similar situation the head moves to the left, then

$$cqa \vdash_{\mathcal{M}} q'cb.$$

These *local reconfigurations* generate the entire relation $\vdash_{\mathcal{M}}$. Indeed, $c \vdash_{\mathcal{M}} c'$ if and only if $c = xvy$ and $c' = xwy$ such that $xy \in \Gamma^*$ and $v \vdash_{\mathcal{M}} w$ is a local reconfiguration.

We shall prove that, for every machine $\mathcal{M}$ (with a set of states Q and working alphabet Γ), the set of those words over $Q \cup \Gamma \cup \{\diamond\}$ that are *not* successful runs of $\mathcal{M}$ is a context-free language.

Indeed, what can go wrong in a word w that is not a successful run? Either:

(i) it begins or ends with a letter different from $\diamond$; or

(ii) between some two consecutive $\diamond$'s there are zero or more than one letters from Q; or

(iii) the letter from Q between the first two $\diamond$'s is not an initial state of $\mathcal{M}$, or the letter from Q between the last two $\diamond$'s is not an accepting state; or

(iv) w has a subword of the form $\diamond c \diamond c' \diamond$ such that cc' does not contain $\diamond$ and $c \not\vdash_{\mathcal{M}} c'$, that is, either

(iv.1) $|c| \neq |c'|$, or

(iv.2) for some $k \leq |c|$, $c_{k-1}, c_k, c_{k+1} \notin Q$ and $c'_k \neq c_k$, or

(iv.3) for some $k \leq |c|$, $c_k \in Q$ and $c_{k-1}c_kc_{k+1} \not\vdash_{\mathcal{M}} c'_{k-1}c'_kc'_{k+1}$.

Properties (i)–(iii) are regular. Property (iv.1) is clearly context-free. So are properties (iv.2) and (iv.3); this can be seen with a variant of the argument used in Problem 106.

Since context-free languages are closed under unions, the language of all the words that are not successful runs of $\mathcal{M}$ is context-free. It is straightforward to provide an algorithm that, given a machine $\mathcal{M}$, produces a grammar that generates this language. Consequently, if the universality problem was decidable, one could also decide the emptiness problem for Turing machines. ∎

Solution to Problem 180

All three problems are undecidable.

(1) For an instance $u_1, \ldots, u_n \in \Sigma^*$ and $w_1, \ldots, w_n \in \Sigma^*$ of the Post correspondence problem, consider the context-free grammar

$$S \rightarrow u_i^{\mathrm{R}} w_i \,\big|\, u_i^{\mathrm{R}} S w_i \qquad \text{for } i = 1, \ldots, n,$$

where u_i^{R} is the reverse of the word u_i. The start non-terminal S generates a palindrome if and only if P has a solution.

(2) Undecidability is immediate from item (1) above: the problem is undecidable for $\mathcal{G}_2$ a grammar that defines the language of all palindromes.

(3) Let $u_1, \ldots, u_n \in \Sigma^*$ and $w_1, \ldots, w_n \in \Sigma^*$ be an instance of the Post correspondence problem. Without loss of generality we can assume that $\Sigma \cap \mathbb{N} = \emptyset$. Consider the following context-free grammar over the alphabet $\Sigma \cup \{1, 2, \ldots, n\}$:

$$S \to U \mid W$$
$$U \to iu_i \mid iUu_i \quad \text{for } i = 1, \ldots, n,$$
$$W \to iw_i \mid iWw_i \quad \text{for } i = 1, \ldots, n.$$

Every solution

$$s = u_{i_1} u_{i_2} \ldots u_{i_m} = w_{i_1} w_{i_2} \ldots w_{i_m}$$

gives rise to a word

$$i_m i_{m-1} \ldots i_2 i_1 s$$

with exactly two derivations. Every other word generated by the nonterminal S has only one derivation. As a result, every generated word has exactly one derivation if and only if P has no solutions. ■

Solution to Problem 181

Yes, this problem is decidable. Given a machine $\mathcal{M}$ (with a set of states Q) and a word w, begin to simulate $\mathcal{M}$ on w. Suppose that $\mathcal{M}$ makes the first move right; the other case is analogous. If $\mathcal{M}$ leaves the part of its tape where w is written and, moving to the right over the blank part of the tape, visits the same state twice, then $\mathcal{M}$ will loop and the word w may be immediately rejected. Otherwise, after at most $|w| + |Q|$ steps to the right, the machine $\mathcal{M}$ stops or starts moving to the left. Again, if $\mathcal{M}$ visits the same state twice in the blank part of the tape to the left of w, it will loop and the word w can be rejected. Otherwise, $\mathcal{M}$ stops after at most $|w| + 2 \cdot |Q|$ moves to the left. ■

Solution to Problem 182

This problem is decidable. To see this, first consider the deterministic finite automaton used to show that for a fixed word $w \in \Sigma^*$ the language $\Sigma^* w$ is regular (Problem 81). This automaton, say $\mathcal{A}_w$, has all prefixes of w as its states and w itself as its only accepting state. When $\mathcal{A}_w$ is run on an input word x, it visits the accepting state exactly $\#_w(x)$ times.

As a result, for all fixed w and u, the language of those words x for which $\#_u(x) = \#_w(x)$ is context-free. Indeed, it is recognized by a pushdown automaton that runs the finite automata $\mathcal{A}_u$ and $\mathcal{A}_w$ in parallel (using the product construction) and maintains on the stack the difference between the number of visits of $\mathcal{A}_u$ and $\mathcal{A}_w$ in accepting states (a similar technique was used in Problem 142).

Finally, the language of words of length at least k is regular for each k. By the closure of context-free languages under intersections with regular languages, the language defined in the statement of the problem is context-free for all u, w, and k, and moreover a pushdown automaton recognizing this language can be computed from u, w, and k.

The claim follows as it is decidable whether a given context-free language (presented either as a context-free grammar or as a pushdown automaton) is non-empty. This classical result follows easily from Problem 97: take the grammar defining the language, replace all terminals with ε, and search through all candidates for a derivation of ε within the size bound given in Problem 97. ∎

Solution to Problem 183

Were C computable, one could use the following algorithm to decide whether a given machine $\mathcal{M}$ accepts a non-empty language: given an encoding of a machine $\mathcal{M}$, produce an encoding of a machine $\mathcal{M}'$ that works as $\mathcal{M}$, but always erases the contents of its tape before accepting; compute $C([\mathcal{M}'], \varepsilon)$; if the value is ∞, reject $\mathcal{M}$; otherwise accept.

To approximate C, we use an idea similar to the one in Problem 173, simulating a machine on all short words for a limited time and gradually extending the time allowed:

Input: a pair $([\mathcal{M}], v)$
$C \leftarrow \infty$
for $k \leftarrow 0, 1, 2, 3, 4, \ldots$ **do**
    for all words w of length at most $\min(C, k)$ **do**
        simulate $\mathcal{M}$ on input w for at most k steps
        if $\mathcal{M}$ accepted **and** $\mathcal{M}(w) = v$ **then**
            $C \leftarrow |w|$
    output C.

This produces a non-increasing sequence of values C that eventually stabilizes at $C([\mathcal{M}], v)$. ∎

Solution to Problem 184

Let $\mathcal{G}$ be a monotonic grammar. We transform it into a context-sensitive grammar generating the same language.

In the first stage of the transformation we do the following. For each terminal symbol a we add to the grammar a fresh non-terminal $\boxed{a}$. We replace each rule $w \rightarrow v$ with $\boxed{w} \rightarrow \boxed{v}$, where $\boxed{w}$ denotes the word w with each terminal symbol a replaced by the non-terminal $\boxed{a}$. Finally, we add the rule $\boxed{a} \to a$ for each terminal a.

After the first stage the grammar contains context-sensitive (actually, even context-free) rules of the form $\boxed{a} \to a$, and rules of the form $w \to v$, for w and v consisting solely of non-terminal symbols and $|w| \leq |v|$. The latter rules need not be context-sensitive; in the second stage we replace each of them with several context-sensitive rules, as follows. Let the following be such a rule:

$$A_1 A_2 \ldots A_k \to B_1 B_2 \ldots B_n;$$

recall that $k \leq n$. We add fresh non-terminal symbols $T_1, T_2, \ldots, T_n$ (to be used only for this rule), and replace the rule with the following $k + n$ context-sensitive rules:

$$
\begin{aligned}
A_1 A_2 \ldots A_k &\to T_1 A_2 \ldots A_k, \\
T_1 A_2 \ldots A_k &\to T_1 T_2 A_3 \ldots A_k, \\
&\ \ \vdots \\
T_1 \ldots T_{k-2} A_{k-1} A_k &\to T_1 \ldots T_{k-2} T_{k-1} A_k, \\
T_1 \ldots T_{k-1} A_k &\to T_1 \ldots T_{k-1} T_k \ldots T_n, \\
T_1 T_2 \ldots T_n &\to B_1 T_2 \ldots T_n, \\
B_1 T_2 \ldots T_n &\to B_1 B_2 T_3 \ldots T_n, \\
&\ \ \vdots \\
B_1 \ldots B_{n-1} T_n &\to B_1 \ldots B_{n-1} B_n.
\end{aligned}
$$

Clearly, the new grammar generates all the words of $L(\mathcal{G})$. Since for each eliminated rule we add fresh non-terminals T_i, no other word can be generated. This is because, in order to eliminate the non-terminals T_i, we need to apply the entire sequence of rules above.   ∎

Solution to Problem 185

First we prove that each context-sensitive language can be recognized by a linear bounded automaton.

For a given grammar $\mathcal{G}$, we construct a non-deterministic linear bounded automaton that simulates executing rules of $\mathcal{G}$, backwards. The input alphabet of the automaton is the set of terminal symbols of $\mathcal{G}$; the tape alphabet is the union of the set of terminals and the set of non-terminals. If $\mathcal{G}$ contains a rule $\alpha X \beta \to \alpha \gamma \beta$ then the automaton can replace an occurrence of a block $\alpha \gamma \beta$ on the tape with $\alpha X \beta$. If $|\gamma| > 1$ then the content of the tape to the right of the replaced γ needs to be shifted to the left so that it borders the newly introduced X (the freed cells are filled with blanks B). The automaton accepts if the tape contains a sequence of the form $S\textsc{b}^*$, where S is the start symbol of the grammar.

Thus, the automaton maintains a word from which the input word can be derived following the rules of $\mathcal{G}$. Therefore, if the automaton accepts, the input word can be derived from the start symbol of the grammar. On the other hand, if there is a derivation of a word from the start symbol of the grammar, then this derivation can be simulated backwards by the automaton described above. Hence, the automaton accepts exactly the words that can be generated by $\mathcal{G}$.

Now we prove that each language recognized by a linear bounded automaton is context-sensitive.

Let $\mathcal{A}$ be a linear bounded automaton. We construct a monotonic grammar that is able to derive exactly the words recognized by $\mathcal{A}$; we know from Problem 184 that such a grammar generates a context-sensitive language. The idea is that the rules allow us to: produce any accepting configuration of the automaton, simulate a run of $\mathcal{A}$ backwards, and eliminate all non-terminal symbols, but only if the initial state was reached.

Let Σ be the input alphabet, T the tape alphabet, Q the state set, q_0 the initial state, and $F \subseteq Q$ the set of accepting states of the automaton $\mathcal{A}$. Without loss of generality we may assume that in the initial configuration and in each accepting configuration the head is over the first cell of the tape. We let Σ be the set of terminal symbols, and S the start symbol of the grammar. Additionally, the grammar uses non-terminal symbols $\boxed{a}$ for $a \in T$ and $\boxed{q}$ for $q \in Q$. The following rules generate an accepting configuration; note that we use only non-terminal symbols at this stage of the construction:

$$S \to S\boxed{a} \quad \text{for } a \in T,$$
$$S \to \boxed{q_f} \quad \text{for } q_f \in F.$$

The rules below simulate a run of $\mathcal{A}$ backwards; δ stands for the set of transitions of $\mathcal{A}$:

$$\boxed{q'}\ \boxed{a'} \to \boxed{q}\ \boxed{a} \qquad \text{for } (q, a, q', a', \circlearrowleft) \in \delta,$$
$$\boxed{a'}\ \boxed{q'} \to \boxed{q}\ \boxed{a} \qquad \text{for } (q, a, q', a', \to) \in \delta,$$
$$\boxed{q'}\ \boxed{b}\ \boxed{a'} \to \boxed{b}\ \boxed{q}\ \boxed{a} \qquad \text{for } (q, a, q', a', \leftarrow) \in \delta \text{ and } b \in T.$$

Finally, the following rules eliminate non-terminal symbols:

$$\boxed{q_0}\ \boxed{a} \to a \qquad \text{for } a \in \Sigma,$$
$$b\boxed{a} \to ba \qquad \text{for } a, b \in \Sigma.$$

Every derivation consistent with the above grammar that produces a sequence of terminal symbols does the following things: it first produces a word encoding an accepting configuration, then it simulates a run leading to this configuration, backwards, and finally it transforms non-terminal symbols into the corresponding terminal symbols after reaching the initial state in the left-most position of the tape. Hence, the grammar generates only words from $L(\mathcal{A})$. It is also straightforward to see that each accepting run can be transformed into a derivation producing an input word of this run. As a result, all words from $L(\mathcal{A})$ are generated. ∎

Solution to Problem 186

We shall work with one-tape Turing machines that start their computation with the head over the first blank position to the right of the input word, rather than over the first symbol of the input word; that is, the initial configuration over a word w is $c_0 = wq_0$, where q_0 is the initial state of $\mathcal{M}$. It is clear that this does not change the expressive power of Turing machines, because a machine can easily find the first letter of the input word.

For a Turing machine $\mathcal{M}$ let $\text{Comp}_{\mathcal{M}}$ be the set of words of the form

$$c_0 \diamond c_1 \diamond \ldots \diamond c_n,$$

where $c_0, c_1, \ldots, c_n$ are the consecutive configurations of some run of machine $\mathcal{M}$, and $\diamond$ is a fresh symbol not in the tape alphabet of $\mathcal{M}$. In particular, $c_0 = wq_0$ for some word w over the input alphabet, and c_n is an accepting configuration.

By Problem 185, to prove that $\text{Comp}_{\mathcal{M}}$ is context-sensitive, it suffices to show that it can be recognized by a non-deterministic linear bounded automaton. Such an automaton can easily verify that the first configuration is initial and the last one is accepting. It can also verify that every two consecutive configurations differ only at or next to positions where the head of $\mathcal{M}$ is located, and that the differences are consistent with one of the transitions of $\mathcal{M}$. The comparison can be done letter by letter: the automaton marks the position currently being verified in both configurations, and travels from one configuration to the other comparing symbols and shifting markers by one.

Now let $\mathcal{M}$ be a machine recognizing some recursively enumerable but undecidable language, for instance the language of all Turing machines that accept some word. Without loss of generality we can assume that no transitions in $\mathcal{M}$ lead to the initial state q_0; that is, q_0 is only used in the initial configuration of each run. By our original assumption, the initial state is the last symbol of each initial configuration. Let R be the regular language of words that start with q_0. Then, $\text{Comp}_{\mathcal{M}} R^{-1} = L(\mathcal{M})$. We have thus shown that the right quotient of a context-sensitive language by a regular language may be undecidable. Clearly, a similar argument works for left quotients.

We remark that the decidability of each context-sensitive language follows immediately from Problem 185; therefore, neither context-sensitive languages nor decidable languages are closed under quotients by regular languages. ∎

Solution to Problem 187
Let $\mathcal{M}_1$ and $\mathcal{M}_2$ be one-tape Turing machines. We shall construct a non-deterministic two-tape Turing machine $\mathcal{M}$ that recognizes $L(\mathcal{M}_1)L(\mathcal{M}_2)^{-1}$.

Let u be the input word (given on the first tape). The machine $\mathcal{M}$ first non-deterministically guesses a word v, writing it on the second tape, and then appends it to u on the first tape. Then it runs $\mathcal{M}_2$ over v on the second tape. If $\mathcal{M}_2$ rejects, $\mathcal{M}$ rejects as well. If $\mathcal{M}_2$ accepts, then $\mathcal{M}$ runs $\mathcal{M}_1$ on the word uv on the first tape. If $\mathcal{M}_1$ accepts, then so does $\mathcal{M}$.

Clearly, the machine $\mathcal{M}$ accepts the word u if and only if there exists a word $v \in L(\mathcal{M}_2)$ such that $uv \in L(\mathcal{M}_1)$. This concludes the proof of the closure under right quotients.

To prove closure under left quotients it is enough to observe that recursively enumerable languages are closed under reverse and that

$$K^{-1}L = \left(\left(L^{R}\right)\left(K^{R}\right)^{-1}\right)^{R}.$$ ∎

Solution to Problem 188
In the table below, $\checkmark$ means that a given class is closed under a given operation, and $\times$ means that it is not. Numbers in superscript refer to the items of the explanation below.

Table 8.2 *Closure properties of the Chomsky hierarchy.*

	∪	∩	¬
Type 0	$\checkmark$[1]	$\checkmark$[1]	$\times$[2]
Type 1	$\checkmark$[3]	$\checkmark$[4]	$\checkmark$[5]
Type 2	$\checkmark$[6]	$\times$[7]	$\times$[8]
Type 3	$\checkmark$[9]	$\checkmark$[10]	$\checkmark$[11]

1. These follow from Problem 163 combined with Problem 165.
2. If a language and its complement are recursively enumerable, then the language is decidable (see Problem 175). Therefore, each language that is recursively enumerable and undecidable is a counterexample; for instance, the halting problem for Turing machines.

3. Let context-sensitive grammars $\mathcal{G}_1$ and $\mathcal{G}_2$ recognize languages L_1 and L_2, respectively. Without loss of generality we can assume that the two grammars use disjoint sets of non-terminal symbols. Let S_1 be the start symbol of $\mathcal{G}_1$ and S_2 be the start symbol of $\mathcal{G}_2$. Let the *disjoint union* of grammars $\mathcal{G}_1$ and $\mathcal{G}_2$ be the grammar with a new symbol S as the start symbol, all the rules of $\mathcal{G}_1$ and $\mathcal{G}_2$, and two additional rules $S \to S_1$ and $S \to S_2$. The disjoint union of $\mathcal{G}_1$ and $\mathcal{G}_2$ is a context-sensitive grammar that generates $L_1 \cup L_2$.

4. Let $\mathcal{A}_1$ and $\mathcal{A}_2$ be linear bounded automata recognizing languages L_1 and L_2, respectively. Let us construct a linear bounded automaton $\mathcal{A}$ that first replaces each letter a of the input word with the letter

$$\begin{bmatrix} a \\ a \end{bmatrix},$$

then executes automaton $\mathcal{A}_1$ over the upper copy of the input word, and then, if $\mathcal{A}_1$ accepts, executes automaton $\mathcal{A}_2$ over the lower copy. If $\mathcal{A}_2$ accepts then so does $\mathcal{A}$. The constructed automaton $\mathcal{A}$ recognizes $L_1 \cap L_2$.

5. The fact that the complement of a language recognized by a linear bounded automaton (see Problem 185) is recognized by a linear bounded automaton is a special case of the Immerman–Szelepcsényi theorem. Let us sketch a proof of this specific case.

   Let us fix a linear bounded automaton $\mathcal{A}$. We describe a non-deterministic algorithm to check that no accepting configuration of $\mathcal{A}$ is reachable from the initial configuration, and then argue that it can be implemented by a linear bounded automaton. Let m be the size of the tape alphabet of $\mathcal{A}$, let s be the number of states, and let n be the length of an input word. Let r_k be the number of configurations reachable from the initial configuration in at most k steps. Observe that the number of different configurations of $\mathcal{A}$ equals $K = m^n \cdot s \cdot n$, which means that if a configuration is reachable then it is reachable within at most K steps.

   For a given word w, the algorithm computes r_k for $k = 0, 1, \ldots, K$, where $r_0 = 1$ and the computation of r_{k+1} relies on the value of r_k:

1: **Input:** a word w
2: *prev_count* $\leftarrow 1$
3: **for** $k \leftarrow 1$ **to** K **do**
4:     *new_count* $\leftarrow 0$
5:     **for all** *conf* $\in$ *Configurations*$_\mathcal{A}$ **do**
6:         *count* $\leftarrow 0$
7:         *reached* $\leftarrow$ *false*

```
8:        for all prev_conf ∈ Configurations_A do
9:            if reachable(k − 1, prev_conf) then
10:              count ← count + 1
11:              if successor(prev_conf, conf) then
12:                  reached ← true
13:                  if accepting(conf) then
14:                      reject
15:          if count ≠ prev_count then
16:              reject
17:          if reached then
18:              new_count ← new_count + 1
19:      prev_count ← new_count
20: accept.
```

The subprocedures used above have the following effects:

- *reachable*(k, *prev_conf*) non-deterministically simulates a run of A of length at most k from the initial configuration, attempting to reach configuration *prev_conf*; if it succeeds, it returns *true*;
- *successor*(*prev_conf*, *conf*) verifies (deterministically) that configuration *conf* is reachable from configuration *prev_conf* in one step; it also returns *true* if the two configurations are equal.

The crucial part of the above algorithm is the verification done in line 15. Note that if a wrong non-deterministic choice is made in line 9 and a run reaching *prev_conf* is not found although it exists, then the counts will not match. The only way for a run of the above algorithm to be successful is to make correct guesses in line 9, that is, reach all the reachable configurations, and verify in line 13 that all the configurations reached are not accepting. This proves the correctness and soundness of the algorithm.

We now observe that the algorithm can be implemented by a multi-tape machine with the length of each tape bounded by the length of the input word. Two tapes are devoted to enumerating configurations *conf* and *prev_conf*. Each of the variables k, *prev_count*, *count*, and *new_count* is stored on a separate tape. Since the values of the counters are bounded by K, they clearly can be stored as n-digit numbers in a notation with sufficiently large base. Two more tapes are used to simulate runs of the automaton during the execution of *reachable*(): one to store consecutive configurations, the other to count the length of the constructed run. The calculation of functions *successor*() and *accepting*() can be done 'in place'; that is, they do not require additional tapes.

To complete the proof, we observe that the multi-tape machine can be transformed into a single tape machine using a product alphabet.

6. See Problem 86.
7. See Problem 133.
8. See Problem 101.
9. If languages L_1 and L_2 are generated by regular expressions α_1 and α_2, respectively, then $L_1 \cup L_2$ is generated by $\alpha_1 + \alpha_2$.
10. The language $L_1 \cap L_2$ can be recognized by the product of automata recognizing L_1 and L_2. See Problem 62.
11. If L is regular, then it is recognized by a deterministic automaton. The complement of L is recognized by the automaton obtained by swapping accepting and non-accepting states. ∎

Solution to Problem 189

All the listed functions are space-constructible.

$f(n) = 2n$. We use one work tape. The machine reads the input word 1^n letter by letter; for each symbol of the input word read, the machine writes 1 in two successive blank cells of the work tape and moves to the next blank cell. The machine accepts when ⊲ is reached on the input tape.

$f(n) = n^2$. We use two work tapes. We first describe the procedure of *multiplying by n* with the following specification. Provided that initially the content of the first work tape is 1^m for some positive integer m, while the second work tape is empty (filled with blanks), after performing the procedure the content of the first work tape will become 1^{mn}, while the second work tape will again be empty. The procedure itself will only use $\mathcal{O}(mn)$ cells.

The procedure is implemented as follows. First, rewrite the content of the first work tape to the second one and erase the first work tape. Next, proceed in a loop. The loop starts with the heads of both work tapes at their respective starts. In each iteration, we move the head on the second work tape to the right by one cell, while on the first work tape we copy the input word 1^n to the right of the current position of the head, thus appending 1^n to the content of the first work tape. The copying procedure is performed by scanning the input word cell by cell from left to right and copying symbols until the end marker is encountered on the input tape. Finally, we break the loop once we run out of symbols on the second work tape; that is, when we encounter a blank there. We finalize the procedure by erasing the content of the second work tape. It is clear from the description that the loop is entered once per each symbol on the second tape, and hence the procedure finishes with 1^{mn} on the first work tape.

To show the space-constructibility of the function $f(n) = n^2$, it suffices to write a single symbol 1 on the first work tape and apply the procedure of multiplying by n twice.

$f(n) = n^k$ for any constant k. We proceed in the same manner as for n^2, but we apply multiplying by n exactly k times, instead of just twice.

$f(n) = 2^n$. We use two work tapes. First, we need the procedure of *duplicating* with the following specification. Provided that the first work tape contains the word 1^m for some positive integer m, and the second work tape is empty, after applying the procedure the first work tape contains the word 1^{2m} while the second work tape is again empty. The procedure of duplicating is implemented in the same manner as multiplying by n described above, but instead of copying the whole input in each iteration we just append 11.

In order to show space-constructibility of the function $f(n) = 2^n$, it suffices to put a single symbol 1 on the first work tape, and then apply the duplication procedure n times. This can be done by counting from 1 to n on the input tape: moving the head on the input tape from left to right, we apply the duplication procedure once for each symbol of the input word; we accept after reaching the end marker $\lhd$.

$f(n) = 2^{2^n}$. We use three work tapes. First, as for 2^n, we compute the word 1^{2^n} on the third work tape. Next, by treating the third work tape as the input tape, we use the same method to compute the word $1^{2^{2^n}}$ on the first work tape. It is easy to see that during the computation only $\mathcal{O}(2^{2^n})$ cells are visited in total.

$f(n) = \lceil \log_2(n + 1) \rceil$. If the input word is empty, the machine terminates without writing anything. For non-empty input 1^n, we use one work tape to implement a binary counter. The head on the input tape is being moved from left to right with the following invariant always satisfied: just before the transition that moves this head to the right of the ith symbol of the input word, the work tape contains $\mathrm{bin}(i)^R$ – the binary encoding of the number i, with the least significant bits on the left. We initialize by reading the first 1 of the input and writing 1 on the work tape. Each time the head on the input tape is moved one cell to the right and sees another 1, we implement the procedure of adding 1 to the counter encoded on the work tape: this is done by changing the maximal prefix of 1's into 0's, and replacing the content of the following cell (either a 0 or a blank) with a 1. When the end marker $\lhd$ is reached on the input tape, the work tape contains $\mathrm{bin}(n)^R$, whose length is exactly $\lceil \log_2(n + 1) \rceil$. Therefore, it remains to change all the non-blank symbols on the work tape into 1's.   ∎

Solution to Problem 190

The first five functions are indeed time-constructible. To see this, it suffices to examine the machines given in the solution of Problem 189. It is not hard to verify that, in all cases, the machine not only traverses at most $\mathcal{O}(f(n))$ cells in total, but in fact uses only $\mathcal{O}(f(n))$ time.

We are left with the last function $f(n) = \lceil \log_2(n + 1) \rceil$, which is in fact not time-constructible. To prove this, suppose that, on the contrary, there is an off-line Turing machine $\mathcal{M}$ that, given word 1^n, computes $1^{f(n)}$ using at most $k \cdot f(n)$ steps, for some constant k. Since $f(n) = \lceil \log_2(n + 1) \rceil = o(n)$, there exists $n_0 \in \mathbb{N}$ such that for all $n \geq n_0$ we have $k \cdot f(n) < n$. Consider the run of $\mathcal{M}$ on the word 1^{n_0}. Since the machine accepts within strictly less than n_0 steps, it cannot reach the end marker $\lhd$ on the input tape. Hence, the machine will behave in exactly the same manner for any $n \geq n_0$, always computing the same number on the first work tape. This is a contradiction since $f(n)$ is not eventually constant. ∎

Solution to Problem 191

Let f and g be the two functions in question. Suppose f and g are computed by machines $\mathcal{M}_f$ and $\mathcal{M}_g$, respectively. For simplicity suppose that both f and g map Σ^* to Σ^*, and that $\mathcal{M}_f$ and $\mathcal{M}_g$ use Σ as their tape alphabet; the generalization for different input, output, and tape alphabets is immediate. Without loss of generality we may assume that both $\mathcal{M}_f$ and $\mathcal{M}_g$ use the same number c of work tapes, and each of them uses at most $\mathcal{O}(\log n)$ space on any word of length n.

The natural idea would be to run $\mathcal{M}_g$ on the input word w, store the output $g(w)$, and run $\mathcal{M}_f$ on it. However, the problem is that the word $g(w)$ may be too large to be stored in logarithmic space. To solve this problem, we will emulate the access of $\mathcal{M}_f$ to its input tape by running $\mathcal{M}_g$ from scratch whenever $\mathcal{M}_f$ needs to read a symbol of $g(w)$.

The first step is to observe that the output of $\mathcal{M}_g$ on an input word w can be indexed in logarithmic space. Since $\mathcal{M}_g$ uses at most $k \cdot \log_2 n$ working space on words of length n, we have that $|g(w)|$ is bounded by the number of possible configurations of $\mathcal{M}_g$, which is bounded polynomially in $n = |w|$. Hence, $|g(w)| \leq \ell \cdot n^{\ell}$ for some constant ℓ (dependent on c, k, and $|\Sigma|$). Consequently, positions of $g(w)$ can be indexed using $\mathcal{O}(\log |w|)$ bits.

We now construct a machine $\mathcal{M}$ that computes $f \circ g$ in logarithmic space. The machine will use $2c + 2$ work tapes. The first c tapes of $\mathcal{M}$ will be devoted to simulating the machine $\mathcal{M}_f$, while the next c tapes will be devoted to simulating the machine $\mathcal{M}_g$. The remaining two auxiliary tapes are used to emulate access to the input tape of $\mathcal{M}_f$. On the first of the two, which we call the *index tape*, we always store in binary the index of the cell over which the head of the input tape of $\mathcal{M}_f$ is placed. The second auxiliary tape will be called the *counter tape*.

The machine $\mathcal{M}$ simulates the transitions of $\mathcal{M}_f$ using its first c working tapes as the work tapes of $\mathcal{M}_f$. The transition of $\mathcal{M}_f$ depends on the symbols under the heads on the work tapes, which are stored directly by $\mathcal{M}$, but also on the symbol under the head on the input tape. Hence, before each simulated transition of $\mathcal{M}_f$, the machine $\mathcal{M}$ computes this symbol. For this, it simulates the machine $\mathcal{M}_g$ using the second c-tuple of work tapes as the work tapes of $\mathcal{M}_g$, and the original input tape as the input tape of $\mathcal{M}_g$. Every time $\mathcal{M}_g$ outputs a symbol, $\mathcal{M}$ increases a binary counter stored on the counter tape. Once the counter on the counter tape reaches the index stored on the index tape, we know that the symbol output just now is the one needed to determine the transition of $\mathcal{M}_f$. We store this symbol in the state of $\mathcal{M}$ and simulate the transition. Note that the transition of $\mathcal{M}_f$ may involve movement of the head over its input tape. This movement is simulated by updating the content of the index tape – incrementing or decrementing it by one.

In total, the machine uses $\mathcal{O}(\log n)$ space on the first c work tapes, $\mathcal{O}(\log n)$ space on the second c work tapes, and $\mathcal{O}(\log n)$ space for the binary counters on the index and counter tapes. Therefore, $\mathcal{M}$ works in logarithmic space. ∎

Solution to Problem 192
Let $\mathcal{M}$ be a machine that recognizes L. We will show that the language L^* can be recognized by a machine $\mathcal{M}'$ that works in deterministic polynomial time but additionally makes $\mathcal{O}(n^2)$ calls to $\mathcal{M}$; that is, it simulates the runs of $\mathcal{M}$ on $\mathcal{O}(n^2)$ inputs. It follows that if $\mathcal{M}$ certifies that L belongs to P, NP, or PSPACE, then $\mathcal{M}'$ will certify the same for L^*. We describe the machine $\mathcal{M}'$ as an algorithm; turning it into a proper Turing machine is straightforward.

Suppose w is the input word and n is its length. For indices $1 \leq i \leq j \leq n$, let $w[i..j]$ be the infix of w between positions i and j, inclusive; for $i > j$, we declare $w[i..j]$ to be the empty word. The machine $\mathcal{M}'$ first computes boolean values $A[i,j]$ for $1 \leq i \leq j \leq n$, defined as follows:

$$A[i,j] = (w[i..j] \in L).$$

In other words, $A[i,j]$ describes whether the infix $w[i..j]$ belongs to L or not. Note that all relevant values of $A[i,j]$ can be computed using $n(n+1)/2$ calls to $\mathcal{M}$.

Using the values $A[i,j]$ we check whether w can be decomposed as a concatenation of words from L using dynamic programming. Specifically, for consecutive $j = 0, 1, \ldots, n$ we compute boolean values $D[j]$ defined as follows:

$$D[j] = (w[1..j] \in L^*).$$

It can be easily seen that values $D[j]$ satisfy the following recurrence:

$$D[0] = \text{true},$$
$$D[j] = \bigvee_{0 \le i < j} (D[i] \wedge A[i+1,j]) \quad \text{for } j > 0.$$

Thus, all the values $D[j]$ can be computed in polynomial time using the values $A[i,j]$. The output of $\mathcal{M}'$ is the value $D[n]$.   ∎

Solution to Problem 193

It is not hard to see that NL is closed under Kleene star. Indeed, assume $K \in$ NL. Then, membership in K^* can be decided by a non-deterministic Turing machine working in logarithmic space as follows. The machine guesses a factorization of the input word, factor by factor, and for each guessed factor checks if it belongs to K (also non-deterministically). Because the machine cannot write on the input tape, it uses three binary counters to represent the beginning and the end of the currently checked factor, as well as the current position of the head on the input tape. This allows emulating the restricted input tape of the simulated machine testing membership in K. Hence, if L $=$ NL, then L is closed under Kleene star.

For the remaining implication, we use the reachability problem for directed graphs, which is known to be complete for NL with respect to L reductions. We represent graphs via incidence matrices: an $n \times n$ matrix with binary entries represents the graph over vertices $\{1, 2, \dots, n\}$ in which (i,j) is an edge if and only if the matrix has 1 at the position (i,j). Such a matrix can be represented as a binary word of length n^2 by concatenating its rows. The variant of reachability we shall use is the language R of words $w \in \{0,1\}^{n^2}$ for $n \in \mathbb{N}$ such that, in the graph represented by the incidence matrix encoded by w, there is a path from 1 to n.

We shall exhibit a language $K \in$ L such that the language R can be reduced in logarithmic space to K^*; that is, there exists a function f computable in L such that $w \in R$ if and only if $f(w) \in K^*$ for all words $w \in \{0,1\}^*$.

To see that this gives L $=$ NL assuming that L is closed under Kleene star, note that each problem in NL can be solved by reducing first to R, then to K^*, and finally solving the instance of K^*. Both reductions are in L, and under our assumption also $K^* \in$ L. Since by Problem 191 compositions of functions computable in L are also computable in L, we get a solution in L for any given problem from NL.

For an integer m, let $\underline{m} = \langle \mathrm{bin}(m) \rangle \in \{\langle, \rangle, 0, 1\}^*$. The language K contains words of the form

$$\underline{k}\,\underline{k+1}\,\underline{k+1}\ \ldots\ \underline{n}\,\underline{n}\#w\#\underline{1}\,\underline{1}\ \ldots\ \underline{l-1}\,\underline{l-1}\,\underline{l}$$

for $k, l, n \in \mathbb{N} - \{0\}$ such that $k, l \le n$, the word w is in $\{0, 1\}^{n^2}$, and either $k = l$ or the symbol at the position $(k-1) \cdot n + l$ of w is 1. The idea is that the word between the two occurrences of # encodes an incidence matrix that has 1 at position (k, l) unless $k = l$.

The reduction assigns to a given word w of length n^2 the word

$$\underline{1}\,\underline{2}\,\underline{2}\ \ldots\ \underline{n}\,\underline{n}\,(\#w\#\underline{1}\,\underline{1}\ \ldots\ \underline{n}\,\underline{n})^{n-2}\#w\#\underline{1}\,\underline{1}\ \ldots\ \underline{n-1}\,\underline{n-1}\,\underline{n}.$$

This word is in K^* if and only if it can be factorized into

$$\underline{j_1}\,u_1\underline{j_2}\,\underline{j_2}\,u_2\underline{j_3}\ \cdots\ \underline{j_{n-1}}\,u_{n-1}\underline{j_n},$$

where $j_1 = 1$, $j_n = n$, and $\underline{j_i}\,u_i\underline{j_{i+1}} \in K$ for all $i \in \{1, 2, \ldots, n-1\}$. By the definition of K, this is equivalent to saying that

$$(j_1, j_2), (j_2, j_3), \ldots, (j_{n-1}, j_n)$$

is a path from 1 to n in the graph represented by w.

It is not difficult to verify that both K and the reduction are in L. ∎

Solution to Problem 194

First we show that this problem is in NP. To this end, we show that if there is some word w generated by an expression e which contains all letters from the alphabet Σ, then there is such a word of length at most $p(n)$, where n is the length of the expression e plus the size of the alphabet Σ, and p is some fixed polynomial independent of Σ and e.

Let $\mathcal{A}$ be the non-deterministic automaton recognizing the set of words generated by e, constructed in the standard way. Then $\mathcal{A}$ has at most $q(n)$ states, for some polynomial q independent of e and Σ. Suppose that w is the shortest word which is accepted by $\mathcal{A}$ and which contains all letters from Σ. We claim that w has length at most $|Q| \cdot (|\Sigma| + 1)$, where Q is the set of states of $\mathcal{A}$. Indeed, let ρ be an accepting run of $\mathcal{A}$ on w. Define a function

$$\alpha \colon \{0, \ldots, |w|\} \to Q \times \{0, \ldots, |\Sigma|\}$$

by setting $\alpha(i) = (s, k)$ if the ith state (counting from 0) in the run ρ is s and the number of distinct letters in the prefix of w of length i is equal to k. If $|w| + 1 > |Q| \cdot (|\Sigma| + 1)$ then there are two numbers i and j such that $i < j$ and $\alpha(i) = \alpha(j)$. Let v be the word obtained from w by unpumping the infix beginning at position $i + 1$ and ending at position j. It is easy to see that $\mathcal{A}$

accepts v and that v contains all letters from Σ. This contradicts the minimality of w. Hence

$$|w| < |Q| \cdot (|\Sigma| + 1) = q(n) \cdot (n + 1),$$

and the claim holds with $p(n) = q(n) \cdot (n + 1)$.

It follows easily that the problem is in NP: a non-deterministic algorithm can guess a word w of length at most $p(n)$, and verify that it contains all symbols from Σ and can be generated by the expression e; both these tests can clearly be performed in polynomial time.

To show NP-hardness, we give a polynomial-time reduction from CNF-SAT. Let the given instance of CNF-SAT be the conjunction of clauses $c_1, c_2, \ldots, c_n$ over the set of variables $x_1, x_2, \ldots, x_k$. We shall construct a regular expression over the alphabet $\{1, 2, \ldots, n\}$ that generates a word containing each letter from the alphabet if and only if there is an assignment to the variables that satisfies each clause. For $i = 1, 2, \ldots, k$, let pos_i be the concatenation of all j such that the clause c_j contains a positive occurrence of the variable x_i, and let neg_i be the concatenation of all j such that the clause c_j contains a negative occurrence of the variable x_i. The regular expression is

$$(pos_1 + neg_1)(pos_2 + neg_2) \ldots (pos_k + neg_k).$$

It is easy to see that choosing one of the two options in each subexpression $(pos_i + neg_i)$ corresponds exactly to choosing the value 1 or 0 for the variable x_i. Thus, the word contains all letters from $\{1, 2, \ldots, n\}$ if and only if each clause contains a positive occurrence of a variable with value 1 or a negative occurrence of a variable with value 0. ∎

Solution to Problem 195

It is obvious that the problem is in NP, since the subfamily $\mathcal{E}$ we ask for may serve as a certificate that can be verified in polynomial time. We proceed with proving that the problem is NP-hard.

We give a polynomial-time reduction from the 3SAT problem. Let φ_0 be the input instance of 3SAT. First, we adjust φ_0 slightly so that there is a constant upper bound on the number of occurrences of each variable, while the satisfiability of the formula is preserved. This can be achieved by the following transformation. For a variable x of φ_0, let $n(x)$ be the number of occurrences of x in φ_0. Replace x with $n(x)$ new variables $x_1, x_2, \ldots, x_{n(x)}$ and introduce new clauses:

$$x_1 \Rightarrow x_2, \quad x_2 \Rightarrow x_3, \quad \ldots, \quad x_{n(x)} \Rightarrow x_1.$$

Recall here that implication $y \Rightarrow z$ can be encoded as $\neg y \vee z$. Finally, modify the clauses of the original formula φ_0 as follows: for each variable x and each $i \in \{1, 2, \ldots, n(x)\}$, replace the ith occurrence of x in φ_0 by the variable x_i. Thus, the constructed formula φ has a set of variables containing $x_1, x_2, \ldots, x_{n(x)}$ for each variable x of φ_0, while its set of clauses contains both the modified clauses of the original formula φ_0 and implication cycles involving the variables created to replace an original variable of φ_0. Observe that in any satisfying assignment for φ, all the variables within one implication cycle must have the same value. Hence, it is clear that satisfying assignments for φ are in one-to-one correspondence with satisfying assignments for φ_0, so the transformation described preserves the satisfiability of the formula. However, in φ, every variable appears in at most three clauses. Hence, by applying this transformation, we can assume without loss of generality that we start the reduction from an instance of 3SAT in which every variable appears in at most three clauses. Moreover, we can assume without loss of generality that no clause contains a variable and its negation at the same time (such clauses can be skipped).

We now give a reduction mapping an instance of 3SAT with the properties mentioned above to an instance of EXACT COVER. As the universe U we take $V \cup C$, where V and C denote the variable and clause set of φ, respectively. Then, for every variable x of φ, let A_x^{false} and A_x^{true} be the sets of clauses of φ containing x that become satisfied when x is set to false and true, respectively. Note that since the two sets are disjoint and x appears in at most three clauses, we have that $|A_x^{false}| + |A_x^{true}| \leq 3$. We define the family $\mathcal{F}$ as follows:

$$\mathcal{F} = \left\{ \{x\} \cup B \ : \ x \in V \text{ and either } B \subseteq A_x^{false} \text{ or } B \subseteq A_x^{true} \right\}.$$

Observe that since $|A_x^{false}| + |A_x^{true}| \leq 3$, for each $x \in V$ we add at most eight sets to $\mathcal{F}$. Thus, the construction of $\mathcal{F}$ can be carried out in polynomial time.

It remains to verify that the reduction is correct. Suppose first that φ admits some satisfying assignment $s \colon V \to \{false, true\}$. To each clause $c \in C$ assign an arbitrary variable $v(c)$ that satisfies it under s. Then, define $\mathcal{E}$ as follows:

$$\mathcal{E} = \left\{ \{x\} \cup v^{-1}(x) \ : \ x \in V \right\}.$$

Obviously, $\mathcal{E}$ forms a partition of U. Moreover, $v^{-1}(x) \subseteq A_x^{s(x)}$ for each x. Hence $\mathcal{E} \subseteq \mathcal{F}$, so the constructed instance of EXACT COVER has a solution.

In the other direction, suppose $\mathcal{E} \subseteq \mathcal{F}$ is a solution to the constructed instance of EXACT COVER. Each variable $x \in V$ has to be in exactly one set $D_x \in \mathcal{E} \subseteq \mathcal{F}$. By the construction of $\mathcal{F}$, we have that $\mathcal{E} = \{D_x \ : \ x \in V\}$ and each $D_x - \{x\}$ is a subset either of A_x^{false} or of A_x^{true}. Let $s(x) = false$ if the former holds, and let $s(x) = true$ if the latter holds (if both conditions hold, choose $s(x)$ arbitrarily). We claim that the assignment $s: V \to \{false, true\}$ satisfies φ. Indeed, take any clause $c \in C$. Since $\mathcal{E}$ forms a partition of U, there exists some $x \in V$ for which $c \in D_x$. By the construction of s, the condition $c \in D_x$ implies that $c \in A_x^{s(x)}$, which means that the value of x under the assignment s makes c satisfied. As c was chosen arbitrarily, we conclude that s does satisfy φ. ∎

Solution to Problem 196

Again, membership in NP is obvious, because the desired subset of $\mathcal{S}$ may serve as a certificate that can be verified in polynomial time.

To prove NP-hardness, we give a polynomial-time reduction from EXACT COVER, whose NP-hardness was established in Problem 195. Take the input instance $(U, \mathcal{F})$ of EXACT COVER, and let $|U| = n$ and $|\mathcal{F}| = m$. The main idea is to encode subsets of the universe as numbers in base-N representation for some large N, so that taking the union of two sets (with multiplicities) corresponds to adding the numbers encoding them. In order to avoid problems with carry, we need to make the number N sufficiently large.

More precisely, we set $N = m + 1$. Let us arbitrarily enumerate U as $\{e_0, e_1, \ldots, e_{n-1}\}$. For each set $A \in \mathcal{F}$, define the number s_A as follows:

$$s_A = \sum_{i:\ e_i \in A} N^i.$$

Then take

$$\mathcal{S} = \{s_A : A \in \mathcal{F}\} \qquad \text{and} \qquad t = \sum_{i=0}^{n-1} N^i.$$

It is clear that binary representations of the numbers s_A and t can be computed in polynomial time, so we can also construct the instance $(\mathcal{S}, t)$ of SUBSET SUM in polynomial time. It remains to prove that the input instance $(U, \mathcal{F})$ of EXACT COVER has a solution if and only if the output instance $(\mathcal{S}, t)$ of SUBSET SUM has a solution.

Consider any subfamily $\mathcal{E} \subseteq \mathcal{F}$. Observe that

$$\sum_{A \in \mathcal{E}} s_A = \sum_{A \in \mathcal{E}} \sum_{i:\ e_i \in A} N^i = \sum_{i=0}^{n-1} N^i \cdot |\{A \in \mathcal{E} : e_i \in A\}|.$$

For each $i \in \{0, 1, \ldots, n-1\}$, we have $|\{A \in \mathcal{E} : e_i \in A\}| \le |\mathcal{F}| < N$. Hence, if we denote

$$t_{\mathcal{E}} = \sum_{A \in \mathcal{E}} s_A,$$

then the numbers $| \{A \in \mathcal{E} : e_i \in A\} |$ can be uniquely decoded from $t_\mathcal{E}$ as the digits of the base-N representation of $t_\mathcal{E}$. In particular, $t_\mathcal{E} = t$ if and only if all these numbers are equal to 1. We conclude that the mapping $\mathcal{E} \to \{s_A : A \in \mathcal{E}\}$ is a one-to-one correspondence between the solution sets of the input instance of EXACT COVER and of the output instance of SUBSET SUM. In particular, the former has a solution if and only if the latter does. ∎

Solution to Problem 197

We prove that the reduction used in the standard proof of Cook's theorem can be performed in L.

First observe that the following standard reduction from CNF-SAT to 3SAT can be performed in logarithmic space: replace each clause

$$(\ell_1 \vee \ell_2 \vee \ell_3 \vee \cdots \vee \ell_{k-1} \vee \ell_k),$$

where $\ell_1, \ell_2, \ldots, \ell_k$ are literals, with the conjunction

$$(\ell_1 \vee z_1) \wedge (\neg z_1 \vee \ell_2 \vee z_2) \wedge (\neg z_2 \vee \ell_3 \vee z_3) \wedge \cdots$$
$$\cdots \wedge (\neg z_{k-2} \vee \ell_{k-1} \vee z_{k-1}) \wedge (\neg z_{k-1} \vee \ell_k),$$

where $z_1, z_2, \ldots, z_{k-1}$ are fresh variables. As we have seen in Problem 191, the composition of two functions computable in logarithmic space is also computable in logarithmic space. Hence, it suffices to give a reduction to CNF-SAT, which can then be composed with the above reduction from CNF-SAT to 3SAT to yield a logarithmic-space reduction to 3SAT.

Let L be a language in NP, recognized by a non-deterministic Turing machine $\mathcal{M}$, and let $p \colon \mathbb{N} \to \mathbb{N}$ be a polynomial such that $p(n)$ is always strictly greater than the running time of $\mathcal{M}$ on all inputs of length n. Our goal is to compute, using only logarithmic space, a formula in CNF that is satisfiable if and only if $\mathcal{M}$ accepts a given input word w. Without loss of generality, we assume that $\mathcal{M}$ uses a single, right-infinite tape, and that its input and working alphabets are the same alphabet Σ. We may also assume that whenever $\mathcal{M}$ has an accepting run on a word w of length n, it also has an accepting run on w taking *exactly* $p(n)$ steps; this is because we can modify $\mathcal{M}$ in such a way that it loops after reaching any accepting state.

To perform the reduction, we introduce the following variables:

- For all $0 \leq i, j \leq p(n)$ and $\sigma \in \Sigma$, introduce variable $x_{i,j,\sigma}$ with the following intended meaning: $x_{i,j,\sigma}$ is true if and only if at time j (that is, after the jth step) the ith cell of $\mathcal{M}$'s tape contains the symbol σ.
- For all $0 \leq i, j \leq p(n)$, introduce variable $h_{i,j}$ with the following intended meaning: $h_{i,j}$ is true if and only if at time j the head of $\mathcal{M}$ is over cell i.

- For all $0 \leq j \leq p(n)$ and $q \in Q$, where Q is the set of states of $\mathcal{M}$, introduce variable $s_{j,q}$ with the following intended meaning: $s_{j,q}$ is true if and only if at time j the state of $\mathcal{M}$ is q.

It remains to construct clauses binding the above variables in such a way that satisfying assignments of the output CNF formula correspond to accepting runs of $\mathcal{M}$.

First, we add clauses ensuring that:

- for each $0 \leq i,j \leq p(n)$, exactly one of the variables $x_{i,j,*}$ is true;
- for each $0 \leq j \leq p(n)$, exactly one of the variables $h_{*,j}$ is true; and
- for each $0 \leq j \leq p(n)$, exactly one of the variables $s_{j,*}$ is true.

Here and in the sequel, $*$ stands for all possible values of the corresponding index. In all three cases this is done in the same manner. We add one clause that expresses the disjunction of all the variables in question, thus forcing at least one of them to be true. Then, for each pair of those variables, we add a clause that expresses the disjunction of their negations, thus forcing at least one of the pair to be false.

Then, we make sure that the first and last configurations are correct. For this, we add unit clauses (that is, clauses of length one) specifying the exact shape of the configuration at time zero, which is encoded by variables $x_{*,0,*}$, $h_{*,j}$, and $s_{0,*}$. In this configuration, the input word w is written at the beginning of the tape, the rest of the tape is filled with blanks, the head is positioned over the first cell, and the state is set to the initial state. To make sure that the last configuration is accepting, we add a clause expressing the disjunction of the variables $s_{p(n),q}$, where q ranges over accepting states. We also ensure that the left-most cell always contains the start marker $\triangleright$ by adding unit clauses specifying the values of variables $x_{0,*,*}$.

We still have to ensure the correctness of transitions between consecutive configurations. For all $0 \leq i \leq p(n)$ and $1 \leq j \leq p(n)$, we create a set of clauses $C_{i,j}$ which guarantee that at time j information about the ith cell is correctly updated. The clauses of $C_{i,j}$ involve variables:

$$V_{i,j} = \left\{ x_{i,j,*}, \ h_{i-1,j}, \ h_{i,j}, \ h_{i+1,j}, \ x_{i,j-1,*}, \ h_{i,j-1}, \ s_{j,*}, \ s_{j-1,*} \right\}.$$

In the case $i = 0$ or $i = p(n)$, the corresponding variable $h_{i-1,j}$ or $h_{i+1,j}$ is omitted. Note that the number of variables in $V_{i,j}$ is at most $2|\Sigma| + 2|Q| + 4$, which is a constant. The clauses of $C_{i,j}$ enforce the following conditions on the variables in $V_{i,j}$:

- If at time $j - 1$ the head is not over cell i, then the symbol in cell i is unchanged. There are no constraints imposed on the values of variables $h_{i-1,j}$, $h_{i,j}$, $h_{i+1,j}$, $h_{i,j-1}$, $s_{j,*}$, and $s_{j-1,*}$.
- If at time $j - 1$ the head is over cell i, then the values of variables in $V_{i,j}$ must represent a valid transition of $\mathcal{M}$. More precisely, there is a transition of $\mathcal{M}$ that starts in the state encoded by the variables $s_{j-1,*}$, with the symbol encoded by the variables $x_{i,j-1,*}$ under the head, finishes in the state encoded by the variables $s_{j,*}$, writes the symbol encoded by $x_{i,j,*}$ on the tape, and moves the head to the cell indicated by $h_{i-1,j}$, $h_{i,j}$, $h_{i+1,j}$.

In order to encode the above requirements by a CNF formula, we inspect all of the at most $2^{|V_{i,j}|}$ boolean assignments to the variables in $V_{i,j}$; recall that $|V_{i,j}|$ is bounded by a constant. Let $\Phi_{i,j}$ be the set of those assignments that do not satisfy the conditions above. Then for each assignment $\eta \in \Phi_{i,j}$, we add one clause ensuring that the variables in $V_{i,j}$ are not evaluated according to η. This clause is a disjunction over $V_{i,j}$, where each variable is taken with the opposite polarity as under η. The conjunction of all such clauses guarantees that, on each $V_{i,j}$, one of the correct assignments is selected.

It is clear from the construction that each satisfying assignment of the constructed formula encodes an accepting run of $\mathcal{M}$ on the input word. On the other hand, if $\mathcal{M}$ accepts the input word, then it can accept it in exactly $p(n)$ steps, using no more than $p(n)$ tape cells, and hence there is an assignment to the variables that satisfies the output formula. We conclude that the input word is in the language L if and only if the output formula is satisfiable, and hence the reduction is correct.

Let us see how the reduction can be implemented in logarithmic space. Note that each variable of the output formula can be represented by an identifier of length $\mathcal{O}(\log n)$: such an identifier consists of the type of the variable (x, h, or s), binary encodings of at most two indices with values bounded by $p(n)$, and some additional constant-size information, such as a symbol of the alphabet or a state of the machine. It is straightforward to implement a logarithmic-space procedure which, given indices i and j, produces the clause set $C_{i,j}$. Thus, the clauses of all the sets $C_{i,j}$ may be computed in logarithmic space by iterating through the two binary indices i and j, and outputting $C_{i,j}$ for each pair of i and j. The other clauses of the output formula can be computed in logarithmic space similarly. ∎

Solution to Problem 198

Clearly, the problem is in NP, because a proper tiling may serve as a certificate that can be verified in polynomial time. We prove NP-hardness.

We present two solutions. In the first solution we adapt a proof of Cook's theorem to the TILING problem. That is, we reduce in polynomial time an arbitrary language $L \in$ NP to TILING directly: we encode the existence of an accepting run of a non-deterministic Turing machine recognizing L as an instance of TILING. This proof strategy is more insightful, but there are multiple technical details that would require our attention in a fully formal argument. Therefore, we only sketch this proof, and then resort to giving a fully formal reduction from the 3SAT problem as the second solution.

Sketch of the first solution. Suppose the language L is recognized by a non-deterministic Turing machine $\mathcal{M}$ with a single, right-infinite tape, that runs in time bounded by $p(n)$ on inputs of length n, where $p \colon \mathbb{N} \to \mathbb{N}$ is a polynomial. We need to construct, given an input word w of length n, an instance of TILING that has a solution if and only if $\mathcal{M}$ has an accepting run on w. The idea will be as in the proof of Cook's theorem. We create a large square of size (roughly) $p(n) \times p(n)$, where the rows will encode the configurations of the machine at consecutive points in time. More precisely, the tile at the intersection of the jth row and ith column describes the content of the ith cell before the jth step of the machine. Now we need to carefully design the set of available tiles S to make sure that tilings of the large square correspond to accepting runs.

Each tile of S has one designated *central colour c* that encodes the information stored in the tile. Intuitively, this information consists of all that we need to know about one cell at a given point in time to determine what can happen to it: the symbols in the cell and in the neighbouring cells, the position of the head in relation to the cell, the state of $\mathcal{M}$ if the head is nearby, etc. We need to make sure that this information is consistent between neighbouring cells. For this, we use the colours of the sides of the tile. More precisely, if the central colour c is *consistent*, in the sense to be defined, with the central colour c' of the tile placed to the left, then we allow the colour (c', c) on the left side of the tile. Thus, the sides of the tiles will be coloured by pairs of central colours. The set S is composed of all the tiles where the side colours form consistent pairs of central colours. Note that consistency in the vertical direction will be defined differently than consistency in the horizontal direction.

Before we describe the relation of (vertical and horizontal) consistency, we need to specify more precisely what the central colour will encode. The information encoded is as follows:

- the symbols written in the cell and the two neighbouring cells;
- one of five options about the position of the head, i.e., either it is at least two cells to the left, or one cell to the left, or over the cell in question, or one cell to the right, or at least two cells to the right; and
- the state of the machine.

Horizontal consistency checks that the central colours of two cells neighbouring horizontally (along the left side of one and the right side of the other) contain consistent information: the symbols in the cells match, the relative positions of the head do not contradict each other, and the stored state of $\mathcal{M}$ is the same. Similarly, vertical consistency checks that the neighbourhood of the cell is modified according to a possible transition of $\mathcal{M}$. As explained before, the notion of consistency sketched above gives rise to the set of available tiles S. It is not hard to see that possible tilings of a $k \times k$ square correspond to k-step runs of $\mathcal{M}$ on a tape of size k.

It remains to encode the other features of an accepting run, in particular to force that the initial configuration contains the input word and the final configuration is accepting, using the condition that the sides of the large square have to be coloured with colour 0. We leave filling these details, as well as formalizing the idea from the previous paragraph, to the reader.

Second solution. We give a polynomial-time reduction from the 3SAT problem. Suppose that φ is a given propositional formula in CNF with clauses of length three whose satisfiability is in question. We may assume without loss of generality that the number of variables in φ is equal to the number of clauses, because otherwise we introduce either dummy variables that do not participate in any clause, or dummy clauses that are always satisfied (say, $x \vee \neg x$ for some variable x). Also, by copying literals if necessary, we may assume that each clause of φ contains exactly three (not necessarily distinct) literals.

Let us enumerate the variables as $x_1, \ldots, x_m$ and the clauses as $c_1, \ldots, c_m$; without loss of generality we assume that $m \geq 3$. Set the size of the large square in the output instance of TILING to $N = m + 2$.

For the sake of readability we use the following set of colours:

$$\mathcal{C} = \{0, 1, 2, \ldots, m+1\} \cup \{v_{i,s} : 1 \leq i \leq m,\ s \in \{false, true\}\} \cup$$
$$\cup \{c_{j,t} : 1 \leq j \leq m,\ t \in \{1, 2, 3\}\}.$$

Note that the number of colours is linear in m; we can represent them as integers between 0 and $|\mathcal{C}| - 1$. The intuitive meaning of these colours is as follows. Colour 0 will be always placed at the boundary of the square. Colours

$\{1, 2, \ldots, m + 1\}$ will be used to count along the sides of the square, so that the whole tiling is 'rigid' due to a forced behaviour on the boundary. Finally, colour $v_{i,s}$ represents assigning value s (*true* or *false*) to the variable x_i, while colour $c_{j,t}$ represents the tth literal of clause c_j.

Before we formally define the set S of available tiles, let us briefly discuss the intuition. Each row of the table, except the first and the last, will correspond to one variable of φ. Similarly, each non-boundary column will correspond to one clause of φ. We first carefully define the set of tiles that need to be placed on the boundary. Their placement will have to satisfy the requirement that the boundary of the large square is coloured with the distinguished colour 0, but we will have some freedom. For each non-boundary row, we can choose among two possible colours for the right side of the left-most tile in this row; this models choosing whether the corresponding variable is set to true or false. Similarly, for each non-boundary column we can choose among three possible colours for the bottom side of the top tile in this column; this models the choice of the literal to be satisfied in the corresponding clause. Finally, we define the set of tiles that can be placed in the interior of the large square so that in the intersection of the ith non-boundary row and the jth non-boundary column the following check is verified: if x_i was chosen to be the variable satisfying clause c_j, then the value assigned to x_i indeed makes c_j true.

We proceed to the formal description. The set of boundary tiles S_{bnd} consists of the tiles

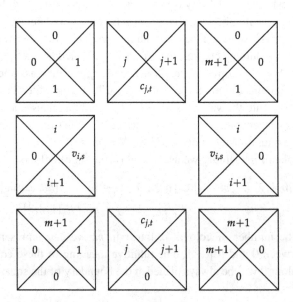

for $i,j \in \{1,2,\ldots,m\}$, $s \in \{false, true\}$, and $t \in \{1,2,3\}$. The two possibilities indicated by $s \in \{false, true\}$ in the ith non-boundary row correspond to the choice of the value of the variable x_i, whereas the three possibilities indicated by $t \in \{1,2,3\}$ in the jth non-boundary column correspond to the choice of the literal that will satisfy the clause c_j.

All the other tiles that we are going to define will not have colour 0 on any of the sides. Hence, the four tiles depicted in the corners in the picture above are the only ones containing two 0's, so in any proper tiling they must be placed in the corners as well. Moreover, the sides of the large square must be tiled using the remaining four types of boundary tiles: the ones with 0 on the left must be used for the left side, etc. Using the requirement that the colours must match along each of the sides, it is not hard to see that the tile in the first column and the ith non-boundary row must be

$$(0, i, v_{i,false}, i+1) \quad \text{or} \quad (0, i, v_{i,true}, i+1),$$

and similarly for the other sides of the large square (recall that the colours of the sides in the quadruples are given in clockwise order, starting from the left).

Now we define the set of available interior tiles S_{int} as follows. For $t \in \{1,2,3\}$, let $i(j,t)$ be the index of the tth variable appearing in the clause c_j. Then, for all $1 \le i,j \le m$, add to S_{int} the tiles

for all $s \in \{false, true\}$ and $t \in \{0,1,2\}$ such that if $i = i(j,t)$ then assigning boolean value s to x_i makes c_j satisfied. Finally, let $S = S_{bnd} \cup S_{int}$ be the set of allowed tiles; this concludes the description of the reduction.

It remains to check that the reduction is correct. Suppose first that the input formula φ admits some satisfying assignment

$$s \colon \{1,2,\ldots,m\} \to \{false, true\}.$$

For every index $1 \le j \le m$, choose $t(j) \in \{1,2,3\}$ so that the assignment s satisfies the $t(j)$th literal of c_j. Then, for all $i,j \in \{1,2,\ldots,m\}$, place tile

$$(v_{i,s(i)}, c_{j,t(j)}, v_{i,s(i)}, c_{j,t(j)})$$

at the intersection of the ith non-boundary row and the jth non-boundary column. Since s is a satisfying assignment, it follows from the construction that all these tiles belong to S. It is also easy to see that the tiling of the non-boundary cells can be extended to the boundary using tiles from S_{bnd}.

For the other direction, suppose we have some proper tiling of the large $N \times N$ square. As noted before, the boundary must be tiled using the boundary tiles S_{bnd} so that the tile at the intersection of the ith non-boundary row ($1 \le i \le m$) and the first column has to be

$$(0, i, v_{i,false}, i+1) \quad \text{or} \quad (0, i, v_{i,true}, i+1),$$

while the tile at the intersection of the first row and the jth non-boundary column has to be

$$(j, 0, j+1, c_{j,1}), \quad (j, 0, j+1, c_{j,2}), \quad \text{or} \quad (j, 0, j+1, c_{j,3}).$$

Define $s: \{1, 2, \dots, m\} \to \{false, true\}$ and $t: \{1, 2, \dots, m\} \to \{1, 2, 3\}$ in such a way that the aforementioned tiles are

$$(0, i, v_{i,s(i)}, i+1) \quad \text{and} \quad (j, 0, j+1, c_{j,t(j)}).$$

It follows from the construction of S that all the non-boundary cells must be tiled with tiles from S_{int}. In all tiles from S_{int}, the left and right sides have the same colour, and so do the top and bottom sides. It follows that the tile placed at the intersection of the ith non-boundary row and the jth non-boundary column has to be

$$(v_{i,s(i)}, c_{j,t(j)}, v_{i,s(i)}, c_{j,t(j)}).$$

Now take any clause c_j, and let x_i be the variable appearing in the $t(j)$th literal of c_j. By examining the intersection of the ith non-boundary row and the jth non-boundary column, we conclude that tile

$$(v_{i,s(i)}, c_{j,t(j)}, v_{i,s(i)}, c_{j,t(j)})$$

had to be included in S_{int}, which means in particular that assigning $s(i)$ to x_i makes c_j satisfied. Hence s is a satisfying assignment for φ. ∎

Solution to Problem 199

To see that the considered problem belongs to PSPACE, we first show that, if $\mathcal{A}$ rejects some word, then the shortest rejected word has length at most 2^n, where n is the number of states of $\mathcal{A}$ (Problem 64 shows that this bound is tight). Indeed, assume that $\mathcal{A}$ rejects some word, and let w be a rejected word of minimal length. Let Q_u be the set of states of $\mathcal{A}$ reachable from the initial state while reading the word u. Towards a contradiction, assume that $|w| > 2^n$. By the pigeonhole principle, there exist two different prefixes s and st of w for which we have $Q_s = Q_{st}$. We can unpump t from w: if $w = stu$, we also have *su* $\notin L(\mathcal{A})$, which contradicts the minimality of $|w|$. This fact is used in our PSPACE algorithm as follows.

The algorithm is non-deterministic. We guess a word w of length at most 2^n and check that it is rejected by $\mathcal{A}$. In order to avoid using exponential space, we guess w letter by letter. For the prefix v of w generated so far, we maintain the set Q_v and additionally $|v|$ (in binary). If at some moment Q_v contains no final state, we know that $v \notin L(\mathcal{A})$, so the algorithm accepts. On the other hand, if this does not happen, but the length counter exceeds 2^n, the algorithm rejects. It follows directly from the fact proved at the beginning that if $\mathcal{A}$ rejects some word, then the algorithm has an accepting run. The converse is immediate. The algorithm uses only polynomial memory, because it does not need to remember the prefix v: it only stores the set of reachable states and the length counter, guesses the next letter, and updates the set of states and length accordingly. The algorithm is non-deterministic, so we have actually proved that the problem is in NPSPACE, but by Savitch's theorem, NPSPACE = PSPACE.

Now we show PSPACE-hardness. Let $\mathcal{M}$ be a Turing machine with a single, right-infinite tape that recognizes a PSPACE-complete language and uses space $p(n)$ for some polynomial p. For a given word w, we construct in polynomial time a non-deterministic automaton $\mathcal{A}_w$ such that $\mathcal{A}_w = \Sigma^*$ if and only if $\mathcal{M}$ rejects w. In this way, we reduce the PSPACE-complete language $L(\mathcal{M})$ to the problem whether a given automaton rejects some word, which implies that the latter problem is PSPACE-hard.

The idea is that $\mathcal{A}_w$ recognizes words that are *not* encodings of correct accepting runs of $\mathcal{M}$ on w. We encode runs as words of the form $\$w_1\$w_2\$ \ldots \$w_k\$$, where $w_1, w_2, \ldots, w_k$ encode consecutive configurations of the machine. Each w_i is a word of length $p(|w|)$ in which the letter at position j represents the content of the jth tape cell, together with the information whether the head of $\mathcal{M}$ is in this cell and the state of $\mathcal{M}$ if the head is there. Thus w_i is a word over the alphabet $\Gamma \times (Q \cup \{\bot\})$, where Γ is the tape alphabet of $\mathcal{M}$, Q is the set of states of $\mathcal{M}$, and $\bot$ indicates that the head is elsewhere.

The automaton $\mathcal{A}_w$ looks for errors in the encoding. It is a union of several non-deterministic automata, each responsible for detecting a particular kind of error:

- the word does not start with $\$$ or does not end with $\$$;
- some consecutive occurrences of $\$$ are not at the distance $p(|w|)$;
- w_1 does not represent the initial configuration (w followed by blanks, the head over the first cell in the initial state) or w_k does not contain the accepting state; and

- for some i the words w_i and w_{i+1} do not represent two consecutive configurations of $\mathcal{M}$.

The first condition can be checked by a constant-size automaton. The second and third conditions are also easy to test, but they require automata of size $\mathcal{O}(p(|w|))$.

The automaton testing the fourth condition moves along the input word until at some point it non-deterministically chooses to test if a given cell evolves correctly. To be able to do this, it stores the content of the given cell and the two neighbouring cells to the left and to the right. After reading the third of these cells, the automaton moves to the right in w for $p(|w|)$ steps. The position it reaches corresponds to the middle stored cell in the next configuration, so its correct contents can be determined based on the stored letters and the transitions of $\mathcal{M}$. The automaton accepts if the letter actually seen is different from the correct one. This automaton also has $\mathcal{O}(p(|w|))$ states.

As the union of the four automata described above, $\mathcal{A}_w$ has size polynomial in $|w|$.   ∎

Solution to Problem 200

To show that the problem belongs to PSPACE we proceed as in Problem 199. Assume we are given k automata, each with at most n states. If there is a word accepted by all these automata, there is one of length at most n^k, because the product automaton recognizing the intersection of their languages has at most n^k states. Thus, the polynomial-space algorithm can keep guessing a word letter by letter, together with the runs of the automata over this word. It does not maintain the entire guessed word and the runs, but only the word's length and the most recent states of the runs, and updates this information each time a new letter is guessed. If at some point all automata accept, the algorithm accepts. If the length of the word exceeds n^k, the algorithm rejects. By Savitch's theorem, this non-deterministic polynomial-space algorithm can be realized in PSPACE.

To show PSPACE-hardness, we modify the polynomial-time reduction from Problem 199. For a fixed Turing machine $\mathcal{M}$ with a single, right-infinite tape, working in space $p(n)$ over inputs of length n, and a given word w, we construct $3 + p(|w|)$ deterministic automata whose languages have a non-empty intersection if and only if $\mathcal{M}$ accepts w. The automata simply test that all four conditions listed in the solution of Problem 199 are unsatisfied. The negation of the first condition is easily verified by a deterministic automaton of constant size. The negations of the second and third conditions can be verified by deterministic automata of size $\mathcal{O}(p(|w|))$. To verify the negation of the last condition we use $p(|w|)$ deterministic automata: the jth automaton ensures that the jth cell of the tape (enriched with the information about the state and the location of the head) evolves correctly. This is done by comparing triples of letters at positions $j - 1, j$, and $j + 1$ after consecutive occurrences of \$, as in Problem 199. ∎

Further Reading

Arora S. and B. Barak. *Computational Complexity: A Modern Approach.* Cambridge University Press, 2006.

Cooper S. B. *Computability Theory.* Chapman & Hall/CRC Mathematics Series. Chapman & Hall, 2004.

Eilenberg S. *Automata, Languages, and Machines. Volume A.* Pure and Applied Mathematics. Academic Press, 1974.

Eilenberg S. *Automata, Languages, and Machines. Volume B.* Pure and Applied Mathematics. Academic Press, 1976.

Garey M. R. and D. S. Johnson. *Computers and Intractability: A Guide to the Theory of NP-Completeness.* W. H. Freeman, 1979.

Herken R., editor. *The Universal Turing Machine: A Half-Century Survey.* Springer, 2nd edition, 1995.

Holcombe W. M. L. *Algebraic Automata Theory.* Cambridge Studies in Advanced Mathematics. Cambridge University Press, 2004.

Hopcroft J. E., R. Motwani, and J. D. Ullman. *Introduction to Automata Theory, Languages and Computation.* Pearson Addison-Wesley, 3rd edition, 2007.

Kozen D. C. *Automata and Computability.* Springer, 1st edition, 1997.

Linz P. *An Introduction to Formal Languages and Automata.* Jones and Bartlett, 4th edition, 2006.

Moore C. and S. Mertens. *The Nature of Computation.* Oxford University Press, 2011.

Papadimitriou C. H. *Computational Complexity.* Addison-Wesley, 1994.

Sipser M. *Introduction to the Theory of Computation.* PWS Publishing, 1997.

Turing A. M. On computable numbers, with an application to the Entscheidungsproblem. *Proceedings of the London Mathematical Society*, 2(42): 230–265, 1936.

Index

Terms used in solutions are usually listed only if they are not used in the respective problem statemements. Page numbers in bold indicate definitions.

Printed in the United States
by Baker & Taylor Publisher Services